GAELIC SCOTLAND
THE TRANSFORMATION OF
A CULTURE REGION

GAELIC SCOTLAND

The Transformation of a Culture Region

Charles W J Withers

ROUTLEDGE
London and New York

First Published in 1988 by
Routledge
11 New Fetter Lane, London EC4P 4EE

Published in the USA by
Routledge
in association with Routledge, Chapman & Hall, Inc.
29 West 35th Street, New York, NY 10001

Printed and bound in Great Britain by Mackays of Chatham PLC, Chatham, Kent

British Library Cataloguing in Publication Data

Withers, Charles W.J.
   Gaelic Scotland: the transformation of
   a culture region: — (historical
   geography series).
   1. Highlands (Scotland) — Civilization
   I. Title
   941.1'5   DA880.H7
ISBN 0-415-00459-4

Library of Congress Cataloging-in-Publication Data
ISBN 0-415-00459-4

CONTENTS

FIGURES

This book is an essay in cultural and regional historical
geography. It explores the cultural transformation of the
Highlands of Scotland, the <u>Gaidhealtchad,</u> or Gaelic
Scotland. It is written both from a feeling that a
cultural perspective upon geographical change has been
neglected in writings on the Highlands and in the hope that
it will stimulate interest from all those involved in
questions of regional identity and transformation. The
main period covered is from 1609 - the Statutes of Iona -
to the 1886 Crofters Act and the Highland 'Land Wars' of
the late nineteenth and early twentieth centuries although
consideration of several events and processes earlier and
later has meant that discussion has ranged beyond and
before these dates. But no all-embracing
historical-cultural geography or cultural history of the
Highlands has been attempted. Rather, in drawing upon some
of the concerns of cultural geography, from a wide range of
source material, and a notion of culture from Marxist
cultural theory, I have sought to put an understanding of
the cultural transformation of the Highlands on a more
equal footing with other explanations of change. The
'transformation' of the title refers not to questions of
physical landscape change (though elements of landscape
change in this sense are discussed), but rather to 'the
making' of the people of the region and to their transformation as a socially-constituted process or set of processes
which took a certain expression over a given period of
time.

The Highlands did not exist as a cultural region within
Scotland until the late 1300s. Distinct in language -
Gaelic - and in the prevalence of a clan-based social
system, largely separate from the rest of Scotland in terms
of agricultural economy and without a base in manufactures,
the Highlands remained distant and to an extent unknown
until the seventeenth and eighteenth centuries. From that
period, they were 'discovered' and subject to agrarian

change, industrial development, religious unification, anglicisation through education, and to a whole suite of policies of 'improvement' geared toward the transformation of Highland society and culture. Improvement and transformation are not just material 'things' however. They involve questions of attitude and ideology, of changes not just in language as a given attribute and in established material practices but also questions of regional identity, of consciousness. I have tried to show here how the transformation of the Highlands as a culture region has been effected intellectually and ideologically as well as materially and to show how the effects of this combined ideological and material transformation varied by class within Highland society, by place and district within the region as a whole, and over time. In so doing I have tried to understand and explain the views and values of those people experiencing the transformation - to consider their needs and capacities - as well as documenting the concerns and intent of those directing and initiating the processes of transformation. This concern itself stems from a feeling that explanations of social and cultural change in the Highlands have too often been couched in terms of an immutable progression - from clan to class, from Gaelic to English, from 'traditional' to 'modern' - a transformation without either opposition or internal contradiction. Understanding the historic Highlands has also been hindered by being too commonly represented in terms of Highlands 'versus' Lowlands with change coming only 'from outside and above' with little thought given to differences of class, of mental outlook or other distinctions within the Highlands. These criticisms are not true of all writing on the Highlands - Dodgshon, Hunter, and Richards stand as notable exceptions - but they are relevant to much that has been written about the region and its people. In considering these and other issues in what follows, questions of that varying historiography that has attached itself to the Highlands will be seen to be no less important than the actual transformation of the region.

ACKNOWLEDGEMENTS

This book owes much to many people for their advice, guidance, and patience. I have reviewed and discussed the work of a large number of people here but I am particularly indebted to Malcolm Gray, James Hunter, Annette Smith, Bob Dodgshon, Eric Richards, Anand Chitnis, and David Stevenson for allowing me to draw upon their work in the way I have. Several people have commented on earlier drafts of various chapters and have discussed with me the intriguing problems of Highland historical geography - I should like to thank Ronald Black, John Christie, David Daiches, Nick Fisher, Mike Heffernan, Lindsay Hewitt, Jean Jones, Peter Jones, Peter O'Brien, Susan O'Brien, John MacInnes, Rudiger Schreyer, and Rick Sher for their help in this way. I am particularly grateful to Bob Dodgshon and William Gillies for their scholarship and critical advice freely and warmly given, and to Robin Butlin I owe special thanks for his perceptive comments and patience as Series Editor. I acknowledge with thanks the permission granted from the Syndics of Cambridge University Press to reproduce data published in M.Flinn (ed.), Scottish Population History from the 17th Century to the 1930s, especially from Tables 5.3.1; 5.4.1; and 5.5.5 reproduced in part here as Table 4.3. For permission to reproduce illustrations, I am grateful to Annette Smith (Figure 2.3); Hugh Stevenson and Glasgow Museums and Art Galleries (for Faed's Last of the Clan (Figure 2.2); the Mitchell Library and City of Glasgow District Council (for Figure 6.2); and to The Illustrated London News Picture Library (for Figure 6.3). For sending me a list of Scottish planned villages and allowing me to draw upon his unpublished material on planned villages (shortly to appear with John Donald Publishers Ltd.), I am particularly grateful to Douglas Lockhart. My colleagues in the School of Geography and Geology have with good humour tolerated, perhaps enjoyed, my absence for periods of research on which this book is based. To them I extend my thanks. Parts of this book have been presented in seminars at Loughborough University, Edinburgh University, Aberdeen University, and All Souls, Oxford, and I should like to record my thanks to the respective audiences. I am especially indebted to the librarians, archivists, and staff of those libraries and record offices I have worked in: the Universities of Aberdeen, Edinburgh, Dundee, Glasgow, and Oxford; the Sandeman Library, Perth; the City Archives and Local History Library, Dundee; Central Region and Grampian Region Record Offices; Strathclyde Regional Archives; the City Library and City Archives, Edinburgh; the National Library of Scotland; and, chiefly, the Scottish Record Office, Edinburgh. I am grateful to the Keeper of the Records and to the Registrar General of Scotland for permission to use and quote from documents in their care. Financial assistance has come from the British Academy, the Nuffield Foundation, the Institute of Historical Research and the College of St. Paul and St. Mary. Sheila Taylor, Erica Breuning, Mary Lailey, and Gill Hunt have all turned rough drafts of maps and text into finished copy with cheerful professionalism. Peter Sowden of Croom Helm has been tolerant and a source of much good advice. But perhaps chiefly I am grateful to my wife Anne for her support and patience and to my children who helped keep things in perspective: to them, with love, this work is dedicated.

INTRODUCTION: THE SCOTTISH HIGHLANDS AS CULTURE REGION

The Highlands is a very general name for a large
tract of the Kingdom, which appears to be best
defined by the boundary of the Gaelic language.1

The Highlands of Scotland, together with the outlying
western islands, present a region both distinct from the
Lowlands and itself characterised by areas of individuali-
ty. Geologically, the Highlands are divided from the
Lowlands by the Highland Boundary Fault which runs from
Stonehaven on the east coast to Helensburgh on the west and
divides the Precambrian rocks of the west and north from
the younger Palaeozoic sedimentary rocks of the Midland
Valley to the south and east.2 To the geographer, this
upland massif to the north and west is separated from the
Lowlands by the 'Highland line' and represented as the
'Highland counties' - Argyll, Ross and Cromarty,
Sutherland, Inverness - together with parts of northern
Perthshire and western Caithness (Figure 1.1). The
Highlands region as a whole is seen as one whose climate is
cool and wet, whose underlying geology has determined a
scanty soil cover and where the incised lochs and
mountainous terrain have made communication difficult,
human settlement limited, and cultivation of the land an
uncertain affair. Compared to the rest of Scotland, the
Highlands are ill-provided with natural resources such as
coal and iron. The relief, with much of the area over
250m, has limited land use largely to rough pasture and
forestry.3 Population is today thinly scattered,
concentrating in several towns along the coastal margins.
Even in the past when numbers and distribution were
different from today, Highland Scotland was never as
densely populated as the Lowlands, although shifts in
balance between population and resources in the rural
Highlands occasioned levels of poverty and hardship more
widespread and severe there than in the Lowlands.
    Whilst the Highlands and Islands may be considered

The Scottish Highlands as Culture Region

Figure 1.1   Scotland and the Highland Line

distinct in a number of ways from Lowland Scotland, the region should neither be seen as uniform in its characteristics nor wholly separate. Not all to the north of the 'Highland Line' is typically Highland: the soils are not everywhere thin and unproductive nor the land everywhere dissected by narrow lochs and high ranges. The division between Highlands and Lowlands is not a simple division between north and south but much more one between the 'farming Highlands' to the south and east and the 'crofting Highlands' to the north and west. The soils of coastal eastern Ross and Cromarty and parts of eastern Sutherland, for example, are closer in type and productive capacity to those of the Lowlands than to soils in the upland west of those counties. The narrow coastal strip around Inverness, in the northern parishes of Moray, Nairn and the eastern upland areas of Aberdeen, has a richness of landscape now and an agrarian economy in the past more Lowland than Highland in nature. Discussion of the geography of Highland Scotland must needs recognise this diversity within unity; in the way people drew a living from the land, in the balance between population and resources, and in the connections different parts of the Highlands had with outside influences.

In the past the Highlands as a whole, both the hill country proper and the coastal plains, have been considered as the area within which the Gaelic language was spoken or the clan was the predominant social system. Definition of the Highlands by language, the Gaelic-speaking culture area or <u>Gaidhealtachd</u> is particularly important. But although it is common today to separate Highlands from Lowlands on the basis of agrarian economy, geology or even topography and climate, and, for the geography of the past more proper to distinguish between the two areas on the basis of social system and language, the terms 'Highlands' and 'Lowlands' describing two cultural provinces within Scotland have not always been in existence. Neither the terms themselves nor the division within Scottish culture and geography they denote had any meaning before the end of the fourteenth century.

THE EMERGENCE OF THE HIGHLANDS

Several reasons may be advanced to explain the social and geographical emergence of the Highlands as a distinct region within Scotland by the late 1300s. Firstly, those changes in society and on the land attendance upon the extension of feudalism in medieval Scotland were felt less in those parts north of the Forth and Clyde than in the

Lothians or the Scottish borders. In the upland north and west, such changes - the expansion of burgh economies, the role of justiciars, baronies and other feudal controls on land and society - were hardly felt. Secondly, the simple fact of distance and the remoteness from authority allowed the population in the Highlands to exist largely unaffected by events in the south. In addition the Gaelic language underwent a major decline in social and political status during the medieval period. In the eleventh century, Gaelic, known as the Scottish language by virtue of its political prestige and nationalist associations was predominant throughout Scotland and in use, to varying degrees, from the Tweed to the Pentland Firth. But by the late fourteenth century Gaelic had retreated into its Highland habitat and had lost its connotations as the Scottish language.4 At the same time as it was retreating from the Lowlands, Gaelic, was being replaced by English as the language of civility and status. As a result of its rise up the social scale and the connotations of Gaelic with geographical and social inferiority, the English language in use throughout Lowland Scotland became known as 'Scottis' or Scots; Gaelic, in losing its nationalist and political associations, became known as 'Irish' or 'Erse' in reference to its Irish origins. This paralleled the emergence of the Highlands-Lowlands division in the then Scottish consciousness. The result of these changes was, by about 1400, the appearance of a dualism in Scotland's geography between the Gaelic Highlands and the Scots or English-speaking Lowlands. The Highland-Lowland boundary line is thus a construction from a particular period in Scottish history. The terms 'Highlands' and 'Lowlands' have no place in the historical sources surviving from the period before about 1300: 'they had simply not entered the minds of men'.5

This division is, to one author, apparent throughout Scotland's literary history: 'as far back as the literature of Scotland goes, the Lowlanders regarded the Highlanders with the feelings of contempt and dislike which the representative of a higher form of civilisation (as he conceives it to be) cherishes toward the representative of a lower'.6 But it is a distinction that would not have been articulated before the 1400s, and is not one shared exactly by the Gaelic historical and literary tradition. MacInnes notes, 'although Gaels recognise more or less the same division of the country into Highland and Lowland, there are certain subtle differences in that division we are perhaps prone to ignore ... Gaidhealtachd and Galltachd (the Lowlands) are abstract terms, not ordinary place-names, and the areas they designate are not drawn with

4

precise boundaries'.7 Several Gaelic tradition- bearers
and poets extend the idea of the Gaidhealtachd beyond the
Highland line, to encompass those areas of Scotland once
Gaelic but now Lowland, and to claim for Gaelic an historical heritage greater in the past and lost through outside
agency. Alexander MacDonald, the eighteenth-century Gaelic
poet, writing of the 'Miorun mor nan Gall' - the 'great
ill-will of the Lowlanders' - pointed to the need to
re-affirm Gaelic literary tradition as the bearer of a more
truly Scottish culture. Assessment of literary evidence
must, of course, bear in mind the selectivity of the writer
and the historical context of the work, but it is nonethe-
less true that such evidence 'from within' - Gaelic poetry
and historical tradition, native expressions of sentiment
or protest - has been too often ignored by geographers and
historians of Highland Scotland. As MacInnes further
notes, Gaelic tradition has regarded the Highland Line not
as a fixed border line between two cultures but as reflection of the earlier decline of a greater Gaelic Scotland.
But to the Lowlander, when that region now known as the
Highlands entered history and literature, Gaelic cultural
forms and value systems no longer carried with them any
sense of a lost Scottishness or even of contemporary
status. Gaelic had become the language, and, in wider
terms the symbol of a geographical region whose cultural
forms and social order were anathema to the standards of
civilised, English-speaking, Scotland.

Highland society in 'the old order' was structured in a
three or four-fold division of chief, tacksman - a middle
tenant, often related to the chief, who sublet land to
those beneath him - and the peasantry, divided into a
variety of tenants and sub-tenants. The Highland economy
was founded upon the holding and working of land with the
basis to agriculture lying in the working of arable for
subsistence and, from the later 1600s, the export of black
cattle. Cash derived from their sale was from that period
important in meeting cash rents and as exchange for the
import of grainstuffs. The form of agrarian organisation
in the Highlands was runrig. The basic unit of agricultural organisation was the joint farm in which tenants
worked the land co-operatively. Land, held through the
older form of tenure, ward-holding, was allocated through
the clan system. The clan system acted not only as the
basis to the working and holding of land, but also provided
a patriarchal bond, based on military service, between
chief and tenantry. Variations in this system stemmed from
local differences in soil quality or land management. The
extent to which proximity to the Lowlands permitted the
circulation of population, ideas, and capital and allowed

relief in times of hardship or permitted earlier adoption
of change in some parts of the Highlands than in others
also occasioned variations in Highland social and economic
structure. Together with the decline of the language and
the break up of the clan system, changes in the way the
majority of the Highland population derived a living from
the land have been widely recognised as crucial elements in
the transformation of the Highlands.

MODELS OF HIGHLAND TRANSFORMATION

Carter (1971) identifies two explanatory models for the
changes affecting Highland Scotland since about 1700:
political, where explanation centres upon the consequences
of single acts or events, chiefly upon Culloden and its
aftermath; and economic, in which change is seen as the
result of population pressure and 'impersonal economic
forces' which, in combination, drew the Highlands into the
sphere of influence of the English and European market
economy.8 Although neither type of model is categorised as
exclusive nor untouched by the other, and recent scholarship has added to and modified them, this distinction
provides a useful basis to examination.

Political models

Several nineteenth-century works consider change in the
Highlands to be the consequence of political acts. The
concern of Gregory, Maclean, Keltie, and Mitchell was with
the efforts of the Scottish monarchy in the fifteenth and
sixteenth centuries to establish civil control in the
Highlands following the break-up of the Lordship of the
Isles.9 In the late 1490s and early 1500s, steps were
taken by James IV (1488-1513) for the expulsion of many of
the vassals of the old Lordship from their possessions.
Plans were laid to establish justiciars or sheriffs for the
west Highlands.10 James VI (1567-1625) led expeditions to
pacify the Highlands. Although some local government was
established, plans aimed at pacifying the Highlands in this
period were more statements of intent than wholly effective
agencies of civil administration.11 Nor should we suppose
that Highlanders were as outsiders then termed them -
'barbarous for the most parte' - where, in the words of a
royal document of 1527 - '...nane of the officeris of ye
law dar pass for fear of yair lyvis'.12 These early acts
indicate concern within central authority over the virtual
independence of Highland chiefs and the separateness of the

The Scottish Highlands as Culture Region

Highland populations and mark the beginning of a history of legislative control aimed at the Highlands from outside.

More recent work has focussed upon the evolution of political policy toward the Highlands and the role of particular institutions in directing changes in Highland affairs. Campbell has considered Highland history and the history of Gaelic in particular to be one of deliberate extirpation.13 Other writers point to 1609 and the Statutes of Iona as marking the beginning of effective political control by centralised government over the Highlands.14 The Statues sought 'to bring the Hielandis and the Iles to civilitie' through education and reform of chiefs' authority, with the intent of creating a class of English-speaking landowners above the Gaelic peasantry. Gaelic was seen as synonymous with 'barbaritie and incivilitie'.15

Difficulties in administering political control in the Highlands were compounded by the facts of geography and the nature of government. Systems of administration, modelled on the English example following the 1707 Union, supported through patronage and run by Justices of the Peace, were not suited to the Highlands.16 Clan chiefs commanded greater authority than the government until the aftermath of the 1745 Rebellion. But even before then, the structures and loyalties of the clan system might have been turned to greater advantage in securing order in the Highlands had central authority in London or Edinburgh pursued a firmer policy in the first decades of the 1700s. The Disarming Act of 1716 and the Royal Bounty Scheme of 1726 both fell short of their intended aim, for example, and General Wade's schemes for civil control were never fully realised, given 'the difficulty that attends the executive of the processes of the Law in the Highlands'.17 Several institutions were established during the eighteenth century whose purpose was to bring 'civility' to Highland affairs through a combination of industry, the English language, and agricultural improvement. The Board of Trustees for the Encouragement of Manufactures and Fisheries in Scotland was begun in 1727 with the purpose of promoting industry among 'the inhabitants of the north'.18 More influential were the schemes employed on the Forfeited Annexed Estates, set up in 1752 ' for the better civilising and improving the Highlands of Scotland'. 'Good Government, Industry, and Manufactures' went hand-in-hand with the erection of schools on the estates 'for instructing young Persons in Reading and Writing the English Language'.19 The Society in Scotland for Propagating Christian Knowledge (the SSPCK), begun in Edinburgh in 1709, was the chief agency in eighteenth-century Highland education.

A political perspective to explanation of the changes affecting Highland Scotland since the early seventeenth century is important to our overall understanding. Individual figures and institutions, single acts, the evolution of policy must all be accorded a role where necessary. But placing too great an emphasis on political factors alone as turning points in Highland affairs misrepresents the often haphazard nature of government and administration in the Highlands and places unjustified weight on the evidence of intention rather than that of result. The significance of the Jacobite rebellions in the eighteenth century, the 1746 Heritable Jurisdiction Act and other acts before and after Culloden, for example, rests more in their ideological intention than their immediate results, more in their consequences one with another and with other factors than in isolation.[20]

Economic models

Cregeen has pointed to the central role of the house of Argyll as motivators of both political and economic change in the south-west Highlands.[21] The house of Argyll, the senior branch of clan Campbell, rose to prominence through service to the Crown. By the first decades of the 1700s, the house of Argyll was the major land-holder and controlling force in the west Highlands, the indispensable agent of central government and a staunch supporter of Prestbyterianism. Schemes for 'civilising the Highlands' prepared by the Dukes of Argyll in their role as chief of clan Campbell and feudal superiors over a large tenantry sought to unite political and economic objectives; loyalty, obedience and progress through agricultural improvement, industrial advance, and hard work: 'I'm resolved (wrote the third Duke to his chamberlain on Tiree in 1756) to keep no tenants but such as will be peaceable and apply themselves to industry'.[22] The second Duke had earlier changed the whole basis of land-tenure when, in 1710 in Kintyre and 1737 in Mull, Morvern and Tiree, he offered tacks of farms not to kin or even through the tacksman but to the highest bidders, whoever they might be: 'Almost at a single stroke of the pen, clanship and vassalage ceased officially to count in the tenurial system of the largest Highland estate, and this a decade before the '45'.[23] The nature and management of landholding in the south-west and the fact that political loyalty was a pre-condition of tenancy were, however, untypical of the Highlands as a whole. The south-west and eastern Highlands differed from the north and west Highlands in two further respects; in their demographic experiences and in the rate and nature of economic change from the later eighteenth century. All part of the Highlands experienced population growth in the period 1750 to 1850, but those areas south and east of the Great Glen were characterised by moderate increase in contrast to the north and west where overall totals and rates of population increase were greater. In part, this was the result of the policies of landlords in the areas of greatest population increase who, until the second quarter of the nineteenth century, tended to retain population resources to supply labour-intensive developments such as kelp-making. Explanation also lies in the differential scale of out-migration - greater from the eastern Highlands than the north and west - which eased pressure in the eastern districts.24 The more limiting physical environment in the north-west not only meant that the balance between population and resources tipped more easily toward dearth and crisis there than in the south and east Highlands, it also meant that the economic basis for improvement was more restricted.25

Several studies point to this regional variation. Innovations in agriculture were taken up earlier and more successfully in areas on the fringes of the Highlands than in the hill country of the north and west.26 Enclosure, new patterns of rotation and longer leases were followed from the second half of the eighteenth century by the large-scale farming of Cheviot sheep. In the north and west, changes in the agricultural base to society and land-holding and the move away from a labour-intensive communal economy to a system that was land-intensive and profit-seeking were not only later in coming and, in places, more dramatic in impact than in the south and east, they also occasioned a greater hardship given the increase in population, the decline of kelp-making, and the build-up of rent arrears. Failure of the potato crop in 1837 and again in 1846-1847, precipitated further clearance and migration of population and for landlords in debt, necessitated the sale of estates for sheep farms or forestry. Richards work on Sutherland has documented the impact in the north of these processes of change.27 Increased profits to be gained from the sale of wool justified the clearance of population from interior Sutherland in the first quarter of the nineteenth century. Relocation of population on the coasts led to the growth of fishing villages and, not just in Sutherland, to the emergence of that occupational pluralism - part-crofter, part-fisherman - that characterised life for many by the later 1800s.28 In other parts of the Highlands that have provided the focus to more detailed study - Morvern, the eastern areas of Ross and Cromarty and the Black Isle, and on the Forfeited Estates – similar shifts towards a money economy, adoption of new methods of agriculture, establishment of local industry and the clearance of population and sale of estates have been noted.29

In outline, these are the 'impersonal forces' of the economic model of Highland transformation. Thus Smout and Gaskell, and, earlier, Hamilton and Gray, regard change in the Highland way of life as the result of what Gray has termed 'the total impact of the powerful individualism and economic rationalism of industrial civilisation on the weaker, semi-communal traditionalism of the recalcitrant fringe'.30 These economic models may be criticised on the grounds that they are based on the premise of a dual economy within Scotland, and, as Carter notes, on an analogy 'or more strictly a homology, between the economic history of England and that of Scotland'.31 Impersonal economic forces become the chief (if not the only) motivating agents for the change from 'traditional' to 'modern' society. Turnock has assessed these changes for Scotland as a whole in terms of Rostow's model of stages of economic growth and the move from a pre-industrial to a post-industrial society, from traditional social structures to modern social systems.32 Seen in these terms, the commercialisation of Highland agriculture from the 1730s onwards and the interpenetration of progressive methods into an economy that both contemporary and modern commentators commonly note as 'pre-industrial', 'backward', or 'primitive' comes to be regarded as 'improvement', 'modernisation', or 'development' in a way that not only denies other causal factors involved but also codifies the behaviour of Highlanders as passive respondents to outside influence without pausing to consider their role as participants and active agents. Change is unidirectional, irreversible, externally imposed. Richards has recently shown how 'the effort to understand' the Highland problem, in the past as today, has been conceived largely as an economic issue either, in the case of contemporaries, in regard to the policies chosen for Highland 'improvement', or, for modern researchers with the advantage of hindsight, the reasons for the failure of those policies.33 Regarding changes in the Highland economy as later and slower than those characterising Lowland Scotland which, in turn, were later and slower than similar events in England ignores variations in the rate and regional pattern of change, and separates those involved in the changes from the making of their own history; actual historical sequences and social relations are replaced by ideal type constructs.

In addition to work that has focussed on the political

bases to change or economic causes of regional transformation, there has been work of a broadly sociological nature.

Sociological models

Carter has considered the suitability of models of social and cultural pluralism and the ideas of domain and domination in explanation of the changing relationship between clan chief and Highland tenant as one between patron and client. The concept of a plural society, deriving largely from work in a colonial context, revolves around the existence of two or more cultural sectors within a single political unit. In the model, the integration of society depends not upon consensus but upon the domination of one sector over the other through institutions of kinship, religious, legal and educational structures and so on. Differences in land-tenure, kinship and in economy and politics are used by Carter to suggest that eighteenth-century Scotland was characterised by two distinct cultural sectors. But given the continued political ineffectiveness of central authority, the continuance of clan feuds, cattle raiding, and the autonomy of clan society until 1745, Scotland was not a plural society until the later 1700s.

Extending from this framework and also drawing upon work done in a colonial context, Hechter has considered the relationship between England, Lowland Scotland, and the Gaelic Highlands to be one between 'core' and 'periphery'. The Highlands are Scotland's and Britain's 'internal colony'.34 The concept of internal colonialism 'focuses on political conflict between core and peripheral groups as mediated by the central government'. Commercial, industrial and economic relations in trade, credit, and capital are directed through the institutions and authority of the core. In addition, membership of bodies established to facilitate the dependent development of the periphery is usually drawn from the core. The economy of the periphery rests upon a single primary export. It is characterised also by migration and mobility of peripheral workers in response to fluctuations in price of this primary good, the growth of an urban economy in the core and by the deterioration of social structures within the periphery resulting from such things as resource depletion or over-population. The socio-economic basis to internal colonialism is reinforced through juridical, political, and military measures, and within the periphery, there is discrimination on the basis of language, religion and other cultural forms. Many of these factors find expression in Highland Scotland: the erection of forts and barracks to facilitate

military control; the role of the Board of Trustees, the
Forfeited Annexed Estates in stimulating economic growth;
the movement of Highlanders to work in Lowland agriculture
or industry; and those agencies whose end purpose was the
anglicisation, 'improvement', and cultural transformation
of the Highlands. Macleod has considered the policies of
James VI in the early seventeenth century towards his
'Highland frontier' to parallel closely those designed to
settle Ireland and America in the same period.35 And in
the eighteenth century, the SSPCK produced folios on
religious unity and the spread of English in which the
Highlander was equated with the North American Indian.36

Colonisation, whether in Lewis, Kintyre, Ulster or
Virginia, depends on the economic and political dominance
of the core. For Smout, the core-periphery model is
clearly relevant: 'the Highlands provided the most striking
example on the British mainland of an internal periphery....the whole problem of the Highlands is a complex
subset of the problem of Scotland itself as a
periphery.'37 Centre-periphery relationships exist at many
levels, but it is clear that as the term is used by
Wallerstein and others to describe relations in the
accumulation of capital and establishment of manufacturing
industry within a single world-economy, Scotland lay on the
fringes of a core located in the Low Countries, Northern
France and England.38 Just as Scotland sought to shed its
peripheral character in relation to England, particularly
after 1707, so the Highlands have been increasingly subject
to the core influences of Lowland Scotland.39 Those
studies that have sought to explain economic and social
change within Highland Scotland as the result of processes
consequent upon the Lowland-centred expansion of capitalism
as the dominant mode of production recognise the
core-periphery model as of value, though they perhaps place
too much weight on economic forces as causal processes.
Dickson and Clarke consider that

> Despite the great differences between the develop-
> ment of the Highland economy and that of Lowland
> agriculture in the period 1780-1830, both were the
> result of essentially the same kind of forces. In
> both cases, a landowning class increasingly
> oriented to financial gain undertook a more
> thorough commercialization of agriculture in
> response to the particular constraints and market
> opportunities with which it was faced.

They further note

Although class polarization was a feature of agrarian Scotland generally in this period, it assumed a particularly severe aspect in the Highlands. In part, this reflected the geographical and climatic disadvantages of the region and, in particular, its peripheral subordinate position in the British economy.40

Others likewise see the history of the Highlands in terms of regional underdevelopment, arising for one author from 'the process of articulation of modes of production, in particular the articulation of capitalism with precapitalist modes'. 41 For others, the Highland case may be comparable either with Latin American underdevelopment as a feudal periphery of metropolitan monopoly capitalism,42 or with other regional inequalities within Scotland, themselves the result of unequal social appropriation of capital in the past.43 More recent work has adopted a socio-economic welfare approach to Highland life, though not in historical explanation.44

For Carter, the emergence of class relationships within the Highlands, especially those between landlord and tenant replacing those between clan chief and tenant, may be understood in terms of an evolving patron-client relationship of domination.45 Three forms of domination, or, to use Wolf's words upon whom Carter draws, 'types of domain', may be distinguished; 'patrimonial', 'prebendal', and 'mercantile'. Patrimonial domain is control exercised through kinship; 'this control implies the right to receive tribute from the inhabitants in return for their occupance'. In prebendal domain, control is exercised through state officials who draw tribute for state purposes and for their own purposes. Prebendal domain control implies 'a much greater degree of centralizing, a much wider scope of central authority, than patrimonial domain, which exhibits a greater autonomy on the part of the various domain holders'. In mercantile domain, 'land is viewed as private property of the landowner, an entity to be bought and sold and used to obtain profit for its owner'.46 Control is exercised through rent. As Carter notes, we may regard 'the recent history of the Highlands as a change from patrimonial domain to mercantile domain. The chiefs increasingly came to define clan lands as capitalisable assets rather than as land to be handed on to their successors'. The opportunities for the controlling elite to maintain economic dominance and cultural influences were certainly much greater by the later 1700s.47 But in understanding class relationships, the assessment paid to relations between classes and between ideal-typified notions of landlord and tenants has perhaps too often obscured relationships between individuals <u>within</u> classes and occupations.48 When questions of ideology are placed alongside shifts in relationships <u>within</u> the tenantry, the departure of the tacksman, the destruction of the joint-farm runrig system, and penetration by an externally-derived capital-intensive market economy, and considered in terms of a differing consciousness of what the Highlands represented, it is possible to advance explanations that rest more upon resistance to agencies threatening existing social relations and more upon questions of regional identity than upon externally motivated impersonal economic forces.

It is clear from even this limited exploration that a large body of literature exists upon the historic Highlands, and that this literature has drawn upon a number of models and perspectives in the search for explanation.

It is also clear that political and economic models of explanation have enjoyed an unwarranted primacy over explanations that consider the place of the Highland people, their culture and beliefs, or their reaction to change. The Highlands have suffered not only from what one author has called 'the enormous condescension of history',49 but also from a stereotype view of what that history has been. Valuable though much of the above scholarship is, it is still largely true 'that while old simplifications about Highland history have been replaced by scrupulously documented accounts of the ways in which the modern economic structure of the region was established, the people upon whom estate manangement imposed their policies have been almost completely neglected.'50 Further, the transformation of the Highlands was not just economic and political. Less often considered though no less important are the perhaps more subtle shifts in Highland life in the past - the decline of Gaelic, the expansion of schooling, the place occupied by religion, the limited efforts to establish manufactures and extend a 'spirit of industry' as a means of social change. Transformation of the Highlands has been both a material and an intellectual process. Yet little attention has been paid to the policy of school and church authorities and to the ideology and means of control employed by those agencies involved in the region's transformation. Anglicisation and urbanisation, religious unification and education, a new cultivation of mind as well as of land were all closely linked in the past though they are not so commonly linked in modern research.

It is important to understand that the region and its people have long been characterised in the eyes of outsiders and those of different values, class, and language, as 'dissenting' from established religion and by a social and geographical distance from authority. It was this sense in which the Gaelic Highlands were _in_ Scotland but not _of_ it (or, more crucially, held values or were believed to hold values alien to the dominant classes within Scottish society), that provided the rationale to those policies which aimed to extend Lowland influence. From the early seventeenth century onwards, cultural change as a process that was at once economic and political, material and ideological, was seen as crucial to the 'cultivation' and 'improvement' of the Gaelic Highlander and to the incorporation of the Highlands into the British political system and market economy. Anglicisation was a central element in this policy. Nicol Graham, writing of Highlanders in 1747 that 'their want of our language evidently prevents their making improvements in the affairs of common life',51 epitomises a view held by many then and one that has its origins a century or more earlier and a persistence until the later 1800s. The below quote, from a 1760 report to the General Assembly of the Church of Scotland, makes clear not only the disaffection felt for the Gaelic language but also hints at the ideology of, and cultural hegemony practised by, those in authority regarding the continued use of Gaelic in the context of the economic and social development of the Highlands.

> In the western Highlands and islands, the inhabit-
> ants universally speak the Gaelic language, and
> are generally unacquainted with that which is used
> in the other parts of Great Britain. This defect
> alone lays them under great disadvantages, both
> with regard to religion, and to civil life... The
> common people can carry on no transactions with
> the more southern part of Great Britain, without
> the intervention of their superiors, who know the
> English language, and are thereby kept in that
> undue dependence, and unacquaintance with the arts
> of life, which have long been the misery of these
> countries. Till the partition arising from
> different languages be removed, and the common
> language of Great Britain be diffused over the
> Highlands, the inhabitants will never enjoy, in
> their full extent, the benefits of religion and
> civil government.52

What follows is an attempt to understand the efforts made through 'the intervention of superiors' to remove ' the partition'. As we have seen, this is not a novel conception: 'Most of the interest of Highland history...

turns on the efforts that were made to close or narrow the gap between Highland and Lowland living conditions and society.'53 But what is suggested here is that anglicisation and those other means intended to civilise the Highlander - to 'close the gap' - were neither separate one from another nor peripheral to those other 'arts of life' - agricultural change, industrial development and so on - more usually considered in work on the historic Highlands. As Cregeen has rightly noted,

> What destroyed the old Highland social and
> political structure was its growing involvement in
> the general cultural influence of their neighbours
> to the south, that is England and the Scottish
> Lowlands. This influence, expressed in speech,
> manners, clothes, religion, political sympathies
> and activity, trade, seasonal migration and so on,
> was at work in the Highlands long before 1745 and
> reached its climax considerably after.54

Gaelic was a symbol of Highland culture and in some senses, anglicisation may be seen as the focus of cultural transformation but it did not occur in isolation. The formation of class relations, the adoption of new agricultural methods, the implementation of schemes of local industry, the evasion of rent, land wars, and the various geographical and social levels at which these and other changes occurred are inseparable elements in the cultural transformation of the Highlands.

TOWARDS A MODEL OF CULTURAL TRANSFORMATION

An understanding of what is meant here by cultural transformation not only raises at the outset the questions of what is meant by culture and how in particular it has been used in the historical and geographical explanation of given regions and peoples but also of allying an analytic view of culture with observed changes in Highland Scotland.

Culture and cultural geography

Introducing a variety of works whose concern was the cultural explanation of historical and geographical change, Wagner and Mikesell (1962) identified five themes - culture, culture area, cultural landscape, culture history, and cultural ecology - which constituted 'the core of cultural geography'. Culture for them drew attention to communities of persons occupying a certain extended and visually continuous space and on the numerous features of belief and behaviour that are held in common by member [sic] of such communities'. Culture 'rests upon a geographic basis'; 'language .... is obviously a critical component of any culture': in sum, 'cultural geography studies the distribution in time and space of cultures and elements of cultures'.55 We have seen that the Highlands in the past were defined on the basis of the geographical extent of spoken Gaelic, the area over which the clan system held sway as a particular social system and cultural trait, by given material practices, and crucially (yet most indefinably), on the grounds of a separateness rooted in received belief and motivating ideologies: by, on the one hand, the perceptions of outsiders for whom the Gaidhealtachd was unknown, irreligious and uncivilised and, on the other, by the constituent beliefs and practices of Highlanders themselves whose collective regional consciousness of themselves as apart from (even above) Lowlanders was yet also underlain by internal tension between and within the constituent clans and kin groups. Given these factors, it is possible to see Highland Scotland as a 'culture region' or 'culture area', whose distinctiveness rested upon a human population sharing similar or related cultures or single related culture traits or complexes, and whose cultural history has been too often typified as the decline of inherent and 'traditional' Highland cultural forms under the influence of an externally-imposed English-speaking culture complex. The expansion and later retreat of the Gaelic language area, the spread of established religion, and the dissolution of kinship-based social structures and tenurial practices might all be used as 'cultural traits' both to identify the Highland 'culture area' and to shed light on its transformation. The association of relief, rainfall, and cultural characteristics within a given area highlight the Highlands as Scotland's 'heartland' or Gaelic 'cultural hearth', a sort of 'Pura Scotia' in the sense Fox, and later, Bowen, have considered Wales a 'Pays de Galles', with a Welsh cultural core or zone of 'cultural continuity' (Pura Wallia) and a fringe of 'cultural replacement' (Marcha Wallia).56 In both cases, the core is now relict, an 'archaic fringe' to the English-speaking 'core society' more 'modern' in its attributes. Meinig's model of core, domain, and sphere in his study of the Mormon culture region may be placed within the theme of culture area. In this model, the 'core' is that area 'displaying the greatest density of occupance, intensity of organization, strength, and homogeneity of the particular features characteristic of the culture under study'. The 'domain' is where those features are dominant over others not of that culture, and the 'sphere' is that outlying fringe where members of that culture live as a minority among those of a different culture.57 It is tempting to see the emergence of a Highland presence in lowland cities and further afield from the later eighteenth century as 'the sphere' of Gaelic culture, and change in the Highlands as the break-up of 'the core', but in so doing, emphasis is placed more upon description of patterns than explanation of causes.

In another sense, it is suggestive to consider the Highlands as a 'cultural landscape' in which the arrangement, style, and materials of such elements as field boundaries, house types, and settlement distribution together with language, dress and a given natural setting produced a distinctive way of life or 'genre de vie'. In Sauer's terms, 'the cultural landscape is fashioned from a natural landscape by a culture group. Culture is the agent, the natural landscape is the medium, the cultural landscape is the result... With the introduction of a different - that is, an alien - culture, a rejuvenation of the cultural landscape sets in, or a new landscape is superimposed on remnants of an older order'.58 Understanding the Highlands as a cultural landscape would perhaps by limited by our fragmentary knowledge on early occupying groups and 'natural' landscape,59 and the variable quality of later source material,60 but an approach that focussed on this 'interplay between a given human community, embodying certain cultural preferences and potentials, and a particular set of natural circumstances',61 might provide a general framework for study as well as insight into the distribution of cleared clachan settlements, the distribution of sculptured stones, the evolution of estate boundaries, or even the provenance of Gaelic manuscripts as indicators of given cultural landscapes.62 And consideration of landscape change over time would involve ideas of 'culture history' and 'cultural ecology'.

Three principal difficulties arise in review here: first, the distinctions are less clear in practice than in theory; second, they are predicated upon a particular and unquestioning view of culture, and third, culture is seen not only as something universally shared, but also as derivative of political and socio-economic functions. It may be true as Wagner and Mikesell note, that 'any sign of human action in a landscape implies a culture, recalls a history, and demands an ecological interpretation; the history of any people evokes its setting in a landscape, its ecological problems, and its cultural concomitants'.63 As Mikesell later observed, 'although cultural geography, by definition, calls for explicit recognition of the concept of culture, most cultural geographers have adopted a laissez-faire attitude towards the meanings of culture'.64

The word 'culture' has enjoyed a range of meanings. In its early uses, it was a noun of process, the tending or cultivation of something. From the early sixteenth century, the sense of tending nature was extended to a process of human development, both senses remaining in use until the later eighteenth century. From that period, culture became synonymous with civilisation as a social process, with cultivation as an achieved social state.65 Although a further distinction saw culture used to describe artistic or intellectual practices, the meaning in which culture expressed the sense of civilisation, an achieved social state in contrast to barbarism and also a sense of development which implied process and progress, has been of particular significance.66 The idea of culture not as an attribute but rather as a socially-constituted process receives greater attention in what follows. It is not, however, a point made of culture in many geographical studies.

The traditional themes of cultural geography drew their inspiration from later nineteenth-century geography, particularly Ratzel and German geography, with its focus upon the moulding of a natural setting by human groups, and from social anthropologists of the later nineteenth and early twentieth centuries.67 One key influence was Tylor's Primitive Culture (1871). Tylor wrote how 'Culture... in its wide ethnographic sense, is that complex whole which includes knowledge, belief, art, morals, law, custom, and any other capabilities and habits required by man as a member of society'.68 The idea of culture as a complex whole or 'superorganic', an entity or pattern of behaviour irreducible to the actions of individuals yet possessed by human groups, was further outlined by the anthropologists Kroeber and Lowie, elaborated upon by White and adopted amongst geographers most notably by Sauer and others in the early twentieth century. Widespread acceptance of the idea that culture was 'a thing sui generis which can only be explained in terms of itself', and of the view that culture generates its own forms independent of men as its 'carriers' has led to the often uncritical adoption of a particular notion of culture among cultural geographers: a notion that saw man not only as passive but culture as consensual and universally shared. To treat culture in this way ignores explanation of cultural characteristics, disguises the role of individuals and fails to consider that culture is not autonomous but the result of social interaction: to quote Duncan (1980),

> ... there is little or no discussion of social
> stratification, the political interests of
> particular groups, and the conflicts which arise
> from their opposing interests... there is little
> discussion of government and other institutional
> policies, or the effects of business organizations
> and financial institutions on the landscape.69

That there has been little discussion of these issues and
only a slow departure from accepted ideas on culture in
geographical analysis is perhaps understandable given the
general lack of analytic precision attached to the term
'culture'.70 Kroeber and Kluckholn conclude their review
of interpretations of culture by considering six categories
into which all usages could be subsumed: culture is
'enumeratively descriptive' (listing artefacts, social
habits); 'historical' (culture constitutes 'a particular
strain of social heredity'); 'normative' (culture as a
'superorganic' entity of values and norms): 'psychological'
(emphasis being placed on transmitted ways of solving
ecological problems); 'structural' (in the sense that
cultures can be regarded as systems or models of reality
that permit 'patterned ways of behaviour' to be developed);
and 'genetic' (wherein cultural symbols are transmitted
over time and space).71 The last three have been considered by one author to be of greatest significance to human
geography given the need for explanation of patterns of
human occupance.72 For Wagner, in a partial renunciation
of the earlier themes of cultural geography, culture is
both 'structural' and 'genetic' - the constituted and
transmitted behaviour of groups: 'It is behaviour, that is,
meaningful activity, not mere activity as such, that
counts, and behaviour is actively interpreted convention-
ly. The individual alone is not the fitting unit for
description and analysis of meaningful behaviour and its
consequences'. Further, 'culture has to be carried in
specific, located, purposeful, rule-following, and
rule-making groupings of people communicating and inter-
acting with one another'.73 But this definition differs
little from Sauer's earlier and prescriptive claim that
'culture is the learned and conventionalized activity of a
group that occupies an area'.74 Other studies that have
reviewed more recent developments in cultural geography
have been equally reluctant to depart from the totalising
view of culture as shared and learned beliefs.75
    Cultural geographers have been slow to rise to the
challenge in recent years 'to narrow the concept of

"culture" so that it includes less and reveals more'.76
Thus, for Mikesell, 'One may doubt that a separate geographical definition can or should be proposed and yet still
assert that geographers ought to give more serious thought
to how they wish to use the concept of culture'.77   As
Schneider has observed, 'It may be that geographers need to
move more into the upper air, where some "theory" or a bit
of frankly high-flown speculation about culture may be
appropriate'.78   For Duncan,

> The term culture could be saved if it were not
> treated as an explanatory variable in itself but
> used to signify contexts for action or sets of
> arrangements between people at various levels of
> aggregation. 79

These 'contexts for action' and 'sets of arrangements
between people' are understood here in two senses: firstly,
as the relationships people maintain between one another in
the course of their daily life; and secondly, in the more
general dialectic relationship between man and nature in
the satisfaction of social wants and given the means
available to realise them. What follows here in the use of
both senses is neither to propose definitions nor advance
theories; it is rather to speculate that a more critically
analytic concept of culture may prove generally useful in
understanding the links between people and place,80 and
useful particularly in investigating the relationships
between beliefs and social and material practices in the
Highlands of Scotland.81

Culture and class: towards a more analytic model of culture

The conceptual model of culture here employed takes as its
initial premise the view that attempts to use anthropological concepts of culture to analyse social class formations
and transformations are condemned to treat culture either
as a 'given', some sort of reflex attachment to more basic
political-econonmic changes or as a self-determining
phenomenon - a 'superorganic' - over and above the reali-
ties of social class.82   This is no new claim. Blaut has
recognised that the traditional ideas of culture employed
within many explorations of historical and geographical
change neglect 'the fundamental, and almost universal, fact
that cultures are divided into classes'.83   While the
concept of class is dynamic, that of culture based only
upon traditional beliefs, a shared systema of values or
shared use of language, lacks a sense of process deriving

from the ties people have with one another - the social relations of production - and the political and economic bases to these social ties - the forces of material production. Material life is a collective thing, made by people as they transform their natural world and expressed in 'symbolic production'84; styles of language, dress, social conduct, architecture and so on. Culture is a central not a peripheral part of these relationships.

> Without any dynamic structure of its own, ... culture is bound to appear as epiphenomenal, secondary and derivative - as simply a superstruc- ture to be tacked on, and ultimately responsive to, a political-economic base ... . It is a totalizing concept first because everything becomes, or is considered, 'culture'. There is material culture, symbolic culture, ritual culture, social institutions, patterned behaviour, language-as-culture, and values, beliefs, ideas, ideologies, etc. Second, not only is everything in a society 'culture', but the concept is totalizing because everyone in the society is supposed to have the same culture ... or at least to be measured by its standards ...

> ... Whatever the utility of this concept for understanding hunting and gathering bands, or relatively egalitarian village social systems, it is not a very effective concept for analysing class-based societies In situations of class conflict the notion of shared values provides no help in understanding either how upper-class cultural hegemony is imposed on a populace, or how oppositional cultures are formed and asserted. 85

This idea of culture serves to relate the production and reproduction of everyday needs and capacities with the dominant mode of production of a given human population in any geographical area. The relationship between a given environment - nature - and a dominant mode of production - human groups - may be seen as historical and flexible. Men and women make their own history and transform themselves as they transform their landscape; a materialist relation- ship recognised within the cultural geographic tradition, but not fully articulated. As Cosgrove observes, the concerns of cultural geography with human agency and environment have not recognised as they might the dialecti- cal unity between society and nature, a unity mediated through patterns of human production grounded in a particular natural context.86

The relationships underlying this perspective to culture were never fully elaborated by Marx as a formal cultural theory, although a useful start point to critical analysis is the formulation of 'base' and 'superstructure' which appears in outline in the Preface to his <u>A Contribution to the Critique of Political Economy</u>.

> In the social production of their life, men enter into definite relations that are indispensable and independent of their will, relations of production which correspond to a definite stage of development of their material productive forces. The sum total of these relations of production constitutes the economic structure of society, the real foundation, on which rises a legal and political superstructure and to which correspond definite forms of social consciousness. The mode of production of material life conditions the social,political and intellectual life process in general. It is not the consciousness of men that determines their being, but, on the contrary, their social being that determines their consciousness ... With the change of the economic foundation the entire immense superstructure is more or less rapidly transformed. In considering such transformations the distinction should always be made between the material transformation of the economic conditions of production, which can be determined with the precision of natural science, and the legal, political, religious, aesthetic or philosophic - in short, ideological - forms in which men become conscious of this conflict and fight it out. 87

This conception of the determining base and determined superstructure is not without difficulties. Neither 'base' nor 'superstructure' are precise concepts nor discrete and static categories capable of being employed as if they were descriptive terms for observable 'areas' of social life. Simply to see 'the base' as 'the real social existence of man' or 'the real relations of production corresponding to a stage of the development of material productive forces' disguises the fact that the base is not a state but a process: 'And we cannot ascribe to that process certain fixed properties for subsequent deduction to the variable processes of the superstructure'. 88 The framework should be seen not as determining but relational.

> According to the materialist conception of
> history, the ultimately determining element in
> history is the production and reproduction of real
> life. More than this neither Marx nor I have
> every asserted. Hence if somebody twists this
> into saying that the economic element is the only
> determining one, he transforms that proposition
> into a meaningless, abstract, senseless phrase.
> The economic situation is the basis, but the
> various elements of the superstructure - political
> forms of the class struggle and its results, to
> wit: constitutions established by the victorious
> class after a successful battle, etc., juridical
> forms, and even the reflexes of all these actual
> struggles in the brains of the participants,
> political, juristic, philosophical theories,
> religious views and their further development into
> systems of dogma - also exercise their influence
> upon the course of the historical struggles and in
> many cases preponderate in determining their form.
> 89

The conceptualisation of culture as reflexive and
relational - within and across both economic 'base' and
ideological and institutional 'superstructure' - avoids the
distinctions made by some cultural theorists between the
'economic domain' (subsistence technology), and the
'ideational domain' (religion, law, ideology, etc.). It
eschews the position whereby 'Either culture is regarded as
wholly derivative from the forms of social organization ...
or the forms of social organization are regarded as
behavioural embodiments of cultural patterns'.90

In an attempt at further refinement of this base-
superstructure model, Williams has urged that the notion of
'superstructure' move towards a related range of cultural
practices and that the idea of 'the base' be considered not
as a fixed abstraction but as the consequences of 'the
specific activities of men in real social and economic
relationships, containing fundamental contradictions and
variations and therefore always in a state of dynamic
process. Further, the constitutions, institutions and
ideologies which provide the basis to a more flexible view
of superstructure are seen to be related to but not
determined by, the economic 'foundation'.

These institutions and ideologies should also be seen
to operate in regard to particular classes: they 'simply
have to be seen as expressing and ratifying the domination
of a particular class'.91 As has been elsewhere noted, 'In
class society culture is the product of class experience.

24

The common sense reflections of each class upon its own
material experience is part of its struggle with other
classes, each attempting to impose what it sees as the
universal validity of that experience'. And when in class
societies surplus production is appropriated by the
dominant group, 'symbolic production is likewise seized as
hegemonic class culture to be imposed across all
classes'.92 In considering culture as a processual
relationship over and above the simple categorisation of
social life as a material economic base and an
institutional or 'cultural' superstructure, the notion of
class may be likewise understood here and in what follows
in a relational sense; not only in Thompson's terms of 'the
productive relations into which men are born - or enter
involuntarily'93 - but also with respect to the question of
class consciousness as the recognition by one group both
of its own identity in opposition to the interests of
another class or classes.94 The use of class as a
description of divisions in social structure does not, of
course, mark the beginning of those divisions in society,
but the use of 'class' by the early nineteenth century in
place of hitherto commonly-used terms like 'rank' or
'order' both reflected and directed the by then advanced
division of society into layers or groups depending upon
matters of relative economic and political domination.95
Culture as a process simultaneously economic and political
may then be seen as the expression of class relationships
and the imposition in various ways of the domination of one
class over another. Important in this respect is the
question of a dominating ideology which, for the ruling
class, both 'rationalises' its position of economic and
political domination and 'explains' to the subordinate
class why it should accept its subordination.96

Ideology is a complex term.97 Three common connotations have been noted: a system of beliefs characteristic
of a particular class or group; a system of illusory
beliefs - false consciousness - in contrast to 'true' or
scientific knowledge; and the general process of production
of meanings and ideas. If, in class societies, all beliefs
are founded on class position, the concept of ideology may
be equatable with a particular self-interest. But the
expression of the practical consciousness of one group or
class is not independent of material relationships and
social processes.98 It is bound up with them as the arena
in which certain values and beliefs are fought out. If we
consider ideology as that system of beliefs characteristic
of a particular class or group, this is not to separate
those beliefs either from a particular social situation or
from the symbols and meanings through which such values are
expressed and made meaningful. And in the context of

geographical explanation, the notion of ideology may not only be equatable with a particular class or group but with the continued occupance of a given area by that class or people to give what may be understood here as a regional consciousness. This is not regional consciousness imposed 'from without' - a sort of typified image or false consciousness of a region and people - but consciousness 'from within', resulting from what Marx considered that 'historically created relationship to nature and of individuals towards each other' which gave to each and every particular place 'a special character of its own'.99

This relationship between ideas and their geographical, material, and social context was central to Marx's views on cultural analysis.

> The production of ideas, of conceptions, of consciousness, is at first directly interwoven with the material activity and the material intercourse of men, the language of real life. Conceiving, thinking, the mental intercourse of men, appear at this stage as the direct efflux of their material behaviour. The same applied to mental production as expressed in the language of politics, laws, morality, religion, metaphysics, etc., of a people. Men are the producers of their conceptions, ideas, etc., - real, active men, as they are conditioned by a definite development of their productive forces and of the intercourse corresponding to these, up to its furthest forms. 100

'Ideas' and 'material activity' are not simple categories for analysis. Each needs to be grounded in a specific historical and geographical setting.

> In order to study the connection between intellectual and material production it is above all essential to conceive the latter in its determined historical form and not as a general category. For example, there corresponds to the capitalist mode of production a type of intellectual production quite different from that which corresponded to the medieval mode of production. 101

And within the capitalist mode of production, ideas and types of intellectual production were indissoluble from class interests.

> The ideas of the ruling class are, in every age,

> the ruling ideas: i.e., the class which is the
> dominant <u>material</u> force in society is at the same
> time its dominant <u>intellectual</u> force...
>
> ... The dominant ideas are nothing more than the
> ideal expression of the dominant material relation-
> ships, the dominant material relationships grasped
> as ideas, and thus of the relationships which make
> one class the ruling one; they are consequently
> the ideas of its dominance. 102.

Of additional value in exploration of these ideas of
domination within society of one class and its culture and
ideas over others and on the means by which that ideology
and culture was realised in practice is the concept of
hegemony.

Hegemony and the means of cultural transformation

The notion of hegemony as a means of understanding relations between social classes, more especially the cultural
dominance of one class and the means by which that class
maintains its dominance, is best associated with the work
of Gramsci in whose writings, however, the term is both
complicated and ambivalent. Gramsci principally distinguished between 'rule', expressed in overtly political
forms and in periods of crisis by direct coercion or
military intervention, and 'hegemony' which sought to exert
consensual relationships through intellectual, moral,
economic and social forces, expressed and manipulated
through institutions and practically organised by specific
dominant values.103 To an extent, hegemony goes beyond the
ideas of culture and ideology as here defined because it
allows consideration of relations of domination and
subordination as a whole lived experience and because those
institutions, symbols, and values through which a culture
or the culture of a particular class is identified as
hegemonic are not now a 'superstructure' to the economic
'base' nor just a reflection, as dominant ideas, of the
dominant forces of production: they are themselves among
the processes of socio-economic formation.

> It is a whole body of practices and expectations,
> over the whole of living: our senses and assign-
> ments of energy, our shaping perceptions of
> ourselves and our world. It is a lived system of
> meanings and values - constitutive and constitut-
> ing - which as they are experienced as practices

appear as reciprocally confirming. It thus
constitutes a sense of reality for most people in
the society, a sense of absolute because experienced reality beyond which it is very difficult
for most members of the society to move, in most
areas of their lives. It is, that is to say, in
the strongest sense a 'culture', but a culture
which has also to be seen as the lived dominance
and subordination of particular classes. 104

Hegemony is a <u>process</u>, one in which the agencies of
control within civil society - the church, schools, trade
unions, industrial organisations and so on - are key
elements. Hegemony is more specific than questions of
class identity because it relates whole social processes in
which people 'define and shape their lives to specific
distributions of power and influence'. It is more broadly
based than ideology, for 'what is decisive is not only the
conscious system of ideas and beliefs, but the whole lived
social process as practically organised by dominant
meanings and values'.105 And it is more precise than the
notion of social control though it recognises as does that
term the important place of institutions within soci-
ety.106 In discussing the analytic use of the term,
Billinge has noted that representation of hegemony as a
'culture', 'a lived system of meanings and values', not
only allows us to go beyond the relational idea of class in
political and economic terms but also 'gives us an entirely
new perspective from which to view the process of acculturation and the crucial importance of culture itself in
shaping social ideas and social relations'. Hegemony does
not neglect the beliefs and meanings embraced by given
ideologies or the economic and political relations in and
between classes: rather it transforms these ideals and
relationships into practice as they are lived and experienced in everyday life. At any time and as they change
over time in a given area, relationships of dominance and
subordination may be seen 'as in effect a saturation of the
whole process of living - not only of political and
economic activity, but of the whole substance of lived
identities and relationships'.107

In Gramsci's terms, hegemonic domination within civil
society depends upon the role of intellectuals operating
within the classes exercising political and economic
control. He distinguished between 'organic' and
'traditional' intellectuals. The former are closely tied
to the ruling class they represent giving it 'homogeneity
and awareness of its own function' on all levels or
'floors' of society. The latter group comprises, firstly,

creative artists and scholars who are traditionally regarded as intellectuals, and, secondly, the vestiges of organic intellectuals from previous social formations (for example, ecclesiastics). Femia has considered that 'While the traditional intellectuals do not necessarily share the world-view of the ruling group, they eventually effect a compromise with it, in part because of institutional pressures and financial inducements'.

> But the only ideas capable of becoming generally accepted and institutionalised in social life are those which both serve the interests and reflect the experience of either the dominant group or the class that is 'rising' ...

> ... While these successful ideas originate in the minds of great intellectuals, they are transmitted throughout society by lesser intellectuals - teachers, political activists, journalists, priests, etc. - working within an institutional context. 108

Intellectuals propagate and disseminate a class-based hegemony and ideology which is dominant as a consequence of a particular authoritarian structure. This structure should not, however, be seen as monolithic.

In the imposition of any culture, either in the totalising sense of a suite of cultural artefacts to be laid aside as others are adopted or in the sense in which culture is mediated through hegemonic class control, there will always be opposition to and denial of those values. Hegemony may be 'total' in the sense it saturates the consciousness of those people under its sway, but it is not held absolutely by all nor is it without internal contradictions. Hegemony is not an abstract category or even the affirmation of ideology; it is rather the variable assertion to given purposes of elite values and claims and is, therefore, continually active and adjusting.

> We have to emphasize that hegemony is not singular; indeed that its own internal structures are highly complex, and have continually to be renewed, recreated and defended; and by the same token, that they can be continually challenged and in certain respects modified. 109

In discussing opposition to the hegemony of a dominant culture, we may distinguish between alternative hegemony and counter-hegemony.110 The question of class conscious-

ness as oppositional hegemony – not merely in opposition to
but as a <u>revolutionary</u> or at least overtly contradictory
consciousness through which to overthrow the ruling
class-has also been considered in this context.111   By
alternative hegemony is meant the emergence and consolidation of a new hegemonic culture, associated with the rise
to power of a new class. Alternative hegemonies may exist,
however, only in an unrealised state; for Thompson, the
idea is 'inapplicable to a subordinate class which by the
nature of its situation cannot dominate the ethos of a
society'.112   Counter hegemony is simply an opposition to
the prevailing hegemony that may or may not be motivated by
an articulated class consciousness, but is nevertheless
characterised by attempts to limit or constrain the
dominant hegemony. Counter hegemony may take several forms
– mockery, evasion and distancing from dominant claims, or
more politicised forms such as food riots, machine-
breaking, land wars and refusal to pay rent. These last
may initiate domination through rule – military suppression, for example. The formation of counter hegemony or
any form of fully articulated oppositional hegemony may be
limited by such things as the fragmented nature of existing
social relations, the existence or not of a radical party
or institutions of opposition, or as a result of geographical isolation: as Williams notes, 'The degree of existence
of these alternative and oppositional forms is itself a
matter of constant historical variation in real circumstances'.113 We may further consider the distinction between
'residual' and 'emergent' forms of oppositional culture.
By 'residual' is meant those meanings, values and experiences which cannot be expressed in terms of the dominant
culture yet remain lived and practised as part of the
residue of some previous social formation. Such residual
notions may, in time, be incorporated into dominant culture
or fade from memory but certain residual values may survive
within dominant culture. 'Emergent' means not only new
values and practices being created within society, but also
how dominant culture reacts to those new forms. Emergent
cultural forms may be alternative without being oppositional. But as the claims of emergent forms extend, what was
once casual disregard for dominant values may become open
dissent, and the forms and institutions of dominant culture
may need to defend and modify, to incorporate the oppositional claims.114
    Hegemony is thus not only an active process of cultural
control but a gathering together of seemingly separate and
perhaps even disparate meanings and values incorporated
within a dominant culture and an effective social order.
Williams has considered that this process of incorporation

depends critically upon the role of 'tradition', 'institutions', and 'formations'.115 Incorporation and dominance depends also on the mediating role of language. Tradition is more than simply 'the surviving past'. Within any culture and dominant hegemony, only certain meanings and practices are selected to identify and define social structures and cultural values that are not part of the hegemony. Tradition in this sense becomes an aspect of contemporary social and cultural organisation to substantiate the dominance of a specific class. Tradition may also embrace notions of the retrospective affirmation of past practices in the face of hegemonic control, but at a deeper level, tradition is the process through which a dominant hegemony maintains the historical and cultural ratification of a contemporary order; the process of incorporating residual or emergent cultural forms into its own structures.

The establishment and maintenance of dominant hegemony depends crucially on institutions, though not alone: 'it is never only a question of formally identifiable institutions'. In rethinking the concerns of cultural geography, Wagner recognised the significance of 'the traditions embodied in institutions and perpetuated by them as effective cultural subsystems'.116 But important in this context are the personnel involved (the 'greater' and 'lesser' intellectuals), the ideology they espouse, and the hegemony they practise. Institutions mean not only the Church or school authorities, but also the family, the work-place, the community, the clan. For Anderson, Gramsci's 'listing of church and schools as instruments of hegemony within the private associations of civil society puts the application of the concept to the capitalist societies of the West beyond any doubt'.117 Further,

> The educational institutions are usually the main agencies of the transmission of an effective dominant culture, and this is now a major economic as well as cultural activity; indeed it is both in the same moment.
> ... The processes of education; the processes of a much wider social training within institutions like the family; the practical definitions and organisation of work; the selective tradition at an intellectual and theoretical level: all these forces are involved in a continual making and remaking of an effective dominant culture, and on them, as experienced, as built into our living, its reality depends.118

31

But an effective hegemonic culture is more than the sum of its controlling institutions. It derives its influence also from the relations individuals, institutions and ideologies have with particular formations; 'those effective movements and tendencies, in intellectual and artistic life, which have significant and sometimes decisive influences on the active development of a culture, and which have a variable and often oblique relation to formal institutions'.119 And important to these relations is the question of the language used by the dominant cultural class within and across its institutions and formations. In it simplest sense, language arises from the need to communicate but it also derives from particular social relations and a dominant mode of production: 'language like capital, is an instrument of domination a carrier of cultural power'.120

> Each class naturally attempts to turn communication into a tool for imposing its own ideas upon other classes. The class that effectively rules succeeds in presenting its particular use of language as the only correct one. But, in itself language is neither ideological nor derived: it belongs to the basis of all social relations. Endowed with a structure of its own, it does not "reflect" reality, it <u>expresses</u> and <u>represents</u> it.121

The senses in which the phrase 'particular use of language' may be used include the conflict existing between two or more languages both as expressive of certain class values and in the wider meaning of conflict between two cultures. Language is thus at one level a cultural 'given', but at other levels, it may be seen as a medium through which ideological forms establish cultural hegemony as a constitutive and incorporative element of material social practice.

The concept of culture employed here and the ideas from which it derives are not intended to be prescriptive of what culture is. In suggesting the relationships between cultural and socio-economic change to be mutual and reflexive the model allows for diversity and complexity, for variations in the scale, nature and impact of change, for contradictions, and for an understanding of cultural transformation that treats culture as a process not an attribute of more 'basic' social and political change. The crucial concept is that of hegemony. An understanding of cultural hegemony as a process requires analysis of the actual formal institutions engaged in the dissemination of culture, of intellectual formations, of traditions, ideologies, oppositional claims and residual cultures, and of the role of language as the basis to social relations and as 'an instrument of domination, a carrier of cultural power'. With these points in mind, let us now return to the case of the Scottish Highlands as a culture region.

Cultural transformation and the Scottish Highlands

Given the acceptance in the past of the linguistic basis to definition, we may take Walker's enumeration of the Gaelic-speaking parishes in about 1765 to be the Highlands, and thus identify more exactly the arena in which the cultural and social conflict discussed in what follows took place (Figure 1.2 and Table 1.1). Yet however useful definition as a language area is for descriptive purposes and in placing a boundary to the area under study, it will not get us far in exploration of the processes of cultural transformation. For one thing, the Highlands as a language area has declined over time from 1698 (the earliest date for which we know its extent), to the picture provided by the censuses of 1881 and 1981 (Figures 1:3 - 1:5).122 And for another, not everyone in the Gaidhealtachd as defined then or now spoke Gaelic only or Gaelic to everyone for every social purpose. Language patterns were complex and varied according to age, sex, purpose and rank or class. More importantly, English was the language of authority and cultural power, the language through which the processes of material and intellectual change were expressed and legitimated. Maps of a declining language area disguise the processes taking place within the Highlands. For this reason, the cultural transformation of the Highlands should not be seen as the move from a uniform culture area possessed of 'traditional' and commonly-shared values or material artefacts to one identified as 'modern' through use of a different language or other artefacts. To do so reifies culture and assigns it causative power over and above questions of the constituent social and economic relations within the region. Highland culture, and the social relations between people and between Highlanders and their natural setting are seen only from outside and only to respond to external influences. This ignores both the geographical variability of the area and the links in economy and society with the rest of Scotland, and considers Highland society to be implicated in an 'ideal' past where 'traditional' values were held by all. Similarly, to interpret the making of the Highland landscape as simply

Figure 1.2   The Highland parishes and other parishes in study area

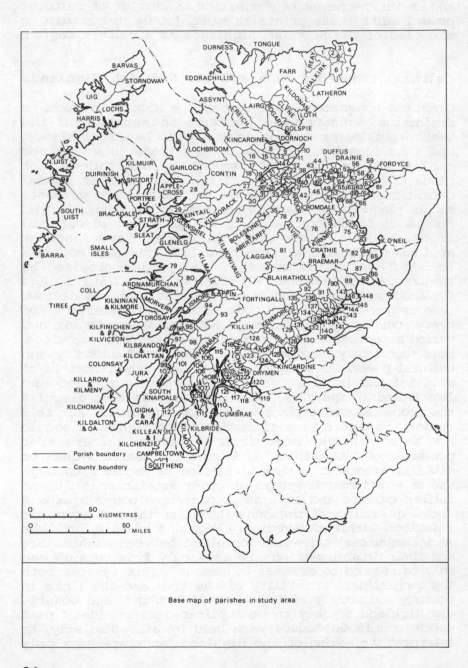

Base map of parishes in study area

Table 1.1

List of parishes in study area (see Figure 1.2)

Number on Figure 1.2	Parish Name	Number on Figure 1.2	Parish name
1	Thurso	33	Inverness and
2	Olrig		Bona
3	Dunnet	34	Dores
4	Cannisbay	35	Daviot and
5	Bower		Dunlichity
6	Watten	36	Croy and
7	Wick		Dalcross
8	Edderton	37	Petty
9	Tain	38	Ardersier
10	Tarbat	39	Nairn
11	Fearn	40	Auldearn
12	Nigg	41	Dyke and Moy
13	Logie Easter	42	Ardclach
14	Kilmuir Easter	43	Forres
15	Rosskeen	44	Kinloss
16	Alness	45	Rafford
17	Kiltearn	46	Edinkillie
18	Fodderty	47	Alves
19	Dingwall	48	Elgin
20	Urquhart and	49	Dallas
	Logie Wester	50	Spynie
21	Resolis	51	St. Andrews
22	Cromarty		Lhanbryd
23	Rosemarkie	52	Urquhart
24	Avoch	53	Birnie
25	Knockbain	54	New Spynie
26	Killearnan	55	Rothes
27	Urray	56	Speymouth
28	Lochcarron	57	Bellie
29	Lochalsh	58	Rathven
30	Kiltarlity	59	Cullen
	and Convinth	60	Deskford
31	Kirkhill	61	Ordiquhill
32	Urquhart and	62	Grange
	Glenmoriston	63	Keith

<u>Table 1.1. (Continued)</u>

Number on Figure 1.2	Parish name	Number on Figure 1.2	Parish name
64	Cairnie	91	Kirkmichael
65	Glass		(Perthshire)
66	Botriphnie	92	Moulin
67	Boharm	93	Glenorchy and
68	Mortlach		Inishail
69	Aberlour	94	Ardchattan
70	Knockando	95	Muckairn
71	Cabrach	96	Kilmore and
72	Inveraven		Kilbride
73	Glenbucket	97	Kilninver and
74	Towie		Kilmelfort
75	Strathdon	98	Kilchrennan and
76	Abernethy and		Dalavich
	Kincardine	99	Craignish
77	Duthil and	100	Kilmartin
	Rothiemurchus	101	Kilmichael
78	Moy and		Glassary
	Dalarossie	102	North Knapdale
79	Arisaig and	103	Kilfinan
	Moidart	104	Stralachlan
80	Ardgour	105	Strachur
81	Kingussie and	106	Kilmodan
	Insh	107	Inverchaolain
82	Glenmuick	108	Dunoon and
	Tullich and		Kilmun
	Glengairn	109	North Bute
83	Logie Coldstone	110	Rothesay
84	Aboyne and	111	Kingarth
	Glentanar	112	Kilcalmonell
85	Birse	113	Saddell and
86	Edzell		Skipness
87	Lochlee	114	Rosneath
88	Lethnot and	115	Lochgoilhead and
	Navar		Kilmorich
89	Cortachy and	116	Arrochar
	Clova	117	Cardross
90	Glenisla	118	Old Kilpatrick

Table 1.1. (Continued)

Number on Figure 1.2	Parish Name	Number on Figure 1.2	Parish Name
119	New Kilpatrick	134	Little Dunkeld
120	Dumbarton	135	Weem
121	Bonhill	136	Logierait
122	Kilmarnock	137	Dunkeld and
123	Aberfoyle		Dowally
124	Port of Menteith	138	Lethendy
125	Kilmadock	139	Caputh
126	Balquhidder	140	Clunie
127	Ardoch	141	Kinloch
128	Muthill	142	Blairgowrie
129	Monzievaird and	143	Rattray
	Strowan	144	Bendochy
130	Crieff	145	Alyth
131	Fowlis Wester	146	Kingoldrum
132	Logiealmond	147	Glentrathen
133	Auchtergaven	148	Kirriemuir

Figure 1.3   The <u>Gaidhealtachd</u> as enumerated in 1698

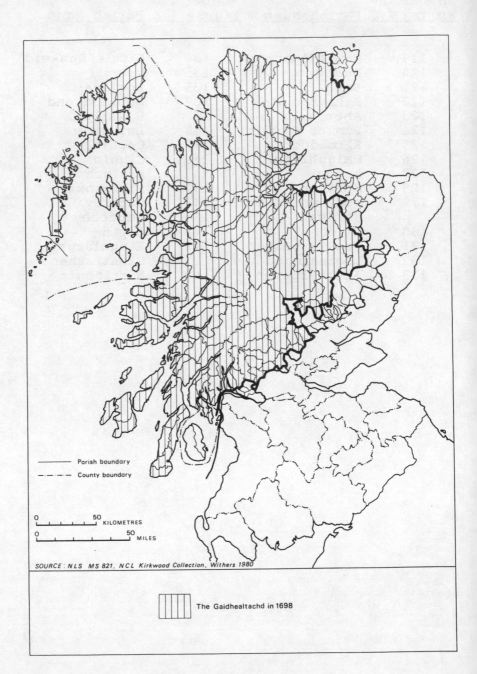

SOURCE: N LS MS 821, NCL Kirkwood Collection, Withers 1980

The Gaidhealtachd in 1698

The Scottish Highlands as Culture Region

Figure 1.4 The <u>Gaidhealtachd</u> in 1881

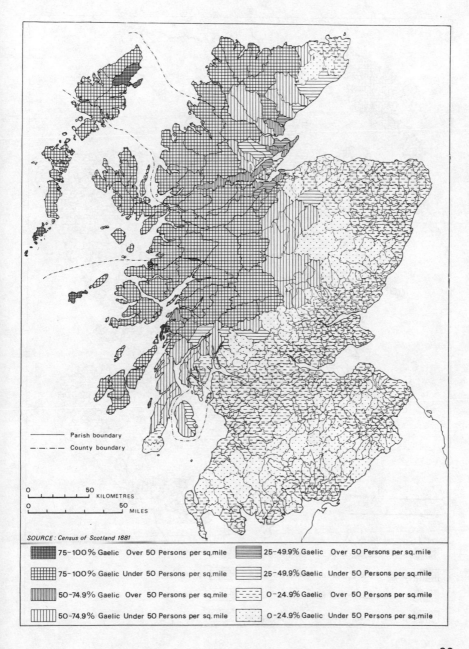

Parish boundary

County boundary

0   50   KILOMETRES

0   50   MILES

SOURCE : Census of Scotland 1881

75-100% Gaelic Over 50 Persons per sq.mile	25-49.9% Gaelic Over 50 Persons per sq.mile
75-100% Gaelic Under 50 Persons per sq.mile	25-49.9% Gaelic Under 50 Persons per sq.mile
50-74.9% Gaelic Over 50 Persons per sq.mile	0-24.9% Gaelic Over 50 Persons per sq.mile
50-74.9% Gaelic Under 50 Persons per sq.mile	0-24.9% Gaelic Under 50 Persons per sq.mile

The Scottish Highlands as Culture Region

Figure 1.5 The Gàidhealtachd in 1981

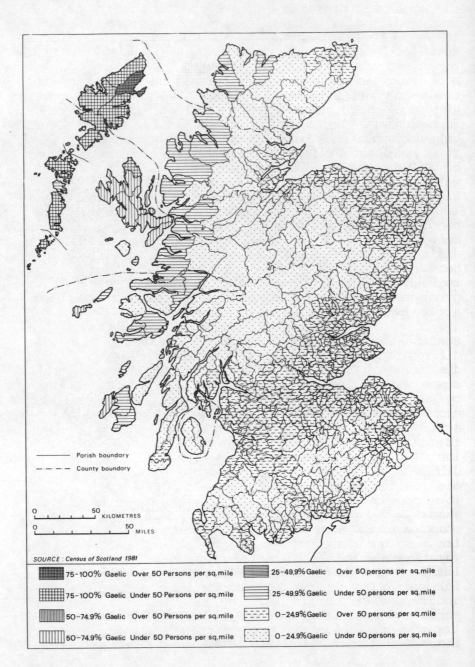

Parish boundary
County boundary

0   50   KILOMETRES
0   50   MILES

SOURCE : Census of Scotland 1981

75-100% Gaelic Over 50 Persons per sq.mile | 25-49.9% Gaelic Over 50 persons per sq.mile

75-100% Gaelic Under 50 Persons per sq.mile | 25-49.9% Gaelic Under 50 persons per sq.mile

50-74.9% Gaelic Over 50 Persons per sq.mile | 0-24.9% Gaelic Over 50 persons per sq.mile

50-74.9% Gaelic Under 50 Persons per sq.mile | 0-24.9% Gaelic Under 50 persons per sq.mile

the move from a 'natural' to a 'cultural' phenomenon without recognising that not everyone in the Highlands or even within particular classes subscribed to the same given values and thus would not have regarded the landscape in the same way, denies the socially-constituted nature of both landscape and culture. Evocation of the disintegration of 'the Highland way-of-life' as the break-up of a traditional culture to a modern society ignores the fact that there was no one Highland genre de vie. It ignores both the relations between and within social classes and the fact that, as several authors have noted, the later history of the Highlands is broadly the history of class formation and the imposition of particular class-related values founded upon political control and economic power. It is true that a close bonding and sense of identity might be deliberately maintained through, say, established marriage patterns.123 But it is also true that many Highland chiefs-cum-landlords looked beyond their own language, land and kin to derive and assert an authority based on capital and political dominance through involvement with people of similar class and ideology in Lowland and English society. And at the same time as many chiefs became part of the new ranks and classes attendant upon the regional articulation of capitalism as the dominant mode of production, some members of Highland society could not accommodate themselves at all

These differences - of material circumstance and sentiment - are as important to recognise as they are difficult to generalise upon. As Hunter notes in his discussion of the making of the crofting community, that community was brought into existence in a relational sense by landlords who decided which areas should be occupied by crofters and which not and because of an increased consciousness of their own identity among crofters; an identity, moreoever, in opposition to that of landlords.124 Given the expressed oppositional interest of the different ranks and emergent classes within the Highlands, one question underlying what follows is the extent to which it is possible to speak not of one regional consciousness shared by all persons but rather of class-based regional consciousness. Both tenants and landlords saw the Highlands as an identifiable region distinct in a number of ways from Lowland Scotland. But what for the first was land held and worked according to established practices was for the latter by the later 1700s a capitalisable asset understood as private property, measurable in terms of acres and rent rolls and amenable in various ways to 'improvement'. It is easy enough, of course, to state that the transformation of the Highlands meant different things

41

to different groups and classes in Highland society (and not just in the Highlands since questions of class and regional identity may have transcended the boundaries of the region). But it is possible to suggest that the increasing economic integration of the Highlands from the late eighteenth century led not to the disintegration of Highland regional consciousness but rather to the re-articulation of that regional identity along class lines.

In broad terms, the economic history of the Highlands from the middle eighteenth century has been a move away from pastoralism as the dominant mode of production with the material forces of production based upon the sale of black cattle and the holding and working of limited arable land through clan-related tenure towards a two-class social structure with control over land deriving from rent and accumulated capital and symbolised in and mediated through the English language. The changes encompassed in this shift have, of course, varied in their geographical impact and social consequences. The house of Argyll led the way in the processes leading to the formation of class relation-ships, but by the early nineteenth century, most Highland landlords had followed their example: 'The commercialisation of the agricultural structure in response to chief-tain's financial necessitousness - an undertaking in which the Campbells were eventually joined by every other leading family in the region - is the great fact of eighteenth century Highland history. From it all else follows'.125 The phrase 'all else follows' covers a multitude of changes not just economic factors. We should not see economic motives as 'leading' agents of changes. To do so relegates political and cultural elements to a secondary role; 'impersonal economic forces' are given under 'determining' prevalence. We need to recognise the complexity of change in the Highlands in a relational sense. The transformation of Highland Scotland as a 'culture region' may then be interpreted to include not just the replacement and incorporation of cultural 'givens' - the Gaelic language, Highland dress and so on - but as both the result and agent of hegemonic class control. Culture as a process and the symbols, values, and ideologies embraced by the term together with the institutions and language through which it is both transmitted and continually adjusting, is and becomes the consequence of dominant class relations. Not until the 'defect' of Gaelic was removed could religion and civil government, 'the arts of life', be brought to the Highlands, and only then through 'the intervention of superiors'. In places, this intervention was opposed by Highlanders themselves and residual elements of Highland culture incorporated into dominant cultural practices

42

though, as we shall see, more common was the renewal and recreation of the ideology and means of hegemony by the dominant classes as institutional policies were re-thought, for example, or new schemes for improvement developed to suit particular circumstances.

In review, what follows seeks to show that those people in the past whose concern was the civilisation and improvement of the Highlands saw that transformation as a unified process, perhaps permitting different emphasis at one time or another, but overall, an incorporation of many elements: 'if the People were at once brought to Religion, Humanity, Industry, and the Low Countrey Language, ... they might yet become a noble accession to the Commonwealth'.126 Anglicisation was a key element in the process not least for the fact that while in general terms policies of anglicisation were directed at 'rooting out their Irish language', the means chosen by the various educational institutions were continually recreated and renewed to meet given ends. What follows suggests how this process took various material forms as it was also made up of various ideological notions; virtue, civility, industry, and improvement. Many of the ideas discussed here have importance because of their contextual significance in the period under review. Given, for example, the widespread acceptance in the eighteenth century of the notion of culture as 'cultivation' and as a process of individual and societal development and the fact, too, that the Scottish Highlands had been understood since the later fourteenth century as a separate culture region, the residence of a 'barbarous' people, it is hardly surprising that the region should have been the focus for cultural transformation.

Figure 1.6 Places mentioned in the text

NOTES

1. J. Walker, <u>An Economical History of the Hebrides and Highlands of Scotland</u> (Edinburgh, 1808), I, p.19.

2. G. S. Johnstone, <u>The Grampian Highlands</u> (Edinburgh, 1973), pp. 1-4 and map between pp. 28-29.

3. See the maps accompanying J.B. Caird, 'Highlands and Islands, geography of', in D. Thomson (ed.), <u>The Companion to Gaelic Scotland</u> (Oxford, 1983), pp.124-132.

4. D. Murison, 'Linguistic relationships in medieval Scotland' in G.W.S. Barrow, (ed.), <u>The Scottish Tradition: Essays in Honour of R.G. Cant</u> (Edinburgh, 1974), pp.71-83.

5. G.W.S. Barrow, <u>The Kingdom of the Scots</u> (London, 1973), pp.362-363.

6. J. H. Millar, <u>A Literary History of Scotland</u> (London, 1903), p.3.

7. J. MacInnes, 'Gaelic poetry and historical tradition', in L. Maclean (ed.), <u>The Middle Ages in the Highlands</u> (Inverness, 1981), pp.142, 154-155, 157.

8. I. Carter, 'Economic models and the recent history of the Highlands', <u>Scottish Studies</u>, <u>15(2)</u>, (1971), pp. 99-120.

9. H.G. Graham, <u>The Social Life of Scotland in the Eighteenth Century</u> (London, 1899); L. Maclean, <u>The History of the Celtic Language</u> (London, 1840); J.S. Keltie, <u>A History of the Scottish Highlands, Highland Clans and Highland Regiments</u> (Edinburgh, 1875); D. Mitchell, <u>History of the Highlands and Gaelic Scotland</u> (Paisley, 1900); D. Gregory, <u>The History of the Western Highlands and Isles of Scotland</u> (Edinburgh, 1881).

10. Gregory, <u>Western Highlands</u>, pp.95-101; <u>Registrum Magni Sigilli regum Scotorum</u> (Register of the Great Seal of Scotland), T. Thomson, (ed.), (Edinburgh, 1814), XIII, pp.96,104,105,114,115, 166,188,200,203,300.

11. <u>Register of the Privy Council of Scotland</u>, J.H. Burton (ed.), (Edinburgh, 1908-1970), V, (1598), p.466; On this period in general in the Highlands, see the excellent work by R. Nicholson, <u>Scotland in the Later Middle Ages</u> (Edin-

burgh, 1974), pp.45, 317,549; Registrum Magni, ibid., TX, p.47; Nicholson, ibid.; I. Grimble, 'The survival of a Celtic Society in the Mackay Country formerly called Strathnaver in Northern Scotland, from the 16th Century', unpublished PhD thesis, University of Aberdeen,1963, p.71,80,198,316.

12. See the 'Sidelights from the Dunvegan Charter Chest' in Scottish Historical Review, II, (1905), pp.356-362.

13. J.L. Campbell, Gaelic in Scottish Education and Life (Edinburgh, 1950), p.21.

14. Nicholson, Later Middle Ages, ibid.; W.C. Dickinson, Scotland from the earliest times to 1603 being Volume 1 of his A New History of Scotland (Edinburgh, 1961), p.42; Register of the Privy Council, VIII, (1608), pp. 93,502,506 Acts of the Parliament of Scotland T. Thomson and C. Innes (eds.), (Edinburgh, 1815-1875), IV, (1608), p.404; Register of the Privy Council, IX, (1609), pp.28-29; Grimble, 'Celtic Society in the Mackay Country', p.71; Register of the Privy Council, X, (1616), pp.671-672.

15. This point is made clearly in the wider context of Irish and Welsh as well in V.E. Durkacz, The Decline of the Celtic Languages (Edinburgh, 1983).

16. R. Mitchison, 'The Government and the Highlands, 1707-1745', in N.T. Phillipson and R. Mitchison (eds.), Scotland in the age of Improvement (Edinburgh , 1970), pp.24-46; A. Murdoch, The People Above': politics and administration in mid-eighteenth century Scotland (Edinburgh, 1980); A.E. Whetstone, Scottish County Government in the Eighteenth and Nineteenth Centuries (Edinburgh, 1981).

17. Scottish Record Office (Hereinafter SRO), State Papers, 54/16, part 2, f.237, 21 October 1715.

18. SRO, NG 1/1/1, f.1, 20 July 1727.

19. Acts of Parliament, 25 Geo II, c.41; Pryde, A New History of Scotland, II, pp.154-155.

20. J. Hunter, The Making of the Crofting Community (Edinburgh, 1976), p.11.

21. E. Cregeen, 'The Changing Role of the House of Argyll in the Scottish Highlands'. in N.T. Phillipson and R. Mitchison, Scotland in the Age of Improvement (Edinburgh,

1970), pp.5-23; see also E. Cregeen ed., <u>Argyll Estate
Instructions in Mull, Morven, Tiree, 1771-1865</u> (Scottish
History Society, Edinburgh, 1964); idem, 'The tacksmen and
their successors: a study of tenurial reorganisation in
Mull, Morvern, and Tiree in the early eighteenth century',
<u>Scottish Studies, 13(2),</u> (1969), pp.93-144.

22. Cregeen, <u>The Changing Role of the House of Argyll,</u>
p.11.

23. Ibid. pp.11-12.

24. M. Gray, <u>The Highland Economy 1750-1850</u> (Edinburgh,
1957), pp.57-66; and see, for example, H. Hamilton, <u>An
Economic History of Scotland in the Eighteenth Century</u>
(Oxford, 1963), pp. 11-13, 17,84,93,136-7; T.M. Devine,
'Highland Migration to Lowland Scotland, 1760-1860',
<u>Scottish Historical Review, LXII(2),</u> (1983), pp.137-149;
C.W.J. Withers, 'Highland migration to Dundee, Perth, and
Stirling, c.1753-1891', <u>Journal of Historical Geography,
11(4),</u> (1985), pp.395-418.

25. Gray, passim; M. Flinn, 'Malthus, emigration and
potatoes in the Scottish north-west, 1770-1870', in L.M.
Cullen and T.C. Smout (eds.), <u>Comparative Aspects of
Scottish and Irish Economic and Social History 1600-1900</u>
(Edinburgh, 1977), pp.47-64.

26. G. Whittington, 'Agriculture and Society in Lowland
Scotland, 1750-1870', in G. Whittington, and I.
Whyte(eds.), <u>An Historical Geography of Scotland</u> (London,
1983), pp.141-164; D. Turnock, <u>The Historical Geography of
Scotland since 1707</u> (Cambridge, 1982), pp.66-81.

27. E. Richards, 'Structural change in a regional economy:
Sutherland and the Industrial Revolution, 1780-1830',
<u>Economic History Review, XXVI(1),</u> (1973), pp.63-76; <u>The
Leviathan of Wealth: the Sutherland fortune in the Industrial Revolution</u> (London, 1973); 'The prospect of economic
growth in Sutherland at the time of the clearances,
1809-1813' <u>Scottish Historical Review, XLIX(2),</u> (1970),
pp.155-156.

28. P. Mewett, 'Occupational pluralism in crofting: the
influence of non-croft work on the patterns of crofting
agriculture in the Isle of Lewis since about 1859',
<u>Scottish Journal of Sociology, 2(1),</u> (1977), pp.31-49.

29. P. Gaskell, <u>Morvern Transformed</u> (Cambridge, 1968);

I.R.M. Mowat, Easter Ross, 1750-1850 (Edinburgh, 1981); A. Smith, Jacobite Estates of the Forty-Five (Edinburgh, 1982).

30. Gray, Highland Economy, p.246.

31. Carter, 'Economic models and the recent history of the Highlands', pp. 99-100, 101; Hunter, Crofting Community, p.5; see also E. Condry, 'The Scottish Highland Problem: some anthropological aspects', unpublished B.Litt. thesis, University of Oxford, 1977, esp. Ch.4.

32. Turnock, The Historical Geography of Scotland, pp.1-11.

33. E. Richards, A History of the Highland Clearances Volume 2: Emigration, Protest, Reasons (London, 1985), pp. 3-178.

34. M. Hechter, Internal Colonialism: the Celtic Fringe in British National Development, 1536-1966 (London, 1975)

35. J. Clive and B. Bailyn, 'England's cultural provinces: Scotland and America', William and Mary Quarterly IX (2), (1954), pp.200-213; W.C. Macleod, The American Indian Frontier (New York, 1958), pp. 152-171.

36. Condry, 'The Scottish Highland Problem', p.16.

37. T. C. Smout, 'Centre and periphery in history; with some thoughts on Scotland as a case study', Journal of Common Market Studies, XVIII(3) (1980), pp. 256-271; see also his 'Scotland and England, 16th-18th Centuries: is Dependency a Symptom or a Cause of Underdevelopment', Review: a Journal of the Fernand Braudel Centre, (1980).

38. I. Wallerstein, The Politics of the World-Economy (Cambridge, 1984).

39. T. Nairn, The Break-up of Britain (London, 1977); C. Craig, 'Nation and History', Cencrastus, 19, (1984), pp.13-16.

40. T. Dickson and T. Clarke, 'The making of a class society: commercialisation and working-class resistance, 1780-1830', in T. Dickson (ed.), Scottish Capitalism: class, state and nation from before the Union to the present (London, 1980), pp. 149-150, 151.

48

41. M. Geddes, 'Uneven development and the Scottish Highlands' Working Paper 17 Urban and Regional Studies Department, University of Sussex (1979), p.2.

42. I. Carter, 'The Highlands of Scotland as an Underdeveloped Region' in E. de Kadt and G. Williams (eds.), Sociology and Development (Tavistock, 1974), pp.279-311.

43. J. Bryden, 'Core-periphery problems: the Scottish case', in D. Seers, B. Schaffer and M-L. Kiljunen (eds.), Underdeveloped Europe: Studies in Core-Periphery Relations (Sussex, 1979), pp.257-277.

44. P. Knox and M.B. Cottam, 'A Welfare approach to rural geography: contrasting perspectives on the quality of Highland life', Transactions Institute of British Geographers, 6 (1981), pp.433-450; M.B. Cottam and P. Knox, The Highlands and Islands A Social Profile (Report for the Highlands and Islands Development Board) (Dundee 1982); see also J. Ennew, The Western Isles (Cambridge, 1980); and J.I. Prattis, 'Industrialisation and Minority - Language Loyalty: the example of Lewis', in E. Haugen, J.D. McClure, and D. Thomson (eds), Minority Languages Today (Edinburgh, 1981), pp.21-31.

45. Carter, 'Economic models and the recent history of the Highlands', pp. 114-120; on this notion, see also A. Pearse, 'Metropolis and Peasant: the expansion of the urban-industrial complex and the changing rural structure', in T. Shanin(ed.), Peasants and Peasant Societies (Harmoindsworth, 1971), pp.69-80.

46. E. Wolf, Peasants (New Jersey, 1966), pp. 50, 51, 52-53.

47. B.P. Lenman, Integration, Enlightenment and Industrialization: Scotland 1743-1832 (Edinburgh, 1981), p.90; J.D. Young, The Rousing of the Scottish Working Class (London, 1979), pp.11-40.

48. Young, ibid., passim; R.S. Neale, Class in English History 1680 - 1850 (Oxford, 1981).

49. Richards, Leviathan of Wealth, pp. 151-168.

50. Hunter, Crofting Community, p.4.

51. 'An Inquiry into the Causes which facilitate the Rise and Progress by Rebellions and Insurrections in the

Highlands of Scotland', Appendix 4 of R.B. Cunningham-Graham, <u>Doughty Deeds: an account of the life of Robert Graham of Gartmore, 1735-1797</u> (London, 1925), p.184.

52. SRO, CH8/212/1, ff. 81-83.

53. Pryde, <u>A New History of Scotland</u>, p.152.

54. E. Cregeen, 'The Changing Role of the House of Argyll', pp.8-9.

55. P.L. Wagner and M.W. Mikesell (eds), <u>Readings in Cultural Geography</u> (Chicago, 1962), pp.1, 2-5, 6.

56. C.A. Fox, <u>The Personality of Britain</u> (Cardiff, 1947); E.G. Bowen, 'Le Pays de Galles', <u>Transactions, Institute of British Geographers,</u> 26, (1959), pp.1-23.

57. D. Meinig, 'The Mormon Culture Region: strategies and patterns in the American West, 1947-1964', <u>Annals, Association of American Geographers</u>, <u>55</u>, (1965), pp.191-220.

58. C.O. Sauer, 'The morphology of landscape', in J. Leighly (ed.),' <u>Land and Life: a selection from the writings of Carl Ortwin Sauer</u> (Berkeley, 1969), pp. 322, 343.

59. On this, see for example, R.A. Dodgshon, <u>Land and Society in Early Scotland</u> (Oxford, 1981), pp.1-25; I.A. Morrison, 'Prehistoric Scotland', in G. Whittington and I. Whyte (eds.), <u>An Historical Geography of Scotland</u> (London, 1983), pp.1-24; G. Whittington, 'Prehistoric activity and its effect on the Scottish landscape', in M.L. Parry and T. Slater(eds.), <u>The Making of the Scottish Countryside</u> (London, 1980), pp.23-44.

60. I.D. Whyte and K.A. Whyte, <u>Sources for Scottish Historical Geography An Introductory Guide</u> (Historical Geography Research Group Publication 6) (1981).

61. Wagner and Mikesell, <u>Cultural Geography</u>, p.11.

62. R. W. Feachem, <u>A Guide to Prehistoric Scotland</u> (London, 1963); A. Small, 'Dark Age Scotland' in G. Whittington and I. Whyte(eds.), <u>Historical Geography of Scotland,</u> pp. 25-45; on forests, see for example, W. Orr, <u>Deer Forests Landlords and Crofters</u> (Edinburgh, 1982); J.M. Lindsay, 'The commercial use of woodland and coppice management', in M. Parry and T. Slater,(eds.), <u>Scottish</u>

Countryside, pp.271-290; on the distribution of sculptured stones, see K.A. Steer and J.L. Bannerman (eds.), Later Medieval Monumental Sculpture in the West Highlands (London, 1977).

63. Wagner and Mikesell, Cultural Geography, p.23.

64. M. W. Mikesell, 'Cultural Geography', Progress in Human Geography, 1(3), (1977), p.460.

65. R. Williams, Keywords (London, 1981), pp.87-93.

66. R. Williams, Marxism and Literature (Oxford, 1977), p.13.

67. J. S. Duncan, 'The superorganic in American cultural geography', Annals, Association of American Geographers, 70(2), (180), pp.181-198.

68. E.B. Tylor, Primitive Culture (London, 1871), p.1.

69. Duncan, 'The superorganic', p.191.

70. The literature on culture is large and contradictory. In addition to the works footnoted here, my thinking has ben directed also by F.M. Keesing, Cultural anthropology (New York, 1959); W.H. Goodenough, Culture, Language and Society (Massachusetts, 1971); M. Freilich(ed.), The Meaning of Culture: a reader in cultural anthropology (Lexington, 1972); C. Geertz, The Interpretation of Culture (New York, 1973); R. Williams, Culture and Society 1780-1950 (London, 1963), pp.258-279; idem, 'Culture' in D. McLellan, Marx: the first 100 years; L.A. White, The Science of Culture (New York, 1949).

71. A.L. Kroeber and C. Kluckholn, Culture: a critical review of concepts and definitions (Harvard University, Papers of the Peabody Museum, 47).

72. W. Rees Pryce, 'The idea of culture in human geography', in E. Grant and P. Newby (eds.), Landscape and Industry: essays in memory of Geoffrey Gullett (London, 1982), pp.131-149.

73. P.L. Wagner, 'The themes of cultural geography rethought', Yearbook, Association of Pacific Coast Geographers, 37, (1978), p.11.

74. C.O. Sauer, 'Foreword to Historical Geography', in

J. Leighly (ed.), Land and Life, p.359.

75. W. Rees Pryce, 'The idea of culture in human geography', passim; W. Norton, 'The meaning of culture in cultural geography: an appraisal', Journal of Geography, 83(4), (1984), pp.145-148; D.E. Sopher, 'Place and location: notes on the spatial patterning of culture', in L. Schneider and C.M. Bonjean, The Idea of Culture in the Social Sciences (Cambridge, 1973), pp. 101-117; S. Williams, The concept of culture and human geography: a review and reassessment (Keele University Geography Department Occasional Paper 5, 1983).

76. F.M. Keesing, 'Theories of Culture', Annual Review of Anthropology, 3, (1974), p.73.

77. M. W. Mikesell, 'Tradition and Innovation in Cultural Geography', Annals, Association of American Geographers, 68(1), (1978), p.13.

78. L. Schneider, 'The idea of culture in the social sciences: critical and supplementary observations', in Schneider and Bonjean, (eds.), The Idea of Culture, p.129.

79. Duncan, 'The superorganic', p.197; this claim was also made, but less explicitly and never elaborated upon, by L. White in his 'The concept of culture', American Anthropologist, 61, (1959), p.235.

80. D. Cosgrove, 'Towards a radical cultural geography: problems of theory', Antipode, 15(1), (1983), pp.1-11.

81. J.A. Agnew and J.S. Duncan, 'The transfer of ideas into Anglo-American human geography', Progress in Human Geography, 5(1), (1981) p.302 note that Marxism may be given one of four meanings - as doctrine; method; heritage; or tradition - and that geographers have not always made explicit in which sense they are drawing upon Marx. I use Marx and others here chiefly in the fourth sense, 'as tradition, in which one claims inspiration from Marx's writing and attempts to use it critically and imaginatively'.

82. G. Sider, 'The ties that bind: culture and agriculture, property and propriety in the Newfoundland village fishery', Social History 5(1), (1980), pp.1-3.

83. J.M. Blaut, 'A radical critique of cultural geography', Antipode, 12(2), (1980), p.27.

84. M. Sahlins, Culture and Practical Reason, (London, 1976), pp.132–136, passim.

85. Sider, 'The ties that bind', p.2.

86. Cosgrove, 'Radical cultural geography', p.5.

87. K. Marx and F. Engels, Selected Works (Moscow, 1962), I. pp.362–364.

88. R. Williams, 'Base and Superstructure in Marxist Cultural Theory', New Left Review, 82 (1973), pp.3–5.

89. Engels in a letter to Bloch, quoted in Williams, Marxism and Literature, pp.79–80

90. Keesing, 'Theories of Culture', p.77; C. Geertz, 'Ritual and social change: a Javanese example', American Anthropologist, 59, (1957), p.992.

91. Williams, 'Base and Superstructure', pp.6–7; idem., Marxism and Literature, p.82.

92. Cosgrove, 'Radical cultural geography', pp.5–6.

93. E.P. Thompson, The Making of the English Working Class, (Harmondsworth, 1980 edition), pp.9–11.

94. R.J. Morris, Class and Class Consciousness in the Industrial Revolution 1780–1850, (London, 1979).

95. A. Briggs, 'The Language of 'Class' in Early Nineteenth-Century England', in A. Briggs and J. Saville (eds), Essays in Labour History (London, 1967), pp.154–177; Williams, Keywords, pp.60–69; G. Stedman Jones, Languages of Class (Cambridge, 1983), pp.1–24.

96. A. Giddens, The Class Structure of the Advanced Societies (London, 1973), p.29; I. Rossi, 'On the assumptions of structural analysis', in I. Rossi (ed.), The Logic of Culture (London, 1982), pp. 3–22.

97. My thinking on the term has been directed principally by Williams, Marxism and Literature, pp.55–71; and also by C. Geertz, 'Ideology as a cultural system', in D.E. Apter (ed.), Ideology and Discontent (New York, 1964), pp.47–76; L. Kolakowski, Main Currents of Marxism (Oxford, 1978), 1, pp.153–155; L. Dupre, Marx's Social Critique of Culture (Yale, 1983), pp.216–275; M. Harris, Cultural Materialism

(New York, 1979), A.R.H. Baker, 'On ideology and historical geography', in A.R.H. Baker and M. Billinge, Period and place: research methods in historical geography (Cambridge, 1982), pp.233-243; H. Fleischer, Marxism and History (London, 1973).

98. Williams, Marxism and Literature, p.55; Dupre, Marx's Social Critique, p.225.

99. Quoted in Fleischer, Marxism and History, pp.21-2.

100. K. Marx and F. Engels, Historisch-Kritisch Gesamtausgabe (Moscow, 1927-1935), 1, (part 5), pp.15-17.

101. K. Marx, Theorien uber den Mehrwert (Berlin, 1956), 1, p.381.

102. Marx and Engels, Historisch-Kritische, 1, (part 5), p.35.

103. Gramsci's writings, and particularly those on hegemony, are lengthy and, indeed, often contradictory. I have based my comments on the following: G.A. Williams, 'The concept of egemonia in the though of A. Gramsci', Journal of the History of Ideas, 21, (1960), pp.486-599; T.R. Bates, 'Gramsci and the theory of hegemony', Journal of the History of Ideas, 36, (1975), pp.351-366; J. Femia, 'Hegemony and consciousness in the thought of Antonio Gramsci', Political Studies, 23, (1975), pp.29-48; W.1. Adamson, Hegemony and Revolution (Berkeley, 1980), pp. 23-61, passim; D. Forgacs and G. Nowell-Smith, Antonio Gramsci - Selections from cultural writings (London, 1983); R. Gray, 'Bourgeois hegemony in Victorian Britain', in The Communist University of London (ed.), Class, Hegemony and Party (London, 1977), pp.73-93; A. Gramsci, Prison Notebooks (London, 1970); Q. Hoare and G. Nowell Smith (eds.), Selections from the Prison Notebooks of Antonio Gramsci (London, 1971).

104. Williams, Marxism and Literature, p.110.

105. Williams, 'The concept of egemonia', pp.588-591; Femia, 'Hegemony and Consciousness', pp.36-37; Williams, 'Base and Superstructure', p.9.

106. A.P. Donajgrodski, Social Control in Nineteenth-Century Britain (London, 1977).

107. M.D. Billinge, 'Hegemony, class and power in later

Georgian and early Victorian England: towards a cultural geography', in A.R.H. Baker and D. Gregory, (eds.), Explorations in Historical Geography (Cambridge 1984), pp.28-67; Williams, Marxism and Literature, p.110.

108. Femia, 'Hegemony and Consciousness', pp.38-39.

109. Williams, 'Base and Superstructure', p.8.

110. Williams, Marxism and Literature, pp.112-113

111. Sider, 'The ties that bind', pp.23-26' Giddens, Class Structure of the Advanced Societies, pp.112-113; D. Cheal, 'Hegemony, ideology and contradictory consciousness', Sociological Quarterly, 20, (1979), pp.109-117; F. Parkin, Class Inequality and Political Order (London, 1971), pp.98-101.

112. E.P. Thompson, The Poverty of Theory (London, 1974), p.74; idem, 'Patrician society - Plebian Culture', Journal of Social History, (1974), pp.388-389.

113. Williams, 'Base and Superstructure', p.10.

114. Williams, ibid., pp.10-11 and see also J. Agnew, J. Mercer and D. Sopher (eds.), The City in Cultural Context (Boston, 1984), p.6.

115. Williams, ibid., pp.10-12.

116. P.L. Wagner, 'The themes of cultural geography rethought', p.12.

117. P. Anderson, 'The Antimonies of Antonio Gramsci', New Left Review, 100, (1976-1977), p.22.

118. Williams, 'Base and Superstructure', p.9.

119. Williams, Marxism and Literature, p.117.

120. R.S. Neale, 'Cultural materialism', Social History, 9(2), (1984) p.209.

121. Dupre, Marx's Social Critique, pp.227-228.

122. C.W.J. Withers, Gaelic in Scotland 1698-1981: the geographical history of a language (Edinburgh, 1984), passim.

123. A.G. Macpherson, 'An Old Highland parish register' (Part I), Scottish Studies, 11, pp.149-192; (Part II), Scottish Studies, 12, (1968), pp.81-111; I. Carter, 'Marriage patterns and social sectors in Scotland and before the eighteenth century', Scottish Studies, 17(1), (1973), pp.51-60; A.G. Macpherson, 'Migration fields in a traditional Highland community, 1350-1850', Journal of Historical Geography, 10(1), (1984), pp.1-14.

124. J. Hunter, The Making of the Crofting Community (Edinburgh, 1976) p.4.

125. Ibid, p.9.

126. SRO, CH1/2/24, Part I, f.7, 28 July 1703.

2

CIVILISATION AND THE MOVE TO IMPROVEMENT

> The people of the Highlands are always Idle and
> sauntering at home and had rather lurk in their
> haunts than remove to the most inviteing settle-
> ments ... and by reason of their barbarous
> Language can have noe manner of Communication with
> others and are upon those two accounts altogither
> as Incapable of being imployed in husbandry,
> fishery, manufactories or handycrafts or of
> settleing in our foraigne plantations.1

> Civility seems part of the national character of
> Highlanders Every chieftain is a monarch, and
> politeness, the natural product of royal govern-
> ment, is diffused from the laird through the whole
> clan.2

The attempts of authority to bring 'virtue and loyalty
through education, religion, and the English language were
inseparably bound up with efforts at improvement of the
material bases to Highland life. With what we shall see of
the assertion of anglicisation as a leading change (Chapter
3), the concern of what follows is in tracing the emergence
of ideas of civilisation and the intellectual productions
underlying the move to improvement. It is suggested here
that changes in material activities in the Highlands
derived potency from the production of ideas of improvement, of culture-as-progress, which, in context with the
extension of political control informed the actions of
anglicising schoolmasters, concerned ideologues, and
improving landlords alike. If it is the case that 'The
production of ideas, of conceptions, of consciousness, is
at first directly interwoven with the material activity
and the material intercourse of men, the language of real
life', it is also true that these relationships must be
considered as historically particular and not conceived 'as
a general category'. Given the concern of eighteenth-

century commentators with civilisation and culture as a process of social advancement – 'natural progress from ignorance to knowledge, and from rude, to civilized manners'3 – it is understandable that the Highlanders should be, in the 1700s especially, the focus of schemes for improvement in the 'arts of life'. Further, with the defeat of the Jacobites at Culloden, the Highlands ceased to be a military threat. Once safe, they were 'discovered' by outside observers. Guided more by cultural preconceptions and a long-standing antipathy towards things Highland than a concern to depict reality, many commentators invested the region and its inhabitants with characteristics that both drew upon and supported contemporary ideas of aesthetic taste, culture, and economic development. All were 'directly interwoven'. Because there was not one in reality, neither can there be here an easy separation between the policies of anglicisation, political control, material transformation, and the intellectual context of improvement in which they were set. It is argued here that the creation of an image of Highlands and Highlander in the mind of the improver laid the basis for material changes on the ground: intellectual and material production were, and are, related elements in Highland transformation. Related but not static and not held by all. Firstly, the ideology of improvement and the views taken of Highland life were largely derived from 'outsiders'. It was they who directed both material change and the shifts in intellectual attitudes toward the Highlands. Secondly, the views held of Highland Scotland have not been consistent. Those of the nineteenth century were not those of earlier. Those of the 1700s vary between the first and second half of the century. All these commentaries reflect the intent of the author and the intellectual and historical conditions of which they are part. And thirdly, whilst the changes affecting the Highlands in the eighteenth century in particular derived emphasis from the then prevailing ideology of 'improvement' and material advance, neither the changes nor the related intellectual context were confined to that period or directed only at Gaelic and the Highlands.

ENLIGHTENMENT, CULTURE, AND IMPROVEMENT

What Young has called 'the imposition of English cultural imperialism', and 'the aping of English language and manners by the Scottish ruling classes' was indeed more common in Scotland after the 1707 Union, but such moves were evident in Scottish life before then and were not always externally derived.4 Throughout the 1600s, the Scottish Parliament and Privy Council passed acts to promote Scotland's economy in advance of eighteenth-century notions of 'progress' and 'enlightenment'. Legislative encouragement was given to the manufacture of linen and to fishing, for example, and restrictions placed on certain exports and imports to encourage commerce. Agricultural improvement began in 1647, and acts of 1661, 1669, and 1695 facilitated further early change in agrarian methods.6 Although the intention of such legislation was not always realised in practice, these acts illustrate the basis to economic change in the eighteenth century provided by innovation in the seventeenth.7 The move to improvement was given renewed impetus after the 1707 Union of Parliaments. Young has argued that as Scottish Society was pushed into a subordinate position after 1707, the move to ape English culture by ' the possessing classes' within Scotland - 'the ambitious and modernising Scottish landed interests, mercantile wealth, the indigenous intellectuals and the Presbyterian church'8 - was evident in three ways: in anglicisation; in sexual repression and matters of public morality; and in the way in which 'the Scottish lower orders were influenced by a total culture in which an insecure and authoritarian elite articulated an obsessive awareness of its own provincial inferiority and backwardness'.9 To these we must add those institutions that carried forward the impulse towards improvement; the Kirk, the Scottish legal and educational systems, formal societies, and the universities, within which Scottish intellectuals re-articulated their relationships to Scottish culture.

Anglicisation, improvement and intellectual production

Although the process of anglicisation among Scotland's ruling classes might be said to have begun with the settlement in the Scottish court of Anglo-Normans from the late eleventh century, the move by literati and intellectuals to adopt English as the language of refinement was most marked in the eighteenth century. Lowland Scots had been declining as a literary language from the late sixteenth century. By the later 1700s, English was the medium for many Scottish writers and the accepted language of cultural refinement.10 In a society open to improvement, the imposition of the English language throughout the Highlands was perhaps the inevitable consequence of its adoption amongst the Lowland elite. Consciousness among the Scottish ruling classes that anglicisation was means to individual improvement and indispensable for national progress received institutional expression in the urban Lowlands in 1761 with the foundation in Edinburgh of the Select Society for Promoting the Reading and Speaking of the English Language in Scotland, an extension of the Select Society of Edinburgh for the encouragement of Arts, Sciences, Manufactures, and Agriculture.11 The aim was to improve the speaking of English given that 'gentlemen educated in Scotland have long been sensible of the disadvantages under which they labour, from their imperfect knowledge of the ENGLISH TONGUE, and the Impropriety with which they spoke it'.12 Although this body did not survive long, its existence points to a general feeling toward English and 'cultivation'. English was not just the language of the polite cultured classes, but was by this period invested with something analogous to the force of law. As Barrell shows for eighteenth-century England, correct linguistic usage marked one as a gentleman and structured social relations on the grounds of deference to and through language: 'the authority of the gentleman and of the ruling class, was reinforced at the level of language, ... a 'correct' English was defined in such a way as to represent it as the natural possession of the gentleman, and to confirm that possession, too, as a source of his political authority'.13 And so in Scotland, 'correct' English became and remained both the symbol and the means of 'improvement': in Neale's words,'an instrument of domination, a carrier of cultural power' (page 32 above).

Evidence for Young's claim that 'In the world-outlook of the Scottish philosophers modernisation did not only entail anglicisation ... but also involved the codification of correct sexual attitudes which ... were certainly useful in keeping some working people "docile" and "oppressed"',14 is less certain, at least for the eighteenth century. Chitnis has pointed out that developments in the Scottish economy by the later 1700s were accompanied by an increase in decadence despite the activities of the Church and others to regularise sexual behaviour.15 Evidence for the Scottish elite being aware of its own provincialism is more clear: partly in their cultivation of English (especially for intellectual and literary writing), and partly also in the way in which distinctions of language and manners between landowners, urban intellectuals, and the majority of the Scottish people were increasingly apparent in terms of rank and social consciousness. Daiches has pointed to this 'paradox in Scottish culture', rooted in the acceptance by the Scottish ruling classes of the English language as polite discourse and the authority invested in it.16 David Hume, for example, who, like other literati consciously avoided 'Scotticisms' in speech, observed, in

Civilisation and the Move to Improvement

1757, 'at a time when we have lost our Princes, our Parliaments, our independent Government, even the Presence of our chief Nobility, are unhappy in our accent and Pronounciation, speak a very corrupt Dialect of the Tongue which we make use of; is it not strange ... we shou'd really be the people most distinguish'd for Literature in Europe?'.17   Distinguished perhaps, if, as has been elsewhere noted, one points for example to Hume's own Essays (1748), Home's Douglas (1756), the works of Black-lock and Wilkie.18 Yet these works were in 'English' and although there was some linguistic (and literary) reaction in the work of Allan Ramsay, Fergusson, and Burns, this was limited.19   Thus, an increasing linguistic separation in Scottish society between the elite and lower orders, apparent from the 1500s and established in the following centuries, was paralleled in literature and evident in the Scottish consciousness in a dialectic or 'disassociation of sensibility'.20   Native culture, either Highland or Lowland, was disparaged in polite society. Culture came to be seen both as the process and the end product of development in and through the common use of a correct English.

Enlightenment and material production

Direct connections between the intellectual context of anglicised enlightenment and material improvement are not easily established. Whilst chronologically, 'the Scottish Enlightenment and capitalism developed side-by-side in the eighteenth and nineteenth centuries',21 the connections were at times tangential and at others closely interwoven rather than simply parallel.22 Many Enlightenment writers were drawn from the professional ranks and had close links with the landed gentry through clubs and societies, as patrons and readers, and as the audience for a culture that was simultaneously social and scientific, philosophical and practical. Lord Kames, for example, lawyer, and moraliser on topics including Scottish sexual attitudes, was also an improving landlord and author of The Gentleman Farmer (1776). He claimed agriculture to be 'the chief of arts' because it combined 'deep philosophy with useful practice' and was, 'of all occupations, the most proper for gentlemen in a private station'.23 His institutional roles included membership of the Board of Trustees for the Encouragement of Manufactures and Fisheries and of the Committee for the Forfeited Annexed Estates. He was patron to others such as John Walker involved in documenting the improvement of the Highlands, and friend to the Duke of Argyll, a powerful politician and influential Highland

improver.24 At the national scale 'the contributions of
the Enlightenment to economic life, while admitted, have to
be evaluated with care'.25 In assessment of the relative
secularisation of Scottish society; the impetus afforded by
the 1707 Union; and the commercial policy – free trade –
which grew out of the Enlightenment, Campbell has pointed
to close links between Enlightenment and improvement and
the stimulus each provided the other. But he cautions
also; 'The influence of the Enlightenment on the economy
was effective not only because its fruition coincided with
particularly favourable historical circumstances but also
because ... circumstances were independently becoming
favourable towards economic growth over a longer period
irrespective of the Enlightenment'.26 Most of these
changes took place within the Lowlands. Agricultural
societies founded in the period 1723 to 1835 were almost
entirely Lowland in location, with the exception of bodies
such as the Badenoch and Strathspey, the Fort George
Agricultural Society and the Ross-shire Farming Society.27
Although the Highland Society of Scotland established in
Edinburgh in 1784 was concerned with Highland cultural and
agricultural affairs 28 (see below), the number and
distribution of improvement societies, agricultural or
otherwise, reflects the principally Lowland impetus toward
development of the Scottish economy.29 Ideas about the
'stages' of human and economic development, particularly in
the work of David Hume, Adam Smith, William Robertson, Lord
Kames, Adam Ferguson, and John Millar, are important in
considering the links between intellectual and material
production. Each was interested in 'the study of social
man': the bonds that held human society together; the
institutions which arose within society; and, in relation
to attitudes towards the Highlands, in understanding
Scotland's progress (as they saw it) from a 'rude' state to
a 'polished' one. Their analysis of the evolution of
society centred on man as an active being, satisfying his
wants by improving his material conditions. Stages of
social development from savagery and barbarism to civilisation, in which last stage distinctions of class and the
possession of property were key elements, were paralleled
by stages or phases of economic development. Each pro-
gressed into the other and was related to a given historical and cultural context: 'The four phases, the primitive,
the pastural, the agrarian and the commercial, while shaped
by their economic characteristics, were also to be seen
consequently as cultural periods of man's past'.30 Thus,
Kames' emphasis on the civilising influence of private
property, Smith's discussions of 'progress' through the
four stages of 'hunting, pasturage, farming, and

commerce', and Millar's 'states' of society - savages, shepherds, husbandmen, commercial peoples - provided a model of development, at once cultural and economic, by which they could delineate social progress. Once delineated, certain questions on the means of progress were of interest; questions of property, justice and law, language, and the division of labour. The possession of private property was seen as the basis to government, which in turn protected property and the authority vested in it through institutions and laws. Division of labour within industrial production was the mark of civilised society, making itself and its members wealthy. A developed language was the means by which authority and industry could control a society at, or moving towards, the most civilised stage of development.

Chitnis claims a four-fold significance for these ideas: firstly, for the historical context in which they were set - the general sense throughout Scotland that the country was moving from barbarism to refinement whilst lagging behind the more advanced neighbour with whom they were now politically united; secondly, in the Whiggish preoccupation with progress and the diffusion of both political liberty and civilised cultural practices to the lower orders in society; thirdly, in the contribution to later developments in industrial society: and, fourthly, in the genesis of Marxist thought.31 There is a further area of significance here; in that Scotland was in a sense not one country but two. Highland Scotland was to Lowlanders what they imagined Lowland Scotland to be to England - less civilised, in need of progress, a 'primitive' region at an earlier stage of culture.

This review of the relationships between the intellectual productions of the Enlightenment and the material changes affecting the Scottish economy has been a partial one. Nevertheless, several points may be made in summary. Important links between intellectual and material changes did exist, in the enlightenment of the eighteenth century especially, in context with, firstly, the favourable historical circumstances of economic improvement then, and, secondly, the basis provided by earlier legislation. The idea of civilisation as cultural progress was underlain by anglicisation of mind and manners. Both received fresh impetus after 1707. The ideas and ideals of culture and improvement were articulated through the 'possessing classes' and by intellectuals, many of whom were speculating, in the context of Scottish social and economic change, upon 'stages' of human development. The claims of the elite to authority derived from and were reflected in the holding of land, membership of institutions, distancing

from the Scottish working 'classes', and in the use of
English. Further, the links between these elements were
forged in 'polite' Lowland Scotland. Within an age of
change, this combination of industry and civility, the
product of an elitist determination 'to rescue their
country from rudeness and barbarity',32 was to provide a
crucial basis for Improvement in the Highlands.

IMPROVEMENT AND INVENTION: 'THE HIGHLANDER DELINEATED',33

It is the claim of one author that 'the aggressive,
forward-thrusting, path-breaking motivation of the Scottish
Enlightenment to impose cultural improvement on the
barbarous Highlands was really inseparable from the
anglicisation of the whole of Scotland'.34 But in focusing
upon the Highlands, we should not assume the process of
imposition to be a simple extension of Lowland 'civility'
over Highland 'barbarity'. These processes took their
historical shape from the institutions and personnel
involved, from the intellectual context in which material
changes were set, and the attitudes that framed the
people's actions towards the Highlands. These derived in
large measure from an ideology of anglicisation; in part
from the geographical separateness of the Highlands which
meant that for many people the region was a threat, in need
of culture simply because it was unknown; partly from the
'discovery' of the Highlands by outsiders, who, once the
region had been tamed, then invested it with qualities of
wildness and barbarism; and partly also from notions of
progress attaching to the move from barbarism to civilisation.

The Highlands geographically apart

Proposals for 'civilising that Barbarous People' in 'Some
Remarks on the Highland Clans, and Methods proposed for
Civilising them' (c.1747) recognised the difficulties
Highland geography presented to civil control: 'the numbers
of woods, mountains, and Secret Glens ... are also great
allurements to incite that perverse Disposition that reigns
amongst all Ranks of them, stimulated by the Rudeness of
their Nature, unrestrained by Law or Religion'.35 Walker,
in his 1765 report on the Highlands, was likewise aware of
these problems; 'the most considerable part of the people
are in a great measure excluded from all religious instruction, by the nature of the country, their access to schools
and churches being cut off by their remote situation, by

dangerous seas, by extensive lochs, rapid rivers, and impassable mountains'.36 The relative isolation of the Highlands was reduced following construction of roads and after opening-up of the area by steamship and railway.37 But even after these events and certainly before, the Highlands were foreign to many. This foreignness was in part perceived image and in part real separation. Each reinforced the other in the sense that the Highlands, for so long regarded as hostile and irreligious, continued uncivil in the Lowland and English mind because of the geographical barriers to effective political administration. Dr. Johnson considered that 'the peculiarities' of the people in 'the rugged region' owed much to its mountainous character which hindered the diffusion of 'good manners': 'As mountains are long before they are conquered, they are likewise long before they are civilized'.38

The Highlands socially apart

The senses in which the Highlands were seen as wild were reinforced by memories of clan feuds within the region, Lowland raiding, and the Jacobite risings. Documents of the seventeenth century on lawlessness in the Highlands speak, for example, of 'the intolerable calamities and violent depradations' resulting from raiding Highlanders, and later sources document actions taken and proposals made in 'taking order with Broaken men and Suppressing theft in ye highlands'.39 Commentators considered the clan system a principal cause of incivility.

> Their notions of virtue and vice, are very different, from the more Civiliz'd part of Mankind; they think it the most sublime virtue, to Pay a servile, and Abject Obedience to the Commands of their Superiors, altho' in Oposition to their Sovereign and the Laws of the Kingdom ... The virtue next to this, in esteem amongst them, is the Love they bear, to that Particular Branch of which they are a part, and in a second degree, to the whole Clan or name, by assisting each other, right or wrong, against any Other Clan, with whom they are at variance: and great barbaritys are often Committed, by one, to Revenge the Quarrells of another.

The author notes also that the sense of unity within clans was strengthened by a common Highland contempt for the

Lowlander.

> They have still a more extensive Adherence one to
> another, as Highlanders, Opposition to the People
> who inhabit the Low Countries, whom they hold in
> the utmost contempt, imagining them inferior to
> themselves in Courage; and Resolution, and the Use
> of Armes; and accuse them, of being Proud,
> avaritious, and breakers of their Word. They have
> also a tradition amongst them, yt the Lowlanders
> were in ancient times, the inheritance of their
> ancestors, and therefore believe they have a Right
> to Commit Depredations, whenever it is in their
> Power to put them in execution.40

To the Lowlander, Highland 'wildness' was at its most
evident in the 1745 Rebellion. To the anonymous author of
The Highlander Delineated (1745), written (as propaganda)
to inform the English public of the Highland character, the
'wildness of their Manners' was ascribed to their 'uncultivated Education', the army compared to a plundering horde:
'this Northern Army of ravenous Mountaineers'.41 One part
of the complex image held of the Highlander stemmed, before
1745 anyway, from genuine concern at their military prowess
and distance from authority. By the end of the eighteenth
century, however, ideas of Highland 'wildness' - borne of
military skill, geographical separateness, perceived
irreligion and a different social system - had been
overlain though not altogether replaced by ideas of the
Highlands as 'wilderness'. From this period we may date
the image of the Highlander as a 'noble savage', remade as
wild in reflection of the taste of urban philosophes.

The Highlands 'discovered'

The opening-up of the Highlands to travellers and tourists
was part of what Martin Martin writing in 1703 called 'The
Modern Itch after the Knowledge of Foreign Places'.42
Smout has identified several trends in the 'discovery' of
the Highlands; first, from the middle of the eighteenth
century, the treatment of the region as natural or anthropological curiosity; second, the later eighteenth- and early
nineteenth-century view of the Highlands as sublime or
picturesque, allied to given historical and romantic
associations; third, 'the vulgar tourism' of the
mid-nineteenth century; and, lastly, twentieth-century mass
tourism.43 The view of the Highlands as a region of
anthropological curiosity was part of a general interest in
antiquarianism and in things Celtic 'as a locus for things

prehistoric', in the eighteenth century.44 In the visual arts and in literary sources, the sublime and the picturesque are of significance here: the former established the view of the Highlands as a savage fearful region though usually without deeming the inhabitants fearsome in the way earlier sources did; the latter, in the context of European ideas of primitivism and interest in the stages of human social development, treated the Highlander as noble savage, a primitive ornament in a primeval landscape. These attitudes developed, notes Smout, 'into an attitude of palpable contempt for contemporary Highlanders along with an attitude of reverence for the imagined 'romance' of the Jacobite and clannish past. It is hard to imagine anything more divorced from reality'.

The late eighteenth-century investiture of the Highlands with qualities of the sublime – inspiring terror and awe of 'wild Nature' – was part of a broader re-working of Man's relationship with Nature and an aesthethic reaction throughout Europe to the regularity of improved and cultivated landscapes. By the end of the 1700s and the early 1800s, 'the educated classes had come to attach an unprecedented importance to the contemplation of landscape and the appreciation of rural scenery'.45 In Europe the Alps, in England the Lake District, and in Wales Snowdonia and the Brecon Beacons provided the setting for escape from town life and cultivated landscapes, and the solitude required for contemplation of wild nature.46 On a European scale, the influence of Rousseau is important in these issues.47 The sense in which he provided (though not alone), the image of the pastoral landscape completed by the presence of the 'good peasant', the 'noble savage' in harmony with a rugged landscape, and the view that man was once more natural, at one with his environment, does find reflection in the Highlands.48 Adam Ferguson (the only Highland-born member of the Enlightenment literati), in his Essay on the History of Civil Society, for example, endows the Highlander with qualities and traditions equivalent to Rousseau's peasants in the Alps.49

In the case of the Highlands, relationships between the wild sublimity of landscape in harmony with a primitive and noble social system received particular emphasis following publication in 1760 of MacPherson's Fragments of Ancient Poetry, collected in the Highlands of Scotland, and translated from the Gaelic or Erse Language. Also important were his Fingal (1761) and Temora (1763), and Hugh Blair's acclamation of MacPherson in his 1763 Critical dissertation on the poems of Ossian, the son of Fingal. The details of 'the Ossianic controversy' need not concern us.50 Some general points are important insofar as they

bear upon the image held of the Highlands. MacPherson
claimed his works to be, in translation, the works of
Ossian, an ancient Caledonian bard. His work was largely
fake, but it drew upon material that was genuine and was
published at a time when interest in things primitive was
widespread. It had considerable impact in Europe.51 The
effect of the Ossianic controversy, in combination with
other events, was threefold: firstly, the debate further
established the Highlands as the romantic local of noble
peasants - barbarians worthy of antiquarian interest but
simultaneously demanding culture as a process of civilisation; secondly, and paradoxically, the interest MacPherson's work generated led to several fabrications of
Gaelic's literary heritage whilst simultaneously ignoring
much genuine Gaelic literature. William Shaw, the
eighteenth-century Gaelic lexicographer, noted how 'Antiqui-
ty being the taste of the age, some acquaintance with the
Gaelic begins justly to be deemed a part of the Belles
Lettres'.52 But this acquaintance ignored or misrepresent-
ed genuine Gaelic cultural traditions and was contemporary
with policies of anglicisation and material change aimed at
'improving' the Highland ways of life. One Gaelic commentator at least was aware of this paradox:

> We cannot however but testify our surprise, that
> in an age in which the study of antiquity is so
> much in fashion and so successfully applied . . .
> this language alone, which is the depository of
> the manners, customs and notions of the earliest
> inhabitants of this island . . . should remain in
> a state of total abandon, but, which is more
> astonishing . . . this people and this language
> should be alone persecuted and intolerated.53

And thirdly, just as for Lowland Scotland, so the image of
Highland Scotland was underlain by a combination of
opposites: policies aimed at anglicisation and material
improvement derived motive force from an intellectual
context which regarded the Highlands as not yet civilised
and which created an idealised Highland life whilst
simultaneously neglecting or overtly attacking actual
Gaelic literature (when it was not considered 'degenerate'). From the late eighteenth century in particular, in
context with European-wide changes in taste, the Highlander
has had his traditions and culture 'invented' for him (not
least in a certain historiographic tradition);54 invented
as distorting and interdependent fabrications: a
primitivism of social system and mental outlook and an
antiquarian literary heritage set within, in both senses

Figure 2.1 'The "Ossianic" Highlands': Glencoe from Fittler's *Scotia Depicta* (1799) (Reproduced with the permission of Edinburgh University Library)

of the Lorn, an 'uncultivated' landscape. Visual representation of the Highland landscape reflects these developments (Figure 2.1). The text accompanying this 1799 depiction of Glencoe reads 'This glen is perhaps the most celebrated of any in Scotland. It is the supposed birth place of Ossian; it is the well known spot of the most dreadful massacre; and it embraces some of the most sublime scenes in this part of the world'. In the works of Runciman, Nasmyth, and later, MacCulloch, but not in Landseer, there is a more realistic representation of Highland landscape and scenery, though the scenes are often without people.55

This creation of the Highlands, not as they were but as they were imagined to be, largely derived from the Lowlands.

> There are few of our countrymen who, at some time
> of their lives, have not visited part of that
> romantic country; and we are sure that all those
> who have done so, will agree in the truth of this
> observation - that more of what they know of the
> character of the Highlanders has been learned in
> the low country than among the mountains.56

And it was a perspective that ignored the view of the people involved.

> It is, further, futile to imagine that the common
> people are sensible of the peculiar charms of a
> mountainous and romantic country. These are
> refinements that belong to education, to the
> cultivated taste. If the Highlander would shew
> you a fine prospect, he does not lead you to the
> torrent and the romantic rocky-glen, to the storm
> beaten precipice of the cloud-capt. mountain. It
> is to the strath covered with hamlets and cultiva-
> tions, or to the extended tract of fertile
> lowlands, where the luxuriance of vegetation and
> wood depends on the exertions of human labour.57

By the later nineteenth century, the Highlander was regarded differently still; as a figure of sentiment, spirituality and natural sensitivity in contrast to the materialism of the Anglo-Saxon.58 An accompanying notion is that of lament for a lost age, represented iconographi-cally in Faed's The Last of the Clan (Figure 2.2).

> The habit of mind promoted by Gaelic influences is
> an ideal treatment of the physical world, and a

Figure 2.2 'The "Lost" Highlands': Thomas Faed's The Last of the Clan (Reproduced with the permission of Glasgow Art Gallery and Museum)

promotion of the sentimental and poetic side of
existence to a more prominent position than the
modern work-a-day world is willing to accord it...
the result of this mental refinement is an
unwillingness, and partial incapacity, to enter
the arena of civilisation.59

The intellectual forces shaping the image of the
Highlands, now and in the past, have been many and their
history complex. The view that the Highlands and the
Highlander have always been considered apart from 'the
arena of civilisation' has, however, been a consistent
one. The sense of wildness and geographical and social
distance with which the Highlands were regarded during the
1600s, was, from the early 1700s, supplemented by
antiquarian interest in primitivism. Drawing upon these
ideas, the modern image derives largely from the later
eighteenth century. From that period, the Highlander, now
'tamed', was celebrated throughout Europe as a
Kulturvolk,60 his habitat an imagined setting for an
outmoded social system, his traditions appropriated to
support the image of a noble savage. The Highlands were
considered a region and people at an earlier phase of
social development - a tribal society of 'barbarians' -
and, in a related way, at an earlier stage of economic
development. In context with contemporary ideas of
civilisation and culture as the process of progress, clan
loyalties, pastoralism, and political disobedience marked
the Highlands as 'backward', in need of material
improvement. To be effective, such improvement had to be
implemented in a region that was politically secure.

THE EXTENSION OF POLITICAL CONTROL 1609-1784

By extension of political control is here meant the
attempts of the Crown and central government to spread
authority into a region that largely ignored the writ of
outside legislation. The belief that the clan system was
'hostile to peace and to settled habits', and that Highlanders did not recognise 'the notion of a body-politic, with
an acknowledged authority over every individual of the
state',61 underpinned and legitimated attempts at political
control. For us, political interest in the Highlands
centres upon three things: firstly, the region's involvement in national affairs, particularly in the seventeenth
century and in the Jacobite rising of 1715 and 1745;
secondly, in the nature and functions of the clan system in
relation to claims upon kin, territory, and tenure in the

Civilisation and the Move to Improvement

Highlands and the interest of outside commentators in heritable jurisdictions and the authority of the chief; and, thirdly, the political bases to material change provided by the annexation of certain Highland estates between 1755 and 1784.

From regional problem to national issue

With the forfeiture of the Lordship of the Isles in 1493, the direct threat to the Scottish monarchy from the Highland clans disappeared. But in the absence of effective authority to replace the rule of Clan Donald, the result in the Highlands was a century or more of factionalism among the clans.62 The Highland policy of the monarchy was, broadly, two-fold from the sixteenth and early-seventeenth centuries: military attempts 'to quell the defection and disobedience of the inhabitants of . . . parties of the Illis and the Hielandis of this realme'63 usually ineffective in the long term, and 'granting authority to great men in or near the Highlands whom they thought they could trust to represent the monarchy and to try to impose some semblance of order'.64 This was begun by James IV (1488-1513). In the southern Highlands, the Campbells were made the king's lieutenants, in the north-east, the Gordons. In the sixteenth century, the rise of Clan Campbell was paralleled by the decline of Clan Ian Mor (Clan Donald South), by the separation of political and cultural ties between the Gaels of Ireland and Scotland, internal factionalism, and, in the figure of James VI and I (1567-1625), by a monarch determined to establish order in the Highlands. An act of 1597 ordered all who claimed rights to land there to produce title deeds, produce security for crown rents, and maintain order amongst kinsmen. Another act of that year provided the basis to the building of towns in Kintyre, Lochaber, and Lewis (see below). These acts and the 1609 Statues of Iona were not alone effective nor do they represent the formal beginnings of a political 'highland problem', but they do mark the start of that 'sustained pressure on the chiefs, year after year, of an increasingly efficient central administration based on the privy council'.65

The extension of political 'rule' in the Highlands should not be seen as the simple overlaying of crown or governmental influence, nor a history involving Highlander ' versus' Lowlander. Within the Highlands, there were groups who saw advantages for self-aggrandisement in service to the crown or parliament, and, consequently, regions whose populations were more 'loyal', warlike, or

distant from authority than others. James VI and I, in his
Basilicion Doron (c.1598), recognised differences between
those 'that dwelleth in our maine land, that are barbarous
for the most parte, and yet mixed with some shewe of
ciuilitie; the other, that dwelleth in the Isles, and are
attulerlie barbares, without any sort or shewe of ciuilitie'.66 Yet at the same time, the general distinction
'Highlander' connoted savagery and barbarism in the Lowland
mind. And in the century from 1644 to 1746, when the
Highlands were a theatre for the acting-out of national
politics, there was much in truth to substantiate this
created image.

The complex political history of the Highlands in the
seventeenth century has been discussed in detail elsewhere
and will not be reiterated here.67 But three points may be
made.   Firstly , the campaigns of Montrose and MacColla
from 1644 to 1647 brought Highland clans together into
national political issues, and did so to the support of the
Stuarts. Stevenson has noted 'If Highland Jacobitism was
to be born in the 1680s, it had been conceived in the
1640s'. Secondly, it was an alliance based on hatred of
common enemies - the Campbells and parliamentary authority. Thirdly, the events of the period 1644 to 1647,
together with the lawlessness of the Highlands after 1660,
intensified the distinction, real and perceived, between
the 'savage' Highlander and the 'civilised' Lowlander. The
separation in sympathies within the Highlands between the
Stewart cause on the one hand and the Campbells and
government on the other not only sharpened this distinction
by the 1700s, but provided, in context with other events,
the political justification for suppression of the clans
and the authority of the chiefs after 1745.

The Restoration of the monarchy in 1660 was welcomed in
the Highlands partly because 'traditional monarchy was much
more acceptable than the rule of English republican
upstarts', and also because Highland chiefs expected (and
got), the restoration of a traditionally ineffective
central government. After 1660, the Highlands were at
their most lawless: this was 'the heyday of the caterans
and sporadic raiding'.68 Stevenson notes, 'The failure of
the Restoration government to take more effective action to
root out Highland lawlessness seems remarkable at first
sight, but the explanation for it is simple. The Highlands
were no longer the area which presented the most direct and
dangerous challenge to the regime. It was the problem of
how to crush opposition to the Restoration religious
settlement that obsessed the king's ministers'.69 Lawlessness within the Highlands was certainly a problem but
loyalty to the crown was not, by the 1670s, in doubt.

74

Indeed, Highlanders were used by the crown – in the shape of the 'Highland Host' in 1678, for example – to suppress Lowland opposition. Support for the crown by Highland clans was both paralleled and undermined by the further extension of Campbell power; an ascendancy which contributed to unrest and disorder. Campbell power was curbed from the 1690s, perhaps too much so for the crown's comfort, since, from that period, the exiled Stuart cause was more completely identified with hatred of the Campbells. Indeed, what had been 'an alliance of expediency' in the 1640s between Stuarts and Highlanders in opposition to the Campbells and central government, became, from the 1690s, a close bonding rooted in a devotion to the cause of James VII and a shared contempt for the house of Argyll. Those acts of 1701 and 1702 aimed at 'securing peace in the Highlands' appear, in expressed intent at least, little different from those of 1597 or 1609. But there had been no one 'Highland problem' in the intervening period.

James VI had been faced with a political system in the West Highlands in which many chiefs were free to wage wars, make alliances with and against each other, and in general conduct their affairs without reference to Edinburgh. But what the chiefs concerned sought through this defiance of central authority was simply the right to ignore it. They did not deny that James was legitimate king of all Scotland. By contrast under William II the Highlanders who resisted rule from Edinburgh were seeking not just to ignore the regime but to overthrow it by force.70

Attention has been paid to the events of the 1600s for two reasons. Firstly, they reveal Highland Scotland as a region of national political significance well before the middle of the eighteenth century. This involvement in wider issues fixed the Highlands firmly in the political consciousness of outside authority; indeed, it may have precipitated 'a much more systematic and brutal attack on clan and culture than would otherwise have taken place'.71 Secondly, however, whilst such involvement made a national issue out of a regional problem, it was not in the 1600s characterised by any real increase in effective authority within the Highlands or by changes directed at the structures of clan loyalty and the authority of chiefs. From the later 1700s it was.

Local administration in the Highlands was often without real power, a state of affairs not helped by the dissolution of the Privy Council in 1708. This 'political vacuum' in regard to Highland administration not only allowed the clans to carry on at a distance from authority, but allowed Jacobitism to surface as it did in 1715 and 1745. Government of the Highlands was weakened by the divided nature of politics in London and the Lowlands, by too few opportunities of patronage to incorporate chiefs into Lowland interests, and by an ineffective system of barony courts, regality courts, and justices of the peace.72 These shortcomings were highlighted by the Jacobite rebellions. The solution, given a prolonged history of internal disorder and a more recent one of increased national significance, was not to persist with traditional policies of allowing chiefs responsibility for maintaining order within and between clans, but to replace altogether clans and the authority of chiefs.

Clans, chiefs, and political obedience

The literal meaning of clann is 'children'. In medieval Highland society, the term was used 'to describe a patrilineal kindred, the members of which descended by known steps from a common ancestor'.73 They were usually divided into septs or branches known as a sliochd, plural sliochdan, within which were small local kin groups called cloinne, sing. clann. Kinship relationships and the authority vested in headship were central to the clan system, but kinship was not alone the basis to Highland social structures. Nor should we suppose a simple distinction in social system between clans (Highlands), and feudalism or, later, capitalism (Lowlands). In practice, the differences between the two areas in the ties that held people together were more often of degree than of type, at least in the seventeenth century. It is true that the clan survived in those parts of early modern Scotland more distant than others from the authority of king and government and apart from the feudal basis to civil control through the holding of land, but the origins of clans and the emphasis placed on kinship or land varied considerably.

If we may talk of a typical clan, it normally consisted of persons with close blood ties to the chief, lesser subordinate 'clans' or septs, dependents brought under the sway of others by conquest or tenurial obligations, 'broken men' - either refugees or members of clans for one reason or another breaking up - and hereditary officials.74 Although over time kinship and blood relationships spread widely throughout the clan and obedience and loyalty held all members together, the most powerful positions within

76

the cadre that advised the chief were usually occupied by immediate relations. These were the daoine uaisle, 'the gentry of the clan', holding land from the chief not only for rent but for their services as military leaders and as advisers to the chief'.75 From the seventeenth century, customary rights to land, mediated through the daoine uaisle, were replaced by written leases or 'tacks' and by the 1700s, the term 'tacksman' was used to describe the members of this layer of Highland society. The tacksman occupied a crucial intermediary function, as functionary and collateral relation between highest and lowest kin and as farm 'managers' and controllers of land and rents.76 Shifts in loyalty from kin to cash from the later 1600s often meant the disappearance of the tacksman or the re-ordering of his role. Some saw him as a 'great oppressor of his subtenants and scallags', 77 but most exercised an important and necessary function in their control over land. We shall meet with and discuss the role of the tacksman and the important relationships between social structure, tenure system and 'ancient possession' again.

Obedience, kinship, land: these three things held clan society together. The sense of loyalty to a chief and clan was often as important as actual blood ties - what one author has called the clan's 'ideological' function. Dodgshon has also examined the behavioural functions of clans as expressed in terms of territory and tenure. The territorial expression of clans was an intrinsic part of their nature. Clans acquired control over an area and maintained control over what may be considered their 'effective space' by tactical marriages, by the acquisition of the lands of lesser clans through Crown grants, or through the overtly feudal means of manrent or bondrent whereby smaller clans 'commended themselves to a larger, more powerful clan, seeking its protection in return for their political and military backing'.78 The question of tenurial arrangements within the clan is less clear: 'Taken at a face value, the available evidence suggests that the typical clansman held his land either by temporary tacks or at will'. We must add to this, however, as Dodgshon notes, the concept of duthchas, which has the more literal meanings of place of birth and customary practice,80 but in tenurial terms connotes a hereditary right of occupation. Occupiers were said to have the duthchas of a given holding which, whilst not having legal authority, seems to have had 'the force of custom behind it'.81 There is a parallel here with the practice of kindly tenure in Lowland Scotland.82 In the case of Highland Scotland, this sense of hereditary and customary right of occupation - an ownership through maintained presence, a rootedness in a given setting at once human and natural - is something we shall see to be implicit in the 1700s and explicit in expressions of protest in the later nineteenth century.

Obedience and loyalty to clan and chief, a persistent belief in customary traditions and rights of occupation and elements of feudal control of land were thus all interwoven elements in the fabric of Highland society. Yet, and despite the fact that these characteristics were found in the early modern Lowlands, these elements were used to stigmatise Highland society as different and, accordingly, inferior in the mind of the Lowlander. Clans arose in part as a response to lawlessness, but, in context with that sense of separation based on given notions of civility and geographical and social distance they came somehow to represent that lawlessness. In a crucial sense then, the image of the clan as a barrier to culture and improvement rested not upon what it actually was and how it worked, ideologically and behaviourally, but upon the significance attached by outsiders to clan society and its constituting bonds (partly as the 'primitive' social system beloved of antiquarians), and to the fact that clans were seen to threaten both local civil order and national political stability.

The authority of the chief over kin and vassals was a common source of complaint. In his 'Tribuum gemitus, or the Highland Clanns sad & Just Complaint' written in 1698, Sir Aeneas MacPherson drew attention to the actions of some chiefs and principal tenants in raising rents, and letting lands 'Clogged with such Conditions as are a perpetuall Check upon the Vassels to be Loyall', as illustrations of 'the opporesion [sic] of their Superiors'. He had three principal points for complaint. First, clan chiefs, and, increasingly, outside landowners taking over clan lands, were restricting by 'pretence of Law' what had been traditional customs and rights of access - fishing rights, wood for construction, 'the use of armes for ffoulling, fishing, and hunting', for example - and were treating their tenantry 'as if (with the froggs in the fable) they were good for nothing but to be Destroyed'. Second, no reward was given for loyalty in war: 'the Loyall and Warlick Clanns have nothing left them but the scares of their wounds, broken fortunes, and the Scorn and Laughter of their Enemies, for a Recompense of their Service'. Third, marrying 'to patch up their broken fortunes' had turned some 'to traitors and men of sordid and mean principles'. MacPherson advanced several proposals to redress these ills; the four most important were to 'annull all vassalages' and make the tenantry responsible to the crown; reduce the number of heritable jurisdictions held by clan superiors; grants and leases other than wadset or 'simple and plain morgage' should not be considered; and 'a Royal Regement of Guards be formed of the Highland Clanns'.83

Highland regiments were recognised as a means of pacifying and diverting the martial spirit of Highlanders to useful ends. The Black Watch was formed from six existing Highland companies in 1739.84 Highland regiments, commanded by Gaelic-speaking officers were of benefit in domestic Highland affairs, their language, military skill and physical endurance making them 'properest for the fatigue of ... getting these thieves best ferreted out of their lurking Holes'.85

The political bases to material change

The attempts at pacification that followed the 1715 Rebellion - the establishment of Lieutenancies, the creation of Highland Companies, forfeiture of estates, the 1716 Disarming Act, construction of roads and bridges, and, later, the establishment of the Royal Bounty Committee - were regarded by central government as important signs of progress in the Highlands. But their effect was variable. The Disarming Act, for example, only disarmed the loyal clans or produced old weapons.86 The structures of clanship and heritable jurisdictions remained untouched. These were, for many, the principal causes of backwardness and disorder. Thus one 'Memorial to General Wade' dated 29 August 1728 noted that

> It will be evident to everyone who is acquainted with the Circumstances of those places that the Gross Ignorance, and Extreme Indolance, and Idleness of the Meaner Sort of People keeps them poor, and their Spirits Low, and in consequence makes them yield a blind obedience to the Commands of their Superiors without Regard to Religion, Law or Reason to which Causes are to be attributed the Multitudes that followed the Disaffected Nobilitie and Gentry in the late Rebellion.87

And for another commentator,

> The Highlanders have been oppressed and inslav'd by their Chiefs, yet oppress'd and inslav'd after Such a Manner, that they have joyfully submitted to their tyrants, and glory'd, nay triumph'd in their base and ignominious Servitude.88

But given the lack of effective local administration and
the weakening of governmental purpose toward the Highlands
from the late 1720s, little direct action was taken against
the authority of chiefs and heritable jurisdictions until
after 1745. From that date, the political attack on
clanship was direct. A range of contemporary sources
illustrate the principal elements involved: action against
the chiefs and against heritable jurisdictions, the
proscription of Highland dress and the carrying of arms,
the forfeiture of estates as a basis to agricultural and
industrial improvement.

In a folio entitled 'Some Hints to [his R.H.] the Duke
of Cumberland concerning ye Highlands of Scotland', we
are told that the 'feudal law' of chief over subject and
distance from 'seats of justice' were the root cause of
'all ye commotions which have happened in this country'.89 For others, 'The civilising of that disorderly
People' likewise involved breaking the bond between chief
and clan, and only then implementing changes in the
economic basis to Highland society as well as extending
local administration. One such source is worth quoting
from at length for the insight it gives into the attitudes
of those who saw political change - particularly 'severing
the bond between clan and chief' - as a precondition to
material transformation.

> I have often censured Cottars and other sub-
> tenants, for the meanness of their Houses, want or
> badness of Gardins, and their general neglect of
> Improvements in the Fields; to which I was
> constantly answered, that they were not so much to
> blame as might be imagined, and that it should
> Rather be imputed to their masters or Superiors;
> who, should they take in their Heads to make any
> Improvements as they wished to do, would give
> their Possession to any of their Own Relations who
> could pay them a triffle of more Rent; and that
> they knew well there would be many to offer for
> them. By this instance of oppression, it plainly
> appears, why the disaffected are so indolent as we
> know they are, and that labour and Industry is
> thereby as Effectually suppressed as if it had
> been studiously intended, and that Lazyness that
> delusive mother of Vice was imprudently Encour-
> aged. Who then that travels among the disaffect-
> ed, and knows these Things, will wonder at seeing
> Mean Hutts, and Uncultivated Fields, and that
> people thus discouraged from labour, Unacquainted

with Law & Religion, and Supported and Protected
when they are guilty of the most attrocious
Crimes, should be the constant prey of Corrup-
tion.90

To this commentator, the clan system shielded law-breakers
and acted as a barrier to effective improvement: the clan
as a social system was inherently incapable of permitting
economic development. His proposals for civilising the
Highlands were, in turn, simultaneously political, economic, and cultural: advance agricultural improvements
especially ley husbandry; annex 'the lands of the disaffected'; plant colonies of 'well-affected subjects'; make
everyone swear an oath of loyalty; establish funds for the
prosecution of thieves and to pay for sufficient constables
and justices of the peace (three in each 'disaffected
parish'); put all vagrants and beggars in workhouses; chase
Catholic priests from the Highlands; quarter troops in the
Highlands; make everyone aged over ten 'attend the hanging
of members of the disaffected clans to set a good impression'; and establish ministers and schoolmasters throughout
the Highlands as a means 'to render the Highland Tongue
unfashionable, & of Course turn it to Contempt'. Similar
suggestions are advanced in other contemporary sources - by
those such as Duncan Forbes, directly involved in the 1745
Rebellion, in his 1745 'Memorial on the State of the
Highlands',91 by those on the margins of the Highlands and
the fringes of political involvement such as Nicol Graham
of Gartmore in his Gartmore Manuscript of 1747,92 and by
persons like William Cross, Sheriff of Lanarkshire and
Professor of Law at Glasgow University, whose 1748 essay on
'The Means of Civilizing the Highlands' was written from
the perspective of the Lowlander concerned to import
progress to 'that little world not subject to Law'.93
    Whilst these sources typify a general concern for
Highland improvement, many point to differences within the
region regarding the civility of the inhabitants. Forbes
considered the south-west Highlands under the Duke of
Argyll more civilised than elsewhere: in Mull, however,
(scene of brutal Campbell repression of the Macleans and
allies in the late 1670s), the inhabitants were 'much more
warlike'.94 The author of 'Some Remarks on the Highland
Clans', so scathing generally of Highlanders, pointed to
local differences in loyalty.

That the whole Highlands may not lye under the
Imputation of guilt common only to some Corners, I
shall here mention the several Districts whose
Inhabitants are most Justly chargable with

Depredations and Cowstealing via Morvein Swinart [Sunart], ardnamurchan, Moydart, arrasack [Arisaig], Glenfinan, Keangerlock, ardgour, Lochaber, Glengery, Knoydard, Glenmorison, Strathglass, Stratharig, Braes of Badenock, Ranoch, Craigcrostan arachar [Arrochar], Braes of Athole and Balquhidder. No doubt there are some Districts in the North Country that might also be mentioned, but were the Inhabitants of the forenamed Districts Civilised those of the North would soon give it up.95

Cross in his 1748 essay distinguished between those Highlanders nearer the Lowlands and those more distant.

They who live near the skirt of low country on the East side, are more civilized, But they who are remov'd and lye more to the west, are wild & Barbarous beyond expression, having no intercourse with the low country, or indeed Knowledge of it, saving what they learn from the Drovers of their cattle, who go once a year to the Low Country Markets.96

These differences within the Highlands are important here because they document in political loyalties and, in a sense, mental outlook what is a constantly recurring theme in the geography of the Highlands. They are also of interest because those acts passed to prohibit the kilt, and the bearing of arms ignored such variation in treating the Highlands as one region.

The 1746 Disarming Act defined the Highlands as

Dumbarton, such parts as lie upon the east, west, and north side of Lochleven, to the northward of that part where the Water of Leven runs from Lochleven, Stirling, north of the Forth, Perth, Kincardine, Aberdeen, Inverness, Nairn, Cromarty, Argyll, Forfar, Banff, Sutherland, Caithness, Elgin, and Ross.97

This act, forbidding the bearing of arms and proscribing Highland dress, was one of several passed after 1745 whose combined purpose was 'to assert an ideology of improvement throughout the Highlands'.98 Heritable jurisdictions were abolished in 1747.99 In 1752, Highland estates of those active in the Jacobite cause were 'forfeit' and annexed to the crown, their rents and produce used 'to civilise the inhabitants'.

Civilisation and the Move to Improvement

The Disarming act was effective, noted James Small, factor on the estate of Strowan in 1755, 'in those places where the troops are stationed' but he could not 'say so much for other places'.100 Wearing 'the Highland Garb' was punishable by six months jail or transportation for a second offence. Whilst there is evidence that Highlanders were arrested for 'wearing a philabeg' [kilt 101], the fact that most convictions were in or near towns with garrisons and in the southern Highlands confirms James Small's observations.102 By 1760, enforcement of the proscription was greatly relaxed. It was repealed in 1782. From that period, in context with the 'discovery' of the Highlands by travellers and royalty, and together with the interest shown in the 'primitive' Highlander, the kilt and tartan were lent a significance in the mind of the Lowlander and in the Scottish identity that they never enjoyed in the Highlands. This 'kilt and tartan' image was, for one author, 'the last stage in the creation of the Highland myth'.103 For many Highlanders, the reality of life was far removed from the created image.

The 1752 Annexing Act was passed

> ... to the purpose of civilising the Inhabitants upon the said estates, and other parts of the Highlands and Islands of Scotland; the promoting amongst them the Protestant Religion, good Government, Industry, and Manufactures and the Principles of Duty and Loyalty to his Majesty, his Heirs, and Successors and to no other Use and Purpose whatsoever.104

Estates had been similarly forfeit after the 1715 Rebellion and controlled by the Barons of the Exchequer 'in order to Raise Money out of them severally for the Use of the Publick'.105 The 1752 act was different in that proceeds deriving from annexation were used to benefit the local area, not collected in a centralised fund. (There is often confusion concerning the title of the body controlling the estates after 1752: the Treasury used the term 'The Commission for the Forfeited Annexed Estates': this title has been accepted elsewhere and is used here 106). The Annexing Act effectively controlled thirteen estates (Figure 2.3). The act recognised the power that the authority of the chiefs had within Highland society. Ward holding was banned as a tenurial system and the act brought in leases (of forty-one years) as a basis to a landholding system that underminded the powers of chief and tacksman. In addition to agricultural affairs, the Board for the Annexed Estates involved themselves in religious and

Figure 2.3   The distribution of the Annexed Estates in the Highlands

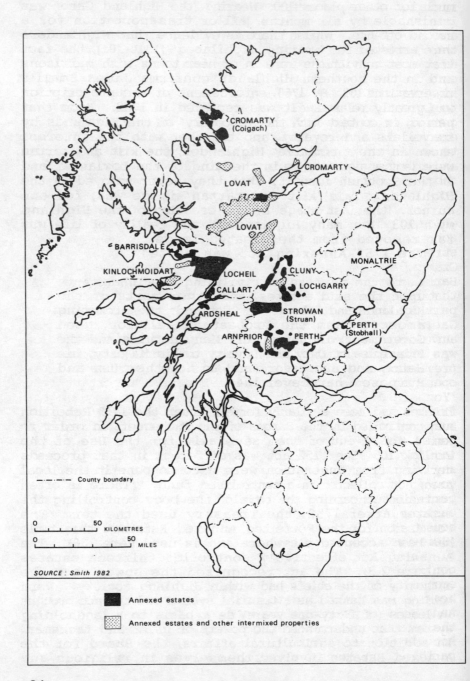

CROMARTY
(Coigach)

CROMARTY

LOVAT

LOVAT

BARRISDALE

MONALTRIE

KINLOCHMOIDART

LOCHEIL   CLUNY

CALLART   LOCHGARRY

ARDSHEAL

STROWAN
(Struan)

ARNPRIOR   PERTH

PERTH
(Stobhall)

----- County boundary

```
0        50
|____|____|  KILOMETRES

0        50
|____|____|  MILES
```

SOURCE : Smith 1982

■ Annexed estates

▨ Annexed estates and other intermixed properties

educational matters, in the development of local industry, and in the building of towns in the Highlands, all with a view to the 'prevention of disorders for the future'. The running of the estates as economic concerns was thus integral with a broader role as focal points for linguistic and religious change and political supervision. Forbes, the factor on Lovat and Cromartie estates, considered education and anglicisation the basis to all else: 'In order therefore to improve & civilize this part of the high-lands, I humbly apprehend that a particular attention to introduce the English Language is of the greatest consequence, and for that purpose schools should be erected'.107 He even proposed (unsuccessfully), that tenancies be refused those who spoke no English.108 There and in other estates, English was diffused through schools and in religious worship though not alone by these means. Proximity to the Lowlands, as it affected material changes in parts of the Highlands, also influenced the extent to which English was known and used. As in the case of SSPCK schools, estate schools in the north and west were less strongly English speaking than those of the central Grampians and Perthshire. The factor to the estates of Barrisdale, Locheil, Ardsheal and Kinlochmoidart reckoned that he operated in the 'most recluse and least civilised' part of the Highlands. Since the relative strength of Gaelic and English in a place marked in the mind of authority the degree of its 'civilization', his observation was 'correct' insofar as we can be certain of the then prevalence of Gaelic in those parts.109 Factors had few operating regulations, but one of the most important read 'You are on no condition to sett a farm to any of the friends [relatives] of the forfeiting persons'. Tenants suspected of connection with the rising were likely to be penalised: 'You [Factors] are to make it your business to inquire which of the tenants have been in rebellion ... If any of the tenants behave in a way not agreeable to you, you are to turn them out so soon as leases expire'.110 As part of this political function, estate surveyors had earlier been given the power of search of 'disaffected' houses and property and, if necessary, the authority to 'Seize and Secure the Same for the use of the King'.111

The 'civilising the inhabitants' involved political control as well as improvement that was simultaneously economic, linguistic and religious. We should be cautious, however, of ascribing to the Annexing Act and to the Annexed Estates a Highland-wide significance or considering the estates concerned entirely successful. The Annexing Act was not implemented until 1755; a delay occasioned by parliamentary laxness as well as by problems surveying the

estates and settling claims on their annexation.112
Throughout its existence from 1755 until 1704 when the
estates were returned to their original families, the Board
was hindered by internal problems. All too often, the
expense of running the estates 'left little room for
grandiose plans for civilising the highlands'.113 Although
in the long-term, Annexed Estates were not wholly successful as experiments in regional development, their cessation
in 1784 marks the end of the overt political 'rule' of the
Highlands.

URBANISATION AND 'COLONIES OF CIVILITY'

If the Annexed Estates represent perhaps the most evident
attempt at maintaining civil control and directing material
advance in the Highlands, a principal means employed to
this general end was the construction of new towns and
villages. Towns were central to the philosophy of the
eighteenth-century improver. One of the concerns of George
Dempster, for example, influential improver, founder member
of the British Fisheries Society, and active ideologue for
Highland 'cultivation', was the lack of towns in the
estates he acquired in Sutherland in 1786. Commenting of
his tenant population, Dempster noted 'They are all besides
far removed from Towns or villages so that they have little
demand for many Articles of their produce, and are ill
supported with things found in Towns, in exchange for their
produce'.114 Villages were central to Dempster's plans for
improvement, on his estate and throughout the Highlands.

> It is one thing to build a village, to which
> people may resort if they choose it, and another
> to drive them from the country into villages,
> where they must starve, unless they change at once
> their manners, their habits and their occupa-
> tions. How much better it would be, gradually to
> introduce spinning wheels and looms into their
> houses, than to drive them from their houses,
> their gardens and their little fields.115

MacPherson, in his prize-winning essay of 1793 on 'The
establishment of inland villages in the Highlands of
Scotland' likewise considered the development of towns in
the Highlands the basis 'to civilization and industry'.116
His essay reflected not only the widespread concern of men
like Dempster interested in the importance of towns and
villages to Highland material transformation in particular,
but also the prevailing ideology of an age in which contem-

poraries such as Adam Smith were discussing the role of towns as motivating forces behind national economic and social development.117 As Youngson notes, 'the town, even the village, appealed to the eighteenth-century mind as a centre of order, as a place of organised activity where the pattern and style of progressive eighteenth-century life could be imposed; as the focus <u>par excellence</u> of civilising influences'.118

Those involved in the Annexed Estates considered towns important not only because the inhabitants could help each other but also since towns would act to suppress lawlessness throughout their local area. These views were held particularly by those planning the settlement of soldiers and sailors in the Highlands.

> It would not only afford Protection to the well
> affected Possessors inhabiting the forfeited
> Estates, and keep unruly spirits there in Awe, but
> would Shed its Influence upon the Countrys around
> when they saw their ill affected Neighbours kept
> in Order, & under Government; so the well dispos'd
> would not only live in Safety, but become terrible
> to their disaffected Neighbours.119

The concern expressed in the debates on annexation for settlement construction and the location there of loyal and industrious inhabitants points also to the strongly-held belief for the industrial development of the Highlands and in the need to focus the marketing of Highland agricultural produce (see below). The erection of these 'colonies' was not always attended by success: 'soldier settlements' designed to accommodate returning soldiers on the Perth estates were almost total failures, for example, and elsewhere the implementation of schemes for village development did not always realise in practice the intent at conception. In places like Callander and Crieff, however, the policy of 'enlargement or new erection' of towns and villages was more successful.120 In the case of other planned villages built for industry or coastal fishing, plans for colonisation and civilisation through urbanisation were successful to varying extents in providing a degree of manufacturing specialisation and a focal point for Highlands-Lowlands commercial intercourse as well as the adoption and spread of the English language. Garrison towns such as Fort George, Fort William, and Fort Augustus fulfilled the additional function of political control.

Yet, whilst recognising the significance attached by contemporary commentators to planned villages and even to small scattered weaving stations and spinning schools, we must be cautious in considering their place in Highland improvement. Terms like 'urbanisation' and even 'town' need qualification in relation to the historic Highlands: what the eighteenth-century mind considered a 'civilizing town' was often little more than a village. Edmund Burt, one of the more realistic commentators on the eighteenth-century Highland scene, commented thus of Highland towns.

> A Highland Town is composed of a few Huts for Dwellings, with Barns and Stables, and both the latter are of more diminutive Size than the former, all irregularly placed, some one way, some another, and, at any Distance, look like so many heaps of Dirt; these are built in Glens and Straths, which are the Corn Countries, near Rivers and Ribulets, and also on the sides of Lakes where there is some Arable Land for the support of the inhabitants.121

Inverness - which Anderson considered 'the point from whence the rays of civilization shone over the surrounding gloom'122 - was the only town of any size in the Highlands. Other 'urban places', like Campbeltown, Dunoon, Callander, Dunkeld, Braemar and Nairn, were situated on the edge of the Highlands: commercially of significance to only limited hinterlands and linguistically on the frontier between Gaelic and English.

Colonisation and cultural transformation

The ideological notion of colonisation - settling loyal subjects and encouraging local industry - as a means of Highland transformation (and it was not only applied in those parts) predated the 1700s by a century or more. It was, in the broadest sense, a cultural policy. Schools were considered focal points for the diffusion of English, and care taken in their siting to ensure greatest effect. Highland libraries, churches, even individual ministers and catechists fulfilled similar functions. The Royal Bounty Committee encouraged 'Collonies of Protestants to settle in Popish Countrys and Islands' to stem the tide of Catholicism and anti-Government sentiment.123 For others, the idea involved a military solution to Highland disorder: settling 'Colonies of the Well-affected Subjects ... in all the Corners of the Highlands possessed by the Disaffected Clans',124 and, operating as the Romans had, in building barracks and forts in key locations.

> Partys of the Troops must, after the Roman manner
> ... be Spread over the Country and encamp'd
> chiefly at the passes and places of Danger, and in
> the Countrys that are most infested with Robberys
> and especially where the Robbers reside.125

The Scottish Parliament recognised the role of towns as outposts of authority in their act of 1597 on 'the bigging [building] of Burrowes Townes in ye Iles and Hielandis'.

> Oure Soveerane Lord [with advice] of ye estaitis
> of this Parliament ffor ye better Intertening and
> continuing [of] ciuilitie and polecie within ye
> hielandis and Iles hes statut and ordanit that
> thair be erectit and buildit within ye boundis
> thairof thre burgheis and burrow tounes in the
> maist conuenient and comodius pairtis meit for ye
> samyn To wit ane in Kintyre Ane uthair in Lochaber
> and the thrid in the Lewis.126

Plans for the settlement in the Highlands of what James VI called 'answerable inlands subjects', [Lowlanders], were only partly successful: the Lochaber scheme was never realised; the settlement in Kintyre at Lochhead (Campbeltown), was slow to develop; and in the case of Stornoway in Lewis, local opposition forced the colonists, the Gentlemen Adventurers from Fife, to depart by 1607.127 During the seventeenth century, however, in combination with the rise in importance of the Campbells who had effectively controlled Kintyre from 1607, the burgh of Campbeltown and adjacent districts was increasingly the focus for schemes of Lowland colonisation: 'Kintyre particularly, and Southern Argyll in general terms, must be looked on as a bridgehead of Lowland influence on the periphery of the Highlands'.128 Lowlanders were planted in Kintyre, in the burgh of Inveraray, and in parts of Cowal throughout the 1600s.129 Estimates based upon a 1678 Rental suggest that about thirty per cent of the population of southern Kintyre were Lowlanders then. Even amongst many native Highlanders, English was being spoken and English-style surnames adopted.130 Although the Lowland presence in parts of the south-west Highlands was marked during the 1600s, not all colonists acted as intended. Kirkwood noted in the 1690s that

> It is very considerable, that in Kintyre (a
> Countrey in the Highlands), whence the Highlanders

were expelled, and where others, who spoke English, were planted in their stead; in process of time, by frequent conversation with the neighbouring Highlanders, many of them, instead of propagating the English language, have learned Irish; so that now they preach once a day in Irish in the chief Churches of the country.131.

In other places, towns and villages did initiate change. In Fort William in 1735, for example, there were 'many hundreds that understands not the Irish'. By 1760, 'the town was largely English-speaking'.132 Lettice (1794) noted that English was commonly spoken in Inverness, Fort George, Fort William and Fort Augustus.133 By the mid-eighteenth century, many of the population of Inverness did not regard themselves as true Highlanders because they spoke English. As Burt noted, the social and cultural division between languages in Inverness corresponded to the town's economic function in the local area:

> ... although they speak English, there are scarce any who do not understand the Irish Tongue; and it is necessary that they should do so, to carry on their Dealings with the neighbouring Country People, for within less than a Mile of the Town, there are few who speak any English at all ... What I am saying must be understood only of the ordinary People, for the Gentry, for the most Part, speak our Language in the remotest parts of Scotland.134

Inverness was the most important market town and trade outlet in the Highlands. Grain prices there regulated prices over the North Highlands and the town was an important supplier of goods for almost all the Highlands.135 Yet the unequal distribution of markets, fairs and towns elsewhere in the Highlands hindered expansion of market forces. Whyte has shown that in the seventeenth century most parts of the Highlands were beyond convenient reach of the economic functions and civilising influences of towns and markets, but that by 1707, trading centres were established in all the large islands of the Inner Hebrides, and in inland Inverness-shire and Perthshire.136 Even so, most of the inhabitants of the Western Isles, for example, had little opportunity to engage in commercial enterprise until the later eighteenth century, and the development of effective market areas for towns like Stornoway, Portree, Fort William and Inverarary was often restricted by limited capitalisation and operated only on

90

local scales.137 The overland movement of meal within as well as into the Highlands, and, more importantly, the export of black cattle, was through towns. This latter trade was of prime commercial importance to those towns and to the Highland economy as a whole. And throughout the western seaboard and islands where the sea joined rather than separated, towns fulfilled local market functions and had longer-distance trade in fish and kelp with the larger commercial interests of the Lowlands. Movement of goods was mirrored by the temporary movement of people to employment in the Lowlands. In these and other ways, the Highland economy was linked with that of the Lowlands and further afield. But the limited number of towns in the Highlands, their small size, and their principally small-scale commercial rather than industrial functions were regarded by contemporary improvers as factors limiting the region's economic development. The intended solution was to initiate local industry and the related notions of virtue and loyalty through planned villages.

Planned villages in the Highlands

Planned villages in Scotland - settlements of regular layout founded by landowners on their estates between about 1735 and 1850 - have their origins in related aspects of natural population increase and structural change in agriculture and in the concern to develop small-scale industries. A number of studies have been made of the geography, chronology of foundation, economic functions and morphology of these settlements.138 Lockhart has recently suggested as many as 393 were established between 1725 and 1850, with a chronology that saw fifty-five founded before 1770, a further 164 between 1770 and 1779, a total of 119 in the period 1800-1819, and the remaining fifty-five between 1820 and 1850.139 Smout has considered that Scotland's planned villages fell into eight geographical groups: coastal settlements along the shores of Caithness, Sutherland, and Cromarty; those in Moray, Banff, and north-west Aberdeenshire - the area of greatest concentration; inland villages in the central Highlands; settlements along the western Highland coasts; a cluster on the fringes of the southern Highlands along Strathmore; those 'within the orbit of Glasgow', principally factory villages; a smaller grouping in the Lothians; and a final group in the south-west Lowlands along the north shore of the Solway.140 He further notes that almost all these planned villages fall into one or other of four economic categories: agricultural; fishing; villages based on small

91

textile industries; or, lastly, factory villages.

Lockhart has advanced a total of 91 planned villages built in the Highlands and Islands between 1725 and 1850: five between 1725 and 1769, thirty-three from 1770 to 1799, forty-two between 1800 and 1819, and the remaining eleven in the thirty years from 1820.141 Most were situated on the coast, intended as fishing villages, others as the location for small-scale textile development in inland sites (Figure 2.4). Both inland and coastal villages and the industry they contained were a response to demographic, economic and moral factors. A number of settlements were built to absorb the local thickening of population on coasts and elsewhere following population clearance and redistribution form the later 1700s. Throughout the 1800s these villages and a number of other settlements appeared and expanded, often rapidly and beyond the capacity of the local environment to afford reasonable subsistence, as the result of population displacements within the Highlands.142

Leaving aside the development of part-time agriculture, the principal industries involved in Highland planned villages were textiles, chiefly linen, and fishing. In addition to the involvement of the Commissioners for the Annexed Estates in the Roman-style <u>colonia</u> of soldiers and sailors, three other organisations were involved in establishment of Highland villages and industries: the Board of Trustees for the Encouragement of Manufactures and Fisheries, concerned to place textile stations in 'the most Centrical Situation';143 the Highland Society, begun in 1784; and the British Fisheries Society, established in 1786. The commitment of the Highland Society to the economic advance of the Highlands was enshrined in their charter and evident in their concern over 'the means of the improvement of the Highlands by establishing towns and villages', and in the premiums awarded to landowners founding, and prizes given for essays on, planned villages.144 Links between these bodies were personal and founded on a shared ideology - the fifth Duke of Argyll, for example, who held high positions in the Highland Societies of London and Edinburgh, was first governor of the British Fisheries Society - and this last body owed its foundation to the work of the Highland Society (of Edinburgh) in encouraging fisheries in the Highlands.145 Returns made to the British Fisheries Society reveal not only the small-scale extent to which fishing was already in existence, but also that almost every major bay and sea loch in the west Highlands was considered or offered as a possible site for a fishing station. John Knox, whose 1786 lecture <u>A Discourse on the expediency of establishing fishing stations or small towns in the Highlands of</u>

Figure 2.4 The distribution of planned villages in the Highlands

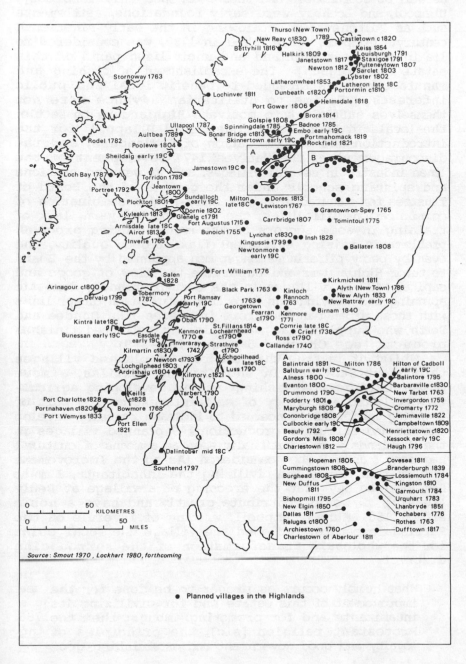

Thurso (New Town)
New Reay c1830   1789   Castletown c1820
Bettyhill 1816   Halkirk 1809   Keiss 1854
Janetstown 1817   Louisburgh 1791
Staxigoe 1791
Newton 1812   Pulteneytown 1807
Sarclet 1803
Latheronwheel 1853   Lybster 1802
Stornoway 1763   Latheron late 18C
Lochinver 1811   Dunbeath c1820   Portormin c1810
Port Gower 1806   Helmsdale 1818
Golspie 1808   Brora 1814
Ullapool 1787   Spinningdale 1785   Badnoe 1785
Aultbea 1789   Bonar Bridge c1813   Embo early 19C
Rodel 1782   Skinnertown early 19C   Portmahomack 1819
Poolewe 1804   Rockfield 1821
Sheildaig early 19C   A   B
Loch Bay 1787   Jamestown 19C
Torridon 1789
Portree 1792   Jeantown
1800
Plockton 1801   Bundalloch
early 19C   Milton   Dores 1813
Kyleakin 1813   Dornie 1802   late18C   Lewiston 1767   Grantown-on-Spey 1765
Arnisdale late 18C   Glenelg c1791   Carrbridge 1807   Tomintoul 1775
Airor 1813,   Fort Augustus 1715
Inverie 1765   Bunoich 1755   Lynchat c1830   Insh 1828
Kingussie 1799   Ballater 1808
Newtonmore
early 19C
Salen   Fort William 1776   Kirkmichael 1811
Arinagour c1800   1828   Alyth (New Town) 1786
Dervaig 1799   Tobermory   Black Park 1763   Kinloch   New Alyth 1833
1787   Port Ramsay   Rannoch   New Rattray early 19C
early 19C   Georgetown   1763   1763   Birnam 1840
1763   Kenmore
Kintra late18C   Oban 1790   Fearran   1771
c1790   Comrie late 18C
Bunessan early 19C   Kenmore   St.Fillans 1814   Crieff 1738
early 19C   1770   Lochearnhead   Ross c1790
Kilmartin c1830,   c1790   Strathyre   Callander 1740
Inveraray   c1790
1742   Lochgoilhead
Newton c1793   late 19C
Lochgilphead 1803   Luss 1790
Ardrishaig c1804   Kilmory c1821

Keills   Tarbert 1790
c1828
Port Charlotte 1828   Bowmore 1768
Portnahaven c1820
Port Wemyss 1833   Port Ellen
1821

Dalintober mid 18C

Southend 1797

0   50
KILOMETRES
0   50
MILES

A
Balintraid 1891   Milton 1786   Hilton of Cadboll
Saltburn early 19C   early 19C
Alness 1800   Balintore 1795
Evanton 1800   Barbaraville c1830
Drummond 1790   New Tarbat 1763
Fodderty 1801   Invergordon 1759
Maryburgh 1808   Cromarty 1772
Cononbridge 1808   Jemimaville 1822
Culbockie early 19C   Campbeltown 1809
Beauly 1792   Henriettatown c1820
Gordon's Mills 1808   Kessock early 19C
Charlestown 1812   Haugh 1796

B
Hopeman 1805   Covesea 1811
Cummingstown 1808   Branderburgh 1839
Burghead 1808   Lossiemouth 1784
New Duffus   Kingston 1810
1811   Garmouth 1784
Bishopmill 1795   Urquhart 1783
New Elgin 1850   Lhanbryde 1851
Dallas 1811   Fochabers 1776
Relugas c1800   Rothes 1763
Archiestown 1760   Dufftown 1817
Charlestown of Aberlour 1811

Source: Smout 1970, Lockhart 1980, forthcoming

● Planned villages in the Highlands

Scotland and the Hebride Isles was influential in forming the British Fisheries Society, proposed forty villages between Dornoch and Arran, each to contain 30 to 40 houses, as well as storehouses and sheds. In fact, only Tobermory, Ullapool, and Lochbay were early foundations, settlements such as Pulteneytown following in the early nineteenth century. Ullapool, established in 1788, was considered to lie in 'the most highland and uncivilized parts of this estate'146 [Coigach]. The establishment of fishing and manufactures was intended to benefit local and public interests. Claims to utilitarian advance were not themselves sufficient to motivate Highlanders to settle; the locals in Lochbroom considered Ullapool 'for the introduction and accommodation of Lowlanders, and the discouragement of the Natives'.147 Development of the linen industry in several villages, and in weaving stations and spinning schools under the control of the Board of Trustees for Manufactures, was limited by a combination of communication difficulties, the high cost of yarn, lack of training in some sectors of the manufacturing process, problems in raising sufficient flax of good quality, and even by petty pilfering amongst men appointed by the Board to tutor Highlanders and supervise the flow of goods and capital.148 In villages in the east Highlands, domestic spinning and weaving was more successful given closer links with those urban manufacturers in places like Dundee and Perth who supplied raw materials and collected finished products (see Chapter 5 pages 289-299).

Whilst it is true that the role of planned villages throughout Scotland in encouraging textiles, a more commercially-oriented fishing, and in developing agriculture reflected a strategy of self-interest on the part of founding landowners concerned to increase rentals, develop markets and stimulate production,149 planned villages in the Highlands were additionally seen as a means of cultural hegemony. John Forbes considered 'As to the Improvement [sic] of this barony and civilizing the inhabitants, I must beg leave to say that the erecting of a village at Beuly [Beauly], ... would contribute greatly and have a noble effect'.150 Mungo Campbell, writing of Inveruie on the Barrisdale estate, reckoned the village the focal point for the wholesale transformation of the surrounding district.

What humbly occurs as proper to be done for the improvement of this estate and for civilizing its inhabitants and for promoting amongst them the Protestant religion [sic], the principles of loyalty and good government and establishing good

husbandry, industry and manufactures is already
hinted at in the settlement proposed to be made at
Inveruie, at which place it is humbly thought that
a seminary or spinning school for the promoting
manufactures of coarse linnen cloath should in
particular be erected.151

As Smout notes , 'These were going to be settlements for a
new morality, towns to bring respectability to the Celtic
fringe'.152 The civil control sought for Highlands through
a harmony of economic, social and political interests in
these settlements was reflected in their ordered plan: the
regular layout not only suited the aesthetic values of the
time but represented in built form the rational and
utilitarian philosophy of individual landowners and the
social values of the improving class. Though clearly
smaller scale than Edinburgh's New Town, the regular
geometry of many planned villages symbolised the same
control over space as in Scotland's capital, and in the
Highlands, stood in representation of the authority of
capital and class over customary relations. New 'prospects' for the region were evident in both senses of the
term - looking outwards in space to new forms on the
landscape and forwards in time to a new order in Highland
society.153

CONCLUSION

This chapter has suggested that attitudes towards the
Highlands were derived both from influences and events
particular to that region and people and part also of
general processes of social, economic, and cultural change
affecting Scotland as a whole. Ideas of civilisation and
improvement, particularly in the eighteenth century (in
which period many 'modern' assumptions and contradictions
regarding the Highlands have their origin), reflected not
only the dominant social and economic relationships within
Scotland, but also prevailing tastes and values throughout
Europe. The ideas of the ruling class on the development
and civilisation of the Highlands were, in general terms,
the 'dominant material relationships grasped as ideas'.
And, in turn, contemporary notions of culture as a
stage-by-stage process of societal development from less to
more advanced, and the ideological claims of improvers to
self-interest, national prosperity and civil authority -
expressed in and maintained through English - provided the
basis to policies of cultural transformation which
involved, simultaneously, anglicisation, political pacifica-

tion, and economic change. In economic terms, the concordance of enlightened self-interest and communal good was perhaps most evident in the work of Adam Smith; as Richards notes, 'His book was a bible to the Highland improvers'.154 But the ideas of progressive improvement sought for Highland Scotland by men such as Smith were not alone or even chiefly economic, however central the doctrine of market forces and the conversion of feudal lords or clan chiefs into capitalist landowners. These ideas, framed and held as ruling ideas by the <u>literati</u> and the landowners, and implemented by a range of institutions whose membership was drawn from these groups and whose policies put the ideology of these groups into practice, were evident before the 1700s and apparent also in literature and language. It may not quite be that 'The soul of the Highlander was won not on the battlefield but in the boardroom by men of the Enlightenment'.155 But civilising the Highlands did involve changes in mental cultivation - for the Highlander new ways and ideas, a different language, new loyalties and beliefs, and, for the outsider, the representation of the region as backward and in need of advance. At the same time, changes were taking place in the material basis to Highland, and Scottish life, changes with which in a variety of ways, these ideas were intimately linked.

NOTES

1. SRO, GD 95.10.57., pp.1-2 [N. Shute, <u>Some Consideration to induce the people of South Brittain to Contribute to the Designe of propagating Christian Knowledge to the Highlands and Isles of North Brittain and of Civilizing the Barbarous Inhabitants of these parts of the Kingdome, 1708</u>].

2. S. Johnson, <u>A Journey to the Western Isles of Scotland</u> (London, 1775), p.25.

3. J. Millar, <u>The Origin of the Distinction of Ranks</u> (London, 1779), p.6.

4. J. D. Young, <u>The Rousing of the Scottish Working Class</u> (London, 1979), pp.11-40.

5. R. H. Campbell, 'The Enlightenment and the Economy', in R. H. Campbell and A. Skinner (eds.), <u>The Origins and Nature of the Scottish Enlightenment</u> (Edinburgh, 1982), pp.17-18.

6. <u>Ibid</u>, p.21; see also I. Whyte, <u>Agriculture and Society in Seventeenth Century Scotland</u> (Edinburgh, 1979), pp.98-101; A. Chitnis, <u>The Scottish Enlightenment</u> (London, 1976), p.13.

7. The innovations and statutes of the seventeenth century, and their effects upon Lowland Scotland in particular, are documented by Whyte, <u>Seventeenth Century Scotland.</u>

8. Young, <u>Scottish Working Class</u>, p.13.

9. <u>Ibid</u>, p.21; see also T. C. Smout, 'Scottish landowners and economic growth 1650-1850', <u>Scottish Journal of Political Economy, XI</u>, (1964), pp. 218-234.

10. D. Daiches, <u>The Paradox of Scottish Culture</u> (London, 1964), p.11.

11. <u>Scots Magazine, 17</u>, (1755), p.129.

12. <u>Scots Magazine, 22</u>, (1761), pp.440-441.

13. J. Barrell, <u>English Literature in History 1730-1780: an equal wide survey</u> (London, 1983), pp.34-5, 50; on the

question of refinement in speech marking class boundaries in the nineteenth century, see K. C. Phillips, Language and Class in Victorian England (Oxford, 1984); and on the way in which the symbolic use of language as the means of authority was vested in institutional structures, see A. P. Donajgrodski, Social Control in Nineteenth Century Britain (London, 1977), pp.13-14.

14. Young, Scottish Working Class, p.21.

15. Chitnis, The Scottish Enlightenment, pp.34-5; on some aspects of nineteenth-century sexual attitudes and behaviour, see T. C. Smout, 'Aspects of sexual behaviour in nineteenth century Scotland' in A. A. MacLaren (ed.), Social Class in Scotland: Past and Present (Edinburgh, 1978), pp.55-85.

16. D. Daiches, The Paradox of Scottish Culture (London, 1964).

17. J. Y. T. Greig (ed.), The Letters of David Hume (Oxford 1932), I, p.255; (Quoted in Chitnis, The Scottish Enlightenment, p.12, and in Janet Adam Smith 'Some eighteenth century ideas of Scotland' in N.T. Phillipson and R. Mitchison (eds.), Scotland in the Age of Improvement (Edinburgh, 1970), pp.107-124).

18. Janet Adam Smith, 'Eighteenth century ideas', p.111.

19. This evidence is discussed at greater length in a number of works on Scottish literature; I have drawn upon the following here: A. Bold, Modern Scottish Literature (London, 1983); M. Lindsay, History of Scottish Literature (London 1977); D. Craig, Scottish Literature and the Scottish People 1680-1830 (London, 1961); K. Wittig, The Scottish Tradition in Literature (Edinburgh, 1958); and D. Murison, The Guid Scots Tongue (Edinburgh, 1977).

20. Daiches, The Paradox of Scottish Culture, pp.20-21; Young, Scottish Working Class, pp.16-17; on the contemporary evidence for the intended neglect of Scots by the landed classes, see, for example, J. Beattie, Scoticisms, arranged in alphabetical order, designed to correct improprieties of speech and writing (Edinburgh, 1797); and J. Sinclair, Observations on the Scotch Dialect (Edinburgh, 1782).

21. Young, Scottish Working Class, p.12.

22. Chitnis, The Scottish Enlightenment p.8.

23. H. Home (Lord Kames), The Gentleman Farmer, being an attempt to improve Agriculture, by subjecting it to the test of rational principles (Edinburgh, 1776), pp.v, xv.

24. See, for example, J. Rendall, The Origins of the Scottish Enlightenment 1707-1776 (London, 1978), p.59; D. Turnock, The Historical Geography of Scotland since 1707 (Cambridge, 1982), p.42: Lord Kames was a major figure in the Scottish Enlightenment - see, for example, G. Bryson, Man and Society: the Scottish Enquiry of the Eighteenth Century (Princeton, 1945), pp.53-77; W.C. Lehmann, Henry Home, Lord Kames, and the Scottish Enlightenment (The Hague, 1971); I.S. Ross, Lord Kames and the Scotland of his day (Oxford, 1972).

25. Campbell, 'The Enlightenment and the Economy', p.8.

26. Ibid., p.17.

27. R.C. Boud, 'Scottish agricultural improvement societies, 1723-1835', ROSC (Review of Scottish Culture), 1, (1984), pp.70-90.

28. R.I. Black, 'The Gaelic Academy: the cultural commitment of the Highland Society of Scotland', Scottish Gaelic Studies, XIV (II), (1986), pp.1-38.

29. The best overall review of these improvement societies, though concerned chiefly with literary and philosophical bodies, is D. McElroy, Scotland's Age of Improvement: a survey of eighteenth-century literary clubs and societies (Washington, 1969); see also Campbell, 'The Enlightenment and the Economy', p.11; I. Hont and M. Ignatieff (eds.), Wealth and Virtue: the shaping of political economy in the Scottish Englightenment (Cambridge, 1982); J. Merrington, 'Town and Country in the Transition to Capitalism', New Left Review, 93, (1975), p.71.

30. Chitnis, The Scottish Enlightenment, pp. 91-123.

31. Ibid., pp.102-106; see also H.T. Dickinson, Liberty and Property: Political Ideology in Eighteenth-Century Britain (London, 1977), pp.124-5.

32. Young, Scottish Working Class, p.24.

33. The title to this section is taken from an anonymous

pamphlet of the same title, published in London in 1745. The pamphlet is composed of a series of notes and articles designed to inform an English public of the inherent barbarity of Highlanders.

34. Young, Scottish Working Class, p.14.

35. NLS, Adv MS 32.4.6., p.2.

36. Scots Magazine, 28 (1766), p.681.

37. A.R.B. Haldane, The Drove Roads of Scotland (Edinburgh, 1952); idem, New Ways through the Glens (Edinburgh, 1962); J. Salmond, Wade in Scotland (Edinburgh, 1936).

38. Johnson, Journey to the Western Isles, p.38.

39. NLS, MS Ch.798 (Contract of James VI and I regarding the suppression of lawlessness in the Highlands, 1612); NLS, MS 7033, f.144 (The King's Answer on the Highlands, 12 July 1667).

40. NLS, MS 2200, ff.60-60a (Papers on situation in the Highlands, n.d., c.1724).

41. Anon., The Highlander Delineated (London, 1745), pp.ii, v-vi (see note 36 above).

42. M. Martin, A Description of the Western Isles of Scotland (London, 1703), p.3.

43. T.C. Smout, 'Tours in the Scottish Highlands from the eighteenth to the twentieth centuries', Northern Scotland, 5(2), (1983), 99-122.

44. M. Chapman, The Gaelic Vision in Scottish Culture (London, 1978), p.37.

45. K. Thomas, Man and the Natural World: changing attitudes in England 1500-1800 (London, 1983), p.267.

46. Thomas, Man and Nature, passim; for an interesting paper on the visual representation of these cultural 'wild' landscapes, see J. Zaring, 'The romantic face of Wales, Annals, Association of American Geographers, 67, (3), (1977), pp.397-418; Smout's 1983 paper draws attention to the visual dimension in the creation of a Highland image, but does not include illustrations.

47. Chapman, Gaelic Vision, p.32; Smouth, 'Tours in the Scottish Highlands', p.102; D.G. Charlton, New Images of the Natural in France (Cambridge, 1984), pp.34, 59.

48. Charlton, New Images of the Natural, p.34; N. Hampson in his The Enlightenment (Harmondsworth, 1984 edition), p.27 has noted that the ideas of the bon sauvage, in the work of Lahontan, may be dated to the first years of the 1700s.

49. Charlton, New Images of the Natural, p.59; a point made also by D. Forbes in his 'Adam Ferguson and the idea of Community' in D. Young et al (eds.), Edinburgh in the Age of Reason (Edinburgh, 1967), p.41.

50. Chapman, Gaelic Vision, pp.29-52; for an authoritative discussion of the debate, see D.S. Thomson, The Gaelic Sources of MacPherson's Ossian (Edinburgh, 1951).

51. Chapman, Gaelic Vision, p.47 notes, from other sources, how editions of Ossian appeared in at least ten different European languages.

52. W. Shaw, An Analysis of the Gaelic Language (London, 1778), p.xxiii.

53. A. MacDonald, Ais-Eiridh na Sean-Chanoin Albannaich: no an nuadh orainiche Gaidhealach (Duneidinn, 1751), pp.vii-viii.

54. H. Trevor-Roper, 'The invention of tradition: the Highland tradition of Scotland', in E. Hobsbawm and T. Ranger (eds.), The Invention of Tradition (Cambridge, 1984), pp.15-42; and the more important H. Gaskill, '"Ossian" Macpherson: towards a rehabilitation', Comparative Criticism, 8 (1986), pp.113-146.

55. J. D. Macmillan, 'Art, Gaelic, in modern times', in D.S. Thomson (ed.), The Companion to Gaelic Scotland (Oxford, 1983), pp.11-14; H. Okum, 'Ossian in Painting', Journal of the Warburg and Courtauld Institutes, 30, (1967), pp.327-356. Valuable work on Landseer and his image of Highland Scotland is being carried out by Trevor Pringle of Loughborough University. It would be interesting to see the degree to which the Highlands of Scotland figures as 'preferred places' in British, and European art, in the sense identified for England and Wales by Peter Howard in his 'Painters' preferred places', Journal of Historical Geography, 11(2), (1985), pp.138-154.

56. Edinburgh Monthly Review, III, (1820), p.490 (Review of P. Larkin, Sketch of a Tour in the Highlands of Scotland (London, 1819)).

57. J. MacCulloch, The Highlands and Western Isles of Scotland (London, 1824), III, p.88.

58. Chapman, Gaelic Vision, p.99; on parallels in European historiography see the valuable paper by P. Sims-Williams, 'The Visionary Celt: the construction of an Ethnic Preconception', Cambridge Medieval Celtic Studies, (1986), pp.71-96.

59. Scottish Review, I, (1882-1883), p.102.

60. Trevor-Roper, 'Highland tradition', p.18; Gaskill, 'Ossian Macpherson', pp.139-140.

61. A. Lang (ed.), The Highlands of Scotland in 1750 (Edinburgh, 1898), p.ix (From Brit. Museum King's MS 104); J. Anderson, Prize Essay on the State of Society and Knowledge in the Highlands of Scotland; particularly in the Northern Counties in 1745 (Edinburgh, 1827), p.60 (Anderson is here quoting from Chalmers' Caledonia, I, p.454).

62. D. Stevenson, Alasdair MacColla and the Highland Problem in the Seventeenth Century (Edinburgh, 1980), pp.6-33, 267-301; G. Donaldson, Scotland James V - James VII (Edinburgh, 1974), pp.228-232, 348-349.

63. J. H. Burton (ed.), Register of the Privy Council of Scotland (Edinburgh 1908-1970), V, (1598), p.466.

64. Stevenson, MacColla and the Highland Problem, p.21.

65. Ibid., p.28.

66. J. Craigie (ed.), The Basilicon Doron of James VI (Edinburgh, 1944-1950), I, p.71; II, pp.120-17.

67. I have drawn heavily upon Stevenson, MacColla and the Highland Problem, not least for the important view it gives of Highland affairs in this period from 'the inside looking out'.

68. I.F. Grant, The Macleods: the history of a clan (London, 1959), pp.319-320; SRO, GD52. 76, Account of losses sustained by robberies of the Highlanders

69. Stevenson, <u>MacColla and the Highland Problem</u>, pp.283-4.

70. <u>Ibid</u>., p.297.

71, <u>Ibid</u>., p.298

72. R. Mitchison, 'The Government and the Highlands, 1707-1745', in N.T. Phillipson and R. Mitchison (eds.), <u>Scotland in the Age of Improvement</u> (Edinburgh, 1970), pp.24-46; A. Murdoch, <u>'The People Above': politics and administration in mid-eighteenth century Scotland</u> (Edinburgh, 1980), p.11; A.E. Whetstone, <u>Scottish County Government in the Eighteenth and Nineteenth Centuries</u> (Edinburgh, 1981), pp. 38-39.

73. W.D.H. Sellar, 'Clans, origins of', in D.S. Thomson, <u>The Companion to Gaelic Scotland</u> (Oxford, 1983), pp.43-44.

74. Stevenson, <u>MacColla and the Highland Problem</u>, pp.10-11; an excellent discussion of the nature and function of the clan is to be found in R. E. Ommer, 'Primitive accumulation and the Scottish <u>clann</u> in the Old World and the New', <u>Journal of Historical Geography 12(2)</u>, (1986), pp.121-141.

75. Stevenson, <u>ibid</u>, p.12.

76. On the tacksman, see, for example, A. McKerral, 'The tacksman and his holding in the south-west Highlands', <u>Scottish Historical Review</u>, <u>26</u>, (1947), pp.10-25; I. MacKay, 'Clanranald's tacksmen of the late 18th century', <u>Transactions of the Gaelic Society of Inverness</u>, 44, (1964), pp.61-93; E.R. Cregeen, 'The tacksmen and their successors: a study of tenurial reorganisation in Mull, Morvern, and Tiree in the early 18th century', <u>Scottish Studies</u>, <u>13(2)</u>, (1969), pp.93-144.

77. J.L Buchanan, <u>Travels in the Western Hebrides</u> (London, 1793), p.63.

78. R.A. Dodgshon, <u>Land and Society in Early Scotland</u> (Oxford, 1981), p.107; Stevenson, <u>MacColla and the Highland Problem</u>, pp.10-15: on the question of marriage patterns maintaining clan integrity and control over a given (and 'traditional') area, see I. Carter, 'Marriage patterns and social sectors in Scotland before the eighteenth century', <u>Scottish Studies</u>, <u>17</u>, (1973), pp.51-60; A.G. Macpherson, 'An old Highland parish register: survivals of clanship and

social change in Laggan, Inverness-shire, 1755-1854'
Scottish Studies, 11, (1967), pp.149-192 and 12, (1968),
pp.81-111; idem 'Migration fields in a traditional Highland
community, 1350-1850', Journal of Historical Geography,
10(1), (1984), pp.1-14.

79. Dodgshon, Land and Society, p.110.

80. E. Dwelly, The Illustrated Gaelic-English Dictionary
(Glasgow, 1973 edition), p.375.

81. Dodgshon, Land and Society, pp.110, 113.

82. A point made by Dodgshon (p.110), and discussed at
greater length, albeit with particular references to the
Lowlands, in M.H.B. Sanderson, Scottish Rural Society in
the 16th Century (Edinburgh, 1982), pp.58-63, 180,188; see
also Whyte, Agriculture and Society, pp.30-31.

83. EUL, Laing MSS, La. III.319, ff.15-16, 19, 22, 25, 29.

84. J. D. Mackie, A History of Scotland (Harmondsworth,
1973), p.271.

85. 'Memorial anent the thieving and Depradations in the
Highlands of Scotland, and the Countries Bordering thereon'
(1747) printed in J. Allardyce (ed.), Historical Papers
relating to the Jacobite Period 1699-1750 (Aberdeen, 1896),
II, pp.500-503; see also NLS, MS 220, ff.65-66; MS 5201,
ff.40, 51.

86. NLS, MS Ch. 2594, 15 December 1725.

87. SRO, CH1/5/51, f.347.

88. Anon., A Second Letter to a Noble Lord, containing A
Plan for effectually uniting and sincerely attaching the
Highlanders to the British Constitution, and Revolution
Settlement (London, 1748), p.14.

89. EUL, MS DC.6.70/2, p.1.

90. NLS, Adv MS 32.4.6., ff.7-8, f.50.

91. NLS, Adv MS 81.1.5.

92. Reprinted as Appendix 4, pp.171-192 of R.B
Cunningham-Graham, Doughty Deeds: an account of the life of
Robert Graham of Gartmore, 1735-1797 (London, 1925).

93. NLS, MS 5201 (Quote from f.6).

94. NLS, Adv MS 81.1.5., f.5.

95. NLS, Adv MS 32.4.6., f.12 (Districts inhabited by cow stealers).

96. NLS, MS 5201, ff.16-17.

97. Acts of Parliament, (19 Geo. II. c.39).

98. B. Lenman, Integration, Enlightenment and Industrialization (London, 1981), p.18.

99. A. Smith, Jacobite Estates of the Forty-Five (Edinburgh, 1982), pp.2-3; Murdoch, 'The People Above', p.35.

100. SRO, E 729. (1).2, p.5.

101. The word 'philabeg' or 'fillebeg' as synonym for kilt from the eighteenth century, is derived from Gaelic feileadh-beag (little kilt), feileadh being originally the whole plaid which, when belted, was an important development toward the modern kilt: Concise Scots Dictionary (Aberdeen, 1985), p.196.

102. J. Telfer-Dunbar, History of Highland Dress (London, 1962), pp.6-8; NLS, MS 5129, f.42 (Disposition of Troops in the Highlands, April, 1749).

103. Trevor-Roper, 'The Highland tradition', p.31.

104. Acts of Parliament, (25 Geo. II. c.41).

105. A. Millar (ed.), A Selection of Scottish Forfeited Estates papers (Edinburgh, 1909), pp.337-339.

106. Smith, Jacobite Estates, pp.21, 25.

107. SRO, E729.(1), p.28.

108. Smith, Jacobite Estates, pp.33, 36.

109. C.W.J. Withers, Gaelic in Scotland 1698-1981: the geographical history of a language (Edinburgh, 1984), pp.42-76.

110. Smith, Jacobite Estates, p.12.

111. SRO, W 701/1, ff.3 4.

112. Smith, Jacobite Estates., pp.38-53; Murdoch, 'The People Above', pp. 73-74.

113. Smith, p.53; Murdoch, pp.78-79, 82.

114. EUL, Laing MSS, La. III. 379, ff.204-207 ('State of the northern parts of Scotland and the means pursued for their improvement', and other letters, 1787-1800).

115. PSA, VII, (1797), p.383.

116. EUL, Laing MSS, La. II. 412, f.3.

117. E. Richards, A History of the Highland Clearances Volume 2: emigration, protest, reasons (Beckenham and Sydney, 1985), pp.14-19; Merrington, 'Town and Country', passim.

118. A.J. Youngson, After the '45 (Edinburgh, 1973), p.37.

119. Smith Jacobite Estates, pp.30-31; NLS, MS 5127, f.108; on plans to settle sailors in the Highlands, see also NLS, MS 5006.

120. Ibid., 126-129; V. Wills (ed.), Reports on the Annexed Estates 1755-1769 (Edinburgh, 1973), pp.4-7, 21-25.

121. E. Burt, Letters from a Gentleman in the North of Scotland to his friend in London (London, 1754), II, p.130.

122. Anderson, Prize Essay on the State of Society, p.127.

123. SRO, CH1/5/51, f.350.

124. NLS, Adv MS 32.4.6., f.18.

125. NLS, MS 2200, f.40.

126. Acts of Parliament of Scotland, (1597), c.34, IV., p.139.

127. Donaldson, Scotland James V - James VII, p.228; D. Macdonald, Lewis A History of the Island (Edinburgh, 1978), pp. 27-28.

128. R.A. Gailey, 'Settlement changes in the Southwest Highlands of Scotland, 1700-1960', unpublished PhD thesis,

University of Glasgow, 1961, p.9.

129. NLS, MS 975; A. McKerral, Kintye in the Seventeenth Century (Edinburgh, 1948), pp.84, 161; D.C. MacTavish, Commons of Argyll (Lochgilphead, 1935); E.R. Cregeen (ed.), Argyll Estate Instructions, 1771-1805 (Edinburgh, 1964).

130. McKerral, Kintyre, pp.84., 161.

131. NCL, Kirkwood MSS, An Answer to the Objection against Printing the Bible in Irish, f.2.

132. T.M. Murchison, 'The Presbytery of Gairloch, 1724-1750', Transactions, Gaelic Society of Inverness, XLIV, (1937-1941), pp.103-104; SRO, CH1/2/113., f.20.

133. J. Lettice, Letters on a Tour through various Parts of Scotland in 1792 (London, 1794), pp.339-340.

134. Burt, Letters from a Gentleman, I. pp.40-41.

135. M. Gray, The Highland Economy 1750-1850 (Edinburgh, 1957), p.9.

136. Whyte, Agriculture and Society, pp. 183-185.

137. Gray, Highland Economy, p.115; F. Shaw, The Northern and Western Islands of Scotland: their economy and society in the seventeenth century (Edinburgh, 1980), p.164; M. McKay (ed.), The Rev. Dr. John Walker's Report on the Hebrides of 1764 and 1771 (Edinburgh, 1980), notes (on p.232, note 7), that trade by sea to Glasgow from Lewis is said to have started about 1710.

138. I have drawn upon the following: J.M. Houston, 'Village planning in Scotland, 1745-1845', Advancement of Science, 5, (1948), pp. 129-132; T.C. Smout, 'The landowner and the planned village in Scotland, 1730-1830' in N.P. Phillipson and R. Mitchison (eds.), Scotland in the Age of Improvement (Edinburgh, 1970), pp.73-106; D. G. Lockhart, 'The Planned Villages' in M.L. Parry and T.R. Slater, The Making of the Scottish Countryside (London, 1980), pp.249-270; idem, 'Planned village development in Scotland and Ireland, 1700-1850' in T.M. Devine and D. Dickson (eds.), Ireland and Scotland 1600-1850: parallels and contrasts in economic and social development (Edinburgh, 1983), pp. 132-145; D. Turnock, The Historical Geography of Scotland since 1707 (Cambridge, 1982), pp.40, 43-44, 48, 82-96; idem, 'The Highlands: changing approaches to

regional development' in G. Whittington and I. Whyte (eds.), <u>An Historical Geography of Scotland</u> (London, 1983), pp.191-216; D.R. Mills, <u>Lords and Peasants in Nineteenth Century Britain</u> (London, 1980), pp. 149-152; M. Storrie, 'Land-holdings and settlement evolution in west Highland Scotland', <u>Geografiska Annaler</u>, <u>47B</u>, (1965), pp.138-160; for a note of communication on the benefits of villages as perceived by contemporaries, see also EUL, Laing MSS, La. II. 105, 2 (Norman MacLeod of MacLeod to John, Fifth Duke of Argyll, 10 October 1790).

139. Lockhart, 'Planned village development', p.133.

140. Smout, 'The landowner and the planned village', pp.83-85.

141. Lockhart, 'Planned village development', p.133; Figure 2:4 is based on the appendix to Smout's 1970 paper and the additions given on Figure 11.1 of Lockhart's 1980 paper above. No map of the ninety-one planned villages in the Highlands put forward by Lockhart (1983) is given in that paper nor exact criteria as to the extent of the Highlands. This accounts for the difference in number of villages on Figure 2:4 here and the estimates of Lockhart.

142. Gray, <u>Highland Economy</u>, pp.61, 72-73, 102-103, 199-200.

143. EUL, Laing MSS, La. II.623, f.32.

144. Lockhart, 'Planned villages', p.251; Black, 'The Gaelic Academy', pp.2-3.

145. J. Dunlop, <u>The British Fisheries Society 1786-1893</u> (Edinburgh, 1978), pp.18-32.

146. Wills, <u>Reports on the Annexed Estates</u>, pp.40-41.

147. Dunlop, <u>The British Fisheries Society</u>, p.51.

148. SRO, NG 1/24/11 (Encouragement of Linen Manufacture in the Highlands, December 1754-April 1763; Precept Book); Turnock, 'The Highlands: changing approaches', pp.196-7.

149. Lockhart, 'Planned villages', p.255; Turnock, <u>The Historical Geography of Scotland</u>, pp.40, 41, 43.

150. SRO, E 729/1, pp.22.

151. SRO, E 729/1, pp. 72-73.

152. Smout, 'The landowner and the planned village', p.80.

153. As Lockhart, Smout and Turnock all note, the form of the villages reflected the aesthetics of the time and often involved major architects: John Baxter, mason to William Adam, laid out Fochabers; William Adam, best known for his work in Edinburgh, together with John, his son, Roger Moriss and Robert Mylne all had a hand in Inveraray; Thomas Telford designed Ullapool and Pulteneytown: Smout, 'The landowner and the planned village', p.86: on the varieties of 'order' imposed upon the Scottish landscape by the architectural forms of the Scottish Enlightenment, see T.A. Markus (ed.), Order in Space and Society: architectural form and its context in the Scottish Enlightenment (Edinburgh, 1982); on the idea of prospect as the social appropriation of space, see D.E. Cosgrove, 'Prospect, perspective, and the evolution of the landscape idea', Transactions, Institute of British Geographers, 10(1), (1985), pp. 45-62.

154. Richards, Highland Clearances: Volume 2, p.18.

155. V. Wills, 'The gentleman farmer and the annexed estates: agrarian change in the Highlands in the second half of the eighteenth century' in T. Devine (ed.), Lairds and Improvement in the Scotland of the Enlightenment (Strathclyde, 1978), p.44.

3

ANGLICISATION AND THE IDEOLOGY OF TRANSFORMATION
1609 - 1872

> In order to improve and civilise the Highlands...
> a particular attention to introduce the English
> language is of the greatest consequence.1

During his tour of Scotland, Daniel Defoe observed of the
Highlands how 'The Face of Reformation and Virtue begins to
appear every-where; and there is reason to apprehend, that
in a few Years, Ignorance, Popery and the Irish language,
will be utterly extirpated; and in their stead, Virtue,
Loyalty, and Industry, will take place.'2   For Defoe, and
for many commentators then and later, the replacement of
Gaelic by English in the Highlands was symbolic as both
means and end of those more general notions of civilisation
and improvement - 'Virtue, Loyalty, and Industry' -
affecting Scotland as a whole since the 1600s.

ANGLICISATION AND AUTHORITY

The continued use of Gaelic acted, in the eyes of the Crown
and Lowland civil authority, as a barrier to effective
control over society in the Highlands. Anglicisation had
to be a crucial first phase in the transformation of
Highland Scotland: only after English had replaced Gaelic
would the Highlands be civilised, loyal, and industrious.

> The Highlands and Isle are remov'd from all Manner
> of Means of Instruction, except what the few
> Ministers they have plac'd amongst them can give
> such as live near them, and what they can pick up
> about their Masters when they see them. Our poor
> people are from the Cradles train'd up in
> Barbarity and Ignorance. Their very Language is
> an everlasting Bar against all Instruction, but
> the barbarous Customs and Fashions they have from
> their Forefathers, of which they are most

> tenacious, and having no other language, they are
> confined to their own miserable Homes... All
> Manner of Pains should be taken that all the
> inhabitants of this famous Isle should have but
> one language, and one Heart, one Religion.3

The General Assembly of the Church of Scotland, much
involved in 'all manner of pains' to this end, considered
that

> The propagation of the English language appears to
> be a most effectual method of diffusing through
> these countries the advantages of religion and
> civil society. The erecting of new parishes, and
> the planting of schools, would be greatly condu-
> cive to this end. Other means would also have a
> powerful effect. We observed with pleasure, that
> the English language is making a very quick
> progress in the neighbourhood of those small
> colonies which have come from the low country, for
> the promoting of manufactures. This agreeable
> observation suggests the happy effects that may be
> expected from the influence which the crown hath
> acquired in those countries. Schools for the
> English language, and examples of industry, may be
> planted with the same pains, without the loss of
> time, and at no expence.4

The development of 'that industriousness' as a characteristic of 'improvement' to which this second quote alludes is
considered in the following chapters. What follows here
examines the role of 'schools for the English language' and
the evolution of policies of educational hegemony and
religious supervision designed to implement the ideology of
anglicisation.

Leglislative action aimed at the replacement of Gaelic
through education has its beginnings in the move to unity
between Kirk and State in Scotland from the late 1500s,
and in the earlier separation between Highlands and
Lowlands in Scottish geography and consciousness. To these
may be added the reaction to the political dissent of parts
of the Highlands towards the Crown during the 1500s, the
need to combat the 'irreligion of the Hielandis' following
the widening gap between the Gaels of Ireland and Scotland
from the early seventeenth century, and the general
embracing of outside, chiefly English, influences following
the Union of Crowns in 1603.5 Given also Gaelic's loss of
prestige, evident in the shift in nomenclature during the
medieval period from 'Scots' to 'Irish' or 'Erse' and the

connotations of the latter usage, the result by the early 1600s was that an association between 'Godliness, obedience and civilitie' and 'vertew, lernying and the Inglische toung' was firmly established within the structures and minds of authority.

To be effective, the incorporation of Highlands and Lowlands within one nation-state had to be based upon the same political and religious authority and mediated and legitimated through the same language. Given the great majority of Highlanders did not understand English, Gaelic had to be used initially at least if the Highlands were not to remain, in the eyes of authority, beyond 'obedience and civilitie'. Yet at the same time as schemes designed to ensure loyalty through the use of Gaelic in religious worship were being initiated, plans were laid to ensure that Gaelic be removed through the agency of schools. That the principal means to the intended aim of anglicisation seem mutually contradictory points to the need for their careful examination. Several questions are important here. Of particular concern is assessment of the evolution of hegemonic policies and of the role of institutions involved in education and religion in the Highlands and how each formulated and operated particular strategies within an overall ideology of anglicisation. Further, given a range of institutions were active in the period 1609 - 1872, we must consider the links between such bodies. Of interest too are the relationships and contradictions between the policy-makers, and those schoolmasters and clergymen, working in the Highlands within particular ideological and institutional contexts, who had to implement them. And lastly, we need to explore variations over time and space in the actual results of these intended means of hegemonic control.

The evolution of educational policy 1609 - 1709

The first body to turn its attention to the role of schools as a means of anglicisation was the Privy Council. They conducted their Highland affairs largely through a sub-committee, the Lords Commissioners for the Affairs of the Isles: (it appears, at times, that this committee operated under other titles such as the Commissioners of Peace in the Highlands, and the Commission of the Privy Council to control the Highlands and Isles.)6 Established in February 1609, the principal brief of the Lords Commissioners was 'to plante religion and civilitie' within the Highlands. This they did in three related ways: first, 'in the cair we haif of the planting of the gospell among these rude, barbarous, and uncivill people'; second, by undermining the control exerted by clan chiefs through their holding of land — 'we noway hold it fitt that ony of these grite chiftanes sould be continewed in their possessions in that quantitie as thay haif formalie acclaymed thame'; and third, through schools. It was the Lords Commissioners who in August 1609 drew up the Statutes of Icolmkill (Iona), the sixth statute of which considered 'that the ignorance and incivilitie of the saidis Iles hes daylie incressit be the negligence of guid educatioun and instructioun of the youth in the knowledge of God and good letters'.7 Highland landowners with a wealth of sixty or more cattle were directed to place their eldest son or if no male children their eldest daughter, in schools in the Lowlands; 'and bring thame up thair quhill thay may be found able sufficientlie to speik, reid, and wryte Inglis- che'. In a statement of 10 December 1616, the Privy Council made clear the role of schools in establishing religious 'obedience' and civil authority in the Highlands.

> Forasmeikle as the Kingis Majestie haveing a speciall care and regaird that the trew religioun be advanceit and establisheit in all the pairtis of this Kingdome, and that all his Majesties subjectis, especiallie the youth, be exercised and trayned up in civilitie, godlines, knawledge, and learning, that the vulgar Inglische toung be universallie plantit, and the Irische language, whilk is one of the cheif and principall causes of the continewance of barbaritie and incivilitie amongis the inhabitantis of the Ilis and Hey- landis, may be abolisheit and removeit; and quhair as theyr is no measure more powerfull to further his Majesties princelie regaird and purpois that the establisheing of Schooles in the particular parroches of this Kingdom whair the youthe may be taught at least to write and reid, and be catechised and instructed in the groundis of religioun.8

This pronouncement is significant for several reasons. Firstly, although the immediate effect was minimal,9 the intention was explicit; the ideology of anglicisation as the basis to cultural transformation was held by all, or at least was without articulated opposition at that time. Secondly, these enactments were the first in a series throughout the 1600s whose concern was to establish schools as formal agencies of cultural change. Thirdly and importantly, legislation to foster education was paralleled by schemes for the recruitment of Gaelic clergy to administer in Gaelic as a basis to political and religious loyalty.

Records of the Privy Council and personnel lists of the Lords Commissioners point to the involvement of members of the upper ranks within Highland society in framing these acts: for example, Archibald, Earl of Argyll; Sir Duncan Campbell of Glenorchy; the Earl of Caithness; and the Sheriff Depute of Inverness.10 The fact that Lowland authority accommodated members of a society they otherwise regarded as uncivil and irreligious - indeed, that they 'actively sought their co-operation as de facto agents of local government' 11 - points to a subtlety in the exertion of outside influence that is not immediately evident in the acts themselves.

The 1616 Act provided for a school to be established in every parish in Scotland. The foundation of schools in every parish was not, however, binding under the 1616 Act: schools were established only 'where convenient meanes may be had'.12 Only following a 1646 Act which made the erection of schools and their financial support compulsory was there an obligation to found a school in every parish. Given this evidence, we may concur with Macinnes that, in their role as heritors, chiefs and principal clansmen would not have been without influence in any decision to erect English schools in Highland parishes and note also his claim that 'The planting of English schools as a first step towards the wholesale extirpation of the Gaelic language was not a policy which commanded either their immediate commitment or the highest financial priority in the early seventeenth century': for Macinnes; 'As a result, the Gaelic language was not directly threatened when the foundations of formal education were laid in the Highlands and Islands'.13 To an extent this is true, but this is only to note a shortfall between ideological intent and practical result in the Acts passed up to 1646; we should not ignore the tenor of legislation. In 1695, the military were empowered to assist bishops in their collection of financial support under the terms of an Act directed toward 'rooting out the Irish language and other pious uses'. This Act underlay the 1696 Act for Settling of Schools, which, in reinforcing the obligation upon parish heritors to establish a school in every parish, stood as the real foundation stone to parochial education throughout Scotland until 1872.14

Although schools were established in the Highlands in the seventeenth century, it is difficult to know exactly their number and location: as Withrington has recently

observed, it is probable that more schools were in existence in the Highlands then than has earlier been supposed,
but not all are locatable and not all operated over periods
of time.15 (Figure 3:1). In addition to noting regional
differences in the establishment of institutions and in
effectiveness of policy, attempts at a more complete
understanding of the evolution and impact of these educational enactments must recognise, too, that for much of the
seventeenth century education was primarily the concern of
the Kirk rather than the State which meant that policies of
education and religious supervision were closely linked.

During the late 1640s, the Church of Scotland began a
series of Acts concerned with the lack of Gaelic-speaking
clergy. Gaelic-speaking boys were trained 'in divinity and
letters' to be used to establish loyalty, through Gaelic
and God, by 'preaching the gospel in those Highland
parts'.16 These schemes for 'bursars' or 'probationers' as
they were called were not intended to benefit the Highland
populations but rather designed to recruit a body of men,
educated in the Lowlands, whose concern was the spiritual
use of Gaelic as an initial stage in the secular advancement of English. Although these schemes were not strictly
geared towards educational ends in the way the Acts of
1616, 1646 and 1696 were, it is important to consider them
here because of the links between education and religion in
the move to 'civilitie', and because an assessment of these
plans illustrates the complex nature of the evolution and
assertion of policies of cultural hegemony.

By 1648, forty 'Hieland boyes of good spirits' were
presented from Argyll.17 From 1648, Highland congregations
were directed to pay forty shillings annually towards
schemes for bursars, but this system was inadequate as
early as 1649. The 1649 Act for a Collection for Entertain-
ing Highland Boyes at Schooles provided for a further
collection but was never everywhere complied with. Some
Synods - Moray, Ross and Caithness - were exempt. The
burden for financial support fell on the Synod of Argyll,
and it was largely in that area that these schemes were
successful. Not until the 1690s did the General Assembly
turn its attention to 'the North': the Synods of Angus and
Mearns, Aberdeen, Caithness, Moray, Ross, Sutherland, and
parts of Perthshire and Inverness-shire. Problems arising
from the shortage of clergy for Gaelic parishes were
intensified by the displacement of ministers before and
after the 'Glorious Revolution' of the 1690s. The General
Assembly was forced in 1694 to despatch Lowland ministers
to serve in the Highlands. This was never effective. In
1695 'a more expedite and certain way of planting the
North' was proposed using Gaelic-speaking clergy from

Figure 3.1   The location of schools in the seventeenth-
              century   Highlands

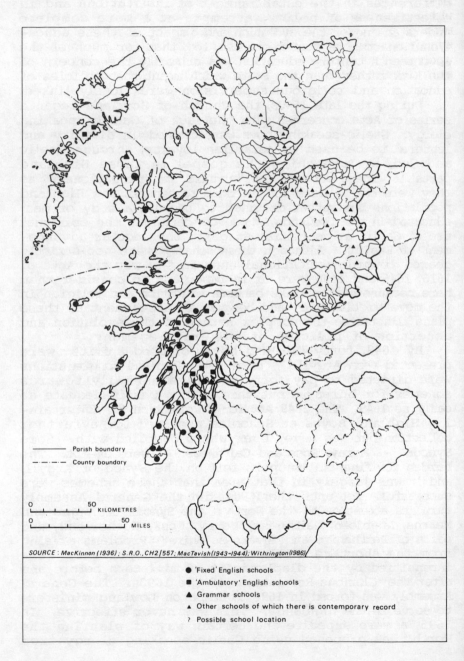

SOURCE : MacKinnon (1936) ; S.R.O., CH2/557; MacTavish (1943-1944); Withrington (1986)

- ● 'Fixed' English schools
- ■ 'Ambulatory' English schools
- ▲ Grammar schools
- ▲ Other schools of which there is contemporary record
- ? Possible school location

Argyll. This Act and later <u>Overtures</u> of 1698 underlay the 1699 Act anent Planting of the Highlands. The clauses of this important Act not only reveal the attitude of the General Assembly towards the educational and religious improvement of the Highlands, but hint also at the way in which assertion of anglicisation depended upon the involvement of a network of formal institutions - universities, synods, presbyteries, schools, kirk sessions - as well as upon the activities of a recruited mediating 'layer' of schoolmasters and clergy.

1. That Ministers and Probationers, who have the Irish Language, be sent to the Highland parishes, and that none of them settled in the Low-Country, till the Highland places be first provided.

2. That Ministers and Ruling Elders, who have the Irish language, be appointed to visit these parts.

3. That where in any Highland Congregation many understand English, and there used once a day to be a sermon in English, Presbyteries be careful to supply them sometimes by preaching in English; and that they catechize them who understand not, by an interpreter, when they cannot get one to preach to them in Irish; and that those, whether ministers or probationers, who have somewhat of the Irish language, but not a facility to preach in it, be sent to these places for the ends forsaid, that by converse they may learn more of the language, and ability to instruct therein.

4. That English schoolmasters be erected in all Highland parishes, according to former Acts of Parliament and General assemblies; and for this end the General Assembly recommends to their commission to address the King and Parliament, to take such course for this, and other pious uses, in the more northern Highland places, as is granted to these of Argyle and that as they shall think fit.

5. That it be recommended to Presbyteries and Universities to have a special regard in the disposal of their bursaries for educating such as it is hoped may be useful to preach the Gospel in the Highlands.18

Assessment of the effectiveness of this twin fold policy - on the one hand, treating Gaelic as a missionary medium through which to extend control over civil society, on the other establishing schools to incorporate English into the Highland way of life - follows in more detail below. But in considering here the evolution of educational policy and noting its seeming contradictions, it is interesting to observe that these Acts - for bursars, schools, financial support and so on - were more effective in Argyll, certainly in the early seventeenth century, than in 'the North'. And in a wider context, it was in the south-west Highlands, in roughly the area embraced by the Synod of Argyll and the Isles, that the absorption of elite personnel into local government was most keenly felt as central authority pursued its policy of incorporating chiefs and principal clansmen into the structures of Lowland society. This development was epitomised in the rise of Clan Campbell, the house of Argyll, following expropriation of the lands of Clan Donald; in Kintyre in 1607, in Islay in 1614, and in Ardnamurchan in 1625.19 It was in Argyll that the move toward the commercial exploitation of Highland estates was most marked in the seventeenth century.20 This latter development reflected the need for cash to support the obligations of chiefs involved in Scottish, not just Highland affairs, and the necessity to recover revenue lost following the devastation of Argyll by Montrose and MacColla.21 Further, Argyll had well-developed trading connections with the west-central Lowlands by the 1600s, and the several colonies of Lowland settlers in Cowal and Kintyre by the 1670s also attests to the way in which Argyll-shire had a regionally leading part in the transformation of the Highlands.

The result of these factors was not so much an evident decay in the fabric of Highland society, in the south-west Highlands or elsewhere, as an emergent tension within the structures of clanship as chiefs were forced, through monetary need deriving from participation in wider commercial and administrative systems, to reinterpret customary relationships with their clansmen. Contradictions deriving from proprietary obligations and involvement with Lowland commerce and authority that was part voluntary, part (and increasingly) necessary were not confined to Argyll. But this tension between the traditional military and social values of clanship and the chiefs' acceptance of commercial values, and the 'cultural dichotomy within Scottish Gaeldom'22 that it prompted, was more marked in Argyll than elsewhere in this period and apparent within the Highlands long before 1745.

Anglicisation and the Ideology of Transformation

It is difficult to know whether such variation in political and ideological sympathies and involvement in outside influences directly affected the establishment of schools and the schemes for Gaelic clergy. It may be, however, that those Acts of the 1640s and 1660s designed to fund bursars were successful chiefly in Argyll because it was only from that area that such persons could then have been drawn. In this regard, we may speculate also that several of those schools erected during the 1600s (Figure 3.1) owed their establishment to the willingness of some heritors to pay for schooling and support an educational system that sought the advancement of values to which they increasingly aspired, as Highland chiefs or as officers of local and Lowland authority. Focusing attention on political Acts should not lead us away from considering the likelihood of conflicting loyalties, within the Highlands or elsewhere, nor from noting that the extension of 'education' in its broadest sense of 'civilitie' was, in the same moment, being paralleled by the gradual re-working of relationships intrinsic to the maintenance of Highland society and by the rise of institutions whose concern was the 'improvement' of that Highland way of life.

Neither the ideology that these institutions espoused nor the incorporative role of education that the above Acts codified was challenged until the late 1600s. It is reasonable to allow that the majority of Highlanders remained then unaffected by the incorporation of their chief into Lowland circles. Most people in the seventeenth-century Highlands remained distant from the work of God and King, and did not regularly send their children or themselves to school. This is not to say that the ordinary Gael was unaware of contemporary events in the Highlands or further afield, but rather to suggest that at that time because of the relative isolation of much of the Highlands, the comparative vitality of Highland society relative to later periods, and the hesitant start to processes of educational hegemony, we should not expect there to have been a conscious and defined opposition to the establishment of schools or the preaching of services in English. Yet much vernacular poetry of the period does reveal an awareness of changing social relationships with the Highlands: for Macinnes, these 'Appeals to the traditions of the Gael ... were essentially attempts to anchor cultural values at a time of rapid political upheaval and social dislocation'.23 Expressions of Highland regional consciousness in opposition to the assertion of a different hegemony may not then have been directed at schemes for 'civilitie' and schools in particular and certainly never took in the 1600s the articulations of violence and protest that characterised the later 1800s, but we should not assume the Highland populations to have been wholly unaware or uninvolved. Of course, opposition need not be rooted in and expressed through the traditions of those experiencing the change. In the case of Highland Scotland, what little formalised counteraction there was in the 1600s to the prevailing ideology of anglicisation and to the means by which civility was to be imposed came from within Lowland institutions.

James Kirkwood's <u>An Answer to the objection against Printing the Bible in Irish, as being prejudicial to the Design of Extirpating the Irish Language out of the Highlands of Scotland</u>, written in the late 1690s, was a rejoinder to the views of authority on education, and schemes then operating for the use of Gaelic texts in the religious supervision of the Highlands.24   Kirkwood's principal criticism was against the use of Gaelic library texts (principally the Irish Gaelic bible, in Latin type, and Gaelic catechisms), in the Highlands. The General Assembly, through their Act approving Overtures anent the Irish Bibles (1690), used these texts in religious adminis- tration but not in schools.25 Kirkwood argued that Gaelic literary texts should be used in Highland schools not only as the means to education throughout the Highlands but as the basis to social advancement generally. The school system and the intellectual formation of anglicisation and civility that evolved during the seventeenth century, typified in the 1696 Act (and in charity schools after 1709) did not afford a place for Gaelic and was, for Kirkwood, entirely unsuitable in its aims and methods.

> Everybody knows that to learne a Language there must be another sorte of Schools to witt, where they are taught to declyne and conjugat to get the particles of speech by heart, and to compose and joyne together words and sentences; for which end Books necessary for learning must be provided, for example, Gramers, Vocabularies, Dictiounaries &c: Besyds all which, care must be taken that they who learn the language converse only with those who speake the same, avoyding all other company for a considerable time. Now as nothing of all this is pretended to, in the Highland Schools, So it is nixt to Impossible, to procure such helpes as are before hinted at for learning English and for extirpating the Irish language out of these parts. If it has been so difficult to get one Schoolmaster to teach a dozen or twenty Children in a parish to read English, how shall

there be got as many Schoolmasters as may be
sufficient to teach all the children of each
parish to read English; and whence shall these
Scholmasters have sallaries? How shall such books
as are necessary for so many children be provyded,
and how shall all the poor boyes and Girls of each
parish be mentained at School untill they be
unabled to speake English and understand Sermons
in that Language? These few Hints (to add no
more) may seem sufficient to convince any persone
of Comon Sense, not utterly blinded with unreasonable prejudice, that it is not possible that the
Irish language should ever be extirpated by such
Schools as are in that part settled in the
Highlands, and that it is nixt to Impossible to
get the other sorte of Schools settled in such
manner as is necessary for teaching all the
Children in that Country (to say nothing of aged
persons) to speake the English language, and
thereby to supersede the necessity of teaching to
read ye Irish Bibles &c.26

Kirkwood's manuscripts, written by someone actively
involved in Highland education, provide evidence of
contradiction <u>within</u> the intended means of cultural
transformation and in so doing illustrate how the establishment of civil control through anglicisation was a flexible
and complex process, and illustrate, too, how policies of
'unreasonable prejudice' were to be realised through
authoritative texts, a recruited body of schoolmasters, and
institutions given their powers from a political authority
geared to removing Gaelic.

POLICIES AND MEANS OF ANGLICISATION 1709 - 1811

Several formal institutions are examined here for their
role in formulating and directing policies of education
and anglicisation during the 1700s; chiefly, the Society in
Scotland for Propagating Christian Knowledge (SSPCK); the
General Assembly (here of significance in schemes for the
recruitment of a Gaelic ministry); and lastly, the limited
educational work of the Commissioners of the Annexed
Estates, and of the Royal Bounty Committee.

The SSPCK as an Institution of cultural hegemony

The SSPCK, established in Edinburgh in 1709, was influenced in its formation by the earlier Society for Reformation of Manners, and by the English-based Society for Promoting Christian Knowledge. Kirkwood, a principal influence behind the SSPCK, had intended that its charity schools use Gaelic in the promotion of Christian values: 'As to ye teaching them the English language it seems somewhat forraign to our first and maine designs viz. ye propagating of ye Knowledge of God Amongst them which must either be done in the language they understand, or else it will be lost labour with respect to the farr greater part of that people, few of whom (in comparison) either young or old understand English'.27 But the possibility of incorporating Gaelic in schools or using Gaelic texts as a basis to literacy had been denied in 1609 and reiterated in 1696. Accordingly, no plans were made to incorporate Gaelic into the schools of the SSPCK. Nor should we expect there to have been. Their intention in 'propagating Christian knowledge' was to ignore Gaelic as an educational medium and to direct 'knowledge' - political loyalty and religious obedience as well as formal learning (reading, writing, arithmetic and music) - only through English. Such Gaelic texts as were available were proscribed from use in schools. No support was given to provide for further texts. English was the recognised and intended means of cultural domination:

> Nothing can be more effectual for reducing these countries to order, and making them usefull to the Commonwealth than teaching them their duty of God, their King and Countrey and rooting out their Irish language, and this has been the case of the Society so far as they could, ffor all the Schollars are taught in English.28

Whilst this statement illustrates the complexion of SSPCK policy, we should not always assume it was adhered to by schoolmasters themselves. By 1719 it was evident to some SSPCK schoolmasters that policies of teaching only in English produced a rote learning amongst Gaelic populations, who could read English and perhaps also speak it, but could do neither with comprehension.29 Resolutions passed in 1720 by the SSPCK sought the assistance of religious authority - ministers and presbyteries - in the Highlands to ensure only English was taught and used and that it was understood.

> Letters should be written to all the Societies
> Schoolmasters, and to the ministers of the
> parishes and presbyteries of the bounds, where the
> said Schools are Lettered, requiring that particu-
> lar care be taken of teaching the Children to
> understand as well as to read the English Lan-
> guage, and that the masters do converse with them,
> and cause them Converse amongst themselves, as
> much as possible in that Language.30

The SSPCK thereby sought to re-affirm its denial of a role
for Gaelic: 'The Societies design was not to discourage
any proper means of Instruction in the principles of
Christianity but to forward the same, and yet not to
continue the Irish Language but to wear it out, and Learn
the people the English tongue'. The 1721 Representation
anent teaching Irish, drawn up by several SSPCK schoolmasters and ministers in the Highlands, suggests that what
constituted 'proper means of instruction' for policy-makers
intent in their pursuit of civility and obedience was not
always accommodated by SSPCK schoolmasters in Highland
parishes. The Representation pointed out how, under
current policy, 'the children are taught to read only in
English which they understand not ... and thus they return
home able indeed to read the Bible but understand not even
the plainest historical part of what they read': further,
'after residing in the Countrey where they hear nothing but
Irish, in a Little time they entirely forget what with much
Labour and long time they acquired'. The schoolmasters
proposed scholars be allowed to translate the Bible and
other scriptural works into Gaelic after being able to read
English: 'which method as it is the only way to make them
capable to understand what they read, and when they return
home to instruct their Ignorant parents who understand not
English, so they take it to be the only way to extirpate
the Irish language'.31

> The Exerciseing of the boys at school to a ready
> Converting of English into Irish and reaching the
> Principles of Religion in both languages, as it
> will instruct themselves, so it will make them
> capable to instruct their Ignorant parents at
> home, who are themselves fond of knowledge and are
> sensible that their Ignorance of the English
> language is their great Loss, by being thereby
> excluded from all Commerce, Conversation and
> Correspondence with the rest of the nation, and by
> the having of it, quo mise to themselves access to
> employments Stations or offices that might afford

them advantage, and the parents having once
understood English, the Babes from the knees would
receive the same as their mother tongue, which
would be the only finishing stroak to the Irish
language.32

The General Committee of the SSPCK, initially reluctant to
embrace this refinement, responded in 1723 with <u>Overtures
for teaching the Societies Schollars to understand and
Speak the English Language</u>. These <u>Overtures</u> rested upon
four points: the schoolmaster was permitted to use Gaelic
translation but only once the pupils could read the
Catechism in English; Gaelic was otherwise banned from use
in schools – 'none who can speak any of it be allowed to
speak Irish except when turning it into English, for the
benefite of those who are Learning the same, and that
Censors be named to delete transgressors therein'; no poor
scholars were able to receive financial aid until they had
made progress in learning English; pupils able to read and
speak English were to be sent to Lowland schools. Additionally, schoolmasters were directed 'to speak to and converse
with their Schollars alwayes in English'. The <u>Overtures</u>
and minutes of the SSPCK were at pains to remind schoolmasters that Highland children 'be not allowed to discourse or
converse with another in the Irish but only in the English
Language'.33
    These <u>Overtures</u> represent an important shift in SSPCK
educational policy. The situation of rote learning without
comprehension was now the basis to an educational system
whereby English was the only language of conversation
permitted and where Gaelic was used only to translate
English. The fact that such translation was not necessarily based upon actual understanding of English but only upon
an ability to read it, meant, in combination with the
proscription of their native tongue, that Gaelic speakers
began to compare and translate the English they were taught
with Gaelic and thus to understand the English they heard
and read. Given that schoolmasters were enjoined to use
and allow English only in daily conversation in and around
the schools, it is likely that English was increasingly
spoken by SSPCK scholars and perhaps also by their 'Ignorant parents at home'. It was the schoolmasters who
prompted this policy shift. Far from disputing the
intended end of 'wearing out' Gaelic or denouncing the
English-only policy as an improper 'means of Instruction in
the principles of Christianity' given the strength of
Gaelic, the schoolmasters sought rather to refine the means
by which the policy operated. Not all Highland schoolmasters or assisting clergy would have thought thus, but it is

likely that the ideology of anglicisation as the basis to civil control was held as firmly by the practising agents as by those framing the enactments. In this sense, policies of anglicisation were not unthinkingly imposed but moulded over time by reflexive and mutually informing relationships between schoolmasters and parent institutions; in Williams' words, 'a lived system of meanings and values ... which as they are experienced as practices appear as reciprocally confirming'. In combination with this alteration, the SSPCK undertook in 1725 to provide a Gaelic-English vocabulary, partly 'for help to the more speedy teaching the Schollars the most usual and familiar English words', but principally 'as a means to Introduce the use of the English language more Universally'.34

> The Instruction of the Youth in The English Language, is thought necessary to promote the charitable Purpose of this Society, and to make these, who can speak only Gaelic, more useful Members in the Commonwealth; and it is certain, that if this were to be carried on, by teaching from Books intirely English, without any Mixture of the Mother-Tongue, it would not be so speedily got done.35

Rethinking the incorporative role of Gaelic texts was necessary in view of the practice of Gaelic-English translation. In 1754, the SSPCK proposed to print a New Testament, with one page in Gaelic and the facing one in English; [this] 'would lend much towards the advancement of Knowledge, and of the English Language in the Highlands'.36 The SSPCK aimed to use the New Testament, which appeared in 1767, as a direct means of extending spoken English through the use of Gaelic in translation. This was related to a further refinement of policy. From 1766, Highland schoolmasters were instructed 'to teach their Scholars to read both Earse and English ... as being ... the most effectual method to make them read, speak and understand the English language'.37 This shift in emphasis was largely motivated by an observation of the SSPCK's General Committee that '... the present practice the teaching of Children to read English only has been found not to have the desired effects; for when they leave the School, they can neither speak nor read English with understanding'.38 This claim should not be taken too literally. We must, of course, allow a difference between use of spoken English, ability to read it, and an actual comprehension of what English was learnt, read, and spoken, and note also that English was being introduced into the

Highlands in other ways than schooling. Even so, there is considerable evidence to suggest that English was understood as the direct result of SSPCK schools well before 1766. As early as 1713, SSPCK schoolmasters in Highland Aberdeenshire, in central Perthshire, and in parts of Inverness-shire reported how their pupils made progress in learning and understanding English.39 Later evidence supports their claims. What is more significant in regard to the amendment of 1766 and the modification of SSPCK policy toward Gaelic texts is the recognition by that body of the role of Gaelic not as an educational medium in itself, but as a necessary stage in 'the desired effects' of extending English. The effect was two-fold, as SSPCK directors noted in 1781: 'not only in opening the minds of the people to knowledge, but in giving a greater desire to learn the English language than they had ever before discovered'.40 Recognition by the SSPCK of the role of Gaelic as a means to the end of anglicisation prompted a further and final change in policy in 1825. The establishment of Gaelic Society schools in 1811 prompted the SSPCK to consider 'the teaching of the Gaelic has been very much neglected'. From 1825, Gaelic, not English, was read first in SSPCK schools, thus holding out an English education as a 'great object of emulation': 'the prejudice of the people against their children learning Gaelic may be more easily overcome, when they have the assurance that ... their children shall afterwards be taught English'.41

The location of SSPCK schools in the Highlands for the years 1755, 1774, 1792, and 1825 may be seen from Figures 3.2 to 3.5. Numbers attending school often varied seasonally, and the average school-going population, although it varied by parish and over time in relation to individual schools, was probably never more than three or four percent of the parish population in any year.42 There is evidence to suggest, however, both that parents were instructed at home by their children, and that the average SSPCK school population increased over time (Table 3.1). These facts are significant given that children attended SSPCK schools for several years in succession: 'None of the children, when they come to the parochial or charity schools, understand a word of English; yet in three years or in four at most, they learn both to read and speak it perfectly'.43

Financial restrictions may have limited SSPCK effectiveness. Although figures on the stock of the society show funds of £13,167 for 1731, £15,822 five years later and £31,171 by 1769, SSPCK stock largely constituted 'money lent on heritable and personal bonds, at 5 per cent interest' from which an annual revenue was derived. In a 1774 Account of the Society, lists of benefactors donating

126

Figure 3.2   SSPCK schools in the Highlands in 1755

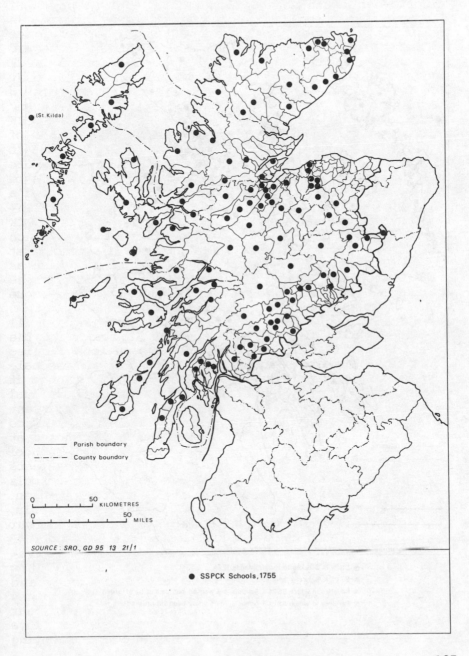

Parish boundary
County boundary

0   50 KILOMETRES
0   50 MILES

SOURCE : SRO., GD 95 13 21/1

● SSPCK Schools,1755

(St.Kilda)

Figure 3.3   SSPCK schools in the Highlands in 1774

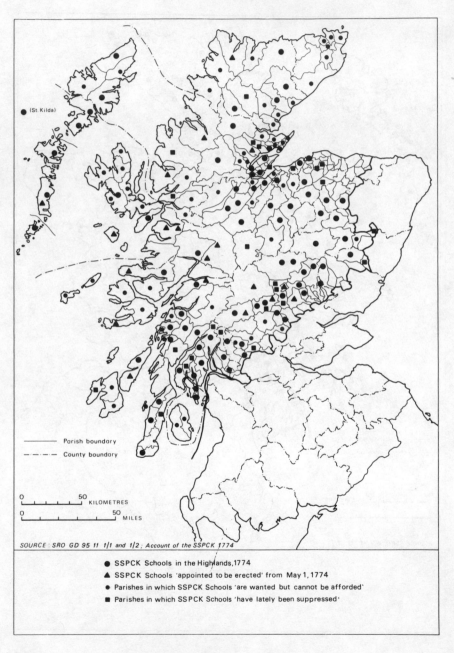

Parish boundary
County boundary

0 —————— 50 KILOMETRES
0 —————— 50 MILES

SOURCE : SRO GD 95 11 1/1 and 1/2 ; Account of the SSPCK 1774

● SSPCK Schools in the Highlands,1774
▲ SSPCK Schools 'appointed to be erected' from May 1, 1774
• Parishes in which SSPCK Schools 'are wanted but cannot be afforded'
■ Parishes in which SSPCK Schools 'have lately been suppressed'

Figure 3.4   SSPCK schools in the Highlands in 1792

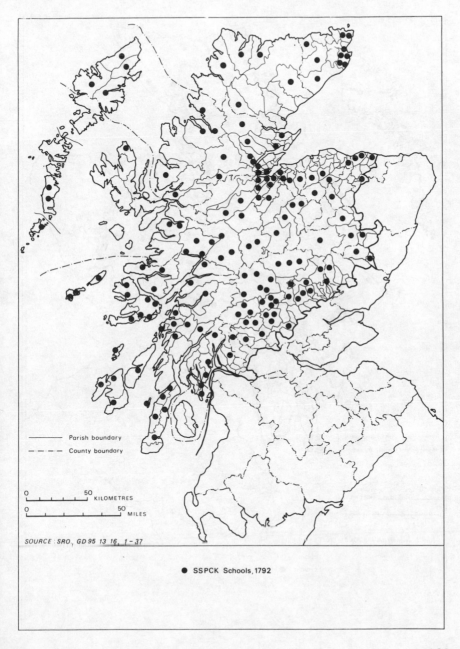

Parish boundary
County boundary

0   50
KILOMETRES
0   50
MILES

SOURCE : SRO., GD 95 13 16, 1 - 37

● SSPCK Schools, 1792

Figure 3.5   SSPCK schools in the Highlands in 1825

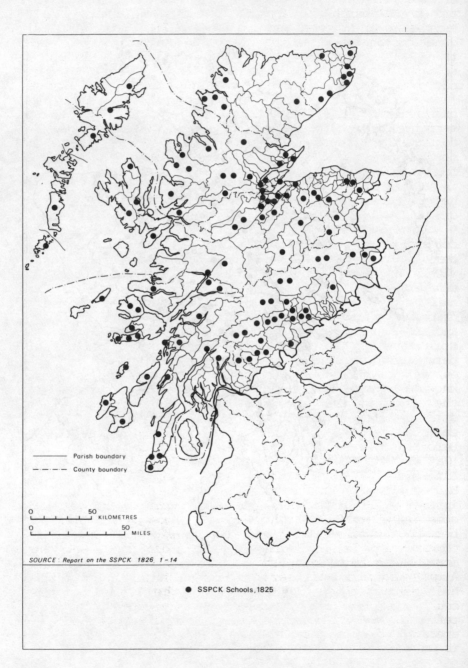

Parish boundary

County boundary

0   50 KILOMETRES

0   50 MILES

SOURCE : Report on the SSPCK 1826 1 – 14

● SSPCK Schools, 1825

more than £50 in a single sum include members of the
Highland gentry as well as the General Assembly of the
Church of Scotland, General Wade, the Lord High Chancellor
of Great Britain, professors and principals at the Universities of Edinburgh and Glasgow and many ministers, urban
merchants and landed gentry (Table 3.2). Many smaller
donations came from other persons of like social rank. In
the 1774 Account, notice is given of parishes 'in which
schools are much wanted, though the Society from the
narrowness of their funds, are unable to maintain them'
(see Figure 3.3), and of how the deficit, 'will, it is
presumed, be reduced by the vacancies of schools which may
happen during the currency of this year'.44 Although the
society may at times have been limited in the schools it
could operate, the SSPCK benefited as a charitable
foundation through donations from persons of status who saw
in the institution the opportunity to articulate a cultural
hegemony founded on those notions of anglicisation,
civility, and urbanity that it and they typified.

On occasions, salaries of SSPCK schoolmasters in
contiguous parishes were combined to provide for Latin
teaching in an attempt at education for the upper ranks
within Highland society. While this had 'an excellent
effect in the education of the gentlemens children ... the
children of the poorer sort are left destitute of the means
of instruction; their ignorance must therefore increase,
and the progress of the English language be stopped'.45
More usually, the SSPCK sited schools in regard to the
particular distribution of population in Highland parishes, and, in parishes where both Gaelic and English were
known and used, by liaising with local clergy to establish
the school in the more Gaelic parts of the parish. In
setting up a school in Port of Menteith in 1721, for
example, the SSPCK decided that the school 'be sent to the
Baronie of Drunkie being an Highland Countrey, whereas
[Gartmore] is Lowland and has no Irish spoke therein'.46
Although SSPCK schools were active in the north-west
Highlands and outlying islands, their main field of
influence lay in the eastern and central Highlands. In
some parishes, SSPCK schools were closed down in 1774
because the directing committees considered them 'low
country', that is, in English-speaking districts, and the
money was needed to operate schools in Gaelic parishes.
Argyll was not well served by SSPCK schools in the
half-century after 1709. Only from the 1770s was the
county more completely covered. It is possible that this
reflected the earlier establishment of parochial schools in
areas of the south-west Highlands (cf. Figure 3.1). There
is no evidence in SSPCK records either to support or deny

Table 3.1

Population attending SSPCK schools in the Highlands, 1719-1825*

Year	Number of schools	Estimated total population	Estimated average school population	Male & Female Scholars as % total school population	
				M	F
1710	5	-	-	-	-
1713	13	-	-	-	-
1715	25	-	-	-	-
1719	26	1,085	42	-	-
1727	78**	2,757	35	-	-
1731	77	3,326	43	74.4	25.6
1742	128**	-	-	-	-
1748	99	5,626	56	67.6	32.4
1755	116	5,034	43	-	-
1758	176**	6,409	36	-	-
1774	84	4,942	59	67.5	32.5
1781	180**	7,000	39	-	-
1792	149	10,526	70	71.8	28.2
1825	128	8,929	72	-	-

* SRO, GD95/1 et seq; GD95/11/6, pp.14-15.

** These totals, given in GD95/95/6, include schools in the Shetland and Orkneys and in Lowland Scotland. There is, unfortunately, no way of knowing the number of schools in the Highland parishes as here defined.

Table 3.2

Assessment by social rank and geographical background of
principal donors to SSPCK, 1709-1773*

Social rank	No. of individuals enumerated	Total sum of donations made by those individuals (to nearest whole £)
Nobility and titled gentry	10(1)	1,639
Professional	31(2)	5,207
Merchants	6	2,550
Military	6	465
[Not given]	[35](3)	10,086
[Institutional donations]	[3]	1,606

Total sum of principal donations = £21,553

Geographical background

Resident in Scotland = 41 individuals
Resident in England = 26 individuals
Resident in Ireland = 4 individuals
Residence not given = 18 individuals

(Continued overleaf.)

Table 3.2 (Continued)

* SRO, GD95/11/1/1 and 1/2; A. Murray and J. Cochrane, An Account of the Society in Scotland for Propagating Christian Knowledge, from its Commencement in 1709 (Edinburgh, 1774), pp.63-66.

1 The King; 3 Baronets; 1 Countess; 2 Dukes; 1 Earl; 1 Lord; 1 Marquis.

2 Bookseller 1; Colonial Governor 1; Lord Chief Baron to Ct. of Exchequer 1; Minister 16; Professor 1; Physician 4; Provost 1; Surgeon 1; Session Clerk 1; University Principal 2; Writer to the Signet 2.

3 General Assembly of Church of Scotland; Edinburgh's Charity Workhouse; unknown Edinburgh shop.

this claim, but given that that body was usually concerned to settle schools in parishes without existing formal education, it may be that the SSPCK turned their initial attention elsewhere, given the relative 'cultivated' status of the south-west Highlands. The author of the 1737 Highland Complaint certainly considered it 'absurd' that the area under the Synod of Argyll should be thought necessary of 'reformation' and 'improvement'.47

In most SSPCK schools, males outnumbered females - in places by eight to one - but more generally in a ratio of about three to one (Table 3.1). Education for females was considered wasteful.

> The great Difference between the Children of the two Sexes, is very remarkable; but the same is the Case all over the Highlands. Wherever there is access to a School, the Boys are carefully put to it; but the Parents consider Learning of any kind as of little Moment to the Girls, on which Account, great Numbers of them never go to any School.48

Evidence on variation in age among SSPCK school populations is less certain though it is likely children taught parents at home, but the general anglicising influence of SSPCK schools cannot be denied. SSPCK directors noted in 1795 how thousands of Highlanders ' have by means of their schools attained to such knowledge of the English language as qualified them for intercourse with the inhabitants of other parts of the British Empire and for deriving all the improvement which that language affords'.49 In Dunoon in 1792, Gaelic was still 'the natural tongue with them, their fireside language, and the language of their devotions', but this was 'changing much ... above all, from our schools, particularly, those established by the Society for Propagating Christian Knowlege'. In Kilfinichen and Kilvickeon parish on Mull and even on distant Barra where spoken Gaelic was less interspersed with English words, English was used and understood because of SSPCK schools.50 The same was the case in other parishes for which we have direct evidence - Alness, Kirkhill, and Rosskeen in the 1790s, The Black Isle in the 1750s, Callander in 1756, Morayshire in 1775, Luss in 1754 51 - and, by implication, for all SSPCK schools operating in the Highlands in the eighteenth and early nineteenth centuries (Figures 3.2 - 3.5). In several SSPCK schools in Gaelic districts, the schoolmaster was unable to speak that language, and even in cases where Gaelic was both known by the schoolmaster and in use in the district, it was seldom

taught. Perhaps the most significant effect of the SSPCK
was to alienate Gaelic from education in the Highland
consciousness. There is little evidence of any formal
opposition from Gaels to the SSPCK, the establishment of
schools or the role of schoolmasters as there was against
the lack of Gaelic clergy or the imposition in a Highland
parish of a non-Gaelic speaking catechist or minister (see
below). The 1774 <u>Account of the Society</u> considered that
earlier attempts at education from 1609 had not been wholly
effective since 'The inhabitants of those countries were
too fond of their own language, to give encouragement to a
scheme, the avowed intention of which was to supplant it'.
Yet by the later eighteenth century if not earlier,
policies of anglicisation and cultural change through
education were effective in actual terms in extending the
use and knowledge of English, and in a related ideological
sense, in devaluing Gaelic in the Highland mind. SSPCK
directors wrote how

> The establishment of charity-schools hath wrought
> a happy change in many places: ignorance hath
> been in a great measure dispelled; the English
> language hath made considerable progress; the arts
> of civilization have been in some degree intro-
> duced; and thousands have been educated in the
> principles of loyalty and the Protestant reli-
> gion.52

On the ideological level, Patrick Butter, touring SSPCK
schools in 1825, noted how 'There seems to be in the minds
of the people ... a very general prejudice against using
the Gaelic as a school language'.53 Highlanders were
separated from literacy in their own language
simultaneously with Gaelic's divorce from contemporary
notions of civility and cultivation.

Attainment of English and the separation of Gaelic from
ideas of status and a means to social progress were not the
result of SSPCK schools alone, however influential that
body as a single institution.

**Highland libraries, the General Assembly and the Royal
Bounty Committee**

In 1699, schemes to establish libraries throughout the
Highlands had been proposed as a means of diffusing 'useful
knowledge' and combating 'the gross ignorance of the people
in these parts'.54 The General Assembly passed Acts on
Highland Libraries in 1704 and 1705. A General Assembly

Committee for the Highland Libraries was appointed to oversee the establishment and operation of the libraries. Although the exact number of these Highland libraries is uncertain, it is likely they were positioned within Gaelic-speaking parishes and near to centres of population in those parishes.55 Perhaps more important is the stock of books they carried, the constitution of their organising committee, and the fact that, from 1706, the General Assembly, under the terms of an Act of that year, directed its Libraries Committee to report on 'the prevalence of Popery', on the extent of 'Paganish customs', and upon those parts of the Highlands in need of schools or Gaelic-speaking clergy or bursars. Their chief function as symbolic outposts of authority in the wilderness of Highland ignorance was as storehouses of Presbyterian literature to be used by ministers, schoolmasters - 'responsible persons' - to civilise the Highlands. The make-up of the organising committee suggests close links with the SSPCK, with the Society for Reformation of Manners, and with those General Assembly committees engaged in providing clergy for the Highlands. Until his death in 1709, Kirkwood was involved with all three bodies. Other influential figures in the operation of these institutions and in the formation of policy toward the Highlands at this time were George Meldrum, Robert Baillie, William Wisheart, Nicol Spence and Neil McVicar. George Meldrum was Professor of Divinity at Edinburgh, minister at Edinburgh's Tron Kirk, 1692 - 1698, Moderator of the General Assembly in 1698 and 1703, a member of the Highland Libraries Commit- tee, of the SSPCK, and of the Society for Reformation of Manners. William Carstares, Principal of New College, Edinburgh, and William Wisheart, an Edinburgh minister, served as committee members of the SSPCK from 1709 as did Neil McVicar and Nicol Spence in Edinburgh. Robert Baillie of Inverness, and Carstares, Wisheart, and Spence were all members of the Highland Libraries Committee. Neil McVicar was minister to the Gaelic community in Edinburgh's West Kirk from 1709 to 1747. Robert Baillie was a minister in Inverness who, despite having little or no Gaelic, was stationed there because the General Assembly needed a loyal presbyterian to serve 'the most considerable Post benorth Aberdeen of greatest influence in the Highlands'.56 Nicol Spence was a member of the Society for Reformation of Manners, Clerk to the Libraries Committee, a member of the SSPCK committee in 1709 and for some years after, and much involved in schemes for Gaelic clergy. Both Spence and Sir Francis Grant of Cullen, a founding and committee member of the SSPCK in 1709, were committee members of the Royal Bounty Committee, established in 1725 'for Reformation of the Highlands and Islands of Scotland'. Spence and McVicar appear on a list of members of that body for 1736.57 This evidence again suggests that the ideology of anglicisation and the way in which it was effected was not through separate institutions, but was rather moulded and articulated within and across institutions whose means of realising intended ends were formulated, in the early decades of the 1700s at least, by a core of intellectuals and mutually-supporting ideologues. Processes of hegemonic practice varied, but they derived potentiality from a sharing of personnel and a uniform purpose in mind: relationships repeated in later periods, and for other institutions and individuals within the same ideology.

Further Acts of the General Assembly directed at the provision of a clergy were passed between 1700 - 1717, and in 1726,1737, 1756, and 1786. The General Assembly intended these Acts to counter religious dissent - 'irreligion', Episcopalianism, and 'trafficking Catholic priests' - at the same time as ensuring loyalty through Gaelic. Emphasis was placed upon the provision of loyal Gaelic clergy: what the 1699 Act had termed 'special regaird in the disposal of their bursaries for educating such as it is hoped may be useful to preach the Gospel in the Highlands'.58 Recommendations of 1701 on 'the great scarcity of probationers having the Irish language' were incorporated in an Act of 1703 which gave the General Assembly control over the distribution of available Gaelic-speaking students, and enjoined them to co-operate with Highland Libraries and existing parochial schools. From 1704, one-half of available funds for bursars in presbyteries in Lowland Scotland were to be used for 'the education of such youths as have the Irish Language'. Acts of 1708 and 1709 forbade Presbyteries from settling in the Lowlands ministers or bursars with Highland experience, or those with only partial ability in Gaelic. Acts of 1710, 1712, 1715, and 1717 required bursars to have testimonial letters from their synod testifying to ability in Gaelic and from their Professor regarding religious proficiency. An Act of 1756 directed that ministers collect at least three shillings per annum to be given to the secretary of the SSPCK 'for educating students for the ministry having the Irish language'. Students were to preach every Sunday in both Gaelic and English.

It is recommended to all the ministers now settled in those parts to do the same. And they are hereby appointed to everything in their power, with the assistance of the Society for Propagating Christian Knowledge, and other friends of our

138

country, religion, and government, to have as many
good schools as may be in that part of the
kingdom, so as the English tongue may spread the
faster, till it be universally understood and
spoken.59

For the author of the mid-eighteenth century 'Some Remarks
on the Highland Clans, and Methods proposed for Civilising
them', more churches were needed in the Highlands: 'the
Publick might be obliged to attend meetings for Divine
Worship' and thus 'induce others who understand and speak
English to attend'.   Both 'might prove a mean to render the
Highland tongue unfashionable, ... turn it to Contempt, and
make it languish to oblivion, a thing which would turn out
of the Greatest advantage and Security to the Nation'.60
New parishes were created in the 1720s to facilitate the
work of the ministry, but the ground to cover was often
extensive, ministerial stipends were not always adequate
despite recommendations that 'as a stimulus to their care
and Diligence, they Ought to be allowed handsome salaries',61 and despite its varied efforts, the Church of
Scotland was continually hindered by too few clergy for its
Highland parishes.   The problem was not confined to the
Established Church: there were too few Gaelic-speaking
Catholic priests in the Highlands in the 1700s, and the
Episcopal Church likewise had difficulties with the
provision of Gaelic staff.62   But lack of clergy amongst
the Established Church is of most significance given
relationships between that body and other institutions and
their shared concern with 'civilitie and obedience'.   Also
of interest is evidence, for various dates but particularly
for the early eighteenth century, that clergy and bursars
resident in the Highlands were not always sufficiently able
in Gaelic to be of use in furthering the intended plan of
loyalty through the use of the native language in worship.
In Inverness in 1703-4, for several bursars in Argyll
between 1708 - 1717, in Weem in 1711, Port of Menteith in
1725, Little Dunkeld in 1723, and in Glenmuick, Tullich and
Glengairn in 1758,63 protests were made by Gaelic-speaking
parishioners at the presence amongst them of men who knew
little or no Gaelic.   These protests, usually in written
form as Representations or Appeals to the Presbytery seem
to have counted for little.   In fact, the settlement of
partly-qualified clergy points to the concern of the
General Assembly to adhere to their 1699 Act which directed
that English services be given 'where in any Highland
congregation many understand English', since in all of the
above places, English was known and used by a proportion of
the native population.   But the presence of men only partly

able to speak Gaelic stemmed chiefly from the concern of the General Assembly to have clergy in the Highlands <u>at all</u>, even if it meant they ignored procedures they had themselves established, and, as was recognised in the Act of 1699, the men involved either had only 'somewhat of the Irish language, but not a facility to preach in it', or, as was noted in an Act of 1709, only the promise that they 'may soon acquire it' [Gaelic]. The words of the Presbytery of Dunkeld in allowing Archibald Campbell, a non-Gaelic speaker, to continue in the strongly Gaelic parish of Weem in 1711 - that he was 'an epitome of righteousness, language tho' obviously here a barrier'64 - typify both the problem and the General Assembly's answer: to establish religious loyalty as the basis to civil control, preferably with but if needs be without Gaelic clergy.

The work of bursars and ministers was aided with the establishment in 1725 of the Royal Bounty Committee, funded by a yearly donation from the King of £1,000 'for the encouragement of Itinerant Preachers and Catechists'. Catechists were to assist ministers to counter 'the spread of popery': 'to ... arm them against the Practices of many Parish Priest that resort thither in order to pervert and seduce them from the Propositions and Principles of the Reform's Religion; Now as the Evil hereof may be of dangerous consequence to Our Government'.65

Both the Royal Bounty Committee, and the Commissioners for the Forfeited Annexed Estates, were concerned with schooling. With the forfeiture of lands of those active on the Jacobite side, legislation was passed 'to erect Public Schools on the said Estates, or in other parts of the Highlands and Islands of Scotland for instructing young Persons in Reading and Writing the English Language'. Several reports from estate factors document the work of these schools; of the school on the Estate of Strowan in Perthshire in 1755, we are told 'The Schools are particularly useful in learning the young ones the English Language as the masters discharge there [sic] Scholars to speak the Irish'.66 The knowledge of estate factors on the lack of education was useful to the SSPCK in the siting of their schools. The Royal Bounty Committee seems not to have founded schools of its own, although it did support the SSPCK, and was concerned in intent at least, in the need for educational policies that were at once 'class'-based, economic, and hegemonic.

Schools [will] remove the Ignorance and Barbarity of the poorer Sort, but it is a loss that for further improving those of a higher Rank and or more than ordinary Pregnant Spirits there are not some few Grammar Schools set up, in the most populous places. This the Government a little after the late happy Revolution, were so sensible of, that, not a Minister but a Schoolmaster with a salarie out of the Bishop's Rents was settled at Maryburgh [Fort William] and continued for some considerable time untill the ffunds for their Maintainance being otherwise dispos'd of, both Ministers and Schoolmaster were oblig'd to leave their posts. The Reviving of these might be of great use not only to the Inhabitants of the Place, but to Gentlemen and Others of Substance in the Neighbourhood, who would send their Children thither, where they would be taught the principles of Religion, Loyalty and Virtue, and the Knowledge of the English Tongue, and further degrees of Learning in Order to fit them to be more useful Members of the Commonwealth.67

Their claims to authority in this respect stemmed from a close relationship with the SSPCK. Nearly thirty per cent of the Royal Bounty Committee's full committee in 1725 (14 out of 48) were members of the SSPCK's executive committees 68: Nicol Spence was most closely involved, as secretary to the SSPCK and sub-clerk to the Royal Bounty Committee, but the lists of lay persons and clergy contain many names of those influential in the evolution of policy within and across both institutions.

The chief importance of the Royal Bounty Committee lay in its use of local catechists to teach 'the Principles and Duties of the true Christian Protestant Religion ... Duty and Loyalty ... and Obedience to the Laws'.69 The involvement of local men in this way meant that the Royal Bounty Committee was not wholly dependent, as was the General Assembly, upon the appearance of candidates among students in the universities, nor, initially at least, upon schemes for financial support. Records of the Royal Bounty Committee suggest that catechists or 'missionaries' modified, as did SSPCK schoolmasters, the original intent of their parent Committee following first-hand experience: rather than move frequently throughout the parish, catechists recognised as early as April 1727 the need to remain in one place and make progress there before moving on.

And some of the Missionaries give it as their opinion, that their Staying too Short a time in one place, Seems not so well to Answer the Design, but that Catechists especially should Remain in

> one place, till they had learn'd a Competent
> Number of the People herein, to Repeat the Shorter
> Catechism, and to understand it in some measure,
> And that being Done, one in a Family may help to
> learn another, which will make way for Ministers
> and Preachers Doing the more good ... And thus in
> Winter Nights in houses, and in Summer in the
> Sheals, the People may be Receiving Instruction,
> with Little Diversion from their work.70

Again, evidence upon the extent of instruction within
Highland families is unclear. Given the limited
availability of the works used, such as Lumsden's
Confessions of the Faith in Gaelic, instruction may not
have been widespread. A 'List of Persons employed' for the
period 1730 - 1740 affords some insight into the location
and number of catechists at work (Figure 3.6). Several
parishes, particularly those with large Catholic
populations, had more than one catechist active and the
records of the Royal Bounty Committee reveal a continued
concern to locate missionaries in strongly Catholic
districts. Lists of May 1725, for example, document areas
in which 'Popery and Ignorance do mostly prevail',
'Memorials concerning Popery' appear throughout the
surviving folios,71 and catechists were re-located more
often to combat a perceived threat of Catholicism amongst
the few - 'the necessity of having that Station Speedily
Supplied by reason of the great Number of Roman Catholics
in it and the Ignorance of the Few Protestants'72 - than
counter a real degree of general irreligion. Several
ministers received financial assistance from the Royal
Bounty Committee (Figure 3.6). The relative levels of
finance needed to sustain eighty catechists and supplement
ministers was a constant drain upon resources and may
explain the decline in influence of this body by the later
1700s. Early records reveal an intention to pay catechists
£40 per annum, but records of salaries paid to catechists
document sums between £4 and £11 per annum with a further
increment of between £1 6s 8d (£1.34) and £1 5s (£1.25)
from the SSPCK. From this, catechists were expected to
subsist, to travel within their parochial bounds and, in
many cases, to move to nearby parishes to officiate there:
'to remove from Contin to the Highlands of Rosskeen, Alness
and Kiltearn'; or, more revealingly, 'to catechise in Muck
for 5 or 6 weeks in summer next, for which he would not be
paid as the funds can bear no more'.73 Although the
evidence suggests that catechists in the Highlands had an
effect beyond a particular parish or district, the shortage
of finance to secure men for all parishes or enable

142

Figure 3.6   Highland parishes in which Royal Bounty
             Committee catechists were active, 1730-1740

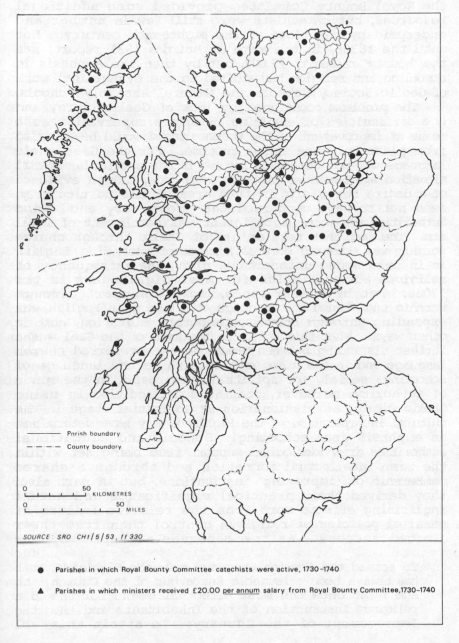

Parish boundary
County boundary

0   50
         KILOMETRES
0   50
         MILES

SOURCE: SRO CH1/5/53, ff 330

●   Parishes in which Royal Bounty Committee catechists were active, 1730-1740

▲   Parishes in which ministers received £20.00 per annum salary from Royal Bounty Committee,1730-1740

full-time work in their regular charges undermined effectiveness. By 1754, the Royal Bounty Committee was noting 'the difficulty there is of getting proper persons to be employed as missionaries in the Highlands'.74 A fund established by the General Assembly in 1726 and operated by the Royal Bounty Committee provided some additional resources, but catechists were still few in number and underpaid by the close of the eighteenth century. Not until the 1830s, in the wake of Baird's 1831 report, was the 'bounty' raised to £2,000, but by then the emphasis in schooling and religion had shifted to the evangelical work of Gaelic Society Schools and General Assembly Schools.

The problems occasioned by lack of Gaelic clergy and the difficulties of ensuring religious supervision as a means of improvement in the Gaidhealtachd would have varied from place to place and over time. For the Gael, their language was not supported by use in one particular social situation and whatever protests were made, though evidence of a desire for Gaelic in that area of life particularly, seem not to have concerned the presbytery and synod authorities whose primary intent was settlement of loyal men. The fact that regular use of Gaelic through church worship was intended more as a means of extending English is in once sense unimportant, given the infrequency of religious administration for most Highlanders in the 1700s. But in another sense, lack of support through worship undermined the language at a time when English was expanding through schools, temporary migration, and in other ways. What this led to in the mind of the Gael was a further distancing between Gaelic as the preferred church language and in the home, and English as the language of schooling; social, not spiritual, progress. In the minds of authority, moreover, continued difficulties in using Gaelic clergy as missionaries as an initial stage in the cultural incorporation of the Highlands may have determined an emphasis upon schooling. Schools and educational authorities drew ideological support from being set within the same intellectual formation and through a shared membership of 'improving' institutions, but in part also, they derived their practical significance and actual anglicising effects more from the relative failure of parallel policies of religious control than from their limited success. As one observer noted,

> To spread the English Language over the Highlands, has always been a laudable Endeavour of the Church and is at once the most effectual means for the religious Instruction of the Inhabitants and the Improvement of the Country. To attain this

Desirable End the Highland Clergy have been enjoined to preach once every Sabbath in English: but instead of promoting, this Regulation, rather frustrates the Design proposed by it. Over most of the Highland Parishes, the number of People is extremely small who understand a Sermon in English, and the Body of the People, being thus excluded from a great part of the Publick Service, they become rather prejudiced against the English Language; a Consequence which ought certainly to be avoided as far as possible. A Sermon in English can only be of use to those who are masters of the Language: It can be of little use to such as understand it imperfectly: and of no service at all in promoting the Language among those who are totally unacquainted with it... A more effectual method of Spreading the English Language over the Highlands, is the Establishment of Schools.75

By the early nineteenth century, emphasis was being placed upon schemes of educational hegemony that incorporated Gaelic and religion.

POLICIES AND MEANS OF ANGLICISATION 1811 – 1872

The Society for the Support of Gaelic Schools

The SSPCK's introduction of Gaelic reading as the basis to an English education, stemmed from the foundation in 1811 of the Edinburgh Society for the Support of Gaelic Schools. Their only concern was teaching Gaels 'to read the Sacred Scriptures in their Native Tongue'.76 Similar societies were established in Glasgow in 1812 and in Inverness in 1818 (both included English from the outset). Gaelic schools (here taken to mean Edinburgh Society) were circulating schools: two terms in a year; November to April, mid-June to mid-September. At the end of the year, schools moved elsewhere in the parish or to other parishes. Classes were held for four to six hours per day, and from six o' clock to ten o' clock in the evenings and on Sundays. These additional 'evening' and 'sabbath schools' as they became known, were chiefly attended by adults. Principal texts used were the Bible, the New Testament, the 1811 First Book for Children in the Gaelic Language, a Second Book from 1816, and, from 1824, collections of Scripture Extracts. From three schools in 1811, Gaelic schools increased to a maximum of eighty-five in 1826, before a gradual decline to seventeen by 1885; a decline interrupted by a brief increase in schools and scholars immediately following the 1843 secession of the Free Church. There is no certain way of knowing whether annual figures of attendance for Gaelic schools enumerate discrete school-going populations, or, as is more likely given their persistence in particular parishes and townships, include persons with previous experience. On average, however, about 3,335 pupils attended Gaelic schools in any year between 1812 to 1860, the greatest annual figure being 8,387 in 1830. By 1885, the population registered as attending had fallen to 599.

What these figures disguise is the work of an institution whose end concern was no less geared to anglicisation through education than the SSPCK or other bodies but whose means differed.

> The general anxiety expressed by many of those who are, as proprietors, most intimately connected with the Highlands and Islands, that the population of these districts should acquire the English, and thus be more amalgamated with the general mass of the people, is the natural result of that intellectual movement, which ... leads men to see that the prosperity of all ranks is promoted by commercial intercourse, and the cultivation ... of similar tastes and habits. Viewed politically, therefore, the introduction of the English language, and its propagation over all the Highlands, is a thing to be desired by every man who contemplates that portion of his country as a portion of the British Empire ... But although it be at once conceded, that the acquisition of the English language would be much for the advantage of the inhabitants of the Highlands and Islands, yet, until the English shall cease to be a foreign tongue, the obligation to communicate to them the knowledge of the language of their fathers remains untouched and altogether imperative.[77]

Of particular significance is the link in Gaelic schools between anglicisation and the maintenance of Gaelic as a spiritual language.

Literacy and the ability to read, in Gaelic or English, was low in the early nineteenth century Highlands. Reports of 1811, 1826, and 1833 testify to this, and further note how Gaelic was preferred as the language of religious administration, even in areas where the inhabitants could generally understand English and use English in church services.78 Given this bond between Gaelic and religion, and the observed disassociation between Gaelic, education, and social progress, the work of Gaelic schools in teaching Highlanders through Gaelic to read the Scriptures in that language had two principal and related effects: firstly, to have reinforced the Highlanders' feeling for Gaelic as a spritual language;79 secondly, to have been an important means of anglicisation. The intended policy of teaching Gaelic scripture reading only was strictly adhered to by the organising committee of the Gaelic Schools Society with the result that ability to read Gaelic led many Highlanders to find support, through the word of God, with which to face contemporary social change in the Highlands. The spiritual basis to instances of protest is reviewed in more detail below (Chapter 6). Of interest here is the fact that the evangelical basis to Gaelic schools – 'that it is essential for every man to read the Word of God in his native tongue, in that language in which he thinks, and which alone he can thoroughly understand' – though partially supporting Gaelic, was deliberately used to extend the knowledge of spoken English: 'the reading of the Gaelic will implant the desire of knowledge, as well as improve the understanding; and thus you insure both the extension and use of the English language'.80 Modifications to the operating policy of Gaelic schools came not through mutually informing relationships between schoolmaster and parent institution as in the case of the SSPCK, but between Gaelic schoolmaster and the Highland population, who paid teachers to go beyond the stated remit and teach them English.

Thomas Ross, minister in Lochbroom, wrote of Badantarbet Gaelic school in his parish in 1813 how 'the people having once got a taste for learning, are not satisfied with their children being able to read Gaelic – a number of them pay the Teacher for instructing them also in reading English, and writing at extra hours'. The Gaelic Schools Society knew of this practice and commended it as a means of furthering English. Teaching English was not incorporated into their educational policy, however, since as was recognised at the outset, teaching Gaelic led on to a desire for knowledge and learning through English.

In the first Report, published by your Society in January 1811, 'to increase the attendance where English is taught', was mentioned as being one of the happy consequences likely to result from the pursuit of the system then adopted by your

Institution. The present Committee are happy to
perceive already, several indications of this
result. 'The people here', say the Rev. Donald
Ross of Kilmuir in the Isle of Skye, 'though they
have not had the benefit of Gaelic Schools long,
are becoming anxious for English Teachers, which
confirms a principle, the truth of which had some
time ago been very much disputed: "<u>That to
cultivate the Gaelic language is a certain though
indirect road to promote the study of English</u>."81

In Kilmallie parish Gaelic school in 1814, scholars 'made
progress in the Gaelic language during the Summer Session;
and, as they have got a taste for learning, they hired a
Schoolmaster to teach the English language, and they are
learning fluently because they have got the Gaelic
before'. In Torosay in 1843, the population 'being able to
compare both versions of the Scriptures, daily add to their
vocabulary of English words'. And for Kiltearn parish in
1839, we are told

The Gaelic School Society, by establishing schools
throughout the country, have done much to eradicate the language ... Those children that had
learned to read Gaelic found no difficulty in
mastering the English; and they had a strong
inducement to do so, because they found in that
language more information suited to their capacity
and taste, than could be found in their own.
English being the language universally spoken by
the higher classes, the mass of people attach a
notion of superior refinement to the possession of
it, which makes them strain every nerve to acquire
it.82

Butter reported 'where these Gaelic schools have been
stationed, the inhabitants express their dis-satisfaction,
not that Gaelic was taught, but that it was not succeeded
by English' and noted how attendance in following years
sometimes declined 'because the inhabitants felt
disappointed in their expectation that the Gaelic teachers
were not authorised to proceed to English after the course
of Gaelic instruction was completed'.83 Of the Gaelic
Society school at Swordle in Ardnamurchan in 1833, we are
told how parishioners there, unable to pay cash to retain
their teacher, 'attempted to stay his departure and pay his
"wages" in potatoes'.84 The 1831 Annual Report of the
Society includes several petitions from Highland parishes
recording the 'incalculable advantages' derived from Gaelic

schools, and a report of 1825 noted 'so universal is the desire of education, that the Society is beset with applications from all quarters for the establishment of Schools' and even in Highland parishes then suffering destitution and over-crowding, residents 'immediately made a subscription for its support, far more than in proportion to their ability'.85 The claim by one minister in 1833 that 'English reading, and English speaking have made greater progress in the Highlands and Isles of Scotland, since the system of Gaelic teaching has been acted upon - that is, during the last twenty years - than it did for centuries before then',86 is not only substantiated in the annual reports of the Society, but we should note, was to a large degree directed by Gaelic speakers themselves.

Figure 3.7 shows the position of all Gaelic schools operating in the period 1811 to 1860, remembering that not all these schools were in operation at the same time. In most cases the location of schools represents a place in the Highlands 'where the Inhabitants ... are now attending to their own Education, either by helping each other forward in the art of reading their vernacular tongue, or by employing Schoolmasters at their own expense'.87 The latter was with the intention of learning English; the former, a means to that end, took several forms: children teaching their parents within and outside school hours; engaging the more educated within their own community to help teach reading; and attendance, by older adults particularly, at sabbath and evening schools. These practices were widespread and commonplace. From one Gaelic school teacher on Mull in 1816, we are told how 'Parents manifested a most earnest desire, all along, to get their Children instructed to read their vernacular tongue', and there and in other townships, 'Parents are instructed by their Children, by hearing them read the word of God in their native language', with the consequence, in the eyes of ministers at least, 'that a wonderful change has been produced on the habits of the people. Their improvements in morals is most visible and striking'. Attendance at Gaelic schools was limited by the needs of labour on the land despite the timing of terms, yet Gaelic schools, for one teacher, made Highlanders so anxious to learn 'that they would sit up day and night if their work would allow them'.88 The twin facts that schools relocated within the parish and that by the 1820s, population distribution had altered so as to congregate people on the coastal margins, may have meant that a greater proportion of the parish population were in touch with Gaelic schools than was the case in regard to the SSPCK. The age range within Gaelic school scholar populations was larger than for SSPCK

Figure 3.7   The location of Gaelic Society schools in the
Highlands, 1811–1860

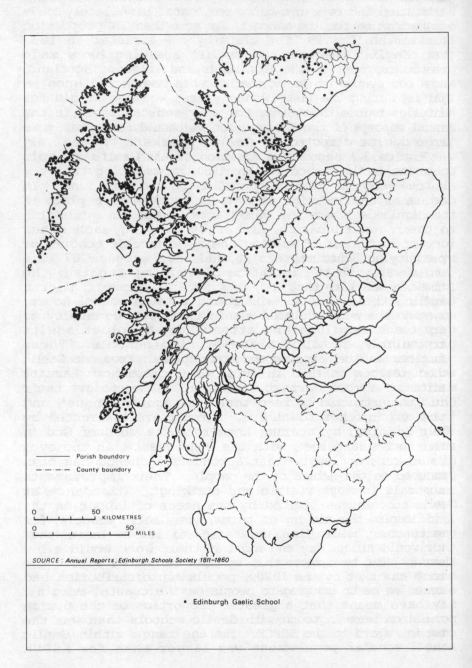

Parish boundary
County boundary

0   50
├──┴──┴──┴──┴──┤ KILOMETRES

0   50
├──┴──┴──┴──┤ MILES

SOURCE : *Annual Reports, Edinburgh Schools Society 1811–1860*

• Edinburgh Gaelic School

schools, and although the relative availability of the
source material must be borne in mind, it is likely that
education outwith the schools was more widespread in the
case of Gaelic than SSPCK schools. What is more certain is
that the sex ratio within Gaelic schools was less biased
toward males than in the SSPCK. In Skeal Gaelic school,
Reay parish, in 1814, for example, fifty-eight scholars are
recorded on the register, males and females equally: of
the males, six were aged between twenty and forty, nine
aged fifteen to twenty years, and fourteen aged less than
fifteen: twenty-one of the females were aged less than
fifteen years and the remaining eight fell within the age
range fifteen to twenty-six years.89 This division by sex
and age is perhaps not typical of all schools since we have
no idea how many persons of what sex and age were being
taught outside of the school, nor how many went to the
sabbath school, but it is illustrative of the much more
equitable balance between the sexes prevailing within
Gaelic schools throughout the period of their operation
(Table 3.3).

The Edinburgh Gaelic Schools Society derived its
principal influence through the operation of a policy which
while effectively denying a formal place for English, had
the end result (and initial intent) of spreading both
spoken English and a desire for knowledge that could only
be fulfilled through English. At the same time, Gaelic
schools in using Gaelic scriptural texts, not only helped
to reinforce Gaelic's place as a church language but
further influenced Highland consciousness in making a
distinction between Gaelic as the language of spiritual
affairs, English of worldly advance. As one minister noted
in 1822, 'although your Committee believe the Gaelic, as
the only language fully understood by the sequestered
Highlanders, to be the only language which can promote
their eternal interest, they are not blind to the advantages which must be conferred on them in regard to their
temporal interests, by giving them the opportunity of
acquiring the English'.90 Assessment, firstly, of the
extent to which Highlanders themselves derived and directed
'incalculable advantages' from being able to read Gaelic
scriptures (albeit that this literacy led to the acquisition of English), and secondly, of the extent of this
separation in the use of Gaelic must consider also that
many clergy, particularly of the Established Church, spoke
against Gaelic as a language of education. Opposition to
Gaelic as a means of social progress was neither new nor
the preserve of the Church alone, but in the latter context
especially, the hostility of some ministers to the language
was part of that broader attitude toward Highland culture

Table 3.3

Population attending Edinburgh Gaelic Society Schools in the Highlands 1812-1885*

Year	Number of schools	Estimated total population	Estimated average school population	Male & Female Scholars as % of total school population	
				M	F
1812	20	650	32	–	–
1823	78	4,522	58	55.4	44.6
1833	58	3,374[1]	58	50.6	49.4
1848	60	2,280[1]	39	–	–
1851	45	2,518[2]	56	50.9	49.1
1860	42	1,668[2]	41	49.0	51.0
1885	17	599	32	–	–

* Annual Reports, Edinburgh Gaelic Schools Society, 1812-1861, 1886

1 Based on returns from 58 schools

2 Based on returns from 40 schools

which blended antagonism and fascination (see above, Chapter 2). Butter commented in 1824 how 'The Clergymen in many cases, whether it is from the difficulty they feel in the use of the language or not often speak unfavourably of it which increases the peoples prejudice against it as a school language'.91 Similar statements on the 'right' of Gaels to have the word of God in Gaelic but the means of social improvement only in English were commonplace.

> I have no prejudice against the Gaelic language
> ... but the most ardent lover of Gaelic cannot
> fail to admit that the possession of a knowledge
> of English is indispensable to any poor Islander
> who wishes to learn a trade or to earn his bread
> beyond the limits of his native isle.92

This separation of language for specific and distinguishable purposes within Highland society as a whole was not always apparent at the level of the individual, nor only a nineteenth-century phenomenon evident just between education and religion. In part, it resulted from expansion of trade networks and rhythms of temporary migration (see below), as well from those earlier schemes for cultural hegemony involving the recruitment of a Gaelic clergy and the incorporative use of Gaelic language and texts as a 'missionary medium' in religious supervision. But in large measure, what we are observing for the 1700s and 1800s in the divergence between the actual uses and perceived value of Gaelic and English stems from long standing notions of anglicisation as the basis to civil control and from the unequal ideological struggle taking place in regard to Gaelic education and religion. Many Highlanders, even those fluent in English, preferred Gaelic church services. Gaelic scriptural texts were deeply treasured. Yet this strength within the Highland consciousness counted for little given that Gaelic texts were being published and distributed by educational institutions whose purpose in extending Gaelic literacy (with what dual result we have seen) was founded upon a network of support from Lowland Missionary and Bible Societies and individual financial donations and set within an intellectual formation compounded of missionary zeal (the righteousness of bringing both salvation and English), and moral superiority (derived from related notions of class consciousness, reflected in and maintained through possession of English).

The Church of Scotland was not as lacking in clergy in the 1800s as in the 1700s but like the Catholic Church, the Episcopal church and, after 1843, the Free Church, they had problems in providing a Gaelic ministry. Protests and petitions against the presentation to Highland parishes of ministers unable to speak Gaelic in, for example, Little Dunkeld in 1825, Avoch in 1831, Dunkeld and Dowally in 1836, Nairn in 1854 93 - stem not so much from the strength of Gaelic there as from the reported inability of a section of the Gaelic population to understand English services. The effect of placing ministers 'who know not a word of the language of the people among whom they are appointed to minister' should not detract from the many who laboured hard to benefit their parishioners, but the result of too few clergy or the use of men unable to preach in Gaelic led, in the 1800s as earlier, to further weakening of Gaelic. Although 'the great want' of Gaelic ministers in the Free Church was more acute in the years immediately following the 1843 Disruption, they were still short of men in the 1870s, and as late as the 1860s, the General Assembly of the Church of Scotland was cautioning its presbyteries in their 'ability to afford religious supervision to the people in their vernacular tongue'.94

Whether Gaelic survived longer as a spoken language and was kept going in a limited way as the language of prayer within the home in part depended upon the possession of a Gaelic Bible or other scriptural texts. This, in turn, reflected the support, in texts and money, or various Auxiliary Societies and Bible Societies. In 1824–25 alone, 5,412 Bibles, 2,532 New Testaments and 2,650 Scripture Extracts were donated by Lowland bodies. An issue-list of books for 1826 records an out-going of 15,832 volumes, the 540 Bibles being the most expensive to purchase and distribute. A footnote to the list estimates that 126,300 books had been circulated in the Highlands since the establishment of the Society in 1811.95 The Ladies' Association in Support of Gaelic Schools in Connection with the Church of Scotland, established in 1845, provided an annual grant of £20 to eight Gaelic schools and grants of between £5 and £10 to a further six. This Association derived an income from donations in excess of £515 between June 1846 and April 1847 which it directed towards schooling in the Highlands.96 The Highland Missionary Society, whose principal aim was 'the promotion of religious instruction in the Highlands and Islands of Scotland, by providing the means for having Preachers of the Gospel sent into those Districts', distributed over £149 in 1824, but only about a third of the total actually reached itinerant ministers.97 The Paisley Society for Gaelic Missions operated on the same principal, but with much reduced funds. Among major donors to the Gaelic Schools Society in 1813 and 1814, for example, were Glasgow Auxiliary Gaelic Society (£300), Paisley and East Renfrew Bible Society and the congregation of Greenock Gaelic School chapel who each gave £50, and Argyll excise officers, many of them Highlanders, who donated £30. Highland regiments provided donations, but the chief source of funding for Gaelic schools came from individual bequests, channelled through Auxiliary Societies. Figure 3.8 shows the location of the principal supporting agencies in 1819 and 1849: a network of agencies whose end concern, like the schools they funded and those individuals whose money they centralised, was to shed light upon the darkness:

> A few years of equal exertion and of equal success ... and what glorious works will be done! - what glorious scenes will be witnessed! The waste lands will be changed into a fruitful field. The light of heaven will be seen illuminating the darkest recessess of the earth; scenes of magnificence and beauty will be unfolded, which were covered with thick darkness.98

Assessment of the names and constituent membership of the directors and committees of management of several of those Auxiliary Societies, especially those in the larger towns and cities, reveals connections between Lowland-resident Highlanders, Highland migrant societies, and the work of the Gaelic Schools Society and other institutions in the Highlands. Among the directors of Glasgow Auxiliary Gaelic School Society in 1834, for example, was the Rev. McLaurin, minister to one of Glasgow's Gaelic chapels and an influential member of Glasgow Highland Society. The President and Treasurer of this Society were ex officio directors of the Auxiliary Gaelic Society. Gaelic Schools, and, by implication, the extension of English they initiated, were supported financially and ideologically not just within the Highlands by persons who paid to be taught English nor alone by a range of concerned individuals from within the structures of Lowland society, but also by elite members of Highland society and Highlanders living in the Lowlands who derived status partly from being members of Highland institutions at work in both Highlands and Lowlands but also from their relative position in the class structures of English-speaking urban Lowland Scotland.

General Assembly schools

The success of the Gaelic Schools Society prompted the General Assembly to establish schools in the Highlands from 1825. The schools were controlled by the Committee of the

155

Figure 5.0 (a) The location of the principal supporting
institutions for the Gaelic Society schools
in 1819

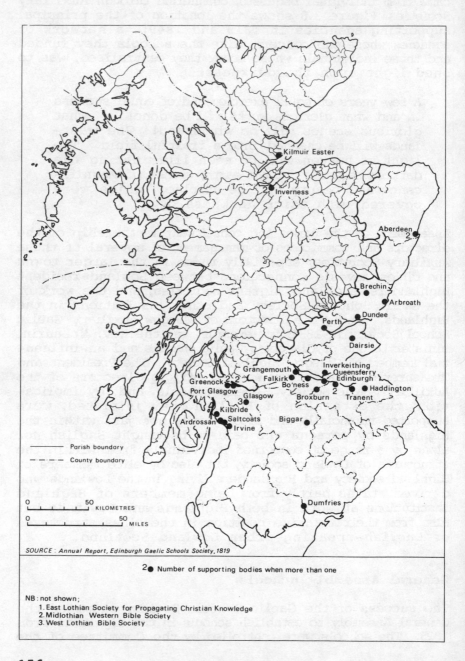

Kilmuir Easter

Inverness

Aberdeen
2

Brechin
Arbroath
Perth • Dundee
Dairsie

Grangemouth
Falkirk
Greenock 2 2
Port Glasgow
3 Glasgow
Kilbride
Saltcoats
Ardrossan
Irvine

Inverkeithing
Queensferry
Edinburgh
Bo'ness 2
Broxburn   Haddington
Tranent

Biggar

Dumfries

———— Parish boundary
—·—·— County boundary

0   50
|———|———| KILOMETRES

0   50
|———|———| MILES

SOURCE : Annual Report, Edinburgh Gaelic Schools Society, 1819

2● Number of supporting bodies when more than one

NB : not shown;
1. East Lothian Society for Propagating Christian Knowledge
2. Midlothian Western Bible Society
3. West Lothian Bible Society

Figure 3.8 (b) The location of the principal supporting
institutions for the Gaelic Society schools
in 1849

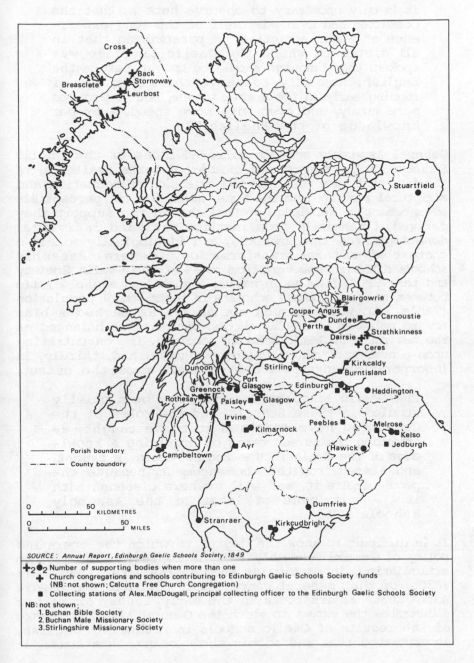

Cross

Back
Breasclete   Stornoway
Leurbost

Stuartfield

Blairgowrie
Coupar Angus
Perth   Dundee   Carnoustie
Dairsie   Strathkinness
Ceres

Dunoon   Stirling   Kirkcaldy
Burntisland
Port
Greenock   Glasgow
Rothesay   Paisley   Edinburgh   Haddington
Irvine   Glasgow
Kilmarnock
Peebles   Melrose
Kelso
Ayr   Hawick   Jedburgh

Campbeltown

Parish boundary
County boundary

0   50
   KILOMETRES
0   50
   MILES

Dumfries

Stranraer   Kirkcudbright

SOURCE : Annual Report, Edinburgh Gaelic Schools Society, 1849

+2 •2 Number of supporting bodies when more than one
  + Church congregations and schools contributing to Edinburgh Gaelic Schools Society funds
     (NB: not shown; Calcutta Free Church Congregation)
  ■ Collecting stations of Alex.MacDougall, principal collecting officer to the Edinburgh Gaelic Schools Society

NB: not shown;
  1. Buchan Bible Society
  2. Buchan Male Missionary Society
  3. Stirlingshire Missionary Society

General Assembly for Increasing the Means of Education and Religious Instruction in the Highlands and Islands. Gaelic reading was taught from the outset as in Gaelic schools.

> It is only necessary to observe here ... that the Committee had availed itself of the long experience of other societies, in prescribing that in all districts where the Gaelic language was spoken, that language should be taught before the English, not only to serve the advantage of reading early in the mother tongue, but to promote more surely, and even with more speed, a proper knowledge of the English.99

General Assembly schools mirrored those of the Gaelic Society: in the nature and number of texts available; in the fact that they prompted the extension of education and scriptural reading into the home, which led to 'perceptible advancement in knowledge of English'; in the support they derived, financially from institutional and individual donations from the Lowlands, and ideologically within a context of cultural transformation. General Assembly schools differed, however, from those of the Gaelic Society and the SSPCK, firstly, in having a much less equable ratio between male and female scholars in their school population (Table 3.4), which though not always as marked a bias toward males as in SSPCK schools, was never as balanced as the sex ratio in Gaelic schools; secondly, in concentrating upon a number of non-circulatory schools; and, thirdly, in incorporating instruction in English from the outset.

> The Gaelic language, however, has been chiefly studied in these Schools, and the roles of the Committee have enjoined it to be taught, as affording the surest means of acquiring a knowledge of the English. The English again is taught, and almost from the commencement, because the people desire it, and will nowhere dispense with it - in none of least of the Assembly Schools.100

It is difficult to know the degree to which the operating policy of General Assembly schools represents either the articulation, in particular form in the later 1820s and 1830s, of that general concern for 'civilitie and obedience' that has its roots in the early 1600s, or rather illustrates the extent to which the General Assembly, aware of the results of Gaelic schools in futhering English, incorporated that end within their means. In a sense, it

Table 3.4

Population attending General Assembly schools in the Highlands, 1826–1838*

Year	Number of Schools**	Estimated total population	Estimated average school population	Male & Female Scholars as % of total population		Numbers learning Gaelic/English as % of total population	
				M	F	G	E
1826	21	1,629	78	65.5	34.5	38.9	67.9
1827	21	1,629	78	68.2	31.8	41.8	74.8
1828	39	3,180	81	65.6	34.4	41.5	82.3
1829	68	5,928[1]	87	59.5[2]	40.5	42.3	77.1
1830	72	5,803[1]	80	66.3[2]	33.7	45.1	85.9
1831	-	-	-	-[3]	-	-	-
1832	72	5,842	81	65.6[4]	34.4	50.7	89.0
1833	72	5,865	81	67.7[4]	32.3	44.9	93.2
1834	72	5,698	79	65.4[5]	34.6	42.7	86.6
1835	76	5,850	76	-	-	34.9	74.2
1838	81	6,545	81	-	-	31.5	80.4

*   Reports, General Assembly, 1827-1838, passim.
** These are schools operating in the Highlands and Islands only
1   No return from Ceannabinn school, Durness
2   Based on returns from 54 schools
3   Based on returns from 53 schools
4   Based on returns from 60 schools
5   Based on returns from 51 schools

is both. In General Assembly schools, we find clear evidence of the shorter-term moulding and re-assertion of anglicisation as the dominant hegemony within a body which, in the longer term and in a broader context, both directed and reflected the transformation of Highland life and consciousness.

Their policy was mediated through selected authoritative texts: English texts outnumbered Gaelic ones and were of a different nature. Most Gaelic texts used were didactic in nature, moralising in tone, and geared towards inciting a learning which could only be furthered through English; 'All the articles are ... very appropriate ... and cannot fail to give the Highlanders a relish for more extensive reading and information'.101 English texts used were generally practically instructive: works on animal husbandry and seamanship in addition to collections of sermons. The Bible and Testaments were the principal texts used in schooling and the General Assembly made them available at reduced prices. Overall, however, the texts available and the way they were employed in Assembly schools, and the other subjects taught - Latin, geography, arithmetic, navigation, and book-keeping - symbolise the authoritarian notions of education through English as the basis to social utility whilst, simultaneously, condemning Gaelic as of little practical value. The 1838 Report of the General Assembly Committee for Increasing the Means of Education ... quoting their schoolmaster in Alness, makes this plain.

> Teach them the common language of the nation - teach them English, to read it, to understand it. Yes, I say, teach them English, for which I would teach them to read the Word of God in their own language, ... a language which must ever continue with them to be language of prayer and devotion; yet, while you do this, you must also teach them the English. Teach it, as the only effectual manner in which it can be taught, through the medium of their own - teach them to write and to count, and circulate among them a few plain and practical books of useful knowledge, and then you require no ground officer or sheriff-officer, to remove them from their poor huts, and transport them from the scene of their present fearful privation.102

The network of Assembly schools grew from twenty-one in 1826 to eighty-one in 1838 (Table 3.4). Using the surviving Annual Reports, it is possible not merely to locate

these schools by parish but also to explore 'the interesting spectacle of the pupils of all ages earnestly engaged
in a conflict with two languages'.103   (Figure 3.9).
Throughout the period for which there is certain evidence
(1826-1838), and for all Assembly schools in the Highlands
and Islands in this period, Gaelic was only once, in 1832,
taught to more than fifty per cent of the total scholar
population.   On average, only an estimated forty-one per
cent of the total school-going population was taught Gaelic
in any year between 1826-1838, whereas, on average,
eighty-one per cent was taught English.   Instruction in
Gaelic declined over time more markedly than was the case
for English (Table 3.4).   It is possible to observe this
'conflict' within individual schools, both for particular
dates and over time.   In several Gaidhealtachd-edge
parishes - Reay, Farr, Mortlach, Alyth, South Knapdale -
not one scholar was being taught Gaelic in 1827, but
English was being learned by all.   In the more strongly
Gaelic central and north and west Highlands, assessment of
the figures for those being taught Gaelic and/or English
reveals a complexity of language use and language instruction that is not assessable from the extant sources of
other educational institutions nor immediately apparent
from the Reports for any single year from the General
Assembly Committee.   Several trends may be observed:
firstly, in the north and west, and parts of the central
Grampians, a higher percentage of the school population was
learning English than Gaelic, but the per cent learning
Gaelic was higher there than in eastern Ross and Cromarty
and the southern parishes of Argyll; secondly, an overall
increase over time in the given evidence on the extent to
which Gaelic teaching encouraged English in and out of
school, to a subsequent knowledge of English (e.g.
Lochalsh parish, 1828-1834); and thirdly, a situation where
levels of English instruction decreased or remained
consistently lower than levels of English instruction - a
reflection perhaps of a more advanced 'stage' of language
change, since English was being universally taught without
the numerical evidence to suggest that a high level of
instruction in Gaelic reading was needed at the outset
(e.g. several schools in the Kintyre and Cowal districts of
Argyll).   Educational Statistics of 1833 suggest that these
differences within and between schools in levels of Gaelic
and English instruction, together with likely sex-based
differences in the 'conflict' between languages in these
and other schools, were paralleled by age differences in
literacy and language ability.   The inability of people
over twenty years of age to read either Gaelic or English
was more marked in the north and west than in the south and

Figure 3.9   General Assembly schools in the Highlands in 1832

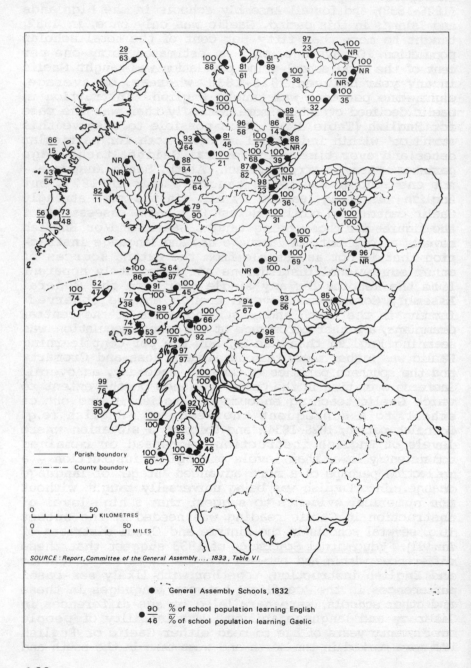

Parish boundary

County boundary

0   50
KILOMETRES
0   50
MILES

SOURCE : Report, Committee of the General Assembly..., 1833 , Table VI

● General Assembly Schools, 1832

$\frac{90}{46}$ % of school population learning English
% of school population learning Gaelic

eastern Highlands and those parishes adjacent to the Lowlands. Whilst this geographical pattern was mirrored in the levels of literacy of persons aged between six and twenty years, the overall level of literacy - the basis to anglicisation - was much higher in the younger sections of the population.104

The work of General Assembly schools, of the Gaelic Societies, the SSPCK, Free Church schools, and a variety of lesser institutions effectively ended with the formalisation of education under the 1872 Education Act. No mention was made of Gaelic in this Act: a reflection of the prevailing ideology that English was the means of social advancement and recognition of the extent to which, even in strongly Gaelic parts, English was known and used, especially by the young, by the end of the nineteenth century. Nicolson, commenting on Skye in 1867, noted how 'the rising generation are growing up in the habits of speaking English and may be heard addressing each other in that language as often as in the mother tongue'.105 Although the 1872 Education Act has been considered a major blow to Gaelic in the modern period,106 it should more properly be seen as the representation and culmination of an ideology articulated and practised since the early 1600s. Protests against the exclusion of Gaelic from the 1872 Act were made, chiefly through the Gaelic Society of Inverness, founded in 1871. But recognition by some persons of the value of teaching in Gaelic, the desire of several school boards and of numerous schoolmasters in the 1870s to participate in any such schemes counted for little given an Education Department which continued to separate Gaelic from social value and amongst whose inspectors were men who regarded 'the teaching of Gaelic in schools in any shape or form as a serious misfortune'. In 1875 a qualifying extension to the earlier act provided that in districts where Gaelic was spoken, children in the second and third standards <u>might</u> be tested in that language, but no condition was imposed on the qualification of teachers or inspectors. The Napier Commission considered, however, that 'all children whose mother-tongue is Gaelic should be taught to read that language ... We think that the discouragement and neglect of the native language in the education of Gaelic-speaking children ... ought to cease, and that a knowledge of that language ought to be considered one of the primary qualifications of every person engaged in the carrying out of the national system of education in Gaelic-speaking districts'.107 From 1885 Gaelic was made a 'specific subject' in Highland schools, but there was no legal compulsion to teach it and not until 1918 were attempts made to gain a statutory place for

Gaelic in education at all successful. Since then, Gaelic education had developed in a number of ways, but these more recent shifts in legislation and in consciousness stand in marked contrast to the earlier evidence.108

CONCLUSION

In what has been discussed above of the role of particular institutions and of the evolution of purposive anti-Gaelic policies of anglicisation, it is clear that the assertion of cultural hegemony in and through the English language in the Highlands in the past was not a story of separable absolutes and was more involved than the straightforward imposition of one language over another or one way of thinking and expression over another through schools and parish churches. Several important and related factors may be identified: the key role of a number of educational institutions; the assertion of a dominant ideology; the policies by which that ideology was effected in and through the various bodies operating in the Highlands (policies that were 'recreated and renewed' as social and geographical circumstances demanded); and, not least, the differences between the ideological intent of anglicisation and the actual result in which we have noted, for example, not only distinctions by age and perhaps even by sex in the extent to which Gaelic or English was known and commonly used as the language of everyday life but also differences between the written and the spoken language and, more generally, between one language and another for specific social purposes such as religious worship, commercial transaction, or schooling.

Each of the several institutional bodies discussed above articulated and practised particular policies of anglicisation during its period of operations in the Highlands. The SSPCK was the most significant educational agency throughout the eighteenth century and for the first part of the nineteenth century, not least for the fact that it continually re-adjusted its operating principles (commonly in accordance with the expressed demands of its own schoolmasters) in order to achieve its intended aim. The location and re-location of SSPCK schools was carefully considered given their expressed intentions. Although financial restrictions hindered school establishment, SSPCK schools served the great majority of Highland parishes (albeit with more regular coverage in the south and east Highlands), in the period 1755 to 1825 (cf. Figures 3.2-3.5). The other principal educational institution was the (Edinburgh) Society for the Support of Gaelic Schools whose schools (like those of the SSPCK were regularly re-located to provide for as large a proportion as possible of the Highland population. Anglicisation was not, however, the result of institutions alone. The SSPCK and the Gaelic Schools derived financial support from a wide range of like-minded individuals throughout Scotland. These donations should be seen as the embodiment of a more widespread sentiment of moral advance and betterment in eighteenth and nineteenth-century Scotland, evident particularly among the upper and middle ranks and classes. At any given moment then, the actual agencies of anglicisation - at the institutional level or at the level of the individual schoolmaster or catechist labouring in his Highland parish - were not only bound together by a common ideology (and in the case of some institutions bound also by a shared membership), but also derived their authority from being set within a particular socio-economic and intellectual 'formation': seventeenth-century 'civilitie and obedience'; eighteenth-century 'improvement'; and nineteenth-century notions of class and class consciousness. There were, for example, some members of Highland society - seventeenth-century and eighteenth-century clan chiefs and landowners, nineteenth-century urban Gaels and church ministers, Highland-born members of the Scottish and British elite who, for one reason or another welcomed, financially supported, and directed policies of civility, improvement, and civilisation. Many Highlanders actively sought English through schooling as a means 'to get on in life', yet they would petition the General Assembly for Gaelic-speaking clergy and protest at any shortage. And there were men like Kirkwood, articulating opposition to the intended means of cultural change from within the structures of authority. The fact, too, that Gaelic schools with their use of Gaelic scriptural texts to develop Gaelic literacy as a means of extending English simultaneously reinforced the deep attachment of Highlanders to Gaelic as a religious medium points to the complex issues underlying the development of education and the spread of English to the Highlands. Furthermore, the 'conflict between the languages' took place at a multitude of levels - within and from the General Assembly, for example, to Synods, presbyteries, clergy and schoolmasters - and at a variety of scales - in schools and churches, between written and spoken forms, between male and female, young and old within counties, in particular parishes and within the minds and lived experiences of individuals.

It is worth noting that similar patterns and processes are observable in the case of Lowland Scots and education. As we have observed above and as Williamson notes in regard

to Lowland Scots in the context of eighteenth-century
intellectual and social development,

> the second half of the 18th century is marked
> particularly by the efforts of many educated and
> professional Scots to acquire and to cultivate a
> brand of Standard English. <u>English had become the
> language of contemporary scholarship in 18th
> century Scotland</u>. The public presentations of the
> intellectual activity that characterised the
> Englightenment were in English, although vernacu-
> lar Scots continued to be the birth-tongue of
> their authors as it was, indeed, of the vast
> majority of Lowlanders in the 18th century.109

The fact that in the eighteenth century and thereafter what
Williamson calls 'the norm of correctness in language for
both speech and writing' was applied to Lowland Scots -
through education as schools 'improved' the native accents
and idiom of the common people - points to intriguing
parallels between Gaelic and Scots in the role of a
standard English in Scotland in expressing and representing
the domination of particular classes. As Phillips has
shown for nineteenth-century England, the question of
refinement in speech was likewise a matter of great
importance.110 In the case of Lowland Scots in the 1800s,
schoolmasters were enjoined to make pupils both speak and
write a standard English and several government reports of
the later nineteenth century in addition note class
distinctions in propriety in use of Scots (a lower class
language often dismissed as 'dialect'), and English, 'the
language of the better classes'.

The ideological association between anglicisation and
cultural transformation has thus not only taken place in
the Highlands. And in that region as in Lowland Scotland
or elsewhere in Britain, the role of language as a means of
social and cultural change derives from the class position
of its users; as claimed above, 'The class that effectively
rules succeeds in presenting its particular use of language
as the only correct one'. In the Highlands, however, as we
shall see, the association between anglicisation and
acculturation from the later 1600s was particularly
important as the basis to, and reflection of, related
processes of material transformation.

Anglicisation and the Ideology of Transformation

NOTES

1. SRO, E.730/25.

2. D. Defoe, _A Tour thro' the Whole Island of Great Britain, Divided into Circuits or Journeys_ (London, 1752), IV, p.241.

3. Anon., _The Highland Complaint_ (Edinburgh, 1737), pp.23-24.

4. SRO, CH8/212/1, ff.89,90.

5. R. Nicholson, _Scotland The Later Middle Ages_, (Edinburgh, 1978), _passim_.

6. D. Masson (ed.), _Register of the Privy Council of Scotland_ (Edinburgh, 1887), Vol.VIII (1607-1610), pp.742-745; Vol.IX (1610-1613), pp.75-80.

7. Ibid., Vol VIII, p.744; IX, pp.28-29.

8. D. Masson (ed.), _Register of the Privy Council_ (Edinburgh, 1891), Vol.X (1613-1616), pp.671-672.

9. A. I. Macinnes, 'Scottish Gaeldom, 1638-1651; the vernacular response to the Covenanting Dynamic', in J. Dwyer, R. A. Mason, and A. Murdoch (eds.), _New Perspectives on the Politics and Culture of Early Modern Scotland_ (Edinburgh, 1984), pp.59-94.

10. Masson (ed.), _Register_, Vol.IX, pp.75-80.

11. Macinnes, 'Scottish Gaeldom', p.65.

12. Ibid., p.62; _Acts of Parliament of Scotland_ T. Thomson and C. Innes (eds.), (Edinburgh, 1815-1875), _V_ (1633), pp.21,216.

13. Macinnes, 'Scottish Gaeldom', p.63.

14. _Acts of Parliament of Scotland_, IX, (1695), p.448; X, (1696), p.63.

15. D. Withrington, 'Education in the 17th Century Highlands', in L. Maclean (ed.), _The Seventeenth Century in the Highlands_ (Inverness, 1986), pp.60-69; see also D. Mackinnon, 'Education in Argyll and the Isles, 1638-1709',

Records of the Scottish Church History Society, 6, (1936), pp.46-54.

16. Acts of the General Assembly of the Church of Scotland (Edinburgh, 1843), (1642), p.55; (1648), p.189; (1649), p.216.

17. Ibid., (1648), p.189.

18. Ibid., (1698), XVII, p.276; (1699), IX p.282; (1694), p.241; (1695), XII, p.250.

19. Macinnes, 'Scottish Gaeldom'. p.65.

20. Ibid., passim; I. D. Whyte, Agriculture and Society in Seventeenth Century Scotland (Edinburgh, 1983), pp.36,157,235; R. A Dodgshon, Land and Society in Early Scotland (Oxford, 1981), pp.277-320; A. McKerral, 'The tacksman and his holding in the south-west Highlands', Scottish Historical Review 26, (1947), pp.10-25; idem, Kintyre in the Seventeenth Century (Edinburgh, 1948); A. Martin Kintyre: The hidden past (Edinburgh, 1984).

21. D. Stevenson, Alasdair MacColla and the Highland Problem in the Seventeenth Century (Edinburgh, 1980), pp.199, 203, 232,240. On the likely impact of plague and the demographic causes of economic change in Argyll at this period, see M. Flinn (ed.), Scottish Population History (Cambridge, 1977), pp. 149-150.

22. Macinnes, 'Scottish Gaeldom', pp.65-67.

23. Ibid., Other illustrations of the vernacular response are contained in D. S.Thomson (ed.), Companion to Gaelic Scotland (Oxford, 1983).

24. The majority of Kirkwood's manuscripts and notes are contained in New College Library, Edinburgh; NCL, MSS L.5.1.6.1., 1-12; Box 2 21(3b); W 13b(2/3); Irish Bible (Box 31); see also the National Library of Scotland, MS 821. For a fuller account of Kirkwood's involvement in schemes for Gaelic texts and in their distribution, see C. W. J. Withers, 'The Highland Parishes in 1698: an examination of sources for the definition of the Gaedhealtachd', Scottish Studies, 24 (1980), 63-88; idem, Gaelic in Scotland, pp. 117-121; V. E. Durkacz, 'The source of the language problem in Scottish education 1688-1709', Scottish Historical Review, LVII (1978), pp.28-39.

25. Durkacz, 'The source of the language problem', passim; Acts of the General Assembly of the Church of Scotland, XI (1690), p.227.

26. NCL, Kirkwood Collection, Box 2 21(3b), Amendment d.

27. NLS, MS 821, pp.291-292.

28. SRO., GD 95.1.1., p.294.

29. SRO, GD 95.2.2., p.308.

30. SRO, GD 95.1.2., p.94.

31. Ibid., pp.104, 170-171.

32. Ibid., p.171.

33. SRO, GD 95.10.79., Overtures for teaching the Societ-ies Schollars to understand and Speak the English Language, 1723.

34. SRO, GD 95.1.4., p.59.

35. A. MacDonald, Leabhar a Theasgarc Ainminnim Nuadhf-hocloir Gaoidhelig & Beurla (Dun-Eideinn, 1741), p.v.

36. SRO, GD 95.1.8., p.122.

37. SRO, GD 95.1.5., p.106.

38. SRO, GD 95.1.5., p.105.

39. SRO, GD 95.1.1., p.191; GD 95.1.2., pp.197-198, 227,; GD 95.1.3., p.132.

40. W. Mackay, 'The teaching of Gaelic in schools', The Celtic Monthly, XIV(2) (1906), p.238.

41. SRO, GD 95.1.8., p.122.

42. Estimates of the average school-going population were calculated by dividing the estimated total school-going population, given in various SSPCK manuscript folios, by the given number of schools. Estimates of the average school-going population as a percentage of the parish population are less accurate: one way is to use Webster's population figures for 1755 as the basis to calculation, or the number of catechisable persons per parish as the basis

to assessment of total population, but both methods are liable to error.

43. Scots Magazine, XXVIII (1766), p.683.

44. A. Belches, An Account of the Society in Scotland for Propagating Christian Knowledge from its commencement in 1709 (Edinburgh, 1774), pp. 45, 67. This appears in the SRO as GD 95.11.1/1 and GD 95.11.1/2; I have quoted here from the printed version.

45. Scots Magazine, XXVIII (1766), p.684.

46. SRO, GD 95.1.2., pp.144-145, 182.

47. Anon, The Highland Complaint (Edinburgh, 1737), p.25.

48. British Museum, King's MS 105.

49. SRO, GD 95.11.3., p.29.

50. J. Sinclair (ed.), The Statistical Account of Scotland (Edinburgh, 1791-1799), II (1792), p.389. (This is usually - and will be here - referred to as the 'Old' Statistical Account (OSA), to distinguish it from the 'New' Statistical Account, of 1831-1845; OSA, XIV (1795), pp.206-207.

51. Withers, Gaelic in Scotland, pp.41-76.

52. Belches, An Account of the Society, pp.3, 52.

53. SRO, GD 95.9.3., p.17.

54. On these Highland libraries, see D. Maclean 'Highland Libraries in the eighteenth century', Records of the Glasgow Bibliographical Society, VIII (1923), pp.36-43; idem, 'Highland libraries in the eighteenth century', Transactions of the Gaelic Society of Inverness, XXXI, (1923), pp.69-97; NLS, MS 3430, ff.130-131, Kirkwood to Meldrum, December 12, 1704; NCL, MS L.5.1.6.1.9 (An Account of a design to erect Libraries in the Highlands of Scotland; as also in Orkney and Shetland; NCL, MS W13 b.2/3 (A Register concerning the Libraries for the Highlands and Islands of Scotland); NCL, MC L.5.1.6.1., (12) (An Overture for founding and maintaining of Bibliothecks in every Paroch throughout this Kingdom, 1699); SRO CH 1/2/23/1. f.77.

55. Estimates vary as to the actual number of Highland

libraries: for a review of the evidence see the above note and Withers, <u>Gaelic in Scotland</u>, pp.54-55; NCL, MS W 13.B.2/3, pp.9, 11; SRO, CH 1/2/30/4, ff/384,385, <u>passim</u>; SRO, CH 1/2/24/3, ff.152,155,156, <u>passim</u>.

56. SRO, CH 1/2/30/1, f.34; see also A. Mitchell (ed.), <u>Inverness Kirk-Session Records</u> (Inverness, 1902), p.120.

57. NLS, MS. 3431, ff.34-35.

58. <u>Acts of the General Assembly</u>, IX (1699), p.282; XVI (1699), pp.287-288.

59. Ibid., VII (1756), p.727; XIII (1704), pp.329-330.

60. NLS, Advocates MS 32.4.6., pp.50-51 (see also NLS, Adv. MS 16.1.14).

61. NLS, Adv. MS 32.4.6., p.57.

62. Scottish Catholic Archives, Box N (1733), Letter of Bishop Hugh MacDonald, 20 August 1733; <u>Report of Bishop MacDonald to Propaganda</u>, 18 March 1732; F. Forbes and W. Anderson, 'Clergy lists of the Highland District, 1732-1828', <u>The Innes Review</u>, XXIX(I), (1968), pp.56-59; J. B. Craven (ed.), <u>Records of the Diocese of Argyll and the Isles, 1560-1860</u> (Kirkwall, 1907), pp.259-260.

63. SRO, CH 1/2/28/5, ff.455, 513; CH 1/2/37/4, f.275; CH 1/2/32/6, ff.547,552,566; CH 1/2/48, ff.205-205; CH 1/5/72, 25 October 1749, 22 November 1759.

64. SRO, CH 1/2/32/6, f.566.

65. SRO, CH 1/5/51, ff.1-3.

66. SRO, E.729 (1), 2, f.3.

67. SRO, CH 1/5/51, f.349.

68. SRO, GD 95.1.1., ff.1-3; GD 95.2.1., ff.9-10; CH 1/5/51, ff.2, 5, 57; CH 1/5/54, Committee Lists 1740; CH 1/5/68, ff.1-3, <u>passim</u>.

69. SRO, CH 1/5/51, f.3.

70. Ibid., ff.188-189.

71. Ibid., ff.9-10; f.73.

72. SRO, CH 1/5/72, 10 August 1758.

73. SRO, CH 1/5/51, ff.330-331.

74. SRO, CH 1/5/56, ff.24-25.

75. Edinburgh University Laing MSS Collection, La. MS 484, f.24.

76. Gaelic Schools Society Annual Report (hereinafter GSSAR, and the year in question), 1811, Laws and Regulations of the Society I, p.10.

77. GSSAR, 1825, pp.1-2.

78. GSSAR, 1811, pp.14-28; Moral Statistics of the Highlands and Islands of Scotland, compiled from returns received by the Inverness Society for the Education of the Poor in the Highlands (Inverness, 1826); Educational Statistics of the Highlands and Islands of Scotland, 1833 (Edinburgh, 1834).

79. Gaelic Schools were known as Sqoilean Chriosd, the 'Schools of Christ'.

80. GSSAR, 1811, Regulation IX.

81. GSSAR, 1815, p.25.

82. GSSAR, 1814, p.50; J. Low (ed.), New Statistical Account of Scotland (Edinburgh, 1831-1845), 7, pp.288-289. (Hereinafter NSA); 14, (1839), pp.322-323.

83. SRO, GD 95.9.3., ff.58-59.

84. GSSAR, 1833, p.12.

85. GSSAR, 1831,p.13; J. Sinclair, An Analysis of the Statistical Account of Scotland (Edinburgh, 1825), Pt.2., Appendix Ch.11, Para XII, p.27

86. GSSAR, 1835, p.36.

87. GSSAR, 1817, pp.32-37.

88. GSSAR, 1818, p.17; 1813, p.33.

89. GSSAR, 1815, p.31.

90. GSSAR, 1822, p.11.

91. SRO, GD 95.9.3., f.18.

92. J. Ramsay, A Letter to the Right Honourable the Lord Advocate of Scotland on the State of Education in the Outer Hebrides in 1862 (Glasgow, 1863), p.4.

93. SRO, CH 1/1/80, f.56; CH 2/106/14. ff.77-78; CH 2/66/7, ff.90-91; CH 2/106/16, ff.90-91; CH 1/1/103, f.264.

94. SRO, CH 1/1/103, f.264.

95. GSSAR, 1827, pp.11-12, 54.

96. First Report of the Ladies' Association in Support of Gaelic Schools in Connection with the Church of Scotland (Edinburgh, 1847), pp.9-15.

97. Fourth Annual Report of the Highland Missionary Society (Edinburgh, 1824), pp.5-6; D. E. Meek 'Evangelical missionaries in the early nineteenth century Highlands', Scottish Studies, 28, (1984), pp.1-34.

98. Extract from the Third Annual Report of the Auxiliary Society of Glasgow (31 January 1815) quoted in GSSAR, 1816, p.94.

99. Report of the General Assembly Committee for Increasing the Means of Education and Religious Instruction in the Highlands and Islands of Scotland (Edinburgh, 1828), p.30. (hereinafter Report, General Assembly).

100. Report, General Assembly, 1832, pp.18-19.

101. Report, General Assembly, 1828, p.17.

102. SRO, CH 1/2/172.

103. Report, General Assembly, 1832, p.19.

104. Educational Statistics..., (Edinburgh, 1834).

105. Education Commission (Scotland), Report on the State of Education in the Hebrides, Parl. Papers, XXV, (1867), p.52.

106. See, for example, M. Macleod, 'Gaelic in Highland Education', Transactions of the Gaelic Society of

Inverness, XLIII, (1966), pp.305-334.

107. Commission of Inquiry into the Condition of Crofters and Cottars in the Highlands and Islands of Scotland, 1884-1885, P.P., XXXII, p.81.

108. A review of recent legislation (c. 1872-1981) on Gaelic in education appears in my Gaelic in Scotland, pp.156-160, 242-246.

109. K. Williamson, 'Lowland Scots in Education: an historical survey', (Part I), Scottish Language, I, (1983), pp.54-77; (Part II) in 2, (1983), pp.52-87. quote from Part I, pp.61-62.

110. K. C. Phillips, Language and Class in Victorian England (Oxford, 1984).

4

POPULATION GROWTH AND THE TRANSFORMATION
OF HIGHLAND AGRICULTURE 1650-1891

> Has not Britain laid out much Greater Sums on
> Colonies abroad of not half the Importance of
> Civilising and Improving this part of Britain
> itself that has been so long a Nuisance and
> Reproach to the Nation? Besides when the Country
> is improved and Trade and Manufactures are
> thoroughly Established, it will repay with Large
> Interest any Expense laid out at present.1

Kirkwood in the 1690s identified four ways in which
Highland culture was then being undermined: 'By Colonies'
[of English speakers in the Highlands]; 'by scattering the
Highlanders all over the Nation'; 'By schools'; and 'By
sending their children to serve in other parts of the
Kingdom and so to learn English'.
    What is considered here are the processes transforming
what Kirkwood termed 'the Conveniences of Life' in the
Highlands, principally in agriculture, in limited industrial production, and more generally, too, in the customary
relationships between people and between people and land.
To the outside observer, it was these customary relationships and practices - the constituting bonds of clanship
with its emphasis on people not profit as the basis to
wealth in land; the practice of runrig; the attention given
to pastoralism and not arable produce as a source of income
- that characterised the region and its people as backward,
at an earlier 'stage' of culture, and in need of development. Improvement was to be centred upon agriculture and
industry

> At this time [c.1747] there is little
> _Agriculture_ in y^e _Highlands_, scarce any indus-
> try; their principal subsistence is by herds of
> Cattle. This probably occasions their great
> idleness, may contribute to their warlike spirit,
> & make depredations so frequent, which were never

175

at a greater height than for some years before ye late Rebellion wch might be one reason for so many resorting to ye Pretenders Standard w^t out ye least provocation from ye govt, as an opportunity for rapine & plunder. Indeed ye situation & nature of ye grounds in many places won't admitt of Agriculture; yet it is certain the country in some places might be cultivated & improved. The granting leases therefore to Tenants under proper Regulations, seems ye most natural scheme for improving such parts of the country as can admitt of agriculture. But what these regulations ought to be, it is impossible for one to suggest, being an entire Stranger to that country.

It is submitted if the introduction of Manufactures into the Highlands, would not prove another great mean to give ye low people in y^t country a taste of y^t independence & liberty, which ye other parts of ye Island have enjoyed ever since the Revolution, & would not prevent ye people's rising & joining in foolish attempts, to disturb ye peace of y^t government which supported & protected them from ye insults and oppressions of their Superiors.2

Yet 'Improvement', as this commentator was aware and more recent scholars have shown, is a vague word amenable of various definitions. The principal tenets, agriculture and industry, meant different things over time and in different parts of the Highlands. The concern of this chapter is in outlining the principal elements of Highland material transformation between about 1650 and 1890, to understand the main changes affecting the economic foundations to Highland life, and to consider what they meant for those involved.

We should not suppose that the Highlands enjoyed, at any time in their past, an unvaried, timeless harmony between people and land and that what is meant by transformation charts the passing of age-old rhythms between social uses and a given physical environment. It is to note that the social relations of production in Highland society, the natural bases on which they were founded, and the processes by which both Highlander and Highlands were transformed contained contradictions and variations, and have been always 'in a state of dynamic process'.

Highland society, from clan chiefs through tacksmen to tenants and subtenants, was based upon several mutually supporting principles: upon loyalty and an understood system of social obligations; upon the holding of land, principally for the grazing of cattle; upon a little arable which, although limited in distribution, and, in the eyes of Lowland farmers, out-dated and inefficient in organisation, was nevertheless productive on a small scale: in short, upon economic and social structures adapted (and adaptable) to given physical resources and accepted social purposes.

> Land in the Highlands, then, was laid out not so much to ensure an effective agricultural economy as to stabilise a class structure and to verify mutual obligations. It passed from proprietor to tacksman (or tenant), from tacksman to subtenant, from subtenant to cottar or servant. At each stage some ground would be kept in immediate occupation, but the rest would be handed down, as an earnest of kinship, or to ensure rent, loyalty, service, each rank linked with the next in mutual obligation. Yet agriculture had to proceed within the framework thus established, and the whole wealth of society, and not least of the aristocracy, depended upon an effective system of pasture and cultivation. There was constant conflict between the demands of productive efficiency and the old obligations of class to class.3

Relationship to land was, at once, demographic, economic, and moral: demographic in the sense of the significance attached to a numerous peasantry as well as in the division of land-holdings, population numbers and so on; economic, involving the production and reproduction of human life and the procedures established to that end within a limited physical environment and an established social system; and moral in the obligations and commitments within and between classes in that system and in the sentiment or consciousness, <u>duthchas</u> even, felt by all toward the social relations of which they were part. Changes in this relationship were also demographic, economic, and moral.

> The bonds of kinship and mutual obligations on which the clan was based effectively precluded the introduction of impersonal money relationships and it was consequently obvious to even the most casual of eighteenth century observers that if a clan's lands were to produce a worth-while rental for its chief the multiple gradations of the traditional society would have to be swept away

177

and the land let directly to men who were willing
and able to work it efficiently and to pay a
realistic money rent for the privilege of so
doing.4

The shift in Highland life toward new demands is first
widely apparent from the later 1700s, but, like so much
else, has its roots in the 1600s and in certain causes more
than others. It begins with Highland landowners, works
downwards through the social hierarchy and outwards from
the south-west and central Highlands in particular. In the
agricultural bases to material life, change begins with a
rise in rents and money income based on the profits from
cattle. It begins also with enclosure, the gradual removal
of runrig, the more general adoption of leases, and with
the weakening of social ties in which the departure of the
tacksman was an important part of the processes of class
polarisation. From the second decade of the nineteenth
century, however, in consequence of falling profits from
kelp, declining cattle prices, and the replacement of
traditional ways by sheep farming on hitherto
unprecendented scales, the economic foundations to Highland
life were much altered. Additionally, from this period,
Highland society had an increasing dependence upon potato
cultivation; a dependence shattered by the Malthusian
crises of the late 1830s and 1840s. The period from the
destitution of 1847-1849 to the Crofters Act of 1886 was,
to an extent, one of recovery. But it was also marked by
the continued sale of estates, the replacement of sheep by
deer, and by continued dependence on limited agricultural
output and part-time industrial pursuits prone to
externally-derived fluctuations in demand and price. Linked
with these events and crucially important in shaping their
specific historical form, were the facts of population
growth and decline.

THE DEMOGRAPHIC FOUNDATIONS TO MATERIAL TRANSFORMATION,
c.1690-1891

Not all is known of the population question in Highland
Scotland, but demographic issues cannot be ignored in
explanation of changes in the production and reproduction
of material life: for Flinn, 'to leave the demographic
developments out of the picture is like presenting Hamlet
without the Prince of Denmark'.5 Two principal themes are
considered in setting demographic issues as foundation to
an examination of material transformation: first, totals,
rates of change, and the geographical patterns of
population change; second, the mechanisms and effect of

population change.

Totals, rates of change, and the geography of population change

The first accurate source for assessment of Highland (and Scottish) population totals is Webster's 1755 'Account of the Number of People in Scotland'.6   Although late seventeenth century poll tax and hearth tax records have been used to calculate population totals for areas partly Highland, general coverage is patchy and evidence must be used with care.7 This deficiency of records for the late seventeenth century is unfortunate since it is likely that one effect of the famine and relative mortality crises that characterised the Highlands in the 1690s may have been a reduction in population growth rate sufficient to postpone that demographic pressure upon resources which so marked Highland affairs from the later eighteenth century. The fact that before 1755 there is no source from which it is possible to estimate a total Highland, or Scottish, population and hence to assess growth rates means we cannot be certain of the longer-term trends in growth in Highland population before the mid-eighteenth century. Nor can we be sure of the degree of short-term instability, particularly in mortality, that would have determined population growth or decline in a region and period whose principal demographic control was recurrent mortality crises, largely from famine and epidemic disease. There were serious crises due to famine in the Highlands in 1604 and 1650, and at other times in the 1600s, Highlanders sought relief from hardship occasioned by cattle murrain or crop failure through visitation to the Lowlands.8 Thus, whilst 1755 is our starting point for investigation of Highland population totals and rates of change, we should not assume preceding periods to have been characterised by some sort of demographic 'stability' nor set out to examine events after 1755 without regard to these earlier patterns.

In 1755, using Webster's Census, Scotland had a population of 1,265,380 persons.9 The four principal Highland counties had a total population in 1755 of 194,707 (15.4 per cent of the national total: Table 4.1a). By 1801, the Highland population (understood here as the population of the counties of Argyll, Ross and Cromarty, Inverness, and Sutherland) had grown to 233,384 persons; 14.5 per cent of the national total. Highland population continued to increase until 1841 - 298,637 persons in the four counties (11.4 per cent of Scotland's total) - from which date, Highland population declined to 264,026 persons

Table 4.1
Population totals and intercensal population change (percentage changes), Highland counties, 1775–1891*

(a) Population totals

Counties	1755	1801	1811	1821	1831	1841	1851	1861	1871	1881	1891
HIGHLANDS	194,707	233,384	248,694	279,879	296,108	298,637	294,298	275,264	268,482	268,839	264,026
Argyll	66,286	81,277	86,541	97,316	100,973	97,371	89,298	79,724	75,679	76,468	75,003
Inverness	59,563	72,672	77,671	89,961	94,797	97,799	96,500	88,888	87,531	90,454	89,317
Ross and Cromarty	48,084	55,318	60,853	68,762	74,820	78,685	82,707	81,406	80,955	78,547	77,810
Sutherland	20,774	23,117	23,629	23,840	25,518	24,782	25,793	25,246	24,317	23,370	21,896
[SCOTLAND]	[1,265,380]	[1,608,420]	[1,805,864]	[2,091,521]	[2,364,386]	[2,620,184]	[2,888,742]	[3,062,294]	[3,360,018]	[3,735,573]	[4,025,647]

(b) Intercensal population change

Counties	1755–1801	1801–11	1811–21	1821–31	1831–41	1841–51	1851–61	1861–71	1871–81	1881–91
					Periods					
HIGHLANDS	19.86	6.56	12.53	5.79	0.85	-1.45	-6.46	-2.46	0.13	-1.79
Argyll	22.61	6.47	12.45	3.75	-3.56	-8.29	-10.72	-5.07	1.04	-1.91
Inverness	22.01	6.87	5.82	5.37	3.16	-1.32	-7.88	-1.52	3.33	-1.25
Ross and Cromarty	17.12	8.05	12.99	8.81	5.16	5.09	-1.57	-0.55	-2.97	-0.93
Sutherland	11.27	2.21	0.89	5.78	-2.88	4.07	-2.12	-3.67	-3.89	-6.30
[SCOTLAND]	[27.10]	[12.27]	[15.81]	[13.04]	[10.81]	[10.24]	[6.00]	[9.72]	[11.17]	[7.76]

*Based on Webster 1755 in Kyd (1952), and Census of Scotland.

in 1891 (6.5 of the national total.) The general pattern
of increasing population until the mid-1800s, followed by
decline in the second half of the nineteenth century, is
differently reflected in individual counties: Argyll
reached its maximum population in 1831, Inverness in 1841,
Ross and Cromarty and Sutherland in 1851. And at the level
of the parish, population totals and rates of growth varied
considerably. With the exception of Lochs whose total
population declined after 1891, every other parish in Lewis
and Harris continued to increase until 1911: elsewhere, the
parishes of the western islands (with the exception of
Barra), were in decline no later than 1851. Our knowledge
of quite when Highland population, at parish, district, or
regional level, reached the point of being too many for
available resources, regardless of numerical maximum, is
less certain.

> It is not possible to set a precise date or even
> decade to the moment when the pressure of Highland
> and Hebridean populations began to press against
> the limits of the capacity of their usable
> resources of land. But evidence, principally in
> the form of substantial emigration, begins to
> suggest that these limits were being approached
> after the middle of the eighteenth century.10

A number of sources that give totals for Highland parishes
at various dates have provided some insight into the growth
of population. Population totals survive for parts of
Caithness in 1722; are included in estate surveys - the
population statistics of the Annexed Estates, for example,
or for Assynt in 1774, or the Argyll Estates in the 1770s -
cover individual parishes over time (Tiree from 1747 to
1808), and provide listings of wider areas at one time -
for 1748, 1750 - or, as in Walker's enumerations, for 1764,
1771, and 1778.11 The Old Statistical Account (1791-1799)
also provides demographic information useful in assessing
totals and rates of growth in Highland population, but the
fact that the volumes were compiled over a period of time
makes their use problematic. Though of limited value in
charting Highland-wide demographic changes, such sources
are valuable in illuminating regional diversity in the
Highland population experience. Cregeen has shown that
from the evidence of the Duke of Argyll's estates, for
example, population there increased by 25 per cent between
1779 and 1792.12 Dodgshon notes that in Ardnamurchan and
Sunart, population rose by almost 90 per cent between 1723
and 1792, two-thirds of the increase occurring after
1755.13 On Tiree, population rose from 1,500 in 1747, to

1,997 in 1770, to 3,308 in 1787, and 3,443 by 1792; even by
1771, the Duke of Argyll described the island as
'over-peopled, and my farms oppress'd with a numerous set
of indigent tenants and cottars'.14 Walker's figures for
the population of thirty-two island parishes for several
dates between 1750 and 1798 and parts of the mainland
Highlands in 1778 are probably suspect for some individual
totals, but the suggestion of a 20 per cent net increase in
population for the period 1755 to 1798 is not unreasonable
given other evidence.15

Assessment of net rates of intercensal population
change reveal that, as a region, Highland population
increased by 19.9 per cent between 1755 and 1801, a
markedly lower rate of increase than for Scotland as a
whole (Table 4.1b). The opening decade of the nineteenth
century saw a 6.6 per cent increase in Highland population,
with a greater rate of increase - 12.5 per cent - in the
period 1811 to 1821. The decline in Highland population
growth begins in the decade 1841-1851 with a decrease of
1.5 per cent. This overall decline was maintained (with
the exception of the years 1871 to 1881), throughout the
nineteenth century and into the twentieth: 'Highland
population declined more slowly than it had grown ... The
rise of population from the first census to its peak on the
eve of the potato famine of the 1840s took just over forty
years: the reversion to 1801 levels took nearly one
hundred years'.16 As Table 4.1 shows, the general pattern
of rising totals and markedly greater rates of change in
the first half of the nineteenth century than in the second
half is not repeated directly at county level. Assessment
at district and parish level reveals further regional
variation in rate of population change (Table 4.2). The
parishes making up the Outer Hebrides, for example,
continued to increase in population throughout the nineteenth century. Other island parishes experienced
similarly high rates of growth in the period 1755 to 1801
before beginning decline by mid-century or, as in the case
of Mull, in the period 1821 to 1831. On the mainland, the
experience of the north and west, particularly Ross and
Cromarty, was not much different from other parts of the
Highlands in terms of net rate of growth between 1755 and
1801, but during the nineteenth century, Wester Ross had a
longer period and higher rate of increase than other
mainland areas. These regional and local variations in the
growth of Highland population are of fundamental importance. Of the parishes making up the Highland counties, 41
per cent (53 parishes of 128) had begun to decline by 1831,
even though the population of the region continued to grow
until 1841. Earlier, Walker enumerated fifty-six mainland

Table 4.2

Intercensal population change (percentage changes) in selected Highland districts and parishes, 1755–1891*

Area	Intercensal Periods									
	1755–1801	1801–11	1811–21	1821–31	1831–41	1841–51	1851–61	1861–71	1871–81	1881–91
Islands										
Outer Hebrides[1]	59.24	12.76	20.39	8.75	11.09	0.95	1.21	8.36	8.48	5.09
Skye[2]	40.31	7.86	22.30	9.40	1.29	-2.36	-12.37	-6.46	-2.16	-6.87
Mull[3]	61.50	9.88	13.09	-0.69	-4.49	-16.84	-12.40	-12.14	-12.68	-9.74
Tiree and Coll	32.55	4.95	0.47	5.95	1.10	-17.41	-17.20	-10.73	-5.16	-11.90
Mainland										
North and West Sutherland[4]	11.90	0.81	0.96	18.43	-1.32	-2.98	1.71	-4.48	-5.20	-4.13
Wester Ross[5]	48.27	23.80	28.05	2.24	2.89	-5.96	0.31	-6.29	-8.46	-8.19
Central Grampians[6]	-14.08	11.67	5.16	5.67	-6.39	2.25	-3.61	-1.95	-9.95	-0.04
Black Isle[7]	22.74	2.39	-2.72	8.94	3.13	6.43	-10.65	-7.40	-10.06	-4.01
Kintyre[8]	41.57	6.93	13.75	0.63	-6.67	-8.41	-11.90	-1.63	3.40	1.73

* Based on Webster 1755 in Kyd (1952), Census of Scotland; see also M.W. Flinn, 'Malthus, Emigration and Potatoes in the Scottish North-west 1770–1870' in L.M. Cullen and T.C. Smout (eds.), Comparative Aspects of Scottish and Irish Economic and Social History 1600–1900 (Edinburgh, 1976), p.48.

Table 4.2 (Continued)

1   Parishes of Barvas, Lochs, Stornoway, Uig, Harris, Barra, North Uist, South Uist.

2   Parishes of Bracadale, Duirinish, Kilmuir, Portree, Sleat, Snizort, Strath.

3   Parishes of Kilfinichen and Kilviceon, Kilninian and Kilmore, Torosay.

4   Parishes of Assynt, Eddrachillis, Durness, Tongue, Farr.

5   Parishes of Applecross, Gairloch, Glensheil, Kintail, Lochalsh, Lochbroom, Lochcarron.

6   Parishes of Abernethy and Kincardine, Alvie, Duthil and Rothiemurchus, Kingussie, Laggan.

7   Parishes of Avoch, Cromarty, Killearnan, Knockbain, Resolis, Rosemarkie, Urquhart and Logie
     Wester.

8   Parishes of Campbeltown, Kilcalmonell, Killean and Kilchenzie, North Knapdale, Saddell and
     Skipness, Southend, South Knapdale.

Population Growth and Highland Agriculture

Highland parishes whose populations had declined between 1755 and the Old Statistical Account, and an additional seventeen in the Highland border parishes of Dumbarton, Argyll, and Perth.17 Gray claims an east-west regional dichotomy in the Highland demographic experience;18 a dichotomy in which the north and west parishes had markedly higher rates of increase than the south and east Highlands (Table 4.2). This regional diversity of population experience and the geographical shifts over time in the areas of high or moderate rate of increase is evident in mapping the percentage population changes from the mid-eighteenth century onwards (Figures 4.1 - 4.3). In the period 1755 to 1801, several north and west parishes more than doubled their population - South Uist, Lochalsh - whilst others more numerous had increases in excess of 50 per cent. But in the eastern slopes of the Highlands, population totals declined over this period (Figure 4.1). By the first half of the nineteenth century, however, to quote Gray, 'the area of disproportionately greater increase has moved slightly to the north; northern Argyll and, indeed, parts of Inverness-shire must now be placed in the southern group'. Some southern parishes increased their population in the period 1801 to 1851, but the far north and west exhibited a continued disproportionate increase in population which, for some parishes, entailed a trebling in the century from 1755, and for all but six in that area, involved a doubling (cf. Figure 4.1 and 4.2). By the second half of the nineteenth century, with the exception of parts of the north and west islands and some Highland mainland parishes centred upon towns - Campbeltown, Inverness, and Dunoon, for example - the region as a whole was losing population (Figure 4.3).

These maps disguise 'local thickening' of population. In southern Kintyre, for example, examination of population distribution from censuses of 1779 and 1792 has revealed a settlement pattern concentrated on land below 500 feet, with considerable coastal clustering on the more fertile soils in the south and west of the Kintyre peninsula.19 Elsewhere throughout Argyll, and in other parts of the western seaboard, both the general coastal distribution of clachan and single farm sites and the actual linear-rectilinear form of the clachans themselves points to a settlement geography in the eighteenth and nineteenth centuries that reflects in its situation on the better lands the overall trends of population growth and the particular nature of agrarian improvement in given localities and, later, in the desertion of clachans and farms, the general facts of Highland depopulation.20 In other parts of the Highlands, population change created and

Figure 4.1   Percentage rates of population change in the Highlands, 1755–1801

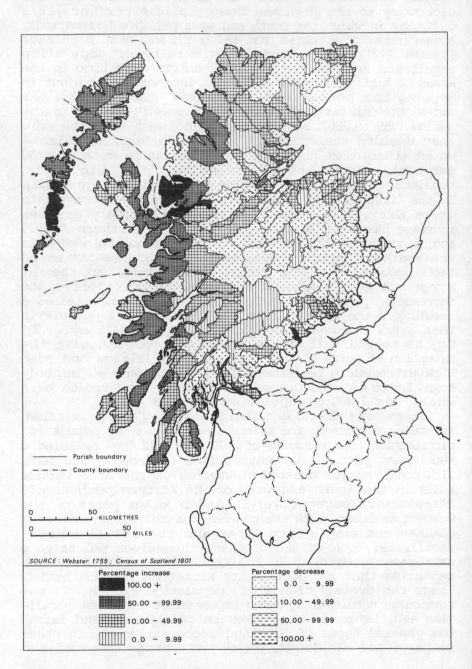

Parish boundary
County boundary

0   50
KILOMETRES
0   50
MILES

SOURCE : Webster 1755 ; Census of Scotland 1801

Percentage increase	Percentage decrease
100.00 +	0.0 – 9.99
50.00 – 99.99	10.00 – 49.99
10.00 – 49.99	50.00 – 99.99
0.0 – 9.99	100.00 +

186

Population Growth and Highland Agriculture

Figure 4.2   Percentage rates of population change
             in the Highlands, 1801–1851

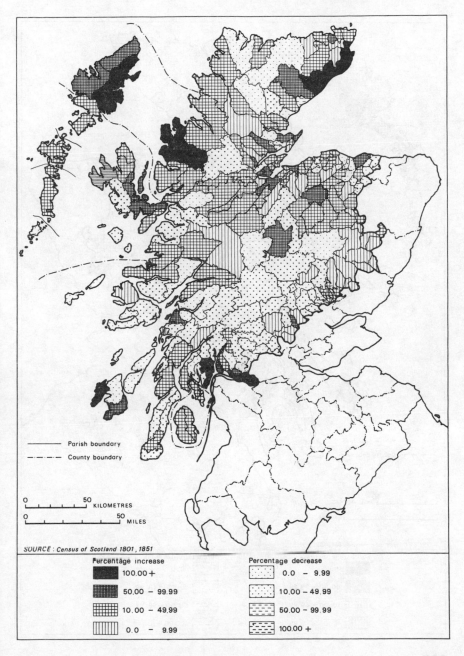

Parish boundary

County boundary

0 ____ 50 KILOMETRES

0 ____ 50 MILES

SOURCE : Census of Scotland 1801, 1851

Percentage increase

100.00 +

50.00 – 99.99

10.00 – 49.99

0.0 – 9.99

Percentage decrease

0.0 – 9.99

10.00 – 49.99

50.00 – 99.99

100.00 +

Population Growth and Highland Agriculture

Figure 4.3   Percentage rates of population change
             in the Highlands, 1851-1891

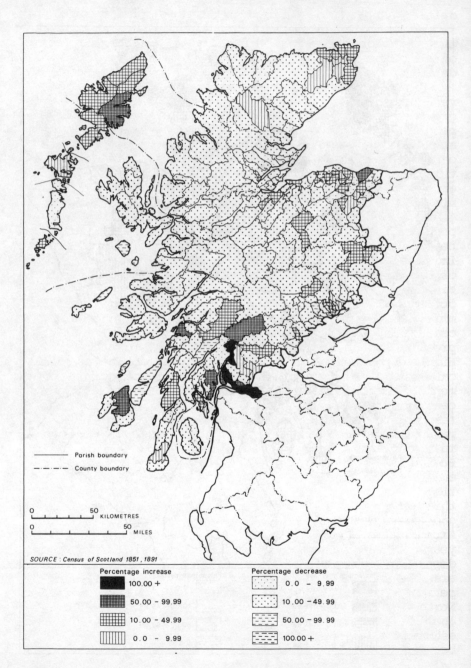

Parish boundary

County boundary

0 ——— 50 KILOMETRES

0 ——— 50 MILES

SOURCE : Census of Scotland 1851 , 1891

Percentage increase		Percentage decrease	
■	100.00 +		0.0 - 9.99
	50.00 - 99.99		10.00 - 49.99
	10.00 - 49.99		50.00 - 99.99
	0.0 - 9.99		100.00 +

destroyed settlement geography as in Sutherland, for example, where clearance in 1831 from the Strath of Kildonan removed one pattern of distribution to create another on the coasts in fishing villages such as Helmsdale.21 And in the Grampian uplands, the retreat of settlement in the later 1700s from the margins of cultivation on the higher slopes in consequence of changing levels of arable production is hinted at but not recorded in detail by the maps of percentage change in population.22

Explanation of these regional and chronological variations in the totals and rate of Highland population growth rests, in part, upon the particular balance between people and resources in the places concerned and in part also upon the policies of landlords (see below). It rests chiefly, however, upon the differential impact of migration. In comparison with Scotland as a whole, the rates of growth in both the late eighteenth century and the early nineteenth century Highlands were relatively low (Table 4.1b). This, and given that the natural increase of population in the early 1800s in the Highlands must have been close to 10 per cent per decade, has been taken to indicate that out-migration was reducing the rate of growth of Highland population from a very early point in the history of the modern rise of population. This was occasioned by overseas migration and by differential migration from the Highlands to the Lowlands. In briefly considering here emigration as a response to population pressure and as mechanisms affecting the growth rate of Highland population, we are limited by a lack of statistical evidence to support the available contemporary comment. We know from several sources of the late eighteenth century that emigration from the Highlands was even then a response to over-crowding and poor harvests as well as the particular circumstances pertaining to Highland settlement in North America after 1763.23 The alarmist remark of Boswell, who, having witnessed the departure of Skye emigrants in 1773, spoke of 'the present rage for emigration', is belied by the relatively small totals leaving in this period. There is evidence of 831 people leaving Ross and Cromarty in 1772-73, of 288 persons leaving Bute and Argyll, and 735 from estates in Sutherland in the same years. Home Office papers record 2,773 and 3,607 persons departing Scotland in 1774 and 1775, the majority Highlanders. We know also of movement from individual parishes: 50 persons from Glenorchy and 77 from Appin in 1775, bound for North Carolina; 150 from Kilmorack in 1801; from Ardnamurchan in 1790; and from Bracadale in 1778 and 1790. The estimated total of 4,000 persons reckoned to have left Skye between 1769 and 1773 - perhaps 20 per cent of the population of the Island was certainly a large loss, but given the probable rate of natural increase of population at that period, these numbers would quickly have been replaced.24 For the Highlands, it is difficult to know the extent to which emigration reduced the rate of population growth. The low rate of the first decade of the 1800s may be partly explained by enlistment in the armed services during the French wars, with demobilisation in the following decade part responsible for the greater rate of growth then. Emigration from the 1830s onwards, to Australia as well as to North America, is more susceptible to numerical investigation. About 100,000 Scots emigrated between 1851 and 1855. Although there is no way of knowing the number of Highlanders in this total, the low natural increase rates suggest that the north and west Highlands - those areas of most rapid growth before 1851 - lost over one-third of its population, perhaps 60,000 persons, between about 1841 and 1854.

To the impact of permanent emigration, only part responsible for overall loss of Highland population before about 1841 but more significant after this date, we must add permanent and temporary migration to the Lowlands. The former cannot be numerically assessed until 1851, the latter is virtually impossible to quantify. Temporary Highland migration to the Lowlands had both demographic and economic effects.25 The temporary movement south of young men and women, and, later in the nineteenth century of members of the older age ranges, altered the age- and sex-structure of the Highland population, the reduction in number of younger partners being particularly responsible for delay in marriage and thus a decline in marital fertility. Temporary movement was, on the one hand an important source of cash income for the Highland economy and of labour for Lowland industries and agriculture, and on the other, a factor acting to alter the constituent demographic structures of Highland population, and to do so differently over time and across space. Gray argues that the east and central Highlands channelled many more persons to the Lowlands than the north and west, and it was this differential out-movement that was responsible for the observed regional dichotomy in rate of growth.26 Although little statistical proof can be adduced for regional variation in migration before the mid-1800s, the evidence from the 1851 census reports onwards of inter-county migration supports this general claim. Most permanent movement from the Highlands was from Argyllshire, Highland Perthshire, and Inverness-shire and was directed toward the towns of the west-central Lowlands (Figure 4.4). Movement to east central Lowland towns was chiefly from the central

Figure 4.4 Highland migration to Paisley, 1851

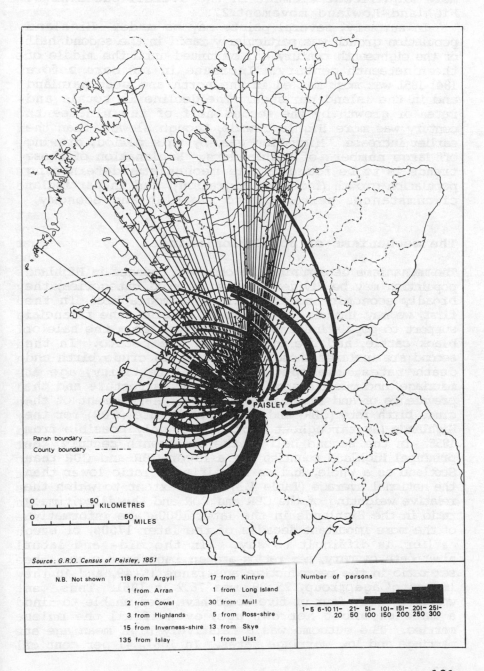

Parish boundary
County boundary

PAISLEY

0   50
|_____| KILOMETRES

0   50
|_____| MILES

Source : G.R.O. Census of Paisley, 1851

N.B. Not shown	118 from Argyll	17 from Kintyre
	1 from Arran	1 from Long Island
	2 from Cowal	30 from Mull
	3 from Highlands	5 from Ross-shire
	15 from Inverness-shire	13 from Skye
	135 from Islay	1 from Uist

Number of persons

1-5 6-10 11-   21-   51- 101- 151- 201- 251-
            20   50   100   150   200   250   300

Grampian parishes, Highland Perthshire, and eastern Ross and Cromarty (Figure 4.5). Only later in the nineteenth century was Highland migration from the north and west a more significant element in the overall patterns of Highland-Lowland movement.27

In summary, several points may be made. Highland population growth was particularly rapid in the second half of the eighteenth century and continued until the middle of the nineteenth century. Increase in numbers before 1841-1851 was most marked in the north and west mainland and in the island parishes. The decline in totals and rates of growth by the second half of the nineteenth century was more Highland-wide, though slower, than the earlier increase. Migration was, by this period, drawing off large numbers of Highlanders. Explanation of these trends is to be found in the mechanisms determining population growth (including migration), and in particular circumstances pertaining to the Highland economy.

The mechanisms of population change

The mechanisms determining the observed changes in Highland population may be divided into two related categories; the broadly economic and the strictly demographic. In the first, we may include the impact of kelping, the financial support to population expansion derived from the sale of black cattle, and the influence of the potato. In the second are included those factors such as crude birth and death rates, age-specific marital fertility, age at marriage, and questions on age- and sex-structure and the prevalence of and response to disease. Assessment of the crude birth rate (CBR) and crude death rate (CDR) for the Highlands (as throughout Scotland) is only possible from 1855. In the second half of the nineteenth century, the principal Highland counties had a lower CBR and CDR than Scotland as a whole, and an illegitimacy ratio lower than the national average (Table 4.3). The extent to which the relative weighting of the CBR and CDR and the illegitimacy ratio in the Highlands in the later 1800s are informative of the more important decades of the later 1700s, or even earlier, is difficult to say. In the mid- and later nineteenth century, sex ratios are an important clue. The sex ratio in the reproductive age-range 15-49, and in the 'marrying' age group, 25-29, was 76.2 in 1861. Thus, one women in every four or five would have been unable to find a mate of about her own age, even if all the males married. The outcome was a relatively high mean age at marriage and low marriage rates. In 1861, 41 per cent of

Figure 4.5   Highland migration to Dundee, 1851

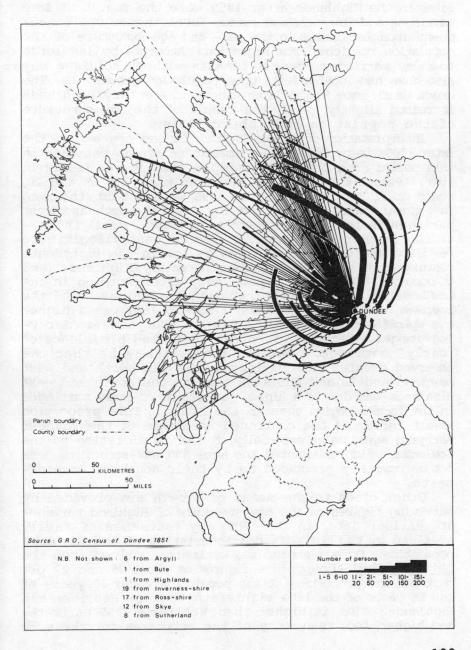

Parish boundary ─────
County boundary ─·─·─·─

0   50
└──────────┘ KILOMETRES

0   50
└──────────┘ MILES

Source: G.R.O., Census of Dundee 1851

N.B. Not shown :   6 from Argyll
                   1 from Bute
                   1 from Highlands
                  19 from Inverness-shire
                  17 from Ross-shire
                  12 from Skye
                   8 from Sutherland

Number of persons

1-5 6-10 11- 21- 51- 101- 151-
          20 50 100 150 200

women aged 25-29 in the Highland counties were married in
contrast to the national figure of 54 per cent. Given that
illegitimacy rates were low, and that age-specific marital
fertility rates were generally low (in comparison with
Scotland as a whole), it is likely that low crude birth
rates in the Highlands after 1855 were the result of late
marriages and low marriage rates, facts themselves consequent upon imbalances in the sex- and age-structure of the
population resulting from migration. Attempts by landlords
to delay marriages amongst tenants without holdings may
also have had local effects upon population growth. 28 The
crude death rate in the later nineteenth-century Highlands
increased slightly, partly the result of the age structure
of the population and tuberculosis.

Interpretation of these factors in the context of the
later 1700s is problematic. Comments on age at marriage in
this period note only, for example, that it was 'early in
life'. Pennant in 1772 records 'men marrying at age 20,
women at 17'.29 For Creich in 1793 we are told 'the men,
in general, marry young', and for several north and west
parishes in the 1790s - Harris, Lochalsh, Small Isles -
similar comments are made.30 Given that illegitimate
fertility was, so far as we know, as low in the eighteenth
century as it was in the nineteenth-century Highlands (and
it occurred often through pregnancy after working in the
Lowlands),31 it is probable that one principal means of the
increase in population between 1755 and 1801 was a higher
age-specific marital fertility rate in the younger 'marrying' ranges especially, given the suggested prevalence of
'early' marriage. And, in turn, it may be that the
observed greater rate of increase in the north and west
mainland and island parishes than in the south and east
Highlands was due to a higher proportion of early marriages
in the former region than in the latter. This proportion
itself reflected the continued residence of the younger
marrying ages, males especially, for whom migration to the
Lowlands, which unbalanced the age- and sex-structure, was
not as commonly practiced as by their southern counterparts.

Other clues to the means of growth are provided by
surviving figures on the age-structure of Highland parishes
at various dates in the 1700s, by estimates of family
size, and by the mortality characteristics of the Highland
population. On age-structure, estimates derived from the
Old Statistical Account give figures of about 26 and 27 per
cent for the proportion of the population under 10 years of
age in parts of the late eighteenth-century Hebrides and
Highlands. This is higher than Webster's 1755 estimates
and higher, too, than many of the estimates for the more

Table 4.3

Crude birth rates, crude death rates, and illegitimacy ratios by Highland counties, 1855-1895*

(a) Crude Birth Rates[1]

| | Periods | | | | | | | |
	1855-60	1861-65	1866-70	1871-75	1876-80	1881-85	1886-90	1891-95
Argyll	26.4	26.9	27.0	25.7	26.1	25.6	24.5	22.4
Inverness	25.3	27.4	27.8	26.5	26.8	25.7	24.5	23.9
Ross and Cromarty	27.9	27.7	26.5	25.1	25.0	26.1	24.9	24.3
Sutherland	24.0	22.9	17.6	22.1	23.6	23.0	22.4	21.9
[Scotland]	[34.1]	[35.1]	[34.9]	[35.0]	[34.8]	[33.3]	[31.4]	[30.5]

(b) Crude Death Rates[2]

	1855-60	1861-65	1866-70	1871-75	1876-80	1881-85	1886-90	1891-95
Argyll	16.3	18.5	17.9	19.2	19.0	17.1	16.6	17.3
Inverness	14.9	18.0	17.7	18.0	17.0	16.8	15.7	17.6
Ross and Cromarty	15.5	17.4	15.6	16.8	16.0	15.7	15.9	17.2
Sutherland	13.7	15.4	12.0	16.2	16.5	16.0	16.2	17.3
[Scotland]	[20.8]	[22.1]	[22.0]	[22.7]	[20.6]	[19.6]	[18.8]	[19.0]

Table 4.3 (Continued)

(c) Illegitimacy Ratios[3]

Argyll	6.62	6.91	7.84	7.77	7.81	7.35	7.62	7.97
Inverness	7.57	7.96	8.01	8.40	8.16	7.59	8.13	7.42
Ross and Cromarty	3.84	4.24	4.86	4.57	4.54	4.78	5.08	4.79
Sutherland	3.78	5.23	6.07	6.90	6.58	7.36	6.53	5.72
[Scotland]	[8.74]	[9.79]	[9.85]	[9.09]	[8.49]	[8.27]	[8.04]	[7.41]

* From Detailed Annual Report of the Registrar-General for Scotland quoted, with permission, from M.W. Flinn, Scottish Population History from the 17th century to the 1930s (Cambridge, 1977), pp.339-340; 350-1; 380-1: Tables 5.3.1., 5.4.1., 5.5.5.

1 Live births per 1000 living, averages of five-year periods.

2 Annual average deaths per 1000 living, averages of five-year periods.

3 Number of illegitimate births per 100 live births, averages of five-year periods.

southern of the Annexed Estates in 1755-1756 (Table 4.4).
These high percentages under 10 years of age suggest a high
birth rate. Estimates derived from these age-structures of
a CBR of 40.31 in the Highlands in the 1790s with a CDR of
24.81 support this claim.32 Detailed estimates for Small
Isles parish in 1764 lend weight to our speculations.
Figures suggest high proportions of total population in the
0-9 age range which, together with a large household size
and reported early marriages, testifies to a high birth
rate and growth in numbers in what we have seen to be a
period and region of particular interest. Estimates of
family size suggest an increase during the later 1700s.
Walker records that a family size of five 'is the best
number that can be allowed for the Highlands and Islands in
general'. He continues 'there is reason to think, that
five and a half would be a nearer calculation . . . the
cause is obvious . . . a greater frequency of marriage'.
33 Estimates of family size from the population statistics
of the Annexed Estates give an average figure of 4.86
persons (Table 4.4). Evidence upon family size and upon
regionally different trends in family size (though both
suggestive of increase in population) needs to be treated
cautiously since both depend upon mortality characteristics
as well as upon fertility rates.

From what is known of mortality in the seventeenth
century, plague and other epidemic diseases were never as
serious nor as widespread in the Highlands as in the
Lowlands, with the possible exception of the plague in
parts of Argyll in the mid-seventeenth century. The
effects of continued harvest failure in the 'seven ill
years' at the end of the 1600s in the Highlands may have
been localised and seasonal mortality crises (though the
varying survival of sources must be taken into account),
with disease (probably typhus) playing a large part in the
mortality. In the 1700s, dearth was no distant memory and
bad harvests in 1740, 1756, 1782 and 1799 likewise prompted
localised peaks in mortality in addition to a more general
out-movement from the Highlands. Cattle murrain and
disease had influenced similar movement in the 1600s.

In the eighteenth century, reports upon the incidence
of smallpox point to that disease and inoculation against
it, as significant mechanisms of population change. Most
of the western isles had smallpox outbreaks of varying
severity during the 1700s; locally severe were outbreaks
of 1784 and 1792.34 Inoculation had been begun in Scotland
in 1726, but was not begun in the isles until 1764.35
Though it was often met with prejudice and misunderstand-
ing, inoculation against smallpox was widely held to have
increased the survival rate and, therefore, population

totals overall by the late 1700s. Reports in the Old Statistical Account for Kilmuir, Duirinish, Strath, and Snizort on Skye, and also for North Uist, Kilmuir Easter, and Logierait all make reference to inoculation against smallpox reducing mortality and permitting population growth, but even in the central Highlands where inoculation was earlier widely practised, difficulties of travel compounded with local opposition meant that not all were inoculated.36 Local outbreaks of smallpox continued to influence the death rate in those parts in 1775 and 1776, for example, and in Lewis in 1820, distrust of inoculation allowed smallpox to spread with severe consequences.37 Infant mortality was generally high, though whether as severe as Adam Smith's remark about it being not uncommon 'for a mother who had borne twenty children not to have two alive'38 is unlikely, even with what few statistics exist.

Other diseases prevalent in the eighteenth century were what locals called 'epidemical fevers', consumption, and an increased incidence of 'civens' or 'cevennes', a form of gonorrhoea introduced by communication with the Lowlands.39 The introduction of cholera and typhus as 'low country' diseases in this way was of greater significance in the 1820s and 1830 especially, and in following decades added to the prevalence of disease associated with failure of the potato crop. The principal source of mortality through disease in the nineteenth century Highlands was tuberculosis.

Speaking of the Hebrides in the 1760s, Walker considered three factors the chief causes of population increase:

> . . . the introduction of inoculation, the manufacture of kelp, and the cultivation of potatoes. By the first the lives of the multitudes are saved; by the second, the quantity of labour, and by the third, the quantity of food has been greatly enlarged.40

This review in brief of the demographic mechanisms of increase for the Highlands as a whole would include, for the later eighteenth century, a high crude birth rate reflecting a high rate of age-specific marital fertility, low illegitimacy rates, and an early age at marriage, the latter perhaps more common in the north and west. Rapid growth of population is indicated, too, by increased family size and relatively high proportions in the younger age ranges. Continued out-movement, different in scale and timing between the north-west and south-east Highlands allowed the areas nearer the Lowlands to shed excess population from the later 1700s, and to build up in the

Table 4.4

Population statistics of the Annexed Estates, 1755–1756*

Estate or barony	Total Population	Proportion of Population under 10 yrs. (as % of total population)	Proportion of Population over 10 yrs. (as % of total population)	Mean Family Size (No. of persons)
Amprior Estate,				
Strathyre barony	289	32.5	67.5	4.1
Barrisdale Estate	249	30.9	69.1	5.9
Cromarty Estate,				
Coigach barony	896	26.9	73.1	5.4
New Tarbat barony[1]	372	16.7	83.3	4.9
New Tarbat barony[2]	151	25.2	74.8	5.0
Strathpeffer barony	780	22.1	77.9	4.5
Lovat Estate,				
Stratherrick barony[3]	869	32.5	67.5	5.7
Lovat barony[4]	597	30.3	69.7	7.4
Lovat barony	630	35.4	64.6	5.5
Beauly barony	835	28.6	71.4	5.9
Monaltrie Estate	139	30.9	69.1	5.6
Struan Estate,				
Slisgarrow barony	516	34.1	65.9	4.6

(Continued overleaf.)

Table 4.4 (Continued)

Kinloch & Murlaggan barony	211	29.9	70.1	3.9
Fearnan barony	286	29.7	70.3	4.6
Glen Errochty & Invervack barony	214	29.9	70.1	4.1
Perth Estate,				
Lix barony	128	34.4	65.6	4.6
Balquhidder barony	257	26.5	73.5	3.8
Comrie barony	777	29.5	70.5	4.3
[Strowan parish]5	99	40.4	59.6	4.7
Muthill parish	1638	25.9	74.1	4.1
Auchterarder barony	261	24.9	75.1	4.2
Kinbuck barony	194	21.1	78.9	5.9
Callander barony	630	22.2	77.8	5.1
Strathgartney barony	414	27.8	72.2	4.1
Milnab barony 6	778	24.8	75.2	3.8
Stobhall barony	1122	24.0	76.0	4.7

* Based on V. Wills, Statistics of the Annexed Estates (Edinburgh, 1973)
1 So much as lies in Kilmuir Easter parish
2 So much as lies in Logie Easter parish
3 So much as lies in Kirkhill parish
4 So much as lies in Kiltarlity parish
5 No barony given
6 Including both the liferented and unliferented parts of the Estate

more distant parishes in the same period. Decline in population in the north and west in the nineteenth century was due to delay in marriage resulting from an imbalance in the age- and sex-structures following migration. To these demographic causes, we must add broadly economic factors; to Walker's potato and kelp, we may add cattle raising and the sub-division of holdings.

Cattle-raising and the export of black cattle permitted the utilisation of poorer quality land and, in exchange for grain crops, allowed for the intake of greater amounts of grain than the areas of arable in the Highlands could produce. In thus increasing total food supply, cattle-raising permitted population increase, yet at the same time was a cause of depopulation in several parishes, chiefly in the south and east Highlands, given that cattle farms demanded fewer people to run them. The seventeen Highland border parishes detailed by Walker as having lost population between 1755 and the 1790s (see page 185 above) mainly did so as a result of the establishment of cattle farms. Population displacement following the expansion of cattle raising in the south and east could be accommodated through movement to the Lowlands. In the north and west, this option was less easy. And throughout the Highlands, the rise in cattle prices during the 1700s - from about £1 per head in the 1740s to £5 or £6 in the 1790s - encouraged an increase in stock to, in some places, the point of a critical dependency upon the export of cattle as the principal source of money income.41 So long as cattle prices remained high and their export ensured the import of grain (or cash) over and above that locally produced, increases in population could be supported. But with the fall in cattle prices after the Napoleonic Wars, this prop to population expansion was weakened. Although prices were to rise again in the later nineteenth century,42 by the middle years of the 1800s, stocks of cattle (realisable capital reserves for peasant and landlord alike) were much reduced in number and a principal source of cash income had been largely removed.

Unlike cattle raising, kelping was chiefly confined to the coastal areas of the north and west mainland parishes and to the outer isles. Kelp was the product of burning seaweed to produce ash useful in chemical processes. Its significance in this context is essentially five-fold. Firstly, in the absence of alternatives, production increased enormously during the wars of 1793 to 1815, an output that augmented the income of landlords who could, therefore, ask an increased rent from an otherwise depressed tenantry if that group were earning cash from participating in kelp manufacture. Secondly, kelping was

labour intensive. In addition to helping retain any
natural increase of population in employment it demanded
large numbers of people to be locally resident. Thirdly,
this labour force had to be coastally located. Kelping
determined landlords to shift tenants from the interior, a
redistribution encouraged by the development of cattle
farming and then by that of large-scale sheep farming.
This concentration on one process, on cash income from it,
and resettlement in coastal locations had the effect,
fourthly, that agriculture was neglected whilst the
landlords' short-term rapacity prevailed over the tenants'
longer-term interests. And, lastly, those lands settled
and worked by the labour force were increasingly
sub-divided to accommodate the increase in population.

The coastal margins of the north-western Highlands and
islands, though very productive land in places, could only
sustain the relative over-crowding in relation to local
resources so long as income from kelp provided the means of
support. Increasingly from about 1810 it did not. The
effect upon Highland demography of the fall in kelp prices
and virtual cessation of the industry by the 1830s was not
alone due to kelp's collapse. But the demands of that
industry had been sufficient to increase population in the
areas of production and then, with its passing, to leave
them without a principal means of monetary income, with an
increased rent, and with too many persons in relation to
agricultural land. This latter fact demanded both the
further sub-division of already small holdings and the
extension of the cultivable area on to land whose potential
returns hardly justified the effort and rent demanded.

Kelp . . . was an extraordinary, even freakish,
growth in the Highland economy which concentrated
a large quasi-proletariat on the absolute fringes
of some of the least auspicious parts of the
west. It encouraged the detachment of population
from the land and their dependence on kelp-income
and potatoes. It enabled landowners not only to
exploit the labour force in a thorough fashion,
but it also reinforced other tendencies to retain
population in the region.43

The demographic influence of the potato in Western
Europe and in the Lowlands of Scotland, had much the same
effect as a means of population change in Highland Scotland
as kelp. The potato was introduced into the Hebrides in
the 1690s, but not widely cultivated until the 1740s. It
became a major item in the food supply of Highlanders by
the end of the eighteenth century. Its advantages were

202

several: it could be grown on poor quality land unable to support grain crops; it could sustain population on smaller acreages per family than required for a principally grain diet; and, in being a subsistence crop, it allowed population to expand irrespective of external markets. As one commentator noted in 1794 in consequence of potato cultivation in Perthshire, ' it had already done more, and is able, by having the cultivation of it farther extended, to do more to keep our people from emigrating, than any other expedient, which has been hitherto devised'.44 Dependence on the potato was greater in the north and west. MacDonald claimed in 1811 that potatoes constituted four-fifths of all nourishment for the population of the Hebrides, and one commentator, writing of Skye and the southern Hebrides in the 1840s, considered population there almost entirely dependent upon potatoes for their subsistence. MacDonald further noted that 'the produce of potatoes . . . promises, by tolerable management, to triple the number of inhabitants every 75 years without ever burdening the country'.45 That population in some parishes did triple over the period 1755 to 1851 (see pages 178-192 above) was due to factors other than just potato cultivation. But the fact of potato crop failure was perhaps the greatest single cause of destitution, population decline and emigration in the mid-nineteenth century Highlands generally. Instances of blight in 1833 presaged the more widespread crop failures of 1836-1837 and 1846-1850. The destitution resulting from these latter outbreaks was especially severe in the western islands and western mainland, but less so in parts of east Sutherland, Caithness or the northern islands. But reports from across the Highlands document an unvarying misery.

> From all accounts, I think it is no exaggeration to conclude that before Winter there will not be one sound Potatoe in all the Highlands and Islands. The failure is universal and total . . . nearly half a million of the population in those districts have before them the prospect of absolute want.46

Understandably alarmed, this comment nevertheless exaggerates the actual scale of failure and the numbers at risk. The potato famine in the Highlands was the cause of terrible hardship, but not of large-scale crisis mortality sufficient in itself to reduce numbers. Emigration, prompted as a means of reducing distress, was more significant. Flinn's estimate of 60,000 persons quitting the western Highlands and Islands in the wake of the potato famine seems not unreasonable. Many parishes in this region experienced sharp falls in population in this period, but it should also be remembered that many others had been losing population before the failure of the potato crop. And in this sense, climacteric or not of Highland history,47 the potato famine stands only as one economic mechanism among many influencing the course of Highland demography.

Whilst these patterns and mechanisms constitute the demographic basis to material change, they did not affect all orders in Highland society equally. The changes in the Highland economy with which they are related did not do so either. Highland social and economic structures were, as earlier noted, held together through a system of mutual obligations founded on land and land management. Should older obligations remain (a persisting moral relationship to land), and a growing population be allowed to reside for whatever reasons, landlords had to be increasingly skilled in balancing increased numbers (demographic factors) with available agricultural resources, levels of rent and cash income (prevailing economic circumstances). Most landlords could not sustain this balance. Population increase and decline greatly affected the cottars and other sub-tenants with no land or fixed right of occupation - 'scallags' as Buchanan perjoratively termed them in 1793 (from the Gaelic sgalag, farm servant). They were the most numerous rank in Highland society and the most prone to the consequences of the collapse of kelp and potato blight. Processes of class formation within Highland society were thus lent particular emphasis by the facts of demography. But they took their historical shape chiefly from the tensions and contradictions between new forms of material production and persistent obligations to increasingly out-moded social bonds and economic practices.

THE TRANSFORMATION OF HIGHLAND AGRICULTURE 1650-1886

Claims to simplistic explanation of changes in Highland agriculture founder on the variety of social relationships and agrarian practices within Highland rural society and on the regional and chronological differences in the nature of change. Highland farms or towns differed greatly in acreage and in the balance within a given acreage between arable and pasture, just as rental evidence shows much variation in patterns of landholding, especially in the proportion held by multiple tenants, tacksmen, sub-tenants, cottars or servants. Contemporary commentators record the predominance of 'traditional' methods in virtually every sphere of Highland agricultural practice and do so for most periods. Their espousal of the need for the replacement of 'custom' by 'modernity ' thus reflects the prevailing ideology at any moment within given historical contexts. For this reason and because both existing practices and the nature of change varied across the Highlands, talk of 'typicality' in Highland agriculture should be seen more as a theoretical notion by which to reveal differences and explore the processes of transformation than as a description of uniform Highland-wide practices, change in which embraced common causes or everywhere followed neat stages.

The central unit of Highland rural life was the joint farm, the essential elements of which were the clachan (small hamlet or group of dwellings), the open arable land divided into 'infield' land and more distant 'outfield', and areas of common grazing. Restricted by aspect, steepness, and soil depth, individual holdings of arable were disposed over the whole of the infield and outfield in parcels or rigs. Periodic reallocation of land, though not essential to runrig, was common and ensured reasonable equitability in use of good or poor land. All land was held in common. Tenants were communally responsible for paying the rent, in money or in kind, to the tacksman or directly to chief or landlord. The rhythms of the rural economy depended upon the rotations practiced on the arable land (those of the outfield being usually longer), on agreed timings for the removal of stock to summer pastures, and upon the sharing of labour. The system was inherently flexible enough to allow the individual or general expansion of arable holdings beyond previous limits given population growth and the availability of land. But once limits to arable cultivation had been determined, almost the only point of flexibility within traditional arable agriculture, given restrictions of soil and custom, was the sub-division of holdings. Arable holdings provided the basis to subsistence, the principal grain crops being oats and barley. The balance between the subsistence production of grain crops and the necessity for the import of grain differed between Highland parishes whose relative proximity to the Lowlands allowed easier import of grain and the north and west parishes more dependent on local production. Cattle everywhere provided cash income for the payment of rent or the introduction of luxuries; 'the only article upon the land which affords money to the tenant, and payment to the landlord.'48

The coincidence of interest and customary obligations between landlord and tenant that underlay the management of this basic system was repeated between tacksman, tenants, and sub-tenants or servants. In simple terms, the tacksman,

usually but not always a collateral relation of the chief,
leased land from the chief, sub-let it to the majority of
the population and lived off the difference. Whilst in the
context of clan structures, the tacksman enjoyed some
agreed formal standing both as 'the middleman in a military
organisation' and as the 'farmer of the rents' in given
districts, there were few, if any, legal bonds between
tacksman and chief. No law recognised the duthchas or
customary rights of the tenantry.49 The ties binding the
subordinate adherents to the land and to other classes in
Highland rural society were likewise set within the context
of customary obligation, without a recognised legality, and
were variable as to their nature in practice. The least
firmly attached was the cottar, sometimes also called
'mealers' or 'mailers' who usually worked a small extent of
arable, and, in return for use of a cow's grazing and
shared access to agricultural implements, was required to
provide labour services on the tenant's land in addition to
a money rent. Crofters, like cottars, held and worked a
small patch of arable, but unlike cottars, this land was
usually compact and was held permanently and directly from
the landowner. Together with servants, contracted for
periods of varying duration for labour on larger farms but
also working small areas of arable for themselves, these
varieties of sub-tenants formed the most numerous class in
the agricultural population. Although it was a system
founded on mutual obligation and agreed customs, Highland
agriculture as a practised and dominant mode of production
was not without internal contradictions or points of
weakness. Tensions existed between the demands of
efficient production from land and the obligations of those
who worked it. Inherent weaknesses were social - the
result of customary practices such as the sub-division of
holdings at the marriage of the son and the lack of leases
- and physical, deriving from restrictions of the natural
setting. Further, the Highland agricultural economy was
not apart from wider economic concerns: the production and
reproduction of material life through agriculture 'involved
nearly every Highland producer in a wider relationship with
the commercial systems of the Lowlands and of England.'50
Change in Highland agriculture was, then, a complex
combination of the adoption and incorporation of outside
influences within existing systems, and the replacement of
established methods by new ones. Written leases, enclosure, and large-scale sheep farming count, in this sense,
as largely 'new' methods. But other factors, principally
levels of money rent, amounts of cash income, and the
associated capitalisation and commercial expansion of

206

Highland agriculture dependent upon involvement in wider issues represent changes of scale in existing practices more than any new beginning in the Highland rural economy.

First signs of change: leases, rents, and money income, c.1650-1755

When, in 1773, an anonymous commentator remarked 'Nothing can exceed the avarice discovered by many of the proprietors in the Highlands, for some time past, in raising their rents'51, he was pointing to one principal element of change in the Highland agrarian economy. Increases in rent, shifts in the balance in rents between money and victual, and the introduction of written leases are normally associated with changes after 1750. There is evidence to suggest, however, that upward pressure upon rent levels and the introduction of more formal leasing arrangements, both of which may be interpreted as first signs of more rationalised and commercially-oriented techniques of land management were known by the early eighteenth century and in the 1600s. Tacksmen have even been recorded in the western isles for the late 1550s, holding tacks of nineteen years, the favoured duration in later periods.

Shaw has documented much variation in the lengths for which written tacks were granted in the seventeenth-century Hebrides, and has also suggested a regional distinction: 'where evidence survives, it shows that tacks granted by proprietors in the more southerly islands of the Hebrides were for much shorter terms than those granted by proprietors further north'. Explanation rests in the fact of earlier feuing of land in the southern Hebrides. Almost all the instances of short tacks - three years or five years most commonly - come from estates of the Campbells of Argyll and Glenorchy. Shaw claims that short tacks encouraged the tenant to work land as fully as possible since there was no automatic longer-term tenancy, and, in addition, short leases allowed the landlord more frequent opportunities to raise rents and ensure security through eviction of disloyal tenants. In contrast, 'The longer tacks of the more northerly isles reflect a society where security and clan loyalties were still felt to matter more than increasing the monetary yield of the estate, and where the more commercial land policies of the Lowlands had not yet filtered through.' Further, 'The greater rents being exacted from the tacksmen of these areas is another sign of the more commercial attitudes of some proprietors in the south-west.'52 McKerral has shown for Kintyre that when lands there first fell into Crown hands in the 1500s, leases were granted only for three years, but once Lowland occupiers had been settled upon lands owned by the Campbells from the 1650s, that is, peopled with loyal tenantry, leases of nineteen years were granted.53 Evidence from parts of eastern Ross and Cromarty generally points to short leases before the later 1700s.54

The extent to which regional differences in length of lease or even in the existence of formal leases, written or not, were passed on to the smaller tenants and sub-tenants in the later 1600s is uncertain. Working people held land from year to year, usually without tacks or other leases. Rent levels for joint tenants over most of the Hebrides show much uniformity for holdings of comparable size in the late 1600s and early 1700s. Whilst it is possible that the average holding of the majority of small tenants in the northern island parishes was smaller than that of their southern or mainland counterparts, there is no reason to suppose that small holding size and general absence of leases permitted easy removal of sub-tenants; indeed, as Shaw notes, 'small tenants in the Western Isles had much greater security of tenure than their legal position might suggest'. Dodgshon's examination of a variety of rentals from Gairloch for 1660 to 1670 and the Macleod estates on Skye in 1678 to a 1769 rental of the Breadalbane estate in Perthshire has revealed great variation in respect of landholding, but no clear regional distinction in relation to the prevalency of either the tacksman system or the dominance of tenants holding land directly to the landowner.55 What is suggested by rentals like that of the McLeans of Duart for parts of Mull in 1674, however, which distinguishes between lands possessed by tenants, those held by tack, or by single tenants, is that more direct proprietor/tenant relationships - so characteristic of the eighteenth century and later - were appearing in the later seventeenth century. Although these relationships did not necessarily involve written leases, this evidence is suggestive of those changes occurring within Highland agriculture before the advent of the 'improver'. Also revealed is a downward trend in the amount of land per tenant, family, or per capita. This, like the above shift in social relationships, was more critical in the 1700s than in the 1600s, but it is a process whose origins lie in the seventeenth century and whose effects then may well have been exacerbated by the increased demands of some landowners for money rent rather than labour services or payment in kind.

The most important part of the tenant's payment was the principal rent. In the Highland parishes bordering on the

Lowlands, it was usually in money with a few bestial. In more distant parishes 'principal rents were often almost entirely in livestock and their products, especially butter and cheese, with a small money payment'.56 Variations existed on this general claim, but also apparent from the later seventeenth century is an increased stress on the cash portion of rents for many Highland estates: the McLeod estates in Harris after 1680; in parts of Lismore after 1660 (in contrast to what is known of rentals there from 1611 to 1660 which show principal rent payments in victual); in Luing and Seil in 1671-2; in Breadalbane in 1692; in parts of Kintyre; and in Skye in the 1670s.57 Many rentals of later date show a balance between cash and kind in payment: for lands in Glendaruel in 1726, for example, where payment in kind included wedders, butter, meal as well as a cash sum of £148.58 In records for estates in Netherlorn in 1727, 1745-47, and 1757, payment in kind was still required, and in a Clanranald rental of 1718 embracing estates in Moydart, Arisaig, Eigg, Canna, and South Uist, the type and proportion of payment in kind varied between places with the money element a constant feature.59 The limited survival of individual records for periods long enough to record shifts in emphasis from kind to money in given estates is a problem. Even so, the general evidence is both that money was increasingly significant as the central element in rent payments by the late 1600s, and that this tendency was first more widely evident in the southern Highlands: 'The old custom of the payment of the rents in victual, and in services and casualties, does in some degree remain, but has of late years been much abridged, the rents in many places being now paid chiefly, if not entirely, in money.'60

This emphasis on money payment thoughout the seventeenth century may be explained by a combination of fashion, expediency, and a necessitiousness perceived and real. The increased involvement of many Highland landlords with broader political and cultural interests, an involvement that necessitated cash for travel, purchase of luxuries and payment of specialised labour, was paralleled by the rise of new market centres, early planned villages, and the expansion of Glasgow's commercial hinterland. The commutation of the principal rents in grain or kind and their replacement by money income in the Highlands at this time originated in the need for increased participation in a developing market economy.

Many of these changes are evident in the re-organisation of estates in Mull, Morvern, and Tiree, and elsewhere on the Duke of Argyll's lands, in the early 1700s. Leases granted for 19 years, the letting of lands directly to tenants, and an increased emphasis upon money payment were all part of tenurial changes by which the tacksman lost control in patronage of land. Cregeen sees 1737 as a watershed between old and new methods in these estates, but also emphasises that the changes took place within a community already open to outside influence and under the direction of leading figures in the introduction of new ways. The picture of land management and tenure provided by the statistics relating to the Forfeited Estates, 1755-1756, thus post-dates a number of important changes in Highland agriculture whilst itself preceding their more complete realisation from the later 1700s. Over all the estates, money rent is important, but not alone so. We can observe the existence of 19 year leases (and longer) dating from the 1740s and earlier and record the introduction of such leases in attempts to establish 'good habits' amongst the tenantry in places where they were unknown. Thus, of Lovat estate, 'When leases are granted to substantiall farmers or strangers that may be intro-duced, I think particular bargains ought to be made with them and suitable encouragement given for improving and inclosing.'61 The introduction of written leases and longer leases, perhaps initially to secure loyalty amongst tenants, was rooted - as was the upward pressure on rents and the emphasis upon money income - in the expanded consciousness and increased commercialism of many Highland landlords. Duncan Campbell of Breadalbane adopted new techniques in his estates in the early 1600s after return-ing from Flanders and France with ideas on forestry and husbandry; Archibald Campbell of Knockbuy from about 1728 raised the rental fourfold in the following sixty years; and on Lewis, the McKenzies were, by 1750, reported to be 'frugal and industrious in their way, and Remarkably disposed to grow rich. They have screwed their Rents to an extravagant Height'.62 Accumulation of capital was replacing loyalty to kin and established ways long before the mid-1700s. And the means by which money income was being augmented - new leasing arrangements and increased rentals - demanded new social relationships.

Processes of class formation and the going of the tacksman

For most landowners, management of agriculture was an indirect affair; proprietorial power and authority was principally vested in the tacksman. The role of the tacksman in Highland social structures has been a conten-tious one, both in historical research and amongst contemporary observers.63 This difference in interpretation is perhaps to be expected given the individual characteristics of different tacksmen and the varying nature of tenancies in which, for example, tacksmen either nominally held land but in actuality sub-let it, wholly or in part, or themselves worked the farm as a single tenant with the help of cottars and crofters from whom various labour dues were demanded. In 1773, Johnson described the tacksman thus:

> Next in dignity to the Laird is the Tacksman; a
> large taker or lease-holder of land, of which he
> keeps part, as a domain in his own hand, and lets
> part to under tenants. The Tacksman is
> necessarily a man capable of securing to the Laird
> the whole rent, and is commonly a collateral rela-
> tion. These tacks, or subordinate possessions,
> were long considered as hereditary, and the
> occupant was distinguished by the name of the
> place at which he resided. He held a middle
> station, by which the highest and lowest orders
> were connected. He paid rent and reverence to the
> Laird, and received them from the tenants. This
> tenure still subsists, with its original opera-
> tion, but not with the primitive stability.64

Johnson goes on to note differences of opinion regarding the tacksman and his role. On the one hand were those who considered the tacksman 'a useless burden on the ground, as a drone who lives from the product of an estate, without the right of property, or the merit of labour, and who impoverishes at once the landlord and the tenant'. On the other hand, argues Johnson, 'If the Tacksman be banished, who will be left to impart knowledge, or impress civility'; tenants would remain uninstructed and negligent; landlords without real influence. Johnson is correct to note the role the tacksman played as middle-man in agricultural affairs, but he omits mention of their principal function in Highland society; that of a soldier holding land in return for military service. It was this fact that distinguished them as a military caste within clan rela-tions. This fact was held by some Lowland authorities in the 1740s to be responsible for the Rebellion and the prevalence of unrest in the Highlands. Nicol Graham of Gartmore considered both the poverty of Highland agricul-ture and political 'disorders and unrest' to stem from the tacksman who could 'bring out' tenants to support the chief in times of war and who, in peacetime, could hinder the development of commercial agriculture through restrictions of letting or the exaction of labour services.65

Population Growth and Highland Agriculture

A good deal of contemporary evidence points to the restrictive role of the tacksman in Highland agriculture, especially insofar as the sub-letting of land was concerned. Walker considered that the sub-letting of lands was 'one great obstacle to the improvement of the Highlands'.

> All the subtenants, who are the great body of the people in the Highlands, are tenants at the will of the tacksman or farmer, and are therefore placed in a state of subjection that is not only unreasonable, but unprofitable, both to themselves and their superiors . . . Their subjection to the tacksman or farmer, on whose ground they live, leaves them no more time than what is barely sufficient to support themselves and their families in life. The tacksman generally has one day in the week of the subtenant's labour the year round, which, with the spring and harvest work, and other occasions, will amount to more than a third of his whole annual labour. He can therefore have neither ability not opportunity to attempt any improvement, which many of those subtenants would undoubtedly do, were they but masters of their time, and independent in their possessions.

Elsewhere, Walker illustrates this influence with reference to Campbell of Shawfield's estates on Islay. There, written leases had been introduced, but in such a way as permitted tacksmen to continue 'letting out Houses and Grounds to the lower People'.

> This unfavourable Circumstance, has defeated the Intention of these long leases and effectually prevented the Improvement of the Island, as these poor People, if they improve their Grounds, must next year pay more Rent or be turned out of their Possessions. Some of the Farms are lett for four times the Rent payed by the original Tacksmen, and the whole, upon an Average, are sublett for three times more Rent than is payed to the Landlord. Such immoderate and unreasonable Profits acquired by these Tacksmen without any Industry, makes them careless about any Improvement, and accordingly, the Lands ly much in the same Situation they were in when the Leases commenced.66

McDonald, writing in 1811 and recognising the manners,

social status and education of many tacksmen, considered also that 'The very circumstances . . . which . . . constituted their respectability, were highly unfavourable to the cultivation of their lands'.

> A tacksman, considering himself and his family as well entitled as any other members of society to the honours and advantages of civilized life, had no idea of enduring the drudgery of a farmer's dull routine . . . The profession of a farmer for any of his family never entered his head.67

MacDonald thus recognised the paradox attaching to the tacksman's role in a changing Highlands: the loss of political status amongst a group who, though they would never have regarded themselves as farmers, were the principal agents in the allocation of land and collection of rents, yet at the same time, a section of Highland population whose intermediary position and functions was almost always considered restrictive of improved methods. But the tacksman was also a valuable even necessary element in respect of local administration or the supervision of runrig or other agreed agricultural practices: 'Without their aid, the efforts of the clergy and officers of justice would be painful and unavailing'. To the extent that we can distinguish within the rank of tacksman a difference between large territorial tacksmen and those whose interests lay within the confines of a single town, it is likely that this organisational and administrative role would have been more evident within the latter type, less demanding beyond rent collection in the former. But whilst recognising role differences in the extent to which individual tacksmen acted either as agents for the land-owner or in their own interests in letting lands, there is widespread agreement that their position as a rank or group within Highland society was increasingly redundant by the mid-1700s.

The establishment of more direct leasing arrangements between landowner and tenant, though a principal means of elimination, should not be held the only cause of the going of the tacksman. For one thing, relationships between tacksmen and chiefs, tacksmen and sub-tenants, were in several cases founded on economic bonds between patron and client as much as on ties of custom. This is particularly true of arrangements made under steelbow tenure whereby tenants received from the tacksman land and cattle as initial capital. Rent was a payment for both stock and land. As McKerral has observed, under this system the tenant was in complete economic thrall to the tacksman;

'to which fact, rather than loyalty founded on the blood
tie, may be ascribed the opposition to the abolition of the
tacksman system by the under-tenants, and their reluctance
to accept leases themselves'.68   And as we have observed,
other 'new' ways - written leases and an increased emphasis
upon money rent - were being introduced into Highland
society without any necessary threat to the tacksman.   But
this depended upon their continued military importance.   It
is interesting to note that the first attempt at letting
directly to the highest bidders - on Morvern, Mull and
Tiree in 1737 - took place on land owned by the Dukes of
Argyll and worked by loyal tenants.   After 1745, without
this military role, the tacksmen were less able to prevent
the march of commercial attitudes that threatened their own
position.   Hunter argues that the going of the tacksman
reflected a change in consciousness within the Highlands.
What had been considered inviolable - the duthchas or
kindly tenure of a holding or extent of land - was now
replaced by a system of money rents and written leases.
Many Highlanders refused to recognise written leases, even
into the later 1800s, arguing that to accept a lease was to
surrender recognised rights.   The re-structuring of
Highland social relations between landlord and tenant
consequent upon the gradual disappearance of the tacksman
as middle layer was not then simply the result of the
imposition of new ways or decline in military prestige.   It
was, for some tacksmen, a conscious rejection of modern
practices rather than any intrinsic inability to function
in a changing agrarian economy.

Many chose emigration and given their intermediate
social position could influence sub-tenants to do likewise.   One anonymous author observed in 1772:

> Such of these wadsetters and tacksmen as rather
> wish to be distinguished as leaders, than by
> industry, have not taken leases again, alledging
> that the rents are risen above what the land will
> bear; but, say they, in order to be revenged of
> our master for doing so, and what is worse,
> depriving us or our subordinate chieftainship, by
> abolishing our former privilege of sub-letting, we
> will not only leave his lands, but by spiriting
> the lower class of people to emigrate, we shall
> carry a clan to America, and when they are there,
> they must work for us, or starve.69

Emigration took place both before and for reasons other
than the gradual elimination of the tacksman, but there is
no doubt it did increase with the departure of tacksmen and

numbers of sub-tenants. Richards has remarked that 'the willingness of the people to follow their natural leaders reflected their poverty, the recurrence of famine, the goad of rising rents and the solidarity of social relations'.70 For the tacksman, as Walker notes, migration symbolised loss of status:

> The tacksmen refused to comply with the offered terms, upon which the lands were let to the inferior people, who had been their subtenants. It does not appear that these tacksmen were induced to leave their country from any wanton desire for change, or any deliberate plan of enterprise; but they found themselves uneasy at home, by alteration in the state of property to which they had not been accustomed, and to which their minds and views could not correspond.71

It should be noted, however, that some evidence points to migration as a response to 'the oppression they meet from their Masters the Tacksmen'.72

In review, it is easy to see the tacksman of the later 1700s only as a sort of agricultural manager, to ascribe their going only to external causes, and to see in their departure the polarisation of social relations into only two classes; landholders and landworkers. The reality was more complex. Many tacksmen were wadsetters, holding land under a wadset or mortgage. In the later 1700s, the redemption of this wadset by tacksmen (for whatever reason) was often a means by which they acquired capital at the expense of established social relations. Further, tacksmen were not always so popular with subtenants that they would automatically follow. If they oppressed the tenantry or displayed patronage towards their own kin, tacksmen were unlikely to be popular. In some parts of the eastern Highlands such as Easter Ross where the bulk of the arable land in the 1700s was held directly from landlords by tenant farmers, tacksmen were never as important as in the west. And in a number of instances, tacksmen were replaced by factors or agents who, without bloodlinks with landowner or tenantry, were often more direct and forceful in the operation of the estate. Yet the position of the tacksman, though restrictive of new ways, was a vital one in the Highland economy. And given that the tacksman was often replaced by a factor or agent, we should not see in their going a simple separation within Highland social structures into the two classes of landowners and a stratified peasantry. Nevertheless, with the decline of military ways and the more common direct letting of land from the 1730s, the tacksman either became an intermediate entrepreneurial figure within an agricultural economy increasingly adopting commercial attitudes and new methods, or he departed the scene altogether. The significance of the tacksman's going was not so much that it left Highland society without a middle layer, but that it indicated 'the literally awesome problem of adjustment which ordinary Highlanders faced'.

> If the tacksmen, men who were usually well educated and knew something of life outside the Highlands, could not adapt to the situation created by the establishment of commercial landlordism, how could the much less well equipped commons of the clans make the still greater adjustments required of them?73

The departure of the tacksman was only one change affecting the agrarian economy although, in some cases, the re-structuring of social relations was itself sufficient to engender changes in other ways. Thus, of Boleskine and Abertarff;

> From the year 1746, the minds of the inhabitants seemed to have taken a different turn; the Wadsetters, finding no longer the importance of their sub-tenants, cottars, and dependants, withdrew their former familiarity and protection; and these thereupon imbibed a spirit of independence, and thinking to their own industry and exertions, many of them quitted their native country, for a better mode of living; and those who remained, being now obliged to pay money-rent in place of their former services, became more attentive to the cultivation of the soil.74

But in most respects, Highland cultivators were not as attentive to their soil as landlords would have liked. And it was to the communal features of Highland agriculture, to the adoption of new crops, new methods, and, not least, to the attempted introduction of a new mentality amongst their tenantry that landlords increasingly turned their attentions.

Runrig, enclosures, and changes in arable agriculture, c.1755–1850

Writing towards the end of the eighteenth century, George

Population Growth and Highland Agriculture

Dempster (who himself owned and ran a farm in the High-lands) outlined eight principal means by which Highland agriculture had been, and could be further, improved. These were longer leases; exemption from personal servic-es; enclosing; use of lime and marl; use of sown grasses, particularly clover; use of turnips 'for feeding cows, oxen and sheep in winter'; 'Potatoes for the same purpose and food'; and paying rents in money and not in kind.75 The introduction and successful implementation of these and other changes in arable agriculture varied over time and space depending upon the attitude of the land-owner, constraints of topography, or the response of the tenantry. Writing to the Duke of Argyll in 1744 on the matter of potato cultivation, Archibald Campbell of Knockbuy considered that 'the ignorance of the people as to the proper culture, times of pulling, in watering, and the cheapest ways of dressing it are the only difficulties to be struggled with'.76 For this observer and for several others, transformation of arable agriculture was simply a matter of instruction. The traditional conservatism attaching to Highland ways was to be expected given the Gaels' general lack of culture and restricted consciousness of the new. Improvement was a matter of contact with people and methods of superior cultivation.

> In the cultivated parts of the country, the farmers are well acquainted with the most profit-able methods of culture, and will not fail to prosecute them, for their own advantage . . . but the case is widely different in the uncultivated parts of the north: There, the labourers of the soil are unacquainted with the improvements that would be most beneficial to themselves and their country. Their knowledge is confined. They are naturally and not blamedly shy to alterations of which they have no experience. Their inclination is to proceed in the old beaten track; but from this they may be allured, by the instruction and example of their superiors; by reasonable prospects of profit and by proper stipulations engrossed in their leases.77

The temptation to cite such evidence to support a view of the means of change in Highland arable farming as simple and unopposed and the results wholly beneficial should be avoided. To disciples of the new, Highland agriculture may have been archaic, its practitioners 'ignorant, aukward and lazy'.78 But what is conservatism to some is to others a set of cultural practices worked out, often over

217

centuries, in the context of a given environmental and social setting. Even when new methods had been taken up, old ones persisted. The cas-chrom or crooked spade could work land horse-drawn ploughs could not and continued to be used long into the nineteenth century; other implements – the cas-dhireach or Hebridean delving spade, or the crann-nan-qad, the one-handed plough – were also employed at a time when new tools and techniques were being introduced. That they were so should not be taken as a sign of intrinsic backwardness.

Changes in arable agriculture took several forms; principally, the abolition of runrig, the engrossing and enclosing of holdings (both of which underlay the emergence of crofting), the introduction of turnips, artificial grasses and new rotations, and a move away from oats and barley to a dependence upon the potato. In the traditional arable sector, cropping on the outfield involved the growing of oats (often continually in given areas of land without manure), and short periods of fallow; in the infield, rotations involved barley, oats, rye or potatoes, which, in receiving what dung the farm produced, thus impoverished the greater part of the land. On some estates, land near the shielings – subsidiary settlements on higher ground where cattle were grazed each summer – was cultivated, but this was not common. Within this openfield system, enclosure was virtually unknown. The only dykes were the head-dykes that divided the arable grounds from common pasture. Head-dykes were not, however, unchanging features. As population increased, so outfield arable was converted to infield, the limits of outfield pushed beyond their previous extent, and areas of land were, in time, distinguished by multiple head-dykes 'sometimes later to be absorbed into developing enclosure patterns, sometimes remaining as mute reminders high up in the glens of the changing economic bases of Highland life during the late eighteenth and the nineteenth centuries'. Gailey considers the question of multiple head-dykes 'one of the seeming paradoxes of eighteenth and nineteenth century Highland economic history'.79 In view of improvements to the arable sector and the growth of population, it might be expected that the arable area would have extended during the later 1700s and throughout the nineteenth century, at the expense of pasture land. But for parts of the south-west Highlands at least, evidence points in the opposite direction. Maximum limits of cultivation were reached by 1800; later periods were characterised only by contraction with the principal period of extension being between 1750 and 1790. In Trotternish on Skye, the maximum limits of cultivation had been reached in 1769. Given the observed patterns and

218

rates of population growth, it is likely that arable cultivation made increasingly intensive use of areas below the head-dyke, areas which in places may even have declined in extent as population increased. Such intensive use resulted from the consolidation of previously scattered holdings.

The destruction of the runrig system stemmed from what Gray has called 'the singularly unanimous abhorrence which the articulate thinkers of the eighteenth century held for anything but individual and permanent tenure of land'.80 This abhorrence was neither eighteenth century in origin nor directed only at the Highlands (see above). In the Highlands, the move to enclose and consolidate holdings was later than in the Lowlands, and the effects varied in result. Several authors have pointed to the Duke of Argyll in 1776 and the Earl of Breadalbane in 1783 as initiators of the move towards consolidation of holdings, at least in the south-west Highlands. The former gave instructions for the lotting of Tiree in 1776, the latter was reorganising lands in Netherlorn in 1783, and, in the 1780s and 1790s, on Loch Tay-side.81 By the end of the eighteenth century, it is argued, most of Argyll's arable was being transformed as compact holdings replaced fragmented runrig; enclosure of holdings followed, and the whole frontier of change moved north and west with such effect that 'by 1850, the old system was virtually extinct'.82

Not all enclosures that followed the going of runrig were for arable. In the east and central Highlands, many were for woods or part of policies whose purpose was aesthetic as well as economic. In Argyll, early enclosure was associated with experiments in controlled stock rearing and grazing. But most were for arable and laid down in concert with the adoption of new crops and crop rotations. For Smith, writing of Argyll:

> Good enclosures are the foundation of all improve-
> ments. Whether lands are employed in tillage or
> in pasturage, enclosures are necessary, in order
> to turn them to the best account. In arable
> lands, they save the ground from being poached
> when wet, and put it in the farmer's power to
> raise green crops with much greater advantage than
> he can do without them. In pasture lands, they
> save the expense of herding; allow the cattle to
> graze freely, without being teazed by herds and
> dogs; and by giving them clean grass and a change
> of pasture as they need it, enable them to thrive
> better than they could do otherwise, and support a
> greater number on the same extent of ground.83

Even in Argyll at that time (1805), however, enclosures were 'chiefly confined to the possessions of proprietors; many of whom have sufficiently enclosed and subdivided the farms in their own hands . . . the general appearance of the country is still naked and open'. Elsewhere, we are told (of Ross and Cromarty in 1810), how 'native farmers have an aversion to inclosures.'84 Over time, however, boundaries known only by custom and tradition were replaced by stone march dykes or 'feal dykes' made of turf divots, and a new geometry slowly imparted to the arable landscape.

Of new crops introduced, potatoes, turnips, and artificial grasses gained ground most rapidly. Neilson, reporting to the Board of Trustees in 1755, noted at Morvern how although potatoes had been known only recently, 'they now find this Root of Such Singular Service that it is planted in great quantitys on the sides of the Hills that were formerly uncultivated'.85 Reports of about the same period relating to the Forfeited Estates document the take-up of clover and turnips, for example, and the evident difficulties some landowners faced in implementing new rotations. Leases insisted on the sowing of clover; rotations including flax, barley, oats, clover and grass were demanded; and prizes were awarded for the improving use of manures such as marl and lime.86 On the more northerly estates, enclosures and new arable methods were slow to be adopted, partly the result of local intransigence - 'They languidly go in the old beaten track' - and partly because of changes in the significance of arable farming given related developments in livestock farming and the growth of kelping. Tenants on South Uist, on first being directed to plant potatoes in 1743, refused, and in consequence were all committed to prison: 'In a very little time however, the inhabitants of South Uist came to know better, when every man of them would have gone to prison, rather than not plant potatoes.' On Barra, where potatoes were first planted in 1752, they provided 'subsistence to the whole inhabitants, above a fourth part of the year' within a decade. And what was happening on Barra was, by the early nineteenth century, widespread in the north and west Highlands and islands.87

The growing of potatoes not only permitted the expansion of population but reduced dependency upon import of grain, and, in allowing steeper slopes or poorer soils to be brought into cultivation, pushed back the margins of arable agriculture. Potatoes were often worked in 'lazy-beds', feannagan taomaidh, where soil or sea-weed was piled into heaps on small plots of land and worked with the cas-chrom.

Before the Introduction of Potatoes, no Care was taken to reclaim any untillaged Earth, but now a great deal of waste land is yearly broke-up, and planted with that Root, in lazy Beds. They always take two and sometimes three Crops of Potatoes off such Land; each Crop being manured either with Dung or Sea Ware.88

Documenting changes in the arable sector of Highland agriculture should not obscure variations between different parts of the Highlands - in remote St. Kilda, for example, arable land had been divided for cultivation since the late 1600s89 - or the fact that change was accompanied both by the replacement of native personnel and the adoption of new methods and new social relations of production by 'old tenantry'. In parts of the eastern Highlands, in upland Aberdeen, Banff, and Morayshire and particularly in the hinterland of Inverness and along the coastal plain of eastern Ross and Cromarty and Sutherland, the going of runrig and the extension of enclosures was more rapid, the landscape more immediately capitalistic in outlook earlier than in the west.

In general, the farther north and west, 'the more backward by 'improving' standards were the agricultural methods used'.90 One commentator writing of the northern Highlands in 1796 reported how the inhabitants there could not 'boast of much improvement in the art of agriculture beyond the remembrance of men living'.91 In the east, central and southern Highlands, change in arable agriculture, though disruptive of traditional methods, was generally complete and rapid enough to allow the adoption of regular and systematic cropping, new enclosures, and the emergence of an independent middle class of employing farmers. This was not the case in the north and west. There, social structures were increasingly distinguished by an upper layer of substantial estate owners, many of whom were outsiders, and the mass of population gathered in a single class of perilously indigent small-holders. For most of this class, lots allocated following abolition of runrig and consolidation of holdings were inadequate. For some people the effect, as in the eastern and southern Highlands, was dispossession and a new life either as a labourer in the more intensive but still unmechanised agriculture or a move to a Highland village or Lowland town. Some emigrated rather than take up new insufficient lots or work as wage labourers. But emigration as an option was restricted following the 1803 Passenger Act. And for most peasant farmers in the north and west, there was little choice but to take up their allotted small

crofts and plots. They did so in a period that was marked
by rising population, with little out-movement, an increased dependence upon one crop - the potato - grown in
holdings too small, and by the subdivision of those
self-same holdings and plots given the continued residence
of landless labourers whose livelihood was more and more
bound up with the limited fortunes of local industries (see
below). In places, planned villages and fishing settlements absorbed excess population and provided employment.
But this was only one aspect of social and geographical
re-adjustment in the northern Highlands. The other, more
widespread, was the emergence in the first two decades of
the 1800s of crofting as a way of life: 'Crofting occupied
a half-way house between the status of an independent
peasantry and that of a totally dispossessed prolet-
ariat'.92 The re-orientation of agricultural social
relations in the north and west owed also to related
changes in pastoral agriculture.

> The miserable, overcrowded townships which
> constituted the most characteristic feature of the
> agrarian system which prevailed on the north-west
> coast of the Scottish mainland for most of the
> nineteenth century were established during this
> period - and settled by people who had been
> cleared from the inland straths and glens in order
> to make way for sheep.93

Cattle, sheep, and changes in pastoral agriculture, c.1764-1850

Most towns and tenants had both native Highland sheep and
cattle. Other livestock included goats and large numbers
of horses. Relatively few pigs were kept. Until the
second half of the eighteenth century, livestock and
pastoral agriculture was largely synonymous with black
cattle. All pasture lands were, in theory, communally
worked by 'souming and rouming', that is, by allocating the
numbers of animals an individual tenant might graze on
common pasture, and by agreed timings for the movement of
stock to and from these upland grounds (usually early May
and the beginning of November).94 Opportunities for
increasing money income through overstocking were
restricted under the souming system, but in other respects,
management of livestock was poor. Cattle sales paid the
rent, or the principal monetary portion of it: 'Cattle
were a logical item of farm produce to trade. There was a
demand for them, their sale did not jeopardize subsistence

222

of the town, they made use of an abundant resource, and they walked themselves to market'. The first half of the eighteenth century is distinguished by an increased attention to the commercial possibilities of cattle-rearing: 'In so far as cattle had long been marketed, this was not outwardly a radical change. But it did represent an important change in attitude, a positive response to the rising level of demand for lean stock from English graziers or fatteners'.95 Again, the pioneers of this new attitude are found on the Argyll estates - men like Archibald Campbell of Knockbuy for example - but an increased emphasis given to cattle-rearing was characteristic of much of the south-west and eastern Highlands by the third quarter of the eighteenth century. This emphasis was, in turn, responsible for early attempts at stock improvement and for early enclosures in districts like Kintyre (see above). In the eyes of one Highlander writing in 1773, 'the leading idea, which one who conducted matters so as to turn a Highland estate to the best account, should always keep in view . . . is to consider this as a country (principally and many parts of it wholly) fit for cattle and pasture, and not for agriculture and tillage'.96

The emphasis given in the eighteenth century to larger-scale commercial cattle-raising, in the south-west and central Highlands particularly, was both sign and symptom of that more general re-orientation of attitudes – the move from a moral to a commercial consciousness – increasingly prevalent amongst the landlord class. Further, the growth of cattle production on new scales underlay an increase in rents contemporary with changes in the subsistence sector of agriculture, but preceding the coming of large-scale sheep farming. New levels of stocking required the engrossing of holdings and the extension of grazing grounds at the expense of arable; changes that themselves demanded replacement of customary herding and 'soum and roum' arrangements. In the decades after 1770, however, a larger-scale transformation in Highland pastoral agriculture was underway, occasioned by the farming of sheep on unprecedented scales. Native highland sheep were kept not for profit and external sale, but for the use of their milk and wool in the domestic economy. Sheep management in modern terms was unknown. The presence of predators meant that sheep could not be allowed to roam untended in large numbers over wide areas. The attention given to cattle by Campbell of Knockbuy in the second quarter of the eighteenth century, for example, was perhaps more than a little influenced by his realisation that sheep husbandry was at that time (1744) unlikely to develop given losses from predators: 'Until the fox is destroyed on the Continent of Argyllshire, as in the Isles thereof, ther can very little improvement be made of our sheep.'97 Because of predators and since little arable land was enclosed, Highlanders housed their seana chaorich cheaga (little old sheep), especially over winter.

Large-scale sheep farming was different in extent, intent, and results from the keeping of sheep within the domestic economy. The principal motive was profit, the principal demand areas the industrialising cities of Lowland Scotland and England. It was a motive that reflected also the attitudes of Highland landlords and Lowland graziers on the seeming wastefulness of not stocking the higher grounds.98 By turning the land over to sheep, landowners could receive an increased rent with regularity.

The chronology and geography of the coming of Lowland sheep and large-scale sheep farming is reasonably well understood. The movement as a whole began in 1752 when Blackface sheep from Ayrshire were introduced into the upland parts of Arrochar, Lochgoilhead and Kilmorich. By 1820, Sutherland had become the stronghold of commercial farming on the very greatest scale, and, by the 1840s, parts of the Outer Hebrides were being enclosed for sheep farms as islands such as Mull and Skye had been earlier. Blackface flocks spread through Argyll and Perthshire, reaching Ross and Cromarty about 1775.99 Smith in his work on Argyll considered the Blackface unsuitable: 'their wool is coarse, loose, and shaggy; and they are subject to a very fatal disease, the braxy, which, before the introduction of these sheep, was totally unknown in the Highlands'.100 Cheviots were better suited than Blackface and were often the breed introduced in later instances. In parts of Perthshire, moves to adopt more modern sheep-farming methods were made in 1765 in the Particular Instructions to Archibald Menzies, the Inspector General of the Annexed Estates. Some were taken up in later improvements; on the Coigach estates, local boys were sent to Teviotdale and elsewhere in the Borders to gain experience in sheep husbandry. But the introduction of commercial sheep farming on the Estates as a whole suffered from restrictive policies of administration and lagged behind the estates of private landlords.101 In eastern Ross and Cromarty, Lowland sheep were first introduced in 1763 on the estates of Sir John Ross of Balnagown and were augmented in 1774 by the addition of Linton flocks tended by Lowland shepherds. In several ways, the introduction of sheep on these estates highlights the general pattern. The experiment was initially unsuccessful: 'The losses of sheep, from the depredations of the people, and from mismanagement, were enormous; and the flocks could not be supported, but by annual importations from the south country, and as frequent changes of the shepherds'. Local opposition came both from the peasantry and local 'gentlemen'. The estate and stock was rented in 1781 to a Perthshire farmer, Geddes, who had also 'to struggle against the prejudices of the people, which were inveterate against the new system of pasturage'. Unlike Sir John Ross, Geddes had to deal with overt violence from the tenants: 'the most wicked and flagrant depredations were committed on Mr. Geddes' flock; numbers were shot, and droves were collected, surrounded, and forced into lakes and drowned'.102 Although the tenantry's reaction was violence against the sheep themselves, the root cause in this instance lay as much in the change of authority from Highland landowner to Lowland rentier as it did in the effects upon tenure and established practices. The removal of small tenant farmers from land in Kildermorie in Alness in 1792 initiated further protest, as did the Sutherland clearances (see below, pages 351-391); elsewhere, as in the conversion of hill districts in Kiltearn parish to sheep grazing from 1811, the process was more drawn-out, less violent. In Caithness, 500 Cheviot sheep were introduced by Sir John Sinclair in 1792; by 1800 his flock totalled 3,000. Kerr of Armadale also introduced large numbers of Cheviots into northern Highland estates in 1791.103

Sutherland was the last county to receive Lowland sheep in any great number: 'Until the year 1806, the native breed of sheep was general among the tenantry of this county'.104 Blackface had been herded in Assynt and Eddrachillis since 1800, but later years saw a change to Cheviots, partly because 1806 witnessed an epidemic of rot and scab killing many native sheep and partly because they were less wandering, equally hardy, and with a wool price per stone four times that of the Blackface. Large-scale sheep-farming really began in Sutherland in 1806 with the leasing to Lowland graziers of lands in Lairg and Strathnaver owned by the Marquis of Stafford; between 1806 and 1819, the 'old order', holdings and social relations, was dramatically altered in these districts. On the islands, sheep from Annandale were introduced to South Uist in 1763 to replace the 'degenerate' native sheep. Lowland sheep were brought to Mull and Skye in 1764 and 1765. Elsewhere at that time, in places like Oronsay, Tiree, Coll, North Uist, and Benecula, 'the aboriginal Race of Sheep still subsists, without any mixture or alteration abroad and without any care to improve it at Home'.105

In a detailed essay of 1807, Patrick Singers considered

the introduction of sheep farming in the Highlands to have
had five principal effects: a rise in rents; 'a valuable
supply of wool has been furnished to the manufacturers and
commercial interest'; a reduction in numbers of black
cattle; reduction 'in the extent of cultivated grounds';
and depopulation - 'the worst effect which has followed the
introduction of sheep husbandry in the Highlands'. This
last was the result of four factors: management of sheep
stocks was unknown to the old tenants; the difficulties
faced by landowners in finding 'new methods of subsistence
for their people' (not least given that 'the people,
dissatisfied with the change, and irritated in their minds,
were generally averse from engaging in any new occupation
on their native soil'); the pull of America; and the
activities of departing tacksmen and middle-tenants in
inducing sub-tenants to quit estates. Singers ends his
commentary on the effects thus:

> This view of the effects produced by sheep farming
> in the Highlands, leads of necessity to the
> following result, viz. that the evils complained
> of, have arisen from an extreme in that system,
> rather than from the nature of the stock intro-
> duced; and that a number of unfortunate circum-
> stances acting in concert, have combined at once
> to produce them. That by judicious management,
> these evils may be avoided or counteracted: That
> sheep, as the principal article of produce, are
> entitled to an evident preference over all the
> Highlands; but that it is unwise and impolitic in
> every view, to make them the sole produce.106

This evidence has been largely substantiated by more recent
research.

Gray argues that the real problem 'was not that sheep
came but that this great increase in production was
achieved by inhibiting rather than by releasing the energy
of the peasantry; sheep created no opportunities for the
small farmers'.107 Some contemporaries advocated the
introduction of sheep-farming alongside old systems of
pastoralism and land management. Walker considered that
'The sheep farming in the Highlands ought not to be greatly
extended beyond what it was in former times . . . whatever
change may be made in the Highlands in the advancement of
sheep farming, it certainly ought not to be sudden and
universal'. But however likely in theory, the possibilities in practice of co-existence between new systems of
sheep-farming, traditional methods and the native tenantry
foundered on reasons both technical and economic. When

hills were given over to sheep, sub-tenants could no longer send cattle to sheilings in summer; grazing was restricted to nearby holdings (themselves under threat from the advance of arable enclosure and Lowland sheep), which, in turn, meant a reduction in numbers of cattle. Sheep pressed hard on arable holdings. Reserves of winter pasture on lower ground were necessary: 'Every successful sheep farmer in the Highlands wanted low ground for his flocks, as well as access to the hills; and it was in this area that he could be satisfied sometimes only at the expense of the small tenants'.108 That these tenants could not themselves become sheep farmers stemmed chiefly from their lack of capital: the optimum flock size to keep a shepherd fully employed was 600 sheep, which cost, at the end of the 1700s, £376 with £50 additional expenses.109 Economies of scale determined that middle-scale sheep-farming was uncompetitive; local tenants had to give way to outside graziers, and had either to re-locate or sub-divide their holdings, often on marginal land.

Profits for graziers of Lowland sheep were great: Cheviot wool, with $7^1/2$ fleeces to the stone, sold at 15-20 shillings in 1792, in contrast to which native wool sold at 7s 6d with ten fleeces to the stone.110 Sheepfarmers continued to take handsome profits from the prices of sheep and wool even during the rise in rents which accompanied the leasing of grazing grounds, and despite slumps in prices in the 1820s. Growth in output of wool from the Highlands not only supplied demand in the Lowlands and England, but prompted renewed attention to the development of a native textile industry, which, as with kelp and fishing, was seen by many landowners as necessary to the useful employment of their dispossessed rapidly-increasing tenantry: evidence such as the 1792 'Proposal for forming an Association to encourage the Woollen Manufacture in the Island of Mull' is revealing of the extent to which sheep farming wool production increasingly dominated the marketing structures of Highland pastoral agriculture by the later eighteenth century.111 For Fraser Darling, leasing for pasture previously arable land and changes in sheep-cattle ratios and the concomitant over-grazing, had a destructive effect on the herbage complex and ecological relationships of the Highlands.112 Changes in the ecology of the Highlands had begun centuries before with the clearance of native pine forests and continued with the often irregular coppicing and management practices of woodland on some Highland estates.113 But sheep farming initiated and accelerated changes in the circulatory systems of the Highland natural environment in a way cattle-rearing did not. Archibald Menzies, who was

at other times critical of the 'incivility' of Highland
ways, commented of the grazing practices on the Barrisdale
estate in 1768 in terms that lend weight to Fraser
Darling's claim.

> They have the grass for each season divided into
> as many divisions as it will admit of, as they
> look upon it [as] of consequence to change their
> grass often . . . It is remarkable the skill they
> show in chusing their pasturages for the different
> seasons. It is not the local situation but the
> quality of the grasses they study. Every farmer
> is so far a botanist as to be able to distinguish
> the particular season each grass is in perfec-
> tion.114

Clearance of tenantry for sheep was not just a Highland
phenomenon. Yet clearances in the Highlands were on a
larger scale and prompted more social protest than in the
Southern Uplands or in the east and coastal Lowlands.
Early clearances for sheep in the south and west followed
quite closely the out-movement occasioned by commercial
cattle-raising and the rise of rents. Many reports in the
Statistical Accounts document for the replacement by sheep
of men: the 1845 report upon Glenorchy and Inishail
summarises the evidence of many by the mid-nineteenth
century:

> The introduction of sheep constitutes an era of
> great importance in the history of this, as of
> almost every other Highland parish. It effected,
> everywhere in the Highlands, a complete revolution
> in the condition of the population. It snapped
> the tie which bound the occupant to the owner of
> the soil . . . the anticipated result followed.
> Vast tracts of our straths and valleys, of our
> moors and mountains, exchanged stock and
> occupants . . . One or other of three alternatives
> was adopted by the unfortunate mountaineer, - that
> of removing to some of the manufacturing towns of
> the south, - of emigrating to America, - or of
> contenting himself with a small patch of land,
> with the keep of a few cows, in some assigned
> locality in his native strath or valley.115

The coming of na caoraich mora (the big sheep) - was a
singularly critical agency in the transformation of
Highland agriculture. Graziers were disliked, sheep-
farmers denounced, native labour devalued, customary

practices overturned and population scattered; as a result of sheep farming perhaps more than other contemporary changes, the soil was increasingly part and parcel of capital.

Prices, rents, and capital accumulation, 1750-1850

Few of the tenantry benefitted from the profits and increased income that followed changes in pastoral and arable agriculture. Most were, however, bound up through rent with those new levels of capital accumulation that came with commercial cattle rearing and sheep farming. In the second half of the eighteenth century and during the 1800s, the course of prices and rents and the levels of money income varied, however, and varied in their impact upon the different classes of Highland society. Bearing in mind the earlier evidence of upward pressure on rents before 1750, it is possible to distinguish three periods or phases in the relationship between prices, rents, and capital in the Highland economy: an expansive phase from 1750 to 1815, a period of decline and collapse from 1815 to 1850, and a period of relative rise in rents and standards of living from 1850 to c.1882.[116]
   The period 1750 to 1815 was characterised by increased rents and prices, the reflection of shifts in consumption preferences and an expanded commercial consciousness. During the later 1700s, revenue from the sale of livestock was the principal source of cash income for most landlords and tenantry. Cash through cattle could even provide - usually with some assistance from other exports such as horses, salted fish, fern ash and kelp - for the money needs of an increasing population. Certainly, whilst prices of grain remained static and those of cattle remained high, and the stocks of the tenant population sufficiently numerous to permit a steady cash income to pay rent and import grain, increases either in total rent or in the money portion of it could be met. But prices, of cattle particularly, were artificially inflated in the later eighteenth and early nineteenth centuries by restrictions on foreign imports during the Napoleonic Wars. With the end of hostilities in 1815, prices of Highland goods dropped rapidly. Cattle prices fell at a time of rising population, when changes in arable agriculture were placing tenants on sub-divided crofter holdings, and during a period of growing dependence upon potato cultivation. They did so, too, at a time of social polarisation and tension between landlord and tenant, accentuated by the incoming of Lowland graziers.

Prices fell but rents did not, at least not at once and not to the same degree. During years of increasing prices, the great part of any cash accumulated by tenants went in payment of money rent. Landlords were, after 1815, dependent upon rent from an increasingly depressed tenantry and on lower returns from sheep farming. They could not afford to lower rents. Rental income fell or stabilised, however, in consequence of the build-up of arrears amongst the tenantry. For some landlords, this meant seriously depleted capital reserves and the sale of estates. But changes in rent-price relationships, within a society where cash reserves were minimal or non-existent and wage-labour not common, were felt chiefly by the tenants and perhaps most acutely by those with small regularised holdings and few stock - the crofting sector of the population: 'In terms of the distribution of income, it seems likely that, from 1815 to about 1850, the crofter class suffered not only an absolute decline in welfare (from the fall of cattle prices) but also a deprivation disproportionate to the rest of the Highland community'.117 Any continuing downward trend in prices, especially of cattle, meant that the tenantry accumulated not capital but cash arrears and other symptoms of dependency that were increasingly difficult to shed. At the same time, landlords and middle-tenants were faced with declining cash income and the prospect of a continual drain upon accumulated fixed capital reserves, given their own expressed standards of living, and the shortfall in cash terms between rent due and actual money payment made, and because of the unlikelihood of a return on any outlay of cash or grain or stock to an under-capitalised labour force ever more restricted in their individual holdings, grazing rights, and economic opportunities.

Changes in rent levels (and quite what they meant in regard to existing or nascent social relations) are not always easy to establish. Understanding regional or local distinctions is made difficult by the differences across the Highlands in the quantity and quality of land, in the balance between income derived from arable or pastoral agriculture, and in the attitudes held toward the accumulation of arrears: 'Thus one must be cautious in drawing inferences from rental series: they do not necessarily represent the pattern of cost changes experienced by the crofter; nor do they represent the net benefits received from landlords, as they ignore investment expenditures, and may not be net of operating expenses'.118 The same problems hold for the accurate statistical assessment of wages and prices: the first because communal sharing of tasks was not based on the cash nexus - 'When People have

230

occasion for more Labour, than that of their own Servants, they borrow their neighbours, so that they have scarce a Price upon a Man's Labour by the Day';119 the second because Highland exports largely operated through local markets thus hindering comparison of different places at separate times. Despite these difficulties, contemporary commentary and a variety of estate evidence is available to illustrate the trends outlined above and to highlight the regional variations in effect and cause of the changing course of prices and rents.

On the Perthshire section of the Breadalbane Estates, rents increased from £2,700 in 1774 to £3,282 in 1778 and £4,129 in 1784 (All figures in pounds sterling). On the MacLeod estates on Skye, the rise may be dated to the early 1700s, with a period of accelerated increase (72 per cent) in the period 1754 to 1769. Rents increased thus: £989 in 1708 to £1,008 in 1724 and £1,188 in 1744; from £1,644 in 1754 to £2,831 in 1769 before a slight (and temporary) decline to £2,473 in 1777.120 In Lochalsh, rents increased by 267 per cent to £1,299 in the forty years from 1748 and in Badenoch by 236 per cent to £1,347 by 1758 over a period of twenty-three years. Several of the early eighteenth century rentals show an attention to money payment that increased in proportion later in the 1700s.121 On the Lochbuie estates on Mull, total rent was £256 in 1743, of which £207 (81 per cent) was in money payment, the remainder in kind. Rent increased to £527 in 1768, to £643 in 1771 and to £1,033 by 1784. By 1805, the rent had risen to £1,430 and stood at £2,298 by 1851. On the Sutherland Estates, Adam has documented total rent increases over the period 1808 to 1815 as high as 336 per cent (for Farr parish), and an average increase of 149 per cent over the eight years for the estates as a whole. At the same time, the victual proportion declined dramatically.122 During the periods of rise, arrears were being built up amongst the tenantry. In 1771, arrears totalling £140 (22 per cent of the rent owed) had been accumulated on the Lochbuie estates; in 1784 the arrears stood at £582 (56 per cent of rent owed). The fact that, by 1805, arrears there had fallen to 4 per cent should not disguise the fact that, even in a period of relative prosperity, landlords might find capital depleted and tenants' cash used to pay debts not rent. A rental of 1786 for the Lochbuie estates includes rent figures exacted that year - 'present rents' - for the thirty-one principal holdings and intended figures for 1787; the 'Rent to be'. Rents were to be increased on all of the holdings: in terms of averages, the mean rent in 1786 of £40 per holding increased by 55 per cent to £62. But on some of the larger farms, the 'Rent to be' doubled within a year, and on one increased by 567 per cent from £45 to £300.123 On MacDonald's estates on Skye, similar farm-by-farm variation in rate of increase is revealed in evidence for the period 1796 to 1809; rental for the farm at Ballamenoch, for example, increased from £30 to £74 over this period, and others doubled. Ballamenoch had been rented in 1731 at £7 5s. Of the twenty-two farms listed in a Rental for 1799 and 1800, fourteen increased in rental, eight decreased (of which two were not let in 1800). The average percentage rate of increase among the fourteen was 61 per cent; for the eight farms whose rent decreased, the average decline was 13 per cent: the estate rent as a whole rose from £5,825 13s 4d to £6,121 19s 4d.124 On the Reay estates, increases over the period 1789 to 1797 were dependent on 'what the said estate may be let for when the whole is out to lease'. The new lease was for sheep farming; 'and for this purpose may be worth double this rent'. Rentals increased for part of the estate by 168 per cent in the period 1789 to 1797 in consequence of this change. On the predominantly arable holdings, rent was rising by £50 every seven years in a fifty-seven year lease. And of estate lands in Tongue parish in 1820, we are told 'All the Small Tenants have no Lease, & [are] understood to be continued only during good behaviour'.125

The general trend of rapid rise in the period 1750 to 1815, based in the northern most Highlands especially upon cattle prices, kelp profits, and commercial sheep-farming, was thus not unambiguous: individual estates contained farms not always let, arrears could accumulate even during periods of prosperity, and the evidence for some places of a difference between intent and effect in attempts at rental increase hints, perhaps, at processes of social negotiation unrecorded in the statistical evidence and certainly at the sometimes irregular path of rise. These variations and contradictions are evident also in the price of cattle or kelp. Walker's evidence on prices and wages and the value of exports for the Hebrides in 1764 and 1771 reveals not only a differential scale of output in any one year between island parishes, in terms of head of cattle or tons of kelp, but also different prices. The base against which rent rose thus varied economically between and even within parishes in relation to prices, people per acre, number of cattle and quality and quantity of kelp. It varied also geographically. In parts of eastern Ross and Cromarty, rents rose in the later 1700s due not to pastoral wealth but to increased arable acreage, itself the reflection of incoming large-scale farmers from the south. Native tenants were unable to purchase lands and farms due

Table 4.5

State of rents, payments and arrears on Lord MacDonald's estates on Skye, by parish, 1823–1824 and 1844–1845*

(a) 1823–1824

Parish	Arrears unpaid 31.7.1823 £	Rent due Whitsun 1824 £	Total sum due Whitsun 1824 £	Total sum received £	Arrears unpaid at 31.7.1824 and as % of rent £	%
Sleat	1582	1898	3487	2389	1092	57.5
Strath	1594	1478	3072	1627	1445	97.8
Portree	2466	1434	3900	1751	2149	149.9
Snizort	2650	1286	3936	2499	1436	111.7
Kilmuir	2500	1082	3583	1767	1815	167.7

(Continued overleaf.)

(Table 4.5 (Continued)

(b) 1844-1845

Parish	Arrears unpaid 30.9.1844	Rent due Whitsun 1844-45	Payment made 30.9.1844- 30.9.1845	Arrears unpaid at 30.9.1845 and as % of rent	
	£	£	£	£	%
Sleat	815	2025	2116	724	35.80
Strath	1511	2432	2561	1382	56.83
Portree	1320	2241	2249	1311	58.52
Snizort	745	1694	1781	658	38.90
Kilmuir	2115	2816	2914	2016	71.61

* SRO, GD221/90/2; GD221/78/35

to a lack of capital, and were under-capitalised and without a well-structured wage-earning sector at just that period of shift towards money and away from victual in payment of rent. And in a region where grain for local consumption and export was much more significant than in the west, crop failures such as those of 1782-3 led to rent arrears and the sale of native farms to Lowland graziers or farmers.

A fall in prices on one hand and, on the other, fixed monetary obligations amongst an under-capitalised tenantry led to an increasing hardship in the Highland economy after 1815. Falling prices did not, however, cause immediate collapse in peasant living standards: 'Having no margin of trivial or luxurious expenditure, tenants passed the deficiency on to what had always been the residual item of expenditure - the rent; the immediate symptom of any drop in income - through, for example, a fall in cattle prices - was a growing list of tenants in arrears'.126 Landlords had little choice but to accept these shortcomings whilst tenants became seriously indebted. If incomes did increase, amounts added were likely to be used to pay off debts; the great part of the fall in money income was passed on to landlords for whom expenditure on the estates was likely to increase given the reasons outlined above. The result was sale of estates, a shortage of capital as restrictive as the shortage of land and continued processes of sub-division, and perhaps, too, a sense of helpless dependency amongst a population whose tenurial position permitted little advance and no sustainable profit.

The gap between rent owed and level of arrears was greatest in the north and west. In places, rental levels diminished, as in part of the Reay Estates in Caithness where rents 'fell a fourth at least' between 1818 and 1828,127 but more common was the build-up of arrears to a level equal to or greater than the annual rent: even if the whole rent had been paid off in any year (impossible for most tenants), debts would have remained. Table 4.5 shows the relationship between rents, payments, and arrears on the MacDonald Estates on Skye in the period 1823-4 to 1844-5. In Snizort, Portree, and Kilmuir parishes, the sum of arrears owed in 1823-4 suggests a serious depletion of cash income for landlords and total indebtedness for the tenantry. A 'List of Arrears due by the Tenants' on these estates drawn up in August 1839 distinguishes between those 'recoverable, doubtful and irrecoverable'. In Sleat parish, 10 per cent of total arrears was considered 'doubtful', 3 per cent 'irrecoverable', and the remainder 'recoverable'. In Portree and Snizort, however, over 30 per cent was reckoned 'doubtful', and in the case of the latter parish (then hard hit by potato blight in addition to the causes outlined above), 16 per cent of arrears was deemed 'irrecoverable'.128 Similar patterns were to be found elsewhere. In Lewis over the period 1814 to 1856-7, for example, rents fell for most of the farms (an average of 52 per cent over the period), but arrears persisted even after the decline (Table 4.6). And in Easter Ross, where a drop in grain prices exacerbated the effect of a fall in cattle prices, rent levels persisted whilst arrears amongst tenantry built up, although the switch in barley for use in distilling diverted the more severe effects of deflation evident in the north and west.

Destitution, famine, and agricultural collapse, 1836-1850

To the extent that Highland material practices were grounded in a natural setting largely restrictive of anything but subsistence agriculture, shortage of food was no stranger. The Highlands endured numerous times of hardship and shortages in food-stuffs before the 1830s, chiefly the result of climate: in 1623-4, 1645-6, 1680, 1688, during the later 1690s, in 1740-1, 1751, 1756, 1763-4, 1771, 1782-3, 1806-8, 1811 and 1816-7. Whether these earlier deficiencies of harvest and their demographic effects may be considered 'famines' comparable with those of 1836-7 and 1846-50, depends partly upon the scale of hardship in any given area and in part, too, upon the impact such earlier events had upon the Highland consciousness and their appearance in the historical record. The majority of recorded shortages and crop failures before 1782 were small-scale events, socially and geographically.

The crisis of 1782-3 appears to have been the first widespread catastrophe (perhaps because it has been better documented than earlier instances). The combination of an extreme winter in 1782 which reduced over-wintered stock, a late and cold spring that delayed planting, and excessive rains at harvest followed by a further cold winter destroyed both potato and cereal crops. Destitution was common and would have been greater but for £17,000 of government aid in peasemeal: 1783 has been remembered as bliadhna na peasrach, the peasemeal year. Flinn has suggested that this crisis had a dramatic effect upon mortality and baptisms in a few parishes but had a longer-term more widespread effect in the form of migration and as a spur to agricultural change. One contemporary believed that the famine of 1782 gave impulse to the replacement of cattle by sheep.129 Between 1782-3 and

236

Table 4.6

Rent increases and the proportion of rent in arrears on selected farms in Lewis, 1814 to 1856–1857*

Farm	Rent in 1814(1) £	Rent in 1856-7 £	Proportion of rent in arrears, 1856-1857 £	Proportion of rent in arrears, 1856-1857 %	Per cent change in rent 1814 to 1856 %
(a) In Stornaway parish					
Garrabost	152.65	51.78	20.13	38.9	− 66.10
Branahuie	21.72	61.40	21.42	34.9	+182.70
Nether Holme	64.67	25.00	7.42	29.7	− 61.30
Nether Coll	171.80	133.65	30.57	22.9	− 22.20
(b) In Barvas parish					
Bragar	217.69	140.00	108.50	77.5	− 35.70
North Bragar	141.85	91.38	76.34	83.5	− 35.60
Arnol	128.72	81.82	43.37	53.0	− 36.40
Upper Barvas	58.87	66.10	10.32	15.6	+ 12.30
Fivepenny Borve	155.00	118.68	32.54	27.4	− 23.40
(c) In Lochs parish					
Arnish	41.52	50.00	25.75	51.5	+ 20.30
Laxay	111.57	86.00	2.18	2.5	− 22.91
Ballallan	212.19	181.00	22.51	12.4	− 14.70
Calbost	118.95	34.00	None	0.0	− 71.40
Knock Carloway	67.54	52.75	8.22	15.6	− 21.90

(Continued overleaf.)

Table 4.6 (Continued)

(d) In Uig parish

Mealista	110.10	105.00	None	0.0	— 4.60
Brenish	135.13	93.67	79.07	84.4	— 30.70
Crowlista	96.92	87.05	64.17	73.7	— 10.20
Valtos	232.37	149.50	81.97	54.8	— 35.70
Breascleit	151.52	112.35	00.11	0.1	— 25.90

* SRO, GD274/19, Lewis Rentals 1814; SRO, GD/475/1-2, Lewis Rentals 1856 – 1857
(1) All rents include sums exacted for road money, school salary, and doctor's salary.

the more striking events of 1846 were several instances of food shortage: in 1806-8, 1812-3, 1816-7, 'the deep and universal distress' of 1831, and the destitution of 1836-7. This last episode, though not as widespread as the famine of 1846-50, was no less severe in scale; together, they bracket a period of collapse in Highland agriculture and destitution for the people who drew a living from it.

Dependence upon the potato was almost total for many people by the early 1800s, in the north and west mainland and islands particularly. For some parishes there, export of potatoes provided valuable cash income. In places, potatoes had been planted in place of grain, earlier shortage of which had been responsible for privation and hardship. But the potato was an unreliable staple. Few varieties were resistant to disease. In the Highlands, however, climatological factors which in their extreme occasioned crop failure, paradoxically protected the potato from infections such as 'curl'. But the region offered no such ecological protection against the 'blight', a condition caused by the fungus phytophtora infestans, which appeared at a time of almost total reliance on the potato. Blight appeared first in Argyll in 1833. Not until 1836 and 1837 was it the cause of widespread crop failure.

The extent of the destitution in the 1830s is revealed in the below letter of 2 March 1837:

> In the range of country and coasts extending from Argyleshire to the northernmost point of Sunder-landshire, including the Hebrides and the Island of Skye, but exclusive of the population in Badenoch, and in the Heights of the Highlands of Aberdeenshire and Perthshire, of which I had no means to form an estimate, there were from 60 to 80,000 persons, who would require a very extensive supply of food, after this month of March till August next, when the new crop may be supposed to come into use. Assuming 80,000 the total number requiring aid, the population of Lewis being 16,000, and bearing the proportion of 1/5 to the whole, 4,400 x 5 or 22,000 Bolls would be required: from which will fail to be deducted any supply by private benevolence or aid . . . this is not the only cause of suffering and distress to be remedied; for the crops not having ripened for the last two seasons, there is the greatest want in the entire extent of the above named districts, of seed barley, oat, and potatoes.130

An estimate of the population of this area, using 1831 population totals, gives a figure of 159,796 persons. Lewis was particularly badly affected. John Cameron, minister in Stornoway parish, writing to Norman MacLeod, secretary of the Glasgow relief committee on 2 February 1837, considered that 'the number of very needy' totalled 2,000 [out of an 1841 population of 6,218]; the potato crop was less than half its usual yield and grain crops were unusable for meal:

> The inclement season prevented the oat crop from filling and ripening - the incessant autumnal rains and the early snow storms injured and even rotted what had been cut - the grain heated and matted in the corn-yards - the meal which had been made of the oats has a frightful colour a bitter unpalatable taste, producing dysentry.131

Elsewhere we are told of one part of Stornoway parish that '163 of the 396 families [are] totally destitute of all supplies of food'. In Uig parish, tenants were 'so depressed in circumstances' as to be unable to support themselves or their families, pay rent, or meet costs of seed granted in relief. An estimated 30 per cent out of the parish population were destitute in Portree in 1837: 'One thousand and seventy-six are wholly without provisions [in an 1841 population of 3,574], and, what is still more deplorable, without the means of procuring them; for they have neither money, or credit, or employment!' The effects of crop failure were made worse by an influenza epidemic and, as they had been in 1831 and 1832, by cholera.132

The 1836-7 famine and attempts at its amelioration highlights not only the depressed state of the tenantry and of landlords' financial capabilities, but also the attitude of central government to the Highland problem. One of the principal resolutions of The Committee of Contributors for the Relief of those suffering from Destitution in the Highlands and Islands, relative to the supply of corn and seed potatoes in 1837, was to grant aid only if the landlord could guarantee to pay half the sum within a year.133 But this was not feasible for many landlords given accumulation of arrears. For most tenants it was virtually impossible; as one commentator observed of Uig parish, 'I see no way of supplying them but by gift'.134 The government was initially unwilling to act unless landlords and charitable relief schemes had been tried; 'it would only be when these two sources of relief had been found to be inadequate, that the funds of the State could have been with justice, and propriety applied for such a

240

purpose'.135 Direct funding was considered inconsistent with the tenets of good management.

> They felt that if any large portion of the subjects of her Majesty were to be impressed with a belief that they had a right to rely upon the interposition of the State in order to supply them with food, the strongest motives to foresight, industry, and frugality would be withdrawn, and a principle would be laid down, inconsistent with the well-being of society.136

The 1836-7 distress was met with local and government relief schemes and harvests recovered sufficiently in 1838 to allow the crisis to pass. But experience of shortage was never far away.

Blight re-appeared in August 1846 and was devastating on a wide scale: 'The failure may be taken as absolute ... Little or nothing will be saved'.137 The effect was felt most in the north and west Highlands and islands where dependence upon the potato was greatest and where kelping and the predominance of crofting had brought people to the coast on small holdings. Unlike some earlier events, however, it was also felt acutely in the eastern parishes of Ross and Cromarty and Inverness, and in Orkney and Shetland. Across all of these areas, the famine was more severe in consequence of its longer duration (over five years), its structural and financial effect upon the agricultural economy, and because of the scale of the relief programme. In Mull and surrounding islands, it was estimated in late 1846 that 18,000 persons in a population of 22,000 were approaching starvation; in Glenelg, two-thirds of the population of 2,729 were seriously destitute; for Latheron, Assynt, and much of Sutherland in 1847, sources speak of 'increasing destitution'; crop returns document districts with two-thirds and upwards of crops, potatoes and grain, 'utterly spoilt'. Failure of the herring fishing over the period added to the misery. A report upon Tiree for 1846 may stand for most of the Highlands:

> I speak of . . . Tyrie [sic] where the population are so enormously redundant that they have exhausted every particle of fuel in the Island, and depend on a distant property for the supply of peat - where upwards of 1400 people are in such a condition that they cannot pay a farthing to the proprietor, nor to any tenant - and are without doubting liable to destitution from (even) a

241

partial failure of any one crop.138

What averted complete catastrophe was relief; from the government, the landlords and private charity.

Government relief from 1846-7 was co-ordinated by Sir Edward Pine Coffin whose experience of Ireland's famine gave him great insight into Highland problems. Coffin realised the extent to which landlords were unable to help their tenants. Grain depots were set up at Tobermory and Portree, but problems of a 'fair' price to set were constant and the immediate burden of aid fell on landlords. Not all landlords responded in the same manner. MacLeod of Dunvegan provided for about 8,000 persons by early 1847; the second Duke of Sutherland (against the advice of James Loch, his principal factor) spent £18,000 on famine relief;139 and on Lewis, in North Morar and on the estate of MacLean of Ardgour, landlords provided relief directly in money or in meal, or initiated road-building and drainage schemes. Where relief was not forthcoming in these ways, many landlords encouraged the younger able-bodied men to seek work in the Lowlands. Some landlords did little, however, most notably Gordon of Cluny, whose neglect of his tenantry on South Uist, Barra and Benbecula at the height of the famine in 1847 earned him widespread hatred. But even well-intentioned land-lords were restricted in their charity; cottars and crofters could pay no rent to reduce landlords' outgoings and landlords had to pay for foodstuffs in those places where crop returns show seriously depleted grain and potato crops. Government help was crucial: 'measures on a large Scale are indispensible, and tho' private Generosity may do much, and the Landlords must do more, yet the Governments active interference is I should think indispensible'.

> It seems to me most important that the Government should thoroughly understand how the resources for the next year are to be provided, seeing that neither the Cottars themselves nor the Proprietors will be enabled to make the same efforts another year which they have done during the last. The little hoards & resources of the smaller occupiers must soon, I should apprehend, be entirely exhausted.140

Further direct involvement was forestalled from February 1847 by the establishment, under government direction, of the Central Board of Management of the Fund for the Relief of the Destitute Inhabitants of the Highlands. This body, whilst taking overall care of policies of fund raising,

242

Population Growth and Highland Agriculture

operated through a series of Local Committees and through two committees, or 'sections', set up in Glasgow and Edinburgh. The Glasgow section was responsible for the Outer Isles, Argyll and western Inverness-shire; the Edinburgh section for Skye, Wester Ross, the eastern mainland, and Orkney and Shetland. Funding for relief through these sections came chiefly from private and public charitable subscriptions in Scotland, but large donations were received from Scots abroad and others. Analysis of subscription lists for 1847-8 reveals many of Edinburgh's Gaelic community to have contributed, as did the Gaelic congregations of Aberdeen and Inverness, Highland regiments, and overseas bodies such as the Boston Scots Charitable Society.141   So successful were the Board's activities, the Government closed its meal depots at Tobermory and Portree in 1847 and sold off the stocks remaining to the Board. The Board itself had intended to operate for only one season. Prospects of its closure were likely in 1847 given its relief schemes over 1846-7 and the seemingly good harvest in prospect. But 1847 was a false dawn.   Autumn rains ruined crops across the Highlands and the Board was forced to resume its operations. Reports from various local committees document the extent of the problem. At any one time on Skye in 1847, between one-quarter and one-half of the population were almost totally dependent on relief for survival.142   In the eastern Highlands, destitution in 1847 was generally less severe than in the north and west, but local instances highlight the poverty of population and collapse of agricultural production;   in Rosskeen, for example, where 'alarming destitution was exacerbated by clearances of the small tenantry';   in Latheron where combined failure of the herring fishing and the potato crop was the cause of destitution;   or in Dores where, notes one commentator, local funding was insufficient and Board assistance needed: 'I both trust & believe that the majority are straining every nerve to meet the distress around them - for none are exempt. It comes to our very door'.143   Food riots along the coasts of Caithness early in 1847 (though not in the more seriously-affected north and west Highlands) are testimony to the extent of destitution, and understandable given that the riots were directed against export of grain from the area at a time of hardship for most.

In 1848 the Board introduced the 'labour test' whereby the meal ration - earlier established at 1 lb 8oz for an adult male - could now only be distributed in return for eight hours' work a day, six days a week. The 'test' was widely disliked, partly for the fact that meal was distrib-

243

uted at rates equivalent to about 5 ^{1}/2d for a family's daily labour at a time when the lowest weekly wages were 6 shillings, and partly because the staff administering the test scheme were well paid. A second change occurred in 1849 to involve landlords in the development of roads, piers, and other aspects of the Highlands' economic infrastructure. Hunter notes: 'These "destitution roads" were the Board's great practical accomplishment, its other development making little tangible impact on the Highland scene'.144 Reports documenting the relative increase and decrease in total numbers of persons on the 'test' and engaged in labour schemes in 1848, 1849 and 1850 show large numbers engaged in these 'public works', others (chiefly women) employed in textiles, and many Highlanders assisted in movement to the Lowlands to look for work. Over 16,800 persons were employed on road schemes in 1849, for example; on average, about 23 per cent of all Highland men seeking relief at any time in 1849 were found employment on the construction of Highland 'relief' roads.145

The Board was a failure in other respects for several reasons. First, it was too ambitious; road schemes intended to stimulate the Highland economy never did so and the Board's under-capitalisation of improvements to agricultural practice, being focussed rather on relief of effects not amelioration or removal of causes, 'served merely to aggravate the damage already done to it by famine and by negligent land management'.146 Second, the appointment from 1848 of Board staff - Overseers, Relief Officers, Sub-Inspectors and Inspectors - to replace Local Committees was neither popular nor successful. Local Committees were regarded by the Board, to use Hunter's phrase, as 'unhealthily democratic'. They had shown 'a lamentable tendency to act as the representatives and advocates of those seeking relief'. Local Committees had failed to engender the spirit of self-help so central to the contemporary assumptions of the middle class as unyielding in its particular prejudices towards Highland relief as it was towards general demands for philanthropy in the new Scottish Poor Law of 1845. This change in personnel meant, thirdly, that few people, certainly at Board level, had experience of the Highland problem. As Hunter has shown, one Board directive of 1848 which laid down that Highlanders were not officially destitute 'until their means are exhausted' rendered useless any effort to save stock or seed, thus undermining any chance of agricultural regeneration by the tenants. In another directive, crofters were refused meal unless they laboured on the Board's projects, rather than on their own land. 'The cultivation of the soil is the most important subject that can engage the Committee's attention', wrote Rev. MacGregor of Kilmuir in 1849, but having offered some local men ground for tillage and seed, he informed the Board of his parishioners' refusal noting that the obligation to the 'test' scheme was 'actually taking away the opportunity of working the soil'.147 And lastly, the Board's failure was founded upon a determination not to alter the social relations of Highland agricultural production. Security of tenure was considered by one inspector to be 'the keystone of every exertion on the part of the crofter', but tenurial change as a basis to relief was never widely considered. Relief was not only distributed 'to make it conducive to increased exertion', but also to preserve the tenurial and social status quo: 'The destitute population were relieved in a mode which left them in their natural position and there was no interference whatever with the ordinary relations of society'.

Demographically, the Highland potato famine was not significant as a major instance of crisis mortality. Flinn advances six reasons why this was so: it affected fewer people than in Ireland; landlords did respond to their conscience; great quantities of food were distributed by the Central Board; public employment schemes made it possible for Highlanders to buy food; the distressed areas being primarily coastal were accessible by sea and relief grain thus easily moved; there were surprisingly high levels of stocks and savings that could be drawn on. As Flinn notes, however, this last was only temporary. In drawing upon savings, many Highlanders were sacrificing future well-being. Famine was more important as a stimulus to migration, both within Scotland following the widespread policy of funding the Lowland-ward movement of labour as a relief measure, and emigration overseas. Migration in the wake of potato famine was not a conscious reaction by the tenantry to changed economic circumstances, but the result of landlords' actions 'who felt that the potato famine had only underlined what they had been coming to think during the previous twenty or thirty years'.149 As Hunter argues, 'the famine of the 1840s served only to intensify Highland proprietors' hostility to the crofting system and to make "redundance of population" an even more "prominent topic of lamentation" in landowning circles'.150 Economically, the famine had several effects; a serious reduction in the stocks and savings of tenants, the deceleration of agricultural production to a point of virtual stagnation for parts of the north and west, and, in turn, a continued decline in profit, levels of capital and income for landlords.

Recovery and legislation: Highland agriculture, 1850-1886

The effect of the destitution in the 1840s was more to heighten and intensify earlier existing processes of transformation than mark any new beginning for Highland agriculture.

Richards has claimed of the period 1850 to 1882 that it 'is in many ways the most interesting and the most enigmatic for the economic and social history of the Highlands'.151 Price trends favoured producers. Wool prices rose by a third between 1850 and 1880. Cattle prices increased two-fold. The standard of living improved 'for almost the entire community'. If they rose at all, crofters' rents did not do so as steeply as those sheep farms or sporting estates: for, claims Richards, 'It is plain the rental policy was discriminatory and that the crofters had become a relatively insignificant source of revenue'. Not until the 1870s did crofting rents start to rise. In this they reflected the trend in rents from sheep farming in prior decades. Sheep farming profited in the Highlands in the 1850s and 1860s as never before. Stocks rose rapidly; in Sutherland the number of sheep rose from 168,170 in 1853 to 240,096 by 1875 (having been 94,570 in 1801); in Ross and Cromarty, sheep stocks increased by over 50 per cent between 1840 and 1869; and in Inverness-shire the total for 1855 was 567,694, that for 1869 a figure of 762,989.152. As numbers and prices rose, so did rents: on estates in Skye, sheep farmers' rents increased by between 50 and 100 per cent in the fifty years from 1830; on Barra the increase was between 30 and 80 per cent, whilst in Knoydart and in Sutherland increases were in the order of 30 to 50 per cent in the 1860s and 1870s. Prosperity for Highland sheep-farmers despite rising rent levels was related also to the effects of climate and outbreaks of disease amongst stock elsewhere in Britain - severe winters in the Border counties in 1859-60; increases of liver-fluke amongst English stocks in 1860 and 1879; rinderpest amongst southern cattle in the mid-1860s. Fluctuations in demand and prices in the 1860s were followed by a brief period of improvement in market conditions in 1870, but by a more serious decline in wool prices after 1872, occasioned by the difficulty of letting farms given the profits to be gained from deer forests and sporting estates and, after 1880, from the introduction of frozen mutton from Australia and New Zealand. Sheep numbers in Ross and Cromarty, Argyll, Inverness and Sutherland fell between 1885 and 1890 as wedder stocks in particular declined: 'With the serious collapse of sheep prices in 1892 and the persistent depression in the wool trade, the demise of wedder farming was imminent'.153 Losses of sheep in the winters of 1878-9 and 1882-3 affected the profits of sheep farmers. The decline of sheep farming was in part also ecological in cause, attributable to over-grazing and the effects of moor burning although more recent work has argued that the importance of a decline in carrying capacity has been exaggerated.154 For these reasons, Highland landlords were, by the 1880s, in a further crisis. The solution for many was a shift from sheep farm to deer forest.

Deer forests - those areas in which other stock were cleared to make room for deer - have their origins in the Highlands in the late eighteenth century. Nine are mentioned in the Old Statistical Account. By 1884 there were 104 covering 1,975,209 acres, mostly in the east-central Grampian Highlands, Inverness-shire north and west of the Great Glen, and Ross and Cromarty, together with pockets in Sutherland and on Lewis and Harris. There were 28 forests formed before 1839, a further 17 in the 1840s, a total of 31 in the period 1850 to 1865, and 31 in the decade from 1865 to 1875. From 1875 to 1880, a further 13 forests were formed. The most rapid growth was in the five-year period from 1880 to 1885 when 29 forests were established before falling to 20 forests formed between 1885-90. Between 1890 and 1900, a further 31 forests were formed.155

Somers in his 1848 Letters from the Highlands considered that the destitution of that period prompted landlords to turn to deer forests and sporting estates as a means of recouping losses.156 This is possible but the more towards a sporting Highlands had begun earlier. William Scrope's The Art of Deer Stalking (1838) has been considered influential here; also significant was the association of the sporting Highlands, especially Deeside, with royalty in the Victorian era, the passing of the Game Act of 1831, and the later expansion of the railway network. The move towards what Smout has called the 'vulgar tourism' of the later 1800s, in which people more often came to the Highlands either to kill in it or to search for spiritual renewal in a 'natural' wilderness than they did to understand it, may be considered part of those several contradictions in then British culture between an urban way of life and a sought-for harmony with a countryside and nature being remade as particular compensating images. The attention devoted to Highland scenery, either as sporting backdrop or as 'wild nature' and the locale of myths and romantic legends, was part of this change in land use in the later 1800s from sheep farm to deer forest, although the view of the Highlands as scenery often overlooked an understanding of it as economic and moral landscape. Estates became 'machines for sport' as Gaskell puts it. His work on the Morvern estates documents the way in which the satisfaction of economic needs by landlords was matched by the gratification of spiritual needs and sporting demands of visitors to the estate. Sheep were cleared; game stocks were preserved by payment of 'vermin money'; scenery walked in, captured on canvas and reduced to photo albums; deer were shot and salmon hooked by foreigners to a created and managed wilderness, led by gamekeepers and 'gillies' (a sportsman's attendant, from the Gaelic gille, pl. gillean, lad or man-servant).157 Nature was appropriated for its use value as social status as well as for its exchange value in economic terms.

Increased acreage of deer forest compensated for falling wool prices. Sporting estates gave higher rents than sheep farms or returns from crofting. The general rise in sporting rents led to an inflation of land prices as well as change in land use. Further, the early years of the second half of the nineteenth century witnessed a renewed attention by landlords to the question of an over-populous under-capitalised tenantry. To the extent that the attitude of landlords in the wake of destitution was one of hostility alone (though some still stood by an obligation part-moral and part-economic to relieve their tenantry), the most common result was, to them, the most evident - the clearance of the small tenants: 'the immediate effect of the famine on land management policies was thus to accelerate and intensify the already existing tendency to make sheep farming the main prop of estate economics in districts where kelping, and therefore crofting, had once been predominant - a development that was necessarily accompanied by the clearance of many of the areas still occupied by crofters'.158

Hunter has considered that the working of the new Scots Poor Law after 1845, which forced an additional financial burden upon landlords and principal estate managers through compulsory payment of given rates of relief, also underlay the determination of landlords to rid their estates of 'dependent population'. The clearances and emigrations of the famine and post-famine years have been documented in detail elsewhere:159 the more important instances were in Glencalvie near Bonar Bridge in Ross and Cromarty in 1845; Sollas on North Uist in 1849; Strathaird in south-west Skye in 1850; throughout the Strathconan district of Easter Ross in the 1840s; Coigach in 1852-3; Suishnish in south-west Skye in 1849, 1852 and 1853; Greenyards in Strathcarron, Easter Ross, in 1854 (for Richards, 'the most sensational of all the episodes of clearances'); and what have been generally considered the most complete clearances of a destitute tenantry by a landlord bent on profit from sheep, those of South Uist, Barra and Benbecula from 1848-51. The move to clear for sheep in these places was not just a post-famine phenomenon. As Caird has shown of the Uists, for example, sub-tenants were systematically evicted from 1826 onwards as leases ended, with the effect that reclamation and partial cultivation of pasture land and over-intensive use of existing arable land on the machairs all occurred.160 But this pre-dated the collapse of kelp and the potato famine and came before the build-up of arrears had undermined investment, profit margins, and processes of capital accumulation. The clearances of 1850s - the climax of the Highland clearances - took place within a society whose cash reserves were seriously depleted and at a time when many tenants seemed destined to permanent dependence upon charity. Consequently, among the landlord class at least, there 'was little opposition to the sponsorship of emigration per se; controversy surrounded the manner of its execution, but not its necessity'.161

Landlords considered the rapid clearance of a proportion of the population necessary to the longer-term economic well-being of the Highlands as a whole. The shared sentiments of a class for whom payment of a trans-Atlantic passage cleared consciences as it also cleared lands are reflected in the role of the Highlands and Islands Emigration Society, largely directed by Sir John MacNeill and Sir Charles Trevelyan and funded by many of the crofting landlords. For this body and those who supported it, estates could neither be run successfully then, nor sold in the future, 'while they are occupied by swarms of miserable tenants who can neither pay rent nor support themselves'.162 Of the effect upon the tenantry, Hunter considers the clearances 'utterly overwhelming catastrophes whose effects - psychological as well as physical - were profound and long-lasting'. Protest against eviction took several forms, discussed in more detail below (Chapter 6). Here it is important to note that, in context with the observed changes in land use from sheep farm to deer forest for many Highland estates in the late 1800s, one principal effect of the clearances was to restrict further the arable holdings and economic opportunities of the remaining crofter and cottar population. Clearances whilst in theory allowing greater opportunity for the expansion of holdings for persisting crofters in practice never did: 'the lands of emigrating tenants are added to some existing sheep farm and the small tenants, whose holding are altogether inadequate for their support, are left just as they were', 'I have never seen that emigration gave more room to people, though it did to sheep. The tendency has been to add more families to places already overcrowded'.163 Rent levels for crofters were always lower, and increased more slowly, than those for sheep farms or sporting estates. The total rental of Inverness-shire in 1845 was about £200,000. By 1871-2 it had risen to £296,353; 'Inverness-shire has its grouse shootings and deer forests in a considerable degree to thank for swelling its rent-roll'. Macdonald notes of 'the advanced portions' of Inverness-shire that rents had been increased for arable farmers at the expiry of leases with the dual effect of stimulating greater production on lands already worked and of reclamation from the waste. Arable acreage increased by 88 per cent in the county between 1854 and 1870.164 In Sutherland, arable acreage increased by 7,418 acres (34 per cent) between 1853 and 1879.165 These changes took place in the south and east of the counties concerned, in areas of better soil, proximity to the Lowlands, and amongst better-off tenants. Expansion of the arable was not possible for most of the crofter and cottar population in the north and west. In many cases, despite an upturn in prices and improved living standards, arrears persisted. On the MacDonald Estates in Skye between 1857 and 1869, for example, arrears were running in some places as high as 48 per cent of the annual rent (Table 4.7); the fact that this represented considerable improvement in degree of indebtedness from thirty or so years before (cf. Table 4.5) is undeniable and hints at a relative recovery, but it is also suggestive of continued financial hardship for many in the crofting regions. Whilst it is true, however, that the clearances of the 1850s acted more to crowd than ameliorate congestion on over-populated town-ships and coastal small-holdings, and rent arrears deter-mined continued dependency, it is also true that the occupation of the hill grazings by sheep following clear-ance of tenantry left those who remained more secure than before (though not better off and still restricted). This paradoxical and quite unforeseen effect left crofters crowded, mostly unable to initiate improvement because of restrictive leases or lack of capital, but it left them alone: 'And the consequent tendency to leave crofters in undisputed occupation of their meagre plots and scanty grazings was enforced towards the end of the 1860s by a falling away in sheep farmers' profits'.166

The 1860s and 1870s were a period of unprecedented stability for the crofting population. Prosperity for crofters (at all times only relative given earlier destitu-tion as a social class and the living standards of other

Table 4.7

State of rents, payments and arrears on Lord
MacDonald's estates on Skye, by parish,
1857-1858 and 1868-1869

(a) 1857-1858

Parish**	Arrears unpaid 31.3.1857	Rent due Whitsun 1858	Payment made at Whitsun 1858	Arrears unpaid at 30.9.1858 and as % of rent	
	£	£	£	£	%
Sleat	159.63	1079.85	741.83	497.65	46.10
Strath	329.42	1353.89	1025.67	657.64	48.60
Portree	130.59	1215.83	1026.57	319.85	26.30
Snizort	6.54	687.69	651.37	42.31	6.15

(b) 1868-1869

Parish**	Arrears unpaid 31.12.1868	Rent from Martinmas 1868 to Martinmas 1869	Payment made at Martinmas 1869	Arrears unpaid at 31.12.1869 and as % of rent	
	£	£	£	£	%
Sleat	763.36	2524.74	2248.81	1039.27	41.20
Strath	1198.04	2625.60	2584.65	1238.97	47.20
Portree	888.76	2600.60	2366.35	1123.04	43.20
Snizort	87.02	1443.66	1427.24	103.44	7.20

* SRO, GD221/160/3/5 (1857-1858); GD221/160/3/2 (1868-1869).
** No returns extant for Kilmuir parish.

social groups) derived both from agricultural prosperity and non-agricultural pursuits. Within agriculture, the principal cause was the rise in cattle prices. Crofters never had many stock, but one or two cattle and a few sheep from small tenant flocks brought in a large proportion of cash with which to pay the rent. Outside agriculture, crofters benefitted to some extent from the rise of wage labouring on Highland estates or in other part-time work. More common was the pursuit of cash through seasonal employment at the fishing or work in the Lowlands. By the later nineteenth century, seasonal migration was not only a necessary adjunct to crofting but was also more common amongst all age ranges and both sexes than it had been in the earlier 1800s or later eighteenth century. Young unmarried women moved to become domestic servants and men to the herring and white fishing of north-east Scotland and eastern England as well as to the waters of the Minch and Pentland Firth.167 Increased levels of real income given more or less static rents and rising wages ushered in a period of relative affluence for crofters. But it was only relative. And, as in the sixty years or so from 1750 to 1815, it was a prosperity founded on externally-determined price levels and wages. It was not founded upon improvement of arable cultivation or of practices of grazing management within the crofting community. Essentially, it was prosperity without security; against the marginal position of most small tenants in the face of a natural setting likely to limit agricultural ouput; a security in money terms likely to be undermined if wage levels in fishing fell or if arrears built-up to beyond the level of the rent itself; and, above all, a lack of tenurial security in law through which crofters could claim a right to the occupance of land and the incentive to improve it. Over-stocking of crofters' stock in an effort to benefit in the short-term from high cattle prices had the long-term effect of pasture degeneration, especially where traditional souming and rouming arrangements had been disrupted and re-allocated by landlords or factors without recourse to local knowledge, stock numbers, or more modern practices of breeding and management. The disproportionate structures of land ownership within Highland agriculture, in the north and west especially, was a cause of real grievance. With the virtual disappearance of the middle tenantry, social relations, rental payments, income levels and agricultural practices were polarised between a numerically small group of principal tenants paying the great proportion of rents, derived chiefly from sheep farms and deer forests, and the small tenants who made up about 80 per cent of the population who paid perhaps 35 per cent of the rent but had less than one-third of available land. The effects of this 'land hunger' amongst the tenant population were made worse by the large numbers of landless squatters and cottars and by differences in land use and quality between restricted tenurial holdings and broad sweeps of hill grazing given over to sheep or deer. The prosperity of one section of the population at the expense of the more numerous was reflected in the deep sense of aggrieved remembrance in the Highland consciousness which recognised, as the laissez-faire economics of the landlords did not, the customary occupations of holdings 'from time immemorial'. Crofters saw in these changes and distributions of land use both the extinction of a practised and lived tradition connecting people to land and people to people through kin and community and also the appropriation of nature then and of future potential. Land was the principal issue. And it was this issue, with its origins in the processes outlined above, that underlay the riots, killing of deer, land wars and protest that began in the early 1780s (see below).

Our understanding of these tensions and their root causes derives in large part from the investigations and reports of the Napier Commission. The Report of the Napier Commission, set up by the government on 26 February 1883 'to inquire into the condition of the Crofters and Cottars in the Highlands and Islands of Scotland', is one of the most important historical documents in all Highland history: 'It represents an unrivalled repository of popular declaration, the finest source for "history from below" in the entire history of the Highlands (and better than available for most of the British Isles for this time)'.168

The Napier Commission took its name from its chairman, Lord Napier and Ettrick. Its other members were Sir Kenneth Smith Mackenzie and Donald Cameron of Locheil, both landowners of large Highland estates; Alexander Nicolson, Celtic scholar and Sheriff Substitute of the Stewartry of Kirkcudbright; Donald Mackinnon, first Professor of Celtic at the University of Edinburgh (largely created through Nicolson); and Charles Fraser-Macintosh, an antiquarian and Liberal MP, who, like the rest of the Commission, was generally favourably disposed at the outset towards the crofters. The Commission began work in May 1883. They asked 46,750 questions of 775 different people in the course of 71 meetings at 61 different locations throughout the north and west Highlands and Islands. The statement of Angus Stewart, crofter at Beinn-a-chorrain in the Braes district of Skye, taken on 8 May 1883, is representative of many.

The principal thing that we have to complain of in
our poverty and what has caused our poverty. The
smallness of our holdings and the inferior quality
of the land is what has caused our poverty; and
the way in which the poor crofters are huddled
together, and the best part of the land devoted to
deer forests and big farms. If we had plenty of
land there would be no poverty in our country. We
are willing and able to work it.169

Elsewhere, statements record the encroachment upon
crofters' arable and grazing lands by sheep farms and deer
forests and the trespassing of the creatures themselves
across crofters' plots; the gathering together of displaced tenants upon the holdings of others; increased rent
demanded for access to grazings traditionally regarded as
common; the absence of leases; and restrictions upon the
use of grazing land: 'The hill pasture is not a day
without from 100 to 200 sheep grazing on it, and we
ourselves are not allowed to graze a head upon it'.
Comments are made, too, about the ecological deterioration
of arable holdings and grazing land, the former
under-manured, the latter over-stocked: 'The places I knew
in my young days where the grass could be cut with the
scythe are now as bare as possible with deer and big
sheep. A wild ass could not get a bite off it'.170 Though
cautious of the nature of the evidence verbally received as
it was from a section of the population whose claims to
occupance rested upon a profound sense of their own history
and the significance attached to management practices and
rent levels 'our fathers knew', the Napier Commission
favoured the crofters and cottars

> The Napier Report effectively exposed the grievanc-
> es and grinding poverty of the crofting community
> and attributed their problems mainly to the
> smallness of their holdings, the insecurity of
> their tenures, the absence of compensation for
> improvements, high rents and a defective economic
> infrastructure.171

The Napier Commission diagnosed the principal Highland
problem as tenurial security. They advocated a central
function for the Highland township as 'the central collec-
tivist institution for the organisation of crofter land and
resources', but whilst this was not embodied in the 1886
Crofters' Act, the resulting legislation did give crofters
unprecedented security of tenure, recognised tenants'
customary rights to grazing, and, in providing for the

foundation of the Crofters' Commission, allowed the population recourse to a statutory body for agreement of fair rents and settlement of claims on improvement. What the Crofters' Act also did, however, was to prohibit any alienation of crofting land, a development which restricted later adaptations: for Richards, 'The crofter system was ossified from the start. The Crofters' Act, always a controversial piece of legislation , has been largely blamed for the failure of crofting to provide adequate scope for material advance'. But in providing any legisla- tion for the majority of the rural population in the north and west, the 1886 Act was a new beginning even though it was not the effective end to those processes of material transformation that had brought about the rise of crofters in the first instance.

CONCLUSION

The transformation of customary relations of property and propriety and established practices of landworking in the Highlands was, for the most part, the gradual working-out of a conflict between two different ways of life. What for most Highland proprietors from the mid-eighteenth century onwards became the challenge of creating alternative material foundations to the Highland economy, was at the same time and for the majority of the Highland people, a major re-working of material relationships towards land and social relations between and within groups in Highland society. The principal issues involved in this transforma- tion have been discussed at length above; several, such as the rise of rents, the processes of capital accumulation, and the variation in levels of capital and cash income between different ranks of people are also considered in what follows in relation to the development of industry in the Highlands. Agricultural transformation was only one change, albeit perhaps the leading one, affecting the 'conveniences of life' in the Highlands. It was closely linked with the industrial 'sector' of Highland life. The creation of a 'surplus' population of labourers, crofters and small tenants - people living on the land but not entirely from it, and dependent to varying degrees upon local handicraft production or other part time industrial employment - was, for example, one of the major consequences of changes in Highland agriculture. It owed also to the patterns and processes of population growth in the Highlands, in the period 1750 to 1850 particularly, and to the different response of landlords in the north and west and islands either to the retention of labour for

kelping or to their shedding, earlier in the nouth and east
mainland, as cattle ranching and then sheep farming on
hitherto unprecedented scales was established.

Three principal points may be made in conclusion here
in ways which bear also upon what follows. The first is
the extent to which changes in agriculture acted to alter
(and were altered by) the constituent structures and bonds
of Highland rural society; the second is the varying rate
of change of the processes affecting population and
agriculture; the third is the regional pattern of agriculture and social change. Underlying them all is the
differing emphasis imparted to material change by the facts
of demography.

Outside observers (and some Highlanders themselves) saw
in the Highlands a society whose internal cohesion derived
not from ownership of property and social structures based
on rent, wages and class, but one whose structures and
operation depended upon affective tradition - customary
occupation without lease or other legal right, established
practices of agricultural management, and a sense of duty
to superiors which outweighed obedience to external
authority. To a considerable extent, policies of agricultural improvement were intended also as means of civic
control, to bring Highlanders to the 'arts of life'
socially and materially. On the Argyll Estates especially,
'Estate policy tended to mix together several diverse
objectives: the pacification of clan rivalry, the extension of ducal authority, and the extraction of rent
increases, were combined with the urge to improved the
country'.172 To do so successfully demanded the effective
re-structuring of Highland social relations. Whether in
the more evident replacement of the tacksman, the appearance of the low-country factor or estate manager, or in the
gradual separating-out between landowner or principal
rentier on the one hand and a stratified peasantry on the
other, the re-structuring of social divisions is one of the
principal themes of change in Highland life. It is a
process that may, however, have acted to limit the forms of
effective re-organisation. Fullarton and Baird considered
that one of the 'evils' affecting the Highlands by the
mid-nineteenth century was the absence of a middle class
'which, in all respects, constitutes the strength and glory
of the British people'. Somers, writing in 1848, noted the
separation of classes in Highland society: 'there are only
two ranks of people - a higher rank and a lower rank - the
former consisting of a few large tenants . . . and the
latter consisting of a dense body of small cottars and
fishermen . . . The proverbial enmity of rich and poor in
all societies has received peculiar development in this

simple social structure of the Highlands'.173 The Napier
Commission was equally aware of the two-fold division in
Highland society, a division founded on money income and
property.

> The severance of the labouring classes from the
> benefits and enjoyments of property (certainly one
> of the elements of civilisation, morality, and
> public order), and their precarious and dangerous
> condition as dependants on capital and mere
> recipients of wages, is a question which engages
> the reflections of those who reason and of those
> who govern.174

Whilst the social relations of production changed in
consequence of changes in the material bases of Highland
life, we should be wary of seeing the process as simply one
of polarisation between landowners or principal tenants and
smallholders, and careful also about attributing to an
earlier Highland society a sense of unity that it never in
fact enjoyed. Historically, as Hunter and others have
shown, Highland society may have been unified with a
cultural consciousness or egalitarianism expressed in terms
of blood relationship and in other ways, but it was 'by no
means an undifferentiated or homogeneous mass'. Differences in status and in caste existed within the ranks of
'traditional' Highland society and were encapsulated also
in divisions within a tenant population: in rent levels,
for example; in the proportion of cash, kind, or labour
dues in the payment of principal rents; or in the way in
which land was held and worked directly of a landowner or
of an intermediary agent. Geographically, parts of the
central and south east Highlands were, from the end of the
eighteenth century, worked by tenants holding land directly
of their landlords. Yet the same process had a very
different effect in the north and west where the policies
of landlords in retaining labour together with the poorer
quality and limited quantity of land worked and the
different course of population growth determined a
different response to the tenantry and perhaps, too,
produced a different tenantry altogether.   The
transformation of Highland agriculture, especially insofar
as rents and levels of money income are concerned, begins
not with the imposition of entirely external improvements
in the wake of military defeat and political control after
1746 but with a more gradual assimilation of commercial
interest, leasing structures, and new methods by Highland
landlords from the mid-1600s. Highland agriculture, in the
importing and exporting of grain and cattle, was bound up

with wider economic interests long before the region
reached a state of critical dependence upon the potato, the
price of black cattle, or demand for wool. Certainly, the
great drive for improvement was most evident after the
1770s and was first felt in the south and west Highlands,
on the Argyll Estates particularly, in the eastern Ross and
Cromarty parishes and in the border parishes of central
Perthshire. But indicators of change for earlier dates and
other places bear witness to what was a gradual evolution
with regional emphasis from the 1600s rather more than a
rapid Highland-wide replacement of one mode of production
by another originating in the later 1700s. In the period
from about 1750 to 1815, arrears were allowed to build up
on some estates during what was otherwise a period of
relative prosperity in the Highlands. Later more
widespread economic recession from about 1815 to about
1850, most marked in the years of the potato famine, had
major effects upon the tenants and their levels of
agricultural production. But tenants were not the only
ones to suffer. Landlords faced (and many met) financial
ruin through allowing irrecoverable arrears to accumulate
amongst a tenantry for whom, whatever the moral commitment
of the landlord, financial obligations were of primary
importance.

These changes had a geography determined by distance
from the markets, the period of introduction, patterns of
population growth and, not least, by the varying qualities
of soil and climate. The 'farming' Highlands to the south
and east of the Great Glen were favoured by soil type,
relative ease of communication and access to markets in
ways that the 'crofting' Highlands of the north and west
were not. In the latter region, the course of population
was much more influential than elsewhere in separating the
common people from a reliance upon runrig and joint farms
to a dependence upon rent levels, the goodwill of the
factor, and returns from holdings themselves subdivided and
restricted in overall acreage.

Directing and reflecting the improvement of cultivation
in agriculture was the related notion of cultivation as a
social process. For Walker, for example, enclosure and
artificial grasses were the leading agricultural agencies
of that more widespread improvement of Highland life then
taking place: 'These are two leading steps of Improvement,
in the uncultivated parts of Scotland, & yet are unknown in
many places . . . They are introductory to every Sort of
polishd Culture'. Elsewhere in his commentaries on the
Highlands, we find him discussing the different types of
economic interest embraced by the term 'improvement'.

There are four separate interests to be regarded.

258

Population Growth and Highland Agriculture

> The interest of the landlord, of the farmer, of
> the inferior people, and of the public at large .
> . . These four interests, though separate, are by
> no means incompatible, or placed at irreconcilable
> variance with one another. They are in most cases
> capable of being justly advanced by the same
> means. In rural economy that measure will always
> be the best which unites and promotes these
> several interests.175

In what we have seen above of agricultural change, the
varied interests of those involved have been far from
compatible.

NOTES

1. NLS, MS 7118, f.17v.

2. EUL, MS Dc. 6. 70/2.

3. M. Gray, <u>The Highland Economy 1750-1850</u> (Edinburgh, 1957), pp.23-24.

4. J. Hunter, <u>The Making of the Crofting Community</u> (Edinburgh, 1976), pp.9-10.

5. M.W. Flinn, 'Malthus, Emigration and Potatoes in the Scottish North-West, 1770-1870, in L.M. Cullen and T.C. Smout (eds.), <u>Comparative Aspects of Scottish and Irish Economic and Social History 1600-1900</u> (Edinburgh, 1977), p.60.

6. A. Webster, <u>An Account of the number of People in Scotland in the Year One thousand Seven Hundred and Fifty Five</u> in J.G. Kyd (ed.), <u>Scottish Population Statistics</u> (Edinburgh, 1952).

7. M.W. Flinn (ed.), <u>Scottish Population History</u> (Cambridge, 1977), pp.51-57.

8. T.C. Smout, 'Famine and famine relief in Scotland' in Cullen and Smout (eds.), <u>Comparative Aspects</u> . . . , p.22; Flinn, <u>Scottish Population History</u>, pp.123-124; I.D. Whyte, <u>Agriculture and Society in Seventeenth Century Scotland</u> (Edinburgh, 1979), pp.11, 12, 40, 246-251.

9. On the accuracy of Webster's 1755 Census, see Flinn, <u>op. cit</u>., pp.58-64.

10. <u>Ibid</u>., p.30.

11. A. Mitchell (ed.), <u>Geographical Collections relating to Scotland made by Walter Macfarlane</u> (Edinburgh, 1906), I, pp.169, 184; EUL, MS La.III; V.Wills (ed.), <u>Statistics of the Annexed Estates 1755-1756</u> (Edinburgh, 1973); R.J. Adam (ed.), <u>John Home's Survey of Assynt</u> (Edinburgh, 1960), pp.68-69;E.R. Cregeen (ed.), <u>Inhabitants of the Argyll Estate, 1779</u> (Edinburgh, 1963); idem, <u>Argyll Estate Instructions: Mull, Morvern, Tiree 1771-1805</u> (Edinburgh, 1964); Flinn, <u>Scottish Population History</u>, pp.58-64; SRO, CH1/5/43; SRO, RH2/4/386, f.81, [A List of the Number of Inhabitants in the Highlands of Scotland, 1778]; on

Walker's population work, see M. McKay (ed.), <u>The Rev. Dr.</u>
<u>John Walker's report on the Hebrides of 1764 and 1771</u>
(Edinburgh, 1980), pp.21-30.

12. Cregeen, <u>Argyll Estate Instructions</u> . . .,
pp.xxviii-xxix.

13. R.A. Dodgshon, <u>Land and Society in Early Scotland</u>
(Oxford, 1982), p.291.

14. Cregeen, <u>Argyll Estate Instructions</u> . . ., p.1.

15. McKay (ed.), <u>Walker's Report on the Hebrides</u> . . .,
p.25.

16. Flinn, <u>Scottish Population History</u>, p.38.

17. J. Walker, <u>An Economical History of the Hebrides and</u>
<u>Highlands of Scotland</u> (Edinburgh, 1808), I, 30-31; II,
414.

18. Gray, <u>Highland Economy</u>, pp.59, 60-61.

19. R.A. Gailey, 'Settlement and population in Kintyre,
1750-1890', <u>Scottish Geographical Magazine</u>, <u>76</u>, (1960),
pp.99-107.

20. H. Fairhurst, 'The Surveys for the Sutherland Clear-
ances 1813-1820', <u>Scottish Studies</u>, <u>8</u>, (1964), pp.1-18;
Gailey, <u>ibid</u>.; idem, 'Settlement changes in the southwest
Highlands of Scotland, 1700-1960', unpublished PhD thesis,
University of Glasgow, 1961; idem, 'The evolution of
Highland rural settlement with particular reference to
Argyllshire', <u>Scottish Studies</u>, <u>6</u>, 1962), pp.155-177;
idem, 'Agrarian improvement and the development of
enclosure in the south-west Highlands of Scotland',
<u>Scottish Historical Review</u>, <u>42</u>, (1963), pp.102-125; M.D.
MacSween, 'Settlement in Trotternish, Isle of Skye,
1700-1958', unpublished PhD thesis, University of Glasgow,
1959; M.C. Storrie, 'Landholdings and Settlement Evolution
in West Highland Scotland', <u>Geografisker Annaler</u>, <u>47B</u>
(1965), pp.138-160; I.D. Whyte, 'The Historical Geography
of Rural Settlement in Scotland: a Review', <u>Research</u>
<u>Discussion Paper 17, Univ. of Edinburgh Dept. of Geography</u>,
1979.

21. Fairhurst, <u>ibid</u>.; see also articles by E. Richards,
J. Hunter and S.R. Sutherland under the general title 'The
Sutherland Clearances' in <u>Northern Scotland</u>, <u>2(1)</u>,
(1974-1975), pp.57-84; R. Forsyth, <u>The Beauties of</u>

Scotland (Edinburgh, 1805-1000), II, pp.379-900.

22. K. Walton, 'Population changes in north-east Scotland, 1696-1951', Scottish Studies, 5, (1961), 16-24; D. Turnock, 'The retreat of settlement in the Grampian Uplands', Northern Scotland, 4(1-2), (1981), pp.83-112.

23. A good review of this is to be found in J.M. Bumsted, The People's Clearance 1770-1815 (Edinburgh, 1982).

24. J. Boswell, Journal of a Tour of the Hebrides (Oxford, 1970 edn.), pp.129, 141, 192; Calendar of Home Office Papers, 1773-1775, No. 585; Flinn, 'Malthus, Emigration and Potatoes . . . ', p.51

25. T.M. Devine, 'Temporary migration and the Scottish Highlands in the Nineteenth Century', Economic History Review, XXXII (3), (1979), pp.344-359; W. Howatson, 'The Scottish Hairst and Seasonal Labour, 1600-1870', Scottish Studies, 26, (1982), pp.13-36.

26. Gray, Highland Economy, p.64.

27. R. Osborne, 'The movements of people in Scotland 1851-1951', Scottish Studies, 2 (1958), pp.1-46; C.W.J. Withers, 'Highland migration to Dundee, Perth, and Stirling 1753-1891', Journal of Historical Geography, 11(4), (1985), 395-418.

28. Hunter, op.cit., p.42; SRO, GD 201/5/1217/46, GD 201/4/97, GD 221/85.

29. Walker, An Economic History . . . ', I, p.32; T. Pennant, A Tour in Scotland and Voyage to the Hebrides (London, 1790), II, p.314.

30. Old Statistical Account [OSA], VIII, (1793), p.368; X, (1794), p.384; XI, (1794), p.425; XVII, (1795), p.279; J. Sinclair, Analysis of the Statistical Account of Scotland (Edinburgh, 1826), p.147.

31. A claim made by Flinn, Scottish Population History, p.363; for one illustration in support, see the New Statistical Account [NSA], V, (1845), p.27 [Kilbride on Bute]; on Highland illegitimacy in general, see L. Leneman and R. Mitchison, 'Scottish illegitimacy ratios in the early modern period, Economic History Review, XL(1), (1987), 41-63.

32. Ibid, p.270.

33. Walker, op.cit., I, p.36; McKay (ed.), op.cit., p.23.

34. OSA, VI, (1793), p.190; XI, (1794), p.425.

35. McKay (ed.), op.cit., pp.29-30; Sinclair, op. cit., p.167.

36. SRO, E.783/68(1)/2; E.788/11, ff.1-4; E.783/87; E.728/57/1, ff.1-20; E.727/63(1)-(5) [Forfeited Estates, Medical Papers].

37. Ibid., passim; SRO, GD46/1/526, F.13.

38. A. Smith, The Wealth of Nations (London, 1776), I, Chapter VII, p.70.

39. OSA, VIII, (1793), p.409 [Kilmallie]; SRO, E.783/68(1)/(2); E.728/57/1, ff.1-4.

40. Walker, op.cit., I, p.27.

41. Gray, Highland Economy, p.142; OSA, III, (1794), p.371; XVI, (1795), p.193.

42. The course of prices (and wages) is difficult to determine with any degree of accuracy for long-term runs: for a recent discussion of the evidence and its limitations, see E. Richards, A History of the Highland Clearances Volume 2: Emigration, Protest, Reasons (London, 1985), pp.504-517.

43. E. Richards, A History of the Highland Clearances Volume I: Agrarian Transformation and the Evictions 1746-1886 (London, 1982), p.133.

44. J. Robertson, General View of the Agriculture of the Southern Districts of the County of Perth (London, 1794), pp.39-40.

45. Correspondence from July 1846 to February 1847 relating to Measures adopted for the Relief of Distress in Scotland, P.P., LIII, (1847), pp.3, 5; J. MacDonald, General View of the Agriculture of the Hebrides (Edinburgh, 1811), p.17.

46. SRO, HD 7/8, f.29.

47. The phrase is Flinn's in Scottish Population History, p.438.

48. Walker, op.cit., I, p.47.

49. E.R.Cregeen, 'The Tacksmen and their Successors: a study of tenurial organisation in Mull, Morvern, and Tiree in the early eighteenth century', Scottish Studies, 13(2), (1969), p.101.

50. M. Gray, 'Economic welfare and money income in the Highlands, 1750-1850', Scottish Journal of Political Economy, II, (1955), p.49.

51. A Highlander, The Present Conduct of the Chieftains and Proprietors of Lands in the Highlands of Scotland (n.p., 1773), p.8.

52. F. Shaw, The Northern and Western Islands of Scotland: their economy and society in the Seventeenth Century (Edinburgh, 1980), pp.50, 56.

53. A. McKerral, 'The tacksman and his holding in the south-west Highlands', Scottish Historical Review, 26, (1947), pp.10-25.

54. I.R.M. Mowat, Easter Ross 1750-1850: the double frontier (Edinburgh, 1981), p.8.

55. Dodgshon, op.cit., pp.276-277.

56. Whyte, Seventeenth Century Scotland, p.33.

57. C. Horricks, 'Economic and Social Change in the Isle of Harris, 1680-1754', unpublished PhD thesis, University of Edinburgh 1974, p.190; SRO, GD 112/9/3, 12, 15, 18, 21, 23-24, 26, 33.

58. SRO, GD 170, ff.261(1), 261 (4), 338/2(1), 338/2(4), 420/1(5), 420/1(7).

59. SRO, GD 201/5/1263.

60. Walker, op.cit., I, pp.47-48.

61. SRO, E.729/1, p.29 Report from Captain John Forbes 30 July 1755.

62. C. Innes (ed.), The Black Book of Taymouth (Edinburgh,

1885), pp.352-356, quoted in Cregeen, <u>Argyll Estate Instructions</u>, p.xi.

63. Richards, <u>Highland Clearances Volume I</u>, pp.60-69; Cregeen, 'The Tacksmen and their Successors . . . '; McKerral, <u>op.cit</u>.; I.MacKay, 'Clanranald's Tacksmen of the late eighteenth century', <u>Transactions of the Gaelic Society of Inverness</u>, <u>44</u>, (1964), pp.61-93.

64. S. Johnson, <u>A Journey to the Western Isles of Scotland</u> (London, 1775), p.78.

65. N. Graham, 'Extracts from the Gartmore MS' in R.B. Cunningham-Graham, <u>Doughty Deeds: an account of the life of Robert Graham of Gartmore, 1735-1797</u> (London, 1925), pp.171-192; E. Burt, <u>Letters from a Gentleman in the North of Scotland to his Friend in London</u> (London, 1754), II, 27; P. Gaskell, <u>Morvern Transformed: a Highland parish in the nineteenth century</u> (Cambridge, 1968), pp.2-3.

66. Walker, <u>op.cit</u>., I, pp.53-55; McKay (ed.), <u>op.cit</u>, p.101.

67. MacDonald, <u>op.cit</u>., pp.74-75.

68. McKerral, <u>op.cit</u>., p.21.

69. Bumsted, <u>op.cit</u>., pp.34-35.

70. Richards, <u>ibid</u>., p.184.

71. Walker, <u>op.cit</u>., I, p.406.

72. R.J. Adam (ed.), <u>John Home's Survey of Assynt</u>, <u>op.cit</u>., p.xxvi.

73. Hunter, <u>op.cit</u>., p.14.

74. <u>OSA</u>, <u>XX</u>, (1798), P.25.

75. EUL, La. III. 379, f.207a.

76. SRO, GD 14/17, f.9.

77. Walker, <u>op.cit</u>., I, pp.66-67.

78. SRO, E.729/1, p.25.

79. Gailey, 'Agrarian improvement and enclosure . . . ',

pp.108, 118; I.M.L. Robertson, 'The Head-Dyke: A fundamental line in Scottish Geography', Scottish Geographical Magazine, 65, (1949), p.14.

80. Gray, Highland Economy, p. 66.

81. Gailey, ibid., p.109; see also L. Leneman, Living in Atholl: a social history of the estates 1685-1785 (Edinburgh, 1986), pp.15,37.

82. Gray, The Highland Economy, p.68.

83. J. Smith, General View of the Agriculture of the County of Argyle (London, 1805), pp.66-67.

84. G. MacKenzie, A General Survey of the Counties of Ross and Cromarty (London, 1810), p.184.

85. EUL, La. II. 623, f.11.

86. J. Smith, Jacobite Estates of the Forty-Five (Edinburgh, 1982), pp.88-107.

87. Walker, op.cit., I, p.251; MacKenzie, General View . . . , p.185.

88. McKay (ed.), op.cit., p.210.

89. Shaw, Northern and Western Islands . . ., pp.87, 101.

90. J. Smith, Jacobite estates . . ., p.58.

91. NLS, MS 1034, f.104.

92. Richards, Highland Clearances, Volume 2, p.356.

93. Hunter, op.cit., p.26.

94. R.W. Munro, Taming the Rough Bounds: Knoydart 1745-1784 (Coll, 1984), pp.18-19; Gailey, 'Agrarian improvement and enclosure . . .',pp.106-107.

95. Dodgshon, op.cit., pp.305, 307.

96. A Highlander, The Present Conduct of the Chieftains . . . , pp.9-10.

97. SRO, GD 14/17, f.4.

98. J. Anderson, Prize Essay on the State of Society and Knowledge in the Highlands of Scotland; particularly in the Northern Counties in 1745 (Edinburgh, 1827), p.102.

99. Gray, Highland Economy, pp.87-88; D.S. MacLagan, 'Stock Rearing in the Highlands, 1720-1820', Transactions of the Royal Highland and Agricultural Society. 6th Series, II, (1958), pp.63-71; M.L. Ryder, 'Sheep and the Clearances in the Scottish Highlands: a Biologist's View', Agricultural History Review, 16, (1968), pp.155-158.

100. J. Smith, General View . . . , p.257.

101. J. Smith, Jacobite Estates . . . , pp.85-87; W. Marshall, General View of the Agriculture of the Central Highlands of Scotland (London, 1794).

102. MacKenzie, General View . . . ,pp.128-129.

103. Mowat, op.cit., pp.35, 45, 145, 152; MacKenzie, General View . . . , pp.130-131; Ryder, op.cit., p.157.

104. J. Henderson, General View of the Agriculture of the County of Sutherland, (London, 1812), p.103.

105. McKay (ed.), op.cit., p.129.

106. W. Singers, 'On the introduction of sheep farming into the Highlands; and on the plan of husbandry adapted to the soil and climate, and to the general and solid interests of that country', Transactions of the Highland and Agricultural Society of Scotland, III, (1807), pp.544-545.

107. Gray, Highland Economy, p.86.

108. Youngson, After the Forty-Five, p.173.

109. J. Robson, General View of the Agriculture of the County of Argyll (London, 1794), pp.45-47.

110. J. Smith, General View . . . , pp.260-261, 272-277.

111. Ibid., p.281; SRO, GD 174/1956.

112. F. Fraser Darling, West Highland Survey (Oxford, 1955), pp.408-410.

113. A. Watson, 'Eighteenth century deer numbers and pine regeneration near Braemar, Scotland', Biological Conserva-

tion, 25(4), (1903), pp.289 305.

114. SRO, E 741/40. p.6.

115. OSA, VI, (1793), p.178; X, (1794), p.470; III, (1792); see also the comments on Moulin, Luss, Aberfoyle, and Killin parishes in the same source - V, (1793), p.54; XVII, (1795), pp.258-259; X, (1794), pp.120-122; XVII, (1795), pp.380-1; Glenorchy and Inishail in NSA, VII, (1845), p.93.

116. Richards, Highland Clearances Volume 2, pp.424-441.

117. Ibid., pp.480, 482.

118. Ibid., p.508.

119. McKay (ed.), op.cit., p.41.

120. R.C. MacLeod (ed.), The Book of Dunvegan 1340-1920 (Aberdeen, 1938), II, pp.79 et seq.

121. SRO, GD 112/9/33; 112/9/49; 112/9/67; Leneman, op.cit., pp.19, 20-27.

122. Adam, op.cit., I, pp.214-215, Appendix A.

123. SRO, GD 174, f.838 (4).

124. SRO, GD 221/40/60; GD 221/2/20.

125. SRO, GD 84, ff.1, 7, 10.

126. Gray, Highland Economy, pp.182-183.

127. SRO, GD 84/2/50, f.14.

128. SRO, GD 221/38/43.

129. Richards, Highlands Clearances Volume 1, p.183.

130. SRO, GD 46/13/199, f.1. Letter to Lord John Russell from J.A. Stewart MacKenzie.

131. Ibid., f.3.

132. SRO, GD 46/13/213; GD 46/13/215, (1)-(6).

133. SRO, GD 46/13/199, f.3.

134. Ibid., f.41.

135. NLS, MS 1054, f.198, Letter of 11 August 1837 from J. Spring Hill to Sir John Neill.

136. NLS, MS 1054, f.197v.

137. Correspondence from July 1846 to February 1847 relating to the Measures adopted for the Relief of the Distress in Scotland, P.P., LIII, (1847), p.8.

138. NLS, MS 9713, Letter of 25 October 1846 to Lord Advocate Rutherford from Baron Maule.

139. E. Richards, The Leviathan of Wealth: the Sutherland fortune in the industrial revolution (London, 1973), pp.262-279.

140. NLS, MS 9702, f.122, Letter of 6 September 1846 from Lord James Robertson to Lord Murray: SRO, GD 46/13/203, f.5, Letter of 1 June 1847 from W.E. Skene to J. Blamire.

141. SRO, HD 16/123 [List of Districts under the charge of the Glasgow Section of the Highland Relief Board for 1848]; HD16/70 [Subscriptions for Relief of Highland Destitution, 1847-1848], Sections 1-13.

142. SRO, HD 20/21.

143. SRO, HD 19/19 (Rosskeen); 19/16 (Latheron); HD 19/6 (Dores).

144. Hunter, op.cit., p.68.

145. SRO, HD 20/71, f.2.

146. Hunter, op.cit., p.70.

147. SRO, HD 14/21, 24 February 1849.

148. SRO, HD 16/95, [Memorandum regarding the mode of relieving destitution by Co-operative arrangements with Proprietors of Estates upon which there is a destitute population].

149. Flinn, Scottish Population History, p.43.

150. Hunter, op.cit., p.73.

151. Richards, Highland Clearances Volume 2, p 485.

152. J. Hunter, 'Sheep and deer: Highland sheep farming, 1850–1900', Northern Scotland, 1(2), (1973), p.201; W. Macdonald, 'On the Agriculture of Inverness-shire', Transactions of the Highland and Agricultural Society of Scotland, 4th Ser., IV, (1872), p.52.

153. Macdonald, 'On the Agriculture of Inverness-shire', p.52; W. Orr, Deer Forests, Landlords and Crofters (Edinburgh, 1982), pp.13, 24.

154. Hunter, 'Sheep and deer . . . ', p.203; J. Macdonald, 'On the Agriculture of the County of Sutherland', Transactions of the Highland and Agricultural Society of Scotland, 4th Ser., XII, (1880), p.65; Watson, op.cit.; J.L. Innes, 'Landuse changes in the Scottish Highlands during the 19th century: the role of pasture degeneration', Scottish Geographical Magazine, 99(3), pp.141–149.

155. Orr, op.cit., pp.168–181.

156. R. Somers, Letters from the Highlands (London, 1848), p.60.

157. Gaskell, Morvern Transformed,pp.56–120; Orr, op.cit., p.40.

158. Hunter, The Making of the Crofting Community, p.73.

159. Ibid., pp.85–87; Richards, Highland Clearances Volumes I and 2, passim.

160. J.B. Caird, 'Land use in the Uists since 1800'. Proceedings of the Royal Society of Edinburgh, 77B, (1979), p.515.

161. Richards, Highland Clearances Volume 1, p.419.

162. Hunter, The Making of the Crofting Community, p.86.

163. Report of the Commissioners of Inquiry into the Condition of the Crofters and Cottars in the Highlands and Islands of Scotland 1884, P.P., XXXII–XXXVI, (1884), Appendix A, Volume XXXII, p.12 [Herinafter referred to as Napier Commission Report].

164. W. Macdonald, 'On the Agriculture of Inverness-shire', pp.2, 17, 22.

165. J. Macdonald, 'On the Agriculture of the County of Sutherland', p.49.

166. Hunter, The Making of the Crofting Community, p.107.

167. Hunter, The Making of the Crofting Community, pp.109-111; Devine, op.cit.; A.C. Cameron, Go Listen to the Crofters (Stornoway, 1986), pp.109-110.

168. Richards, Highland Clearances Volume 2, p.86.

169. Napier Commission Report, XXXII, (1884), p.3, Q.23.

170. Ibid., p.32, Q.547.

171. Richards, Highland Clearances Volume 2, p.298.

172. Richards, Highland Clearances Volume 1, p.12

173. A. Fullarton and C.R. Baird, Present Evils affecting the Highlands and Islands of Scotland, with some suggestions as to their remedies (Glasgow, 1838), p.65; Somers, Letters . . ., p.110.

174. Napier Commission Report, XXXII, (1884), p.109.

175. Walker, op.cit., I, p.14.

5

INDUSTRIOUSNESS AND THE FAILURE OF INDUSTRY

> You are making many human Creatures happy & your
> Country great. You are opening resources of
> population and production to an extent few are
> aware of... Cast your eye over the enterprising
> hardy & virtuous character of its present Inhabit-
> ants and you will discover the hidden treasures
> you are employed in bringing to light.1

> Let me add, that this people will never be
> usefully employed till drawn out of the country,
> and by sheer necessity, bred to Labour. All
> schemes of Industry to be executed in that Country
> are idle dreams.2

Small-scale industrial production - usually for immediate
domestic needs but involving in places the limited making
for sale of woven cloth or the manufacture of shoes by
customer craftsmen - was an integral though minor part of
Highland life. The significance of industry in the
Highland economy rests, however, not upon its essentially
subsistence nature as localised manufactures or in its
subordinate relationship to agricultural production, but
upon the fact that the extension of a commercial basis to
industry in the Highland was considered a means to the
overall civilisation and improvement of the region. The
development of market-oriented industry in the Highlands as
opposed to the continuance of limited subsistence production thus both followed from and itself demanded structural
changes in 'traditional' Highland modes of production and
in the Highland consciousness. Neither subsistence
production nor production for small local markets
encouraged either a growth in investment, capital
accumulation, or the division of labour. Yet these and
other factors were regarded as principal engines of
economic growth, during the eighteenth century especially.
   The expansion of industrial pursuits on Highland

272

estates was seen as a way of re-structuring the social and material relationships of Highland society whilst retaining and utilising the population.

> There are more people than the produce of the land can well maintain; they are on that account obliged to wander to other places in quest of employment, and to become a kind of vagabonds upon the earth. What relief, then, so natural, as to find them employment at home, in a manufacture, which if well conducted, would not only make individuals live comfortably, but, by means of the money which such manufactures would bring in to the country, the soil would be improved, the value of the land raised, and employment found for numbers of the natives in agriculture.3

Industrial employment and that more strictly defined division of labour that it demanded was considered also, as was the related extension of a commercial and monetary basis to social transactions, as a means to a social development no less important than economic advance.

The term 'industry' may be understood here in the dual sense it was understood by articulate thinkers in the past; as, firstly, the institutions and means behind the manufacture of goods for markets wider than the immediate and local (in which context it held with the improvement of husbandry a central place in the progress towards commercialism as a 'stage' of material development); and secondly, in the way industry was synonymous with the quality of 'industriousness', a civil and civilising attribute necessary for social advance and cultural transformation.4 For these reasons, examination of the limited role of industry in the Highlands cannot be divorced from those wider issues affecting the region nor realistically separated from the state of the Scottish economy as a whole or the views of contemporary 'improving' thinkers and theorists.

In review of a wide range of evidence for the state of the Scottish economy by the late eighteenth century, Smout advanced six principal conclusions: the third quarter of the eighteenth century was characterised by 'a modest yet distinct improvement in Scottish GNP per capita'; the benefits of this 'probably accrued much more to the landowners and the bourgeoisie than to the common people'; growth occurred over a range of sectors and was associated with improvement both in internal demand, evident in grain prices and the market for meat and textiles, and external demand evident in cattle, linen, and re-exported tobacco;

a secondary effect of growth was the redistribution of labour, perhaps especially female labour, away from agriculture towards either linen making or town services of all kinds; landowners improved and reorganised their estates with a view to increased rent and productivity, but with the more immediate effect of increasing the labour supply outside the agricultural sector; and lastly, the economy was characterised by a greater spread of monetisation facilitated by the increased commercial significance of banks and the issue of paper money.5 Most of these changes took place in the central and eastern coastal Lowlands with growth and improvement focused in and through expanding urban economies. But the Highlands were not unaffected.6 To this extent, several of the conclusions drawn by Smout for the national economy are applicable to the Highlands as a region. The inadequacy of local grain production pressed many parts of the Highlands unavoidably into dependence on the regions of grain surplus, and in so doing, population growth and food requirements provided a stimulus to internal commercial expansion. The greater spread of monetisation in the national economy was reflected in the Highlands in the observed increased emphasis on money rents, in the patterns of consumption of Highland chiefs and landlords, and particularly in the attention given even by small tenants to the sale of cattle for cash. Capital accumulation, per capita improvement in GNP, and the benefits deriving from monetisation and estate improvement in the Highlands certainly 'accrued much more to the landowners and the bourgeoisie than to the common people'.

Whilst it is true that Highland landlords had participated since the seventeenth century in the commercial markets of the Lowlands and many were politically bound-up with national issues, the fortunes of the Highland economy by the later eighteenth-century did not mirror national trends in all respects. Highland class structure was then largely (and was to be increasingly) polarised between a landlord class and a group of principal rentiers on the one hand and a stratified peasantry on the other without a middle layer of merchants or manufacturers or large tenants able to concentrate or venture capital. Amongst the peasantry, systems and types of occupational pluralism - part-agricultural labourer and part-weaver or fisherman-persisted throughout the Highlands. There was no clearly defined occupational hierarchy or division of labour. And as we have seen, during the 1700s and 1800s a combination of increased rents and persistent arrears and famine swept away what peasant surplus there was. The bulk of the tenantry was at all times caught between relatively

274

fixed obligations and falling money income. The absence of a merchant and manufacturing class and of a commercial infrastructure was both reflected in and directed by the overall shortage of towns to provide market functions and act to concentrate and circulate capital. It was these factors in combination - little commercial basis, few markets and towns, no defined division of labour between agricultural workers and rurally-located manufacturers of goods for national consumption, and no motivating sense of industriousness - that provided the central issues in contemporary comment on plans for Highland industry.

INDUSTRY AND INDUSTRIOUSNESS: INDUSTRY AS A CIVILISING PROCESS

Richards has claimed a central significance for the influence of Adam Smith on thinking about the Highlands.

> His references to the Scottish Highlands, taken together amount to an indictment of feudal social relations, the associated narrowness of the market, and the restricted division of labour to which he attributed the proverbial poverty of the people. His prescription for Highland progress was, therefore, obvious. Smith, indeed, provided much of the inspiration, even a blueprint, for the rapid conversion of the Highlands to market economies in the following half century. The Wealth of Nations of 1776 yielded most of the economic propositions which justified the shift of the region towards sheep production, and away from the labour-intensive self-sufficiency which had characterised the old Highlands. His book was a bible to the Highland improvers.7

Smith comments on the patriarchal power of the Highland chiefs and on their consumption of goods 'in rustick hospitality at home' given the lack of foreign commerce and manufactures. He attached importance in The Wealth of Nations to the cattle trade of the Highlands particularly since the Union of 1707; 'The union opened the market of England to the highland cattle. Their ordinary price is at present about three times greater than at the beginning of the century, and the rents of many highland estates have been tripled and quadrupled in the same time'. Elsewhere we find him remarking how 'Of all the commercial advantages, however, which Scotland has derived from the union with England, this rise in the price of cattle is,

275

perhaps, the greatest. It has not only raised the value of all highland estates, but it has, perhaps, been the principal cause of the improvement of the low country'.8 Smith knew of the financial returns deriving from kelp and realised, too, not only what Richards has called 'the unearned character of kelp profits', but also the additional impact that kelp had on raising rent levels for the participating labourer who suffered rent increases without benefiting from the profits of manufacture. Smith attached great importance to the absence of a division of labour in the Highlands - 'In the lone houses and very small villages which are scattered about in so desert a country as the Highlands of Scotland, every farmer must be butcher, baker and brewer for his own family' - and, in consequence, considered the range of by-employments undertaken by tenants to meet tenurial obligations a sign of intrinsic backwardness.9 It should be noted, however, that the emphasis laid by Smith upon the division of labour as a mark of commercial progress and a means to achieving 'the highest degree of industry and improvement' for the Highlands rested more upon an intended division between persons and groups of people in society than it did upon formal distinctions in the organisation of production processes.10 Wage structures and price levels were likewise poorly developed in Smith's view. Others also comment on this hindrance to Highland industrial and commercial development; Johnson, remarked, for example, how 'In the Western Islands there is so little internal commerce, that hardly any thing has a known or settled rate', and the observations of contemporaries on the absence of a regulated wage economy support this evidence (page 245 above). The limited number of towns and villages inhibited economic development and recognition of this fact underlay moves to establish manufacturing and fishing villages in the Highlands. Smith considered that commercial and manufacturing towns contributed to the 'improvement and cultivation' of countries in three ways: 'by affording a great and ready market for the rude produce of the country'; in the way in which 'the wealth acquired by the inhabitants of cities was frequently employed in purchasing such lands as were to be sold, of which a great part would frequently be uncultivated'; and, lastly, through what may be considered their civilising influence.

> Commerce and manufactures gradually introduced
> order and good government, and with them, the
> liberty and security of individuals, among the
> inhabitants of the country, who had lived almost
> in a continual state of war with their neighbours
> and of servile dependency upon their superiors.11

Industriousness and the Failure of Industry

In this last respect (though no direct reference to the Highlands was made), Smith saw in the expansion of urban commerce and the establishment of smaller manufacturing villages a principal generative means of Highland development.

Whilst agreeing with Richards' claim that Smith's influence on thinking about the Highlands was pervasive, we must for several reasons be cautious about attributing to Smith an individual significance he does not merit. Firstly, as Richards notes, Smith had little personal knowledge of the Highlands and the references he made to the region were in order to substantiate general theories rather than illustrate the particular deficiencies of one regional economy. Secondly, several of the issues he considered important to the development of the Highlands had been recognised by others long before - the role of towns as places of 'civility' and the necessity for industrial employment in context with other 'arts of life'. And thirdly, in an age of so much economic commentary directed at the Highlands, it is difficult to separate out the influence of Smith from that of other commentators and theorists who each discussed the means of exciting 'a spirit of industry'.

Just as Smith's comments on the Highlands cannot be fully understood outside the framework of his model of economic growth and development involving as it did the basic elements of division of labour, expansion of markets and accumulation of capital, so also the suggested influence of Smith cannot be separated from wider debates of the time on industry, manufactures and commercial development. Restrictions of space here preclude detailed appraisal of the historiographic significance of those authors of the 1700s and 1800s who considered the nature of manufactures and the impact of industry more generally. But it is clear from even a limited assessment of those persons who wrote about the Highlands that 'industry' (both as material pursuit and social quality) was not only considered necessary as means to <u>economic</u> improvement but was also regarded, by the thinkers of the Enlightenment especially, as the final stage of <u>cultural</u> development. Lord Kames placed much emphasis on private property as the basis to what he termed a more advanced 'mode of subsistence'; 'Without private property there would be no industry, and without industry, men would remain savages forever'.12 For Millar, property was 'the principal source of authority'. And elsewhere, Millar comments upon the virtues of industry in extending political and civil liberty.

Wherever men of inferior condition are enabled to

277

> live in affluence by their own industry, and in
> procuring their own livelihood, have little
> occasion to court the favour of their superiors,
> there we may expect that ideas of liberty will be
> universally diffused. This happy arrangement of
> things, is as naturally produced by commerce and
> manufactures; but it would be as vain to look for
> it in the uncultivated parts of the world, as to
> look for the independent spirit of an English
> waggoner, among persons of low rank in the
> Highlands of Scotland.13

This comment reflects the concern of Enlightenment thinkers
with industry as industriousness, a quality of civilized
commercial societies. Others were more understanding of
Highlanders' industry.

> Unassisted Exertions of Industry are not to be
> expected from a People still in the Pastoral Stage
> of Society; nor from unenlightened Minds are we
> anywhere to expect the sudden Discontinuance of
> Bad Customs. But, wherever the Highlanders are
> defective in industry, it will be found; upon fair
> Enquiry; to be rather their Misfortune than their
> Fault: and owing to their want of Knowledge,
> rather than to their any want of the Spirit of
> Labour. Disposition to Industry, is greater than
> is usually imagined, and if judiciously directed
> is capable to rise to the greatest Heights.14

Most commentators, less directly concerned with the
science of man and more with the practical problems of
extending Highland industry, devoted their attention to the
best means of development. For some, such as George
Dempster and John Sinclair, the solution was two-fold; a
more rigidly-defined division of labour, and, once an
industrial group within the Highland population had been
freed from agricultural demands, their employment in
manufacturing villages. Others like George Mackenzie
likewise favoured villages.

> Our only means of making the natives industrious,
> is to make them depend on each other for many of
> the necessaries of life, and this can only be done
> by collecting them in towns. This will, at first,
> be found extremely difficult, but a beginning is
> all that is required. If a few can be prevailed
> upon to study different trades, and commence
> business, many will follow their example. At the

same time, when we collect tradesmen into a
village we ought to endeavour to provide employment for the increasing numbers of useful people,
and this is to be obtained by the establishment of
some species of manufacture.15

Sinclair argued for the striking of 'a proper balance
between agriculture and commerce' to promote the welfare of
the country and argued that re-locating population in
villages following estate re-organisation had to provide
sufficient industry to employ all the people meaningfully.

Whenever the population of a village exceeds the
industry of its inhabitants, the place must
decline. When their consumption is greater than
their earnings, and their wants are not supplied
by their labour, the stock of the society must
decrease . . . The body politic may be vitiated,
as well as the natural body. Habits of indolence
eradicate every desire of exertion . . . It is a
wise maxim, therefore, to increase the population
of a village, providing the people are rendered
industrious.16

Others were more sceptical about the idea of villages
of and for industry in the Highlands. Walker considered
implementation of this general policy 'by no means such an
easy matter as is commonly imagined'.

At the towns and villages, either in the Highlands
or their neighbourhood, there is very little
demand for the mechanic arts, though they are
surrounded by extensive countries, containing
great numbers of people. This must occur to an
observer in the case of Crief [sic], Callander,
Inveraray, Oban, Fort William, Fort Augustus, and
Stornoway, but arises from the manners of the
Highlands, where every family, and almost every
person execute most of the mechanic arts that are
necessary for their own accommodation. This
renders the formation of a Highland village
peculiarly difficult. The Highlands do not afford
immediate and profitable employment in any one
place to a number of day labourers, mechanics, and
manufacturers; and without this, the mere
accommodation of a house can, to such persons, be
no inducement. When dislodged from their small
farms, it has been proposed to convert them into
villagers; but no such care has been taken of the

people so dispossessed, nor can any one be assured
of its being taken in times to come. The establishment of a village in the Highlands is easy in
speculation, but difficult in practice, and can
only be done by assigning to each villager an
allotment of land.17

James Anderson, who although he proposed the establishment
of fishing villages as a principal means of exciting 'a
spirit of industry' in the Highlands shared with Walker a
concern with the difficulties in establishing a clearly
defined division of labour and in initiating and maintaining industries which would provide employment and markets
without disrupting agriculture.18 And even on Gigha and
Cara, the minister recognised that inherent Highland
employment structures restricted development: 'Division of
Labour, which is the highest improvement in society has not
yet been carried to such a length, as to entitle the people
of Gigha to the character of being industrious'.19
    Plans for the development of manufactures in the
Highlands thus centred upon the need to promote a motivating spirit of industry and a division of labour which, if
not entirely freeing workers in villages from commitments
on the land, was intended to separate them sufficiently to
allow concentration on manufacturing for a commercial
market. This emphasis placed on property and a more
strictly defined occupational hierarchy acted to separate
the Highlander from what he would have recognised as a more
'traditional' mode of life. Even the emphasis placed on
money, in agricultural rents or in its circulation in
manufactured goods, represented a different medium of
exchange for a people whose social bonds centred upon
place, the clan and family and recognised rhythms of
occupance. This is not to claim that the Highlands were
without industry and Highlanders incapable of industrial
labour (though some commentators considered this so): it
is to note that in a region where established relationships
were mediated through a variety of non-monetary obligations
and recognised concepts of self-sufficiency, the institutions of industry and the ideology of industriousness
themselves represented a form of cultural hegemony.

MANUFACTURES IN THE HIGHLANDS

In his reports to the Board of the Annexed Estates, Walker
recommended the introduction of a variety of manufactures
as principal 'Heads of Improvement'. Included were such
things as the making of ropes, canvas, salt, and soap;

plans to instruct the natives in quarrying; the need 'to pursue the Appearance of <u>Lead</u> and <u>Copper</u> in Coll and Tirey' (<u>sic</u>); create harbours to promote fishing; remove customs on linen to expand textile making; instruct Highlanders in the small-scale collection of a variety of natural productions - green jasper in Rum, eider down and 'Pearls in many places'; and he argued, too, for the advantages likely to result 'if the Gentlemen would form themselves into <u>Oeconomical Societies</u> in the three great counties of <u>Argyll</u>, <u>Inverness</u> and <u>Ross</u>'.20 In places there was limited development of mineral resources - iron working at Furnace and Bonawe, lead mining at Strontian, quarrying at Easdale and Ballachulish - but the Highlands as a whole offered little opportunity for manufactories or extractive industry of this sort. Without the resources and commercial base of the Lowlands but with growing proportions of the native population released from agriculture but still resident on the land as a result of estate reorganisation, Highland manufactures centred upon three areas of production. The making of kelp was concentrated in the southern Outer Hebrides and was particularly important from about 1760 to 1825 although it continued on a smaller scale after that date. Textiles, especially domestic linen, were concentrated in Highland Perthshire and in parts of eastern Inverness, Ross and Cromarty, and Sutherland. The north and west had little or no involvement in this industry. Fishing was a traditional by-employment in the Highlands. As with textiles, the development of fishing as an industry depended upon the establishment of villages for the concentration of population, capital, and the techniques of production. Commercially-oriented fishing centred upon the sea lochs of the north and west mainland, in the waters east of Kintyre, around Lewis, and following the clearance of population in Sutherland in the opening decades of the nineteenth century and their relocation in coastal villages, was of particular importance to eastern Sutherland and Caithness. These three types of manufacture are the main issues discussed in what follows.

The rise and fall of kelp, c.1760-c.1830

The production of kelp involved burning seaweed to give a calcined ash used in making glass, soap and iodine. Kelping was seasonal labour, starting in early June and extending over the following six to eight weeks. The seaweed was burnt in kilns, simply constructed on or near the shore and the tools of production - sickles to cut the weed and long pokers to stir it when burning - were

Figure 5.1 The principal areas of kelp and textile
manufacture in the Highlands

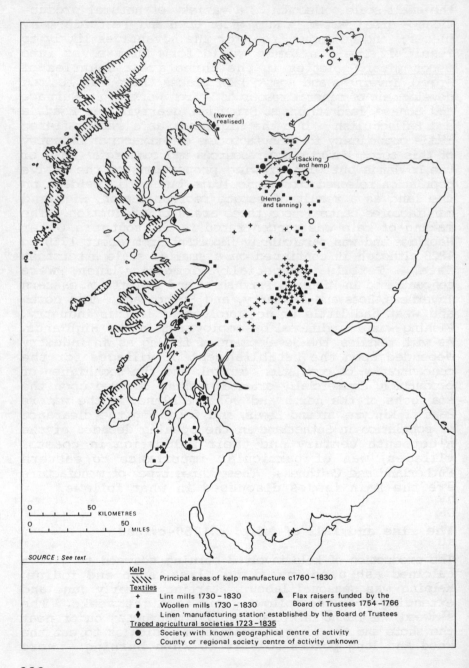

SOURCE : See text

Kelp
\\\\ Principal areas of kelp manufacture c1760 – 1830
Textiles
+   Lint mills 1730 – 1830   ▲ Flax raisers funded by the
■   Woollen mills 1730 – 1830   Board of Trustees 1754 –1766
◆   Linen 'manufacturing station' established by the Board of Trustees
Traced agricultural societies 1723 – 1835
●   Society with known geographical centre of activity
○   County or regional society centre of activity unknown

likewise simple. Burning reduced the weed to 5 per cent of its former weight. The kelp was collected from the shore, sold at twenty-two hundredweights to the ton given impurities of sand, and shipped to London, Liverpool and other southern ports. Kelp making had begun in the 1720s around the Firth of Forth and in the Orkneys and was only introduced to the western isles from the 1740s, chiefly by Irish entrepreneurs. By the 1760s it was well established in the Outer Hebrides, and was by then largely controlled by local landlords.[21] Although there are records of kelp making on parts of the western and northern mainland, the industry was from this period until its demise chiefly confined to the western islands. (Figure 5.1). Until the repeal of the salt duties, growth in foreign trade and the manufacture of artificial substitutes collectively undermined the industry, kelp was a principal contributor to the money economy of this region. The industry had related deleterious effects which have been touched upon above and are considered in what follows. But from about 1760 to 1830, kelp manufacturing provided landlords with cash income from an industry where the raw material was plentiful and free, the techniques and tools of production simple, the labour cheaply available, and, in consequence, the profits enormous.

Prices, costs, and profit margins deriving from kelp are not easily assessed nor always strictly comparable over time given the different qualities of material and the varying costs of manufacture. But 'There can be no doubt about the steep rise and fall or about the periods over which the change was most rapid'.[22] Kelp sold at about £2 5s per ton in the mid-eighteenth century, at £5 by the 1770s, between £9 – £10 by the end of the eighteenth century, up to £20 a ton in the peak price years to about 1810, then began a decline in price to £8 – £11 by the 1820s, to £4 16s 8d by 1830 and sold at about £2 10s by 1840. In some places, prices never achieved these maximum levels and the fall in prices was more rapid than the general trend suggests: in Lewis, for example, where the highest price reached was £11 11s per ton in 1819, and in Uig and Lochs kelp was priced as low as £1 10s a ton by 1833. But by then, the industry had virtually ceased although necessity forced some families to produce small amounts of kelp in the Outer Isles in the 1847–1851 famine. Production levels are also difficult to ascertain. Most of the Outer Isles were making between 50 and 100 tons by the early 1760s (Table 5.1). By the 1790s the area was producing about 5000 tons annually with the peak in production coming in 1810 at about 7000 tons. North Uist was the principal source of output. But production levels rose from both a widening of these areas making limited amounts as well as from intensification in the Uists and Lewis. Output was greatest from a few estates and was usually through direct landlord control of production by tenants. Virtually the only cost to landlords was labour and freight. Total manufacturing costs for Lewis kelp in the later 1790s averaged £1663 per annum with labour costing 53s 6d and other costs totalling £2 per ton.23 With prices at this time ranging from £6 to £10 a ton, profit margins were great. Between 1807 and 1809, Clanranald had an annual average income after costs of £9454 from sale of his South Uist kelp at a time when his land rental was £5297. MacDonald on North Uist took between £14,000 and £20,000 a year from kelp at its peak and smaller landlords made large profits from often even limited amounts.24 Table 5.2 shows the levels of production, prices, and profit figures for Lewis kelp from 1811 to 1836. While many of the more profitable years for Lewis and other places came before 1811 and this table suggests also that overall trends were underlain by annual fluctuations in output and prices, these figures may be taken as representative of the levels of profit to be gained as well as illustrative of the general decline by the 1830s.

Kelp's importance as an extractive industry in the Highlands in the seventy years after 1760 rests on two related facts: firstly, the unequal distribution and accumulation of the cash income derived from its manufacture; secondly, the effect on rents, tenurial relationships and the social relations of production during both kelp's expansion and its more rapid cessation. Almost all profits from kelp making went to landlords. But the unequal appropriation of cash income resulted also from increases in rents which most landlords levied on kelp estates. As we have seen, kelp manufacture demanded the localised coastal concentration of labour at a time of population increase. But because kelping was seasonal and tenants bound to agricultural demands for the rest of the year, no specialised division of labour was possible. Kelp workers remained agricultural tenants. Landlords, however, could increase the dependency of tenants on the returns from kelp making and increase the potential labour supply by sub-dividing holdings and increasing rents. Tenants, unable to meet the rent demanded from the produce of their land alone, were forced into reliance on kelp wages which, in turn, were recovered by the landlords as rental. On the Clanranald Estates, for example, 'the lands were let to the tenantry with a view to the rents being paid in a great measure by kelp manufacture'. Landlords became large-scale employers, fixing wage rates which hardly varied with rise

Table 5.1

Production levels, prices, and value of kelp in the Hebrides, c. 1764*

Island	Annual amount produced (tons)	Price per ton (£)	Total value of annual product (£)
Barra(1)	c. 60	–	–
Benbecula	170–200 tons per annum to total value £166.00		
Coll(2)	c. 40	4	160.00
Colonsay(3)	c. 40	4	160.00
Harris	c.100	3.25	325.00(4)
Islay	'exports some kelp'		
Lewis	50(5)	3.25	162.50
Mull	100	3.50	350.00
North Uist(6)	500	3.50	1625.00
Skye	200	3.75	750.00
South Uist	100	3.25	325.00
Tiree(7)	44	3.25	143.00

* Based on M. McKay (ed.), The Rev. Dr. John Walker's Report on the Hebrides of 1764 and 1771 (Edinburgh, 1980),41,42,54,65,69,76,77,87,88,100,125,155,161,171,187, 207,211- 212, 233; J. Walker, 'An Essay on Kelp, containing the rise and progress of that manufacture in the north of Scotland, its present state, and the means of carrying it to a greater extent', Transactions of the Highland and Agricultural Society of Scotland, I, (1799), pp.1-31; SRO, GD.201/5/1232, Bundles 1, 4, and 5; SRO, GD.46/13/126; M. Gray, 'The Kelp Industry in the Highlands and Islands', Economic History Review, IV, (1951), pp.197-209; idem, The Highland Economy 1750-1850 (Edinburgh, 1957), pp. 124ff; E. Richards, A History of the Highland Clearances Vol. II, p.514.

(Notes to Table continued overleaf.)

(1)   Kelp first made on the Island in 1763.
(2)   Kelp first made on the island in 1754;   25 tons
       made that year.
(3)   In his remarks on Colonsay, Walker notes that 40
       tons of kelp was produced from Jura in 1762 by 'an
       Irish manufacturer' but since that date locals
       have run the industry there.
(4)   Harris exported 300 tons per annum by 1771.
(5)   This figure of 50 tons was for 1763.
(6)   North Uist produced 800 tons in 1762, 1200 tons by
       1790, 1500 tons by 1810, and still produced 1200
       tons in 1842 when kelp making had virtually
       ceased. Kelp making began on nearby Bernera in
       1748.
(7)   Walker notes that kelp making began on the island
       in   1746, started by an Irish entrepreneur.

in price and in places, tenant-labourers received no returns at all from kelp making, remuneration being taken off the rent owed. Direct leasing and wage arrangements and the increased involvement of landlords as entrepreneurs further accelerated the disappearance of the tacksman and controlled a labour force now paying more 'for the employment and the labour which their tenements secure for them, than for the intrinsic value of these tenements themselves'.25 As the costs of labour remained static and kelp prices and rents rose, virtually all the increase came to landlords as profit with the agricultural possibilities for the tenantry being simultaneously eroded. Smaller holdings likewise meant a smaller stock of cattle, a reduction critical to non-kelp income levels. And as Hunter has noted, 'as if that were not bad enough, the kelp industry, by its very nature, resulted in the neglect and consequent stagnation of the crofting economy's agricultural base'.26

Kelping may thus have been an important means of capital accumulation for landlords but it was a short-term gain restrictive of agricultural development: 'On kelp estates the land is almost entirely sacrificed to that manufacture and is at best, with regards to its agriculture, in a stationary condition'.27 Because kelp making was basically an extractive industry with the product processed elsewhere, it did not generate associated trades or manufactures. And because of its seasonal nature and the dependency of the labour force both upon wages and returns from restricted agricultural holdings in the remainder of the year, no division of labour between sectors of the tenant population was possible. No division of labour between processes of production was feasible given the simple techniques involved in its making. The virtual collapse of the kelp industry after 1830 thus had several effects on the economy of those regions in which it had been concentrated. For landlords, a vital source of cash income was removed. Many went bankrupt (though kelp was not the sole cause) and sold their estates. The emphasis in developing the economy of these estates switched from kelp manufactures to sheep farming, a change which necessitated the clearance of that population and labour force previously allowed to accumulate. Arrears built up amongst an over-crowded tenantry whose agricultural base would not meet the rents demanded and whose source of income from part-time industrial employment had been removed. Kelp making continued in places. There were still 400 families engaged in the industry in North Uist in 1837, and 1,872 persons in South Uist at the same date. But the amounts produced, though high quality, were insignificant. At one level, the manufacture of kelp did

Table 5.2
Production levels, prices, and profits for Lewis kelp, 1811-1836*

Years	Annual Amount Produced (to nearest whole ton)	Price per ton (to nearest whole £)	Net proceeds exclusive of process of manufacture (to nearest whole £)	Expense of Manufacture (to nearest whole £)	Free Net Profits (to nearest whole £)
1811	498	—	—	1594	—
1812	730	—	—	2219	—
1813	366	—	—	1184	—
1814	557	—	—	1720	—
1815	459	10–11	3636	1577	2059
1816	725	8–10	4520	2358	2162
1817	380	—	—	1180	—
1818	559	—	—	1794	—
1819	385	9–12	2356	1206	1150
1820	627	8–12	5486	2129	3357
1821	441	6–12	3512	1198	2314
1822	588	4– 9	3668	1624	2044
1823	359	5–10	2744	1049	1695
1824	460	6– 8	2698	1277	1421
1825	488	7	3014	1921	1093
1826	732	4– 7	2793	1059	1734
1827	376	5– 6	3730	1275	2455
1828	546	3– 6	2371	1084	1287
1829	422	5	1592	1641	49 [(+)]
1830	336	5	1266	1113	153
1831	412	2– 5	1399	1018	381
1832	381	5	1536	871	665
1833	328	4– 5	1214	1212	2
1834	414	3	1199	803	396
1835	256	3	711	1080	369 [(+)]
1836	310	3– 4	1119	—	—

* Based on SRO GD 46, *Seaforth Muniments*, Section 13/134; *Select Committee on Emigration, P.P., VI*, (1841), p. 214.
(+) These figures represent losses that year.

Industriousness and the Failure of Industry

provide labour, generate cash income and signal the industrial integration of the Highlands with wider commercial interests. But at another and more fundamental level, the industry was destructive of social and material relationships, geared only to short-term capital accumulation with no investment of profits and the limited wage-economy it determined was in the longer term of no benefit to the labour force it employed.

The textile industry in the Highlands, 1727-1830

In the seventeenth century, the export of coarse linen and woollen cloth was of considerable significance to the Scottish economy. The poor quality of these textiles restricted potential markets before the eighteenth century. During the 1700s, however, the making and export of linen cloth became Scotland's premier industry. Production rose from 8.51 million yards in the period 1750-1754 to 9.58 million yards a decade later and reached 12.36 million yards by the mid-1700s, at which time it had a value of £558,000. 28 By 1818-1822, output of linen was 31 million yards. The expansion of textiles generally and the linen industry particularly in Lowland Scotland in the century from about 1727 was the result of several factors in combination: direct institutional encouragement, especially from the Board of Trustees for the Encouragement of Manufactures and Fisheries (established in 1727), and the British Linen Company; the growth of a rurally-located industrial work force, employed in spinning and weaving within the domestic system or in mills using water power (not until the 1820s and 1830s did the techniques of production and use of steam-power determine a shift to urban locations); the entrepreneurial role of merchants and manufactures in stimulating demand and supplying equipment and capital; and, not least, the encouragement given by landowners and 'improving' gentry to the development of textiles as a source of industry in the sense both of manufactures and industriousness. The landowner's interest in textiles lay not only as Shaw has claimed 'in the incentive which it gave to agricultural improvement, in the broader economic base which it gave to his estate, and in the enhanced estate value which accrued directly or indirectly from the presence of the textile industry', but also in the political and civil control of his tenantry.29 This last concern was likewise considered important by those institutions and individuals who directed the expansion and commercial development of textiles in the Highlands.

The making of linen and woollen textiles were traditional subsistence activities in the Highlands which drew upon
local natural products for dyes, chiefly female labour in
production, and which had an established if minor place in
communal labour patterns. During the eighteenth century,
however, the emphasis on production for commercial markets
drew the Highlands away from production for domestic needs
and into increasingly close association with the textile
industries of the Lowlands. Gray has argued that the
Highland textile industry from this period was based 'not
upon locally grown flax, not upon the organically related
processes of household and village production, but upon the
fission and geographic spread of one of the sub-processes
of the larger developing industry of the Lowland belt'.30
It was this fact that determined the development of chiefly
linen, and, to a degree woollen, textiles in those areas of
the Highlands nearest the main belt of Lowland production:
in Highland Perthshire particularly, in Easter Ross and
eastern Inverness-shire, with yarn manufacture being
locally important in Islay but with the north-west mainland
and islands as a whole being little affected (Figure 5.1).
Later work has additionally revealed the variety of
ways by which the localised expansion of manufactures was
not only drawn into the orbit of a wider economy but also
the effect such integration had upon local economic and
social structures. In the Atholl lands in Perthshire, for
example, efforts to establish a more commercial footing to
linen production through the introduction of spinning
wheels, local growing of lint seed, and the recruiting of
low country weavers to instruct native tenants were made as
early as 1708. Other acts and measures of 1712 and 1719
point to the importance of the industry - the staple for
cash rents in much of the Atholl Highlands - and to the
involvement of landowners before the more institutionalised
interest of the Board of Trustees. In this area, the fact
that tenants took their yarn to Moulin market - 'In the
market of Moulin held the 1st of March, the yarn is sold
for ready money; and the payment of rent depends on that
market' - has been taken to indicate the absence of an
entrepreneurial 'putting-out' system.31 But by the later
1700s in the textile areas of Perthshire generally, there
is evidence of the involvement of urban merchants in the
circulation of raw and finished materials and of a more
direct negotiation between spinner, weaver, and entrepre-
neur over the processes and levels of production. In the
other principal area of production around eastern
Inverness-shire and in Easter Ross, commercial expansion
depended more immediately upon the involvement of urban
merchants and manufacturers.32 Geographical variations in

the distribution and economic importance of textiles in the highlands were thus complemented by distinctions in the organisational bases to production at the household, institutional, and individual level.

The three principal institutions concerned with the commercial expansion of textiles in the Highlands were the Board of Trustees, the British Linen Company, and the Board for the Annexed Estates. The SSPCK was also directly involved, in a small way, in the establishment of 'spinning schools'. The Board of Trustees was established for the encouragement of herring fisheries and the development and regulation of linen, hemp, and coarse wool manufacture. The Board was generally supported by annuities and funds under acts of 1707, 1718, and 1724, but their work in promoting textiles in the Highlands was principally funded by an annuity of £3,000 given in 1753 to run for nine years 'For Encouraging and improving the Linen Manufacture in the Highlands of Scotland'.33 Shaw notes that the Board of Trustees' contribution to the national development of textiles took four forms: control of standards; technical research; industrial training; and construction grants.34 In the Highlands, their involvement after 1753 centred upon the construction of 'manufacturing stations'. The development of spinning in the Highlands (with which the Board had earlier been almost alone concerned) had provided employment for women. The purpose of the manufacturing stations was that they become 'colonies of industry' in which financial resources and the technical means of production would be concentrated and the techniques of production would be taught as a means to the full-time industrial employment of a sector of the population. Four manufacturing stations - part school, part factory - were planned, at Lochbroom, Lochcarron, Glenmoriston, and Glenelg. This last never materialised (Figure 5.1). Each station was placed under the authority of experienced linen merchants: at Lochbroom, the 'principal undertaker' as these men were known was John Ross of Dingwall; at Lochcarron Ninian Jeffrey from Kelso; at Glenmoriston Alexander Shaw from Elgin; at Glenelg the intended operator, Robert Campbell of Edinburgh, never appeared. These men were to instruct natives in converting flax into linen yarn and cloth, growing better quality local lint seed to reduce dependence on imported flax, and to distribute equipment to persons who could not attend school. In addition, the Board of Trustees which had established several spinning schools in 1728 in the Perthshire Highlands directed the founding of further schools 'where the Linen manufacture hath been already introduced but hath not yet arrived to any considerable Degree of perfection',35 and provided funds for flax raisers throughout the Highlands (Figure 5.1).

Records of the Board of Trustees show close links with the British Linen Company, through which body agents acted as putting-out merchants in parts of the Highlands. Hector Scott, a manufacturer in Inverness in 1757, had for the preceding seven years 'been employed in carrying on the Heckling of Flax and Spinning of yarn at Inverness and the adjacent Highlands' and in buying flax from the British Linen Company 'which he carries to the said Country, dresses, and gives it out to spin there'.36 The British Linen Company had been founded in 1746 'to carry on the Linen Manufactures in all its branches'. They employed thousands of yarn spinners in the coastal areas of Ross and Cromarty and Sutherland and, unlike the Board of Trustees, organised production through agents such as Scott who controlled the distribution of flax, the spun yarn, and the payment of spinners. Their policies were important in establishing a more commercial outlook to linen spinning. Price reductions, problems in supplying flax, and overall financial restrictions undermined the involvement of the British Linen Company with spinning by the mid-1760s, however, and by 1773 the Company had ceased any direct involvement with Highland linen spinning.37 The British Linen Company's role in the organisation of spinning in the north-eastern coastal Highlands from 1746 to 1773 was at least regarded as successful by contemporaries: this was not the case for the Board of Trustees.

The Board of Trustees' activities met with only partial success. One of the two surveyors, Richard Neilson, realised the difficulties that the facts of Highland geography imposed on the establishment of manufactures. It was he who proposed the policy of dispersing spinning wheels and other equipment 'throughout the mountainous Countrey' and of annually distributing amounts of flax seed to the inhabitants. Of Morvern, Neilson reported the inhabitants 'the most Civilized and Industrious on the western coast' and 'ready to grasp at every opportunity for instruction',38 but later reports more commonly point to loss of equipment, lodging of false reports by flax raisers, resignation of spinning school teachers and a continued expenditure on material and salaries not equalled by returns on the amount of yarn spun. The three manufacturing stations cost £921 to run annually, construction costs in 1758 totalled £1196, and salaries, the cost of lint seed and wheels accounted for the remainder of the £3000 annually available.39 The British Linen Company took over the supply of yarn from 1759 and the Board of Trustees' involvement in Highland textiles effectively ended in

1762 when the fund was used to support a scheme in Bute.40 Responsibility switched to the Board for Annexed Estates. The fact that in 1766, the Trustees remitted to the above Board an account of £306 as the debt remaining after assisting linen expansion in the Highlands (their funds being then even too small to meet Lowland demands) is indicative of the longer-term failure that their work in the Highlands represented.41

From the mid-1760s until its cessation in 1784, the Board for the Annexed Estates was the sole official body for promoting manufactures in the Highlands. The reports of factors on the annexed estates provide an important source for the understanding of the geography and success of Highland textiles in the mid-eighteenth century. The comment upon Lix barony in Killin parish is representative of many.

> There is no sort of commerce or publick manufac-
> ture carried on here. They buy as much lint with
> what they have growing of their own as serve their
> women to spin and sell the yarn, the produce of
> which and the sale of some cattle is the only fund
> they have for making money for payment of their
> rents and other uses.42

In Callander village, as a result of the importance of the road communications between there and the low country, 'there is the greater reason to expect that several branches of business, commerce & manufacture might succeed in this place'. In most of the eastern estates contiguous to the Lowlands, reports comment on the spinning of linen yarn which is sold in local markets - in Dingwall, Crieff, Inverness, Callander, Logierait, Moulin - and note how in such areas, spinning 'is the staple commodity they have for making money'. Crieff in particular provided the commercial central place functions imagined for all Highland towns and villages.

> There are a good many people in Crieff that deal in
> the mercantile way and carry on a trade in linen
> and woollen cloths, yarn & skins and furnish the
> country round in merchant goods of all kinds . . .
> severals (sic) here deal likewise in the victual
> trade . . .   People of all trades, such as masons,
> joiners, house carpenters, wheelwrights, smiths,
> bakers, butchers, brewers, taylors & barbers are to
> be found in Crieff.43

But in more distant parts, commerce and manufactures were

'hardly known', with what little spinning was practised being winter work for women. The population of the north and west are commonly described as 'idle a great part of their time' with 'little knowledge of manufactures'. Archibald Menzies noted that the schemes for developing textiles in the more remote areas were not working because of the controls the principal undertakers had on the import and cost of the flax seed and given, too, the virtual impossibility of a more clearly defined occupational specialisation since most Highlanders depended on agriculture for their living, and, in the north and west especially, regarded spinning as part-time work for subsistence needs. Walker's observations on the Hebrides in the 1760s point to the limited nature of textile production in those regions. In Lewis, some woollen cloth was made for export but 'They are entire Strangers to all the Proper Methods of executing the Linen Manufacture'. The erection in 1763 of a spinning school by the Board for the Annexed Estates had been beneficial in instructing women to spin but was not accompanied by the settlement of a trained weaver. And even with the spinning school, Walker noted 'there is still a greater Superfluity of Idleness among Women, occasioned by the Want of the Woolen and Linen Manufacture'. Elsewhere in the islands, in Harris, for example, or in North Uist of which Walker noted 'The Linen Manufacture is not anywhere in the British Dominion in a more imperfect state, than in this Countrey', textiles were of minor importance. Only on Islay was linen manufacture well-established, but even there they were without weavers, uninstructed in the techniques of lint preparation, reliant upon poor local flax or expensive imports, and without standard yarn reels: 'The Inhabitants have been very little aided in their Prosecution of the Manufacture, and therefore it still subsists among them in a very rude State, though with proper attention and Encouragement, it might be brought to great Perfection'.44 The 'proper attention' given in the form of the three manufacturing stations was not successful. They remained only local places of instruction in particular processes of manufacture and not the central places for industrial growth intended: 'I understand that the people employed by the public for promoting of manufactures in the Highlands have never proceeded further than the article of yarn, contenting themselves with being a sort of factor for the real manufacturers'.45 As Menzies noted in 1768, the expense of the stations was not justified in the levels of output: 'Immense sums of money were expended in building magnificent structures to carry on manufactures where there are hardly any inhabitants and to push a branch by high

294

praemiums (sic) which has fallen tothe ground so soon as left to itself, as the country could have no access to the rough material'.46 The manufacturing stations were eventually leased to their undertakers in 1770 and finally sold off in 1791.

Smith writes that the Board for The Annexed Estates had four principal lines of approach in attempting to establish trained artisans and a more evident division of labour in the Highlands: apprentice Highland children to tradesmen in the Lowlands; encourage tradesmen and 'artificers' to move to the Highlands as instructors; establish small 'technical' schools; and build new towns or villages in which to concentrate the labour and means of production.47 None of these approaches encouraged manufacturing to any great degree. Apprentice schemes were costly; the scheme to bring in skilled labour foundered on the problem of the extent of agricultural land to give craftsmen; the schools were concentrated in Perthshire where textile manufacturing was at its most advanced and not in the north and west Highlands where they were most needed and their overall longer-term effect was limited; and the plans for settling tradesmen and local population in towns and villages was successful only in the case of Crieff and Callander and not in the 'uncivilized' north and west. Moreover, in concentrating upon linen and upon certain parts of the Highlands, they neglected the perhaps wider benefits to be gained from the commercial manufacture of woollen cloth. As Smith has shown, the Board made few gestures towards encouraging the wool industry despite reports by Menzies and others.48 Linen was considered crucial for Highland industry because it held a primary place in the national economy.

The Board for Annexed Estates was not unique in founding spinning schools. The Board of Trustees had established a few in 1728 and under their second patent, the SSPCK had erected spinning schools from 1738 as a means of extending 'Husbandry, Housewifery', Trades and Manufactures'.49 The SSPCK was concerned both with the local benefits of employment and manufacture and with the national interest in Highland civility.

> It is found by experience, that the breeding up of
> young people to handy labour, trades, and manufac-
> tures, together with learning to read and write,
> will be of great benefit, not only to these young
> people, but likewise to the nation in general, and
> better answer the inclinations of the contributors
> for promoting piety and virtue.50

Most of the SSPCK spinning schools present at one time or

another during the 1700s and early 1800s were located in Argyll, south-west Perthshire, and in eastern Ross and Cromarty (Figure 5.2). They were usually run by the wives of the SSPCK schoolmaster. SSPCK spinning schools were attended exclusively by women and thus, like the Trustees' and Annexed Estates' spinning schools, brought skills and equipment to those already familiar to varying degrees with the techniques of textile production without instructing men as weavers.

Consideration of institutional policies for Highland textiles should not obscure the role of individual agents or firms as entrepreneurs. Merchants in Highland towns acted to distribute goods and capital and in spinning especially, controlled large numbers of workers in given regions of the Highlands. Many were local men, employed by the Board of Trustees or the British Linen Company. William Forsyth, a Cromarty merchant, controlled putting-out systems as far west as Lochbroom; others, like George Ross, who built a hemp factory at Cromarty in 1773, and George Welsh a skinner from the Lowlands who established a successful tannery in Inverness, were industrialists and manufacturers rather than merchants. One of the most important entrepreneurial concerns involved in developing Highland textiles was the firm of William Sandeman and Co. Sandeman was a leading figure and his company a leading agency in the development of linen textiles in eighteenth-century Scotland.51 Sandeman had an establishment at Cromarty in 1750 and further bases at Milntown and Fortrose in Easter Ross from the 1760s from which points the firm controlled the yarn distribution and output levels for an estimated 1800 Highland spinners. Sandeman was also involved with the Board for Annexed Estates in their apprentice schemes. His involvement is illustrative of the way in which the development of textiles in the Highlands took place within the context of national growth. Sandeman's comment of 1763 made in regard to Highland linen manufactures – 'I am afraid . . . it will turn out a losing trade on account of great outlay of money and charge attending correspondence and distance in transporting flax and yarn'52 – provides important clues to why the textile industry in the Highlands, small in scale but locally not unimportant, did not provide the means to longer-term regional transformation.

By the 1830s, textile production had ceased in most parts of the Highlands, though spinning remained locally important.53 The failure of the textile industry in the Highlands stemmed not from a failure of will on the part of those institutions involved in its intended commercial re-orientation, but from a combination of mismanagement,

296

Figure 5.2   SSPCK spinning schools in the Highlands

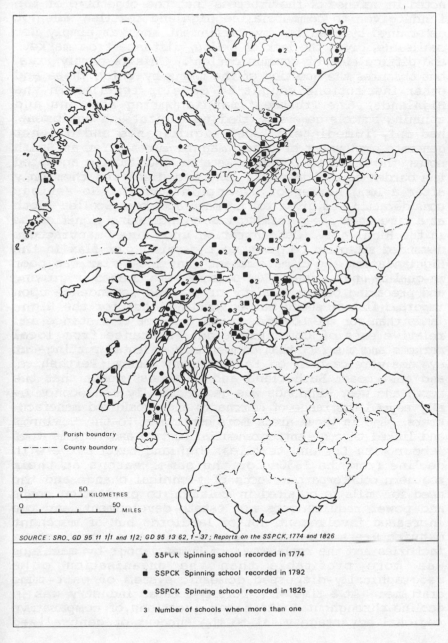

———— Parish boundary

—·—·— County boundary

0   50
|_____| KILOMETRES

0   50
|_____| MILES

SOURCE : SRO., GD 95 11 1/1 and 1/2; GD 95 13 62, 1 – 37 ; Reports on the SSPCK, 1774 and 1826

▲   SSPCK Spinning school recorded in 1774

■   SSPCK Spinning school recorded in 1792

●   SSPCK Spinning school recorded in 1825

3   Number of schools when more than one

comparative economic advantage and geographical location. Whilst recognising that 'Neither the record of the Board of Trustees nor of the Board of Commissioners for the Annexed Estates was distinguished in relation to the objective of establishing the linen industry in the north', Durie has noted in defence of the Trustees that the objective of the funds given to commercialise Highland textiles was not determined by them 'but by Parliament and was simply not realisable, given the lack of skills, distance from markets and difficulties of communication'. This is partly true, but obscures the question of the <u>means</u> by which these and other institutions sought to develop textiles in the Highlands. The Trustees' manufacturing stations and spinning schools generally tied up capital and equipment, had only immediately local significance and did not generate employment or other manufactures. Yet as Smith notes, the Board for Annexed Estates 'uncritically accepted the burden of the linen stations and discarded them only after a long series of disappointments'. No serious consideration was given to the manufacture of woollen cloth at a time when sheep farming was of increasing significance in the Highlands. Concentration upon linen manufacture demanded attention be given to the raising of flax in the Highlands, but the climate meant that local flax was poor in quality and amount. Few persons were trained in growing and preparing better quality crops, and dependence upon imported flax or seeds raised costs higher for the Highlands than for the Lowlands given problems of distance and relative ease of communication. Distance from local markets and the fact that commercially-oriented putting-out systems were centred on Easter Ross, central Perthshire, and east coast Sutherland and Caithness meant that the north and west Highlands was geographically and economically beyond the range of merchants and subsidised manufacturers. And in those areas more contiguous to the Lowlands and linked through entrepreneurial control and movement of labour with Lowland textiles, Highland textiles were in decline from the 1830s for the same reasons as their southern counterparts: facts of technical change and the need for mills to be sited in relation to production costs and power requirements not estate development, and the increased involvement not of landlords but of merchant manufacturers for whom centralisation of productive facilities and the replacement of human labour by machines was more profitable than the organisation of a geographically-dispersed domestic system of part-time craftsmen. At a time when rurally-located industry was in decline throughout Britain and questions of comparative regional advantage vital to the success of centralised

Industriousness and the Failure of Industry

factory-based production, it is unsurprising that even in those Highland areas where textiles had been commercially important and the basis of money rent, the industry should have declined as and when it did. Highland textiles centred upon spinning, giving employment chiefly to women. The relative lack of weaving meant that the industry in the Highlands was only ever partial in productive terms. Highland tenants had no capital to invest in local commercial production. Textile manufactures thus never provided the means to establishing a division of labour within the industry itself or of fostering an occupational diversity in the population generally. Further, textiles did not distract attention from the fundamental task of cultivating the soil. In the north and west - those areas relatively unaffected by the development of textiles - and in other places where a growing population was being displaced to the coasts as a result of agrarian transformation, individual pursuits centred either upon kelp, or more widely, upon fishing.

The fishing industry in the Highlands, 1786-1884

The fishing industry in the Highlands shares a number of features with textiles. Both were traditionally undertaken on a small scale. In undergoing the shift from subsistence practice to commercial production, fishing likewise relied for its expansion more upon the impetus given by formal institutions and the involvement of largely non-active capital and entrepreneurs than upon local initiative. Both were chiefly centred in villages, intended as focal points for industry and commercial advance. Commercial fishing developed in and brought economic benefit to particular parts of the Highlands rather than to the region as a whole, but as for textiles, the expansion of the industry in those areas did not always free the Highlander from dependence upon the land.

'The fishing industry, like so many other aspects of Highland economic life, must be studied in regional sections'.55 We may identify three main 'sections': in the lochs of Argyll and the Clyde estuary, especially around Loch Fyne and Loch Long; in the sea lochs of Wester Ross - Loch Broom, Loch Hourn and others; and the north-east Highland coast, focussing upon Helmsdale, Wick and other villages in Sutherland and Caithness. Each of these areas enjoyed varied importance at one time or another; the first, as the most thoroughly commercial and highly organised and with good boats and equipment, was successful because of its proximity to Lowland markets and the good catches there. For a few, fishing provided the only means of support. The areas north of Mull, including the Outer Isles as well as the mainland, were the focus of much mercantilist attention from the later 1700s but had relatively little commercial success. The north-east fishing was especially important from the nineteenth century and as in the south-west Highlands, the industry there regularly provided money income greater than the returns from agriculture though unlike the south-west, it never separated off a sector of the population from the land. Although in each of these areas (as throughout the Highlands generally), fishing by line or net was chiefly for subsistence purposes, there had been attempts at its commercial orientation since the late 1500s. James V tried to develop fishing within a twenty-mile limit of the Western Isles by encouraging Lowland burghs to build 'busses', boats of between 10 to 90 tons burden. This scheme was unsuccessful largely due to harassment by the natives – Lewismen were reckoned particularly unfriendly towards 'all strangers guha aither in their lawful trade of fishing'. In 1632 the Association of the Fishing was established under the patronage of Charles I, but opposition from the inhabitants of Lewis again hindered this development and the Association's involvement in Hebridean fishing ended in the 1640s. We know from sources of various date in Macfarlane's Geographical Collections that herring fishing was common in several west mainland sea lochs during the seventeenth and early eighteenth centuries, but this was chiefly by Clyde-based concerns or Dutch busses with little or no involvement from Highlanders. East coast highland fishing at this time was likewise the preserve of Lowland or foreign fishermen.56

More direct commercial development of Highland herring fishing began with the Board of Trustees and, later, the Board for Annexed Estates. The former concentrated its efforts on the east coasts more than the west; the latter, after 1763, attempted to stimulate Highland fishing by establishing sailors in fishing villages on the northern and western annexed estates and by providing boats and equipment on loan and by lending capital. As policies, the first quickly failed; the second had variable effect. Most Highlanders at this time depended upon agriculture and regarded fishing only as a supplement. Fishing as a way of life demanded major changes in the social relations of production in Highland society: 'it is no easy task to teach men, habituated from infancy to tend herds on the hillside, to drag for subsistence in the deep sea'.57 Those natives who did see potential for the industry were restricted by poor equipment and boats capable of loch or

300

inshore fishing only, by lack of capital, too few merchants and entrepreneurs, by the monopolies granted to Lowland busses, distance from market, few curing or storing facilities, and by ignorance of commercial fishing techniques. Additionally, the system of private bounties which operated until 1787 (payments on a tonnage basis payable to all fishing vessels) favoured the fleets of larger Lowland busses centred on Campbeltown, Rothesay, and Greenock. Records of these bounties show an increase in the number of busses, in the men employed and in the barrels of herring cured for export: from 87 busses, 865 men and 3052 barrels by 1763-64, for example, to 289 busses, 3326 men and 51,402 barrels by 1776-1777.[58] Local boats in the north-west Highlands could not compete with the scale or organisation of those Clyde-based fleets who fished their waters, a picture repeated for the north-east coast during the 1700s and for the fishing districts of Easter Ross.[59] It was this lack of commercial capital, entrepreneurial skill, even of interest in the utilisation of a plentiful resource for productive purposes that motivated the attempts at establishing Highland fishing. The above agencies were successful only in part. Trends of output are difficult to establish but the Board of Trustees seems to have stimulated herring output at least. The Board for the Annexed Estates had limited success in providing capital and equipment to local fishermen, but no greater reward was possible given the Board's financial difficulties and the continued dependence of tenants on agricultural returns. It was these difficulties and the failure of earlier efforts that prompted the establishment in 1786 of the British Society for Extending the Fisheries and Improving the Sea Coasts of the Kingdom (The British Fisheries Society).

The British Fisheries Society was established in the wake of renewed interest in commercial fishing by parliament, the Highland Society of London (which body had been funding fisheries in the Highlands since its foundation in 1778), and in the works of numerous improving individuals.[60] Richards has shown, for example, how George Dempster was involved with plans for Highland fishing. Mindful perhaps of earlier difficulties, Dempster had written in 1784 of the potential advantages and actual problems involved in developing Highland fishing: 'The seas abound with fish, the Highland (sic) with industrious and good people. It will be the business of the legislature to bring these two to meet. But I fear it would in that country be an easier task for mountains to melt, at least they are at present much nearer to one another'.[61] The Society was influenced in its decision to establish fishing villages along the west Highland coast by Knox's 1786 lecture <u>A Discourse on the Expediency of Establishing Fishing Stations or Small Towns in the Highlands of Scotland</u>. And as Dunlop has noted, the policy of building fishing villages to promote that industry reflected the eighteenth-century ideological pursuit of civility and industry through settlements of good order, moral and physical. On the question of where to build such fishing stations, the Society was largely governed by returns and responses from Highland landlords to its 1787 question-naire, a letter containing queries on where best to establish wharfs and on local advantages of site and situation. Perhaps because fishing in the south-west Highlands was well-established, attention focussed on the north-west mainland and the coast of Caithness. Some existing local projects are revealed in the responses of landlords to the 1787 questionnaire: Campbell of Shaw-field's initiative in building a small quay and fishing station at Bowmore on Islay, for example, or the two small stations at Isle Martin and Tanera in Loch Broom. Overall, however, replies were a mixture of optimistic encouragement for the idea of fishing villages and realisation of the difficulties involved: the reply of Maclean of Torloisk on Mull exemplifies the concern over the likely difference between intent and result given the particular circum-stances of the late eighteenth-century Highlands.

> I must declare the merely building of villages
> will not be sufficient to enable the natives of
> this island to begin the fishery. The poverty in
> which they are immersed makes it utterly impossi-
> ble for almost any of them to purchase boats and
> tackle for the beginning of a voyage.62

Rather than turn to smaller 'stations', the British Fisheries Society established three principal fishing settlements in the western Highlands, at Ullapool, Tober-mory, and Lochbay on Skye (Figure 5.3). The idea of a settlement at Ullapool was not new. The Board for the Annexed Estates considered a village there 'would occasion a concourse of people from all corners of the neigh-bourhood, to be employed either in the fisheries or manufac-tures, and would spread industry along all the western coast'. Neilson in his report to the Board of Trustees had urged commercial development of the site given the abundant herring shoals there.63 The decision of the Society to begin in 1787 with two fishing settlements (Lochbay was not developed until 1795) was certainly based upon their desire to foster fishing in both 'the southern and northern

302

Figure 5.3   The principal fishing villages, deer forests and lesser industries in the Highlands

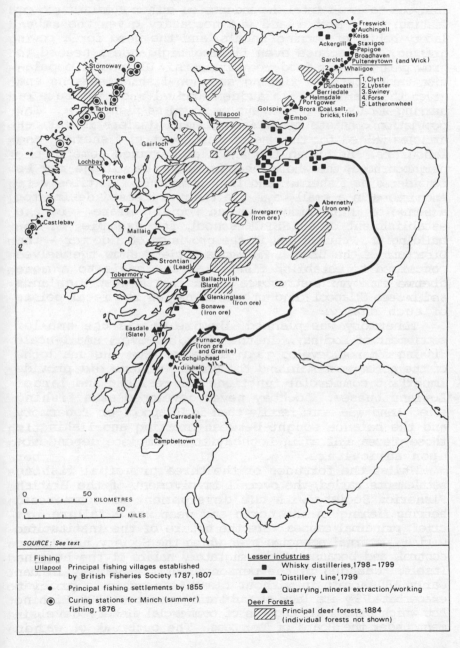

Fishing
Ullapool   Principal fishing villages established by British Fisheries Society 1787, 1807

● Principal fishing settlements by 1855

⊙ Curing stations for Minch (summer) fishing, 1876

Lesser industries
■ Whisky distilleries, 1798–1799

— 'Distillery Line', 1799

▲ Quarrying, mineral extraction/working

Deer Forests
▨ Principal deer forests, 1884 (individual forests not shown)

SOURCE: See text

division of the Highlands', but the choice of Ullapool as the northern settlement may have derived also from those earlier claims. Ullapool was chosen, too, because of the earlier failure of textiles at Lochbroom, and the presence of curing stations at Isle Martin and Tanera.64 Land was laid out to avoid total dependence on either agriculture or fishing; some arable land was necessary given the ambulatory habits of herring shoals, and the need for a cow's grazing, and because even fishing Highlanders needed to grow part of their food requirements. Ullapool's population varied between fishing and non-fishing seasons and given the characteristic sudden arrival and departure of herring shoals was not always employed as fishermen: 'The population consists of artisans, small dealers in various articles wanted for the use of the country, fishermen and labourers. But when the shoal of herrings come to the neighbourhood, the whole inhabitants of the village may be considered as fishermen and fish curers'.65 Textiles were encouraged in a small way. In their expressed desire for a sense of industriousness and social welfare - in the establishment of an SSPCK school, for example, in the building of a church and in the provision of a doctor - the Directors of the British Fisheries Society show themselves concerned to establish fishing as the basis to a more diverse employment structure in the north-west Highlands and to see Ullapool (and other towns) as the focal points of such change.

Tobermory was planned likewise as was the smaller settlement of Lochbay. In the first, however, small-scale fishing did not develop given distance from the sea lochs of the north-west mainland though the village did provide important commercial functions for resident and larger Lowland busses. Lochbay never developed as a fishing site. Land was more fertile than in Ullapoool or Tobermory and the balance sought between crofting and fishing in those places shifted in Lochbay to a complete dependence upon agriculture.

Whilst the fortunes of the three principal fishing settlements varied, the overall involvement of the British Fisheries Society with the development of commercial herring fishing in the north and west was a failure. In brief, principal causes were the nature of the institution, various external agencies over which the Society had little control, and because of the migratory habits of the herring itself. Changes in the personnel of the Society in the early 1800s left it without clear leadership, a problem exacerbated by its lack of publicity and the 1808 Fishing Act which placed all aspects of commercial fishery development under the Board of Trustees. The outbreak of war in

Industriousness and the Failure of Industry

1793 drew many fishermen away and restricted fishing. More important was the continued emigration from the north and west in the late eighteenth and nineteenth centuries. This loss of population was complemented by the coastal reloca- tion of large numbers of people in consequence of changes in agriculture. This movement allowed employment of some persons in commercial fishing but had the more widespread effect of placing excess population on marginal land with too small a plot size to allow for productive agriculture and with no capital and little experience with which to establish even small-scale fishing interests in an industry whose organisation and techniques of production were increasingly geared to larger commercial needs. Markets declined in the early 1800s, especially those in the West Indies. Important, too, was the failure of the herring fishing itself, the result of the migratory habits of the herring which from the later 1700s and early 1800s moved away from the waters of the north and west. Failure of the British Fisheries Society in the north-west did not represent overall failure for the industry. In places in this area, dependence upon fishing was greater than upon crofting and in others, returns from small-scale inshore fishing for herring or white fish formed an important part of the money rent. Herring fishing was important to a few places in the Outer Isles by the later 1800s, but the region as a whole was ill-supplied with capital and entrepreneurial skill, and the nature of the industry was too intermittent either to provide the means of support to a growing population or the basis to other manufactures. From the early 1800s, commercial fishing in the northern Highlands was associated with the east coast of Sutherland and Caithness.

Fishing expanded all along the Scottish east coast during the eighteenth and nineteenth centuries.66 Develop- ment was particularly rapid from the 1790s and in the Highlands centred upon the eastern coast of Caithness in particular and Sutherland. By the opening years of the nineteenth century, Caithness was the basis of 'a greater concentrated fishery than any that had been known in Scotland'.67 It was this concentration of herring fishing and the shortcomings of local harbours that prompted the British Fisheries Society to build Pulteneytown near Wick. Pulteneytown differed from the western settlements in several respects. Firstly, there was already a town close at hand which meant that a population of artisans and traders already existed. Secondly, east coast herring fishing was successful where the west coast fishing was not; the harbour and other facilities at Pulteneytown provided for the further development of an expanding industry not the basis to a struggling one. Thirdly, Pulteneytown and other fishing villages on the north-east coast were successful when the west was not because of the nature and the organisation of the industry in the region. In the north-east, the emphasis lay on the curing of catches using local labour and capital. Capital was commonly invested in plant, new boats and equipment. Lowland concerns were drawn to the Caithness fishing not as exploitative outsiders but as participants in an indigenous industry. Labour was available and was supplemented by seasonal migration. Also important was the fact that for several villages, in Sutherland particularly, the settlements and their constituent holdings had been purposefully designed for fishermen as the intended end result of estate reorganisation.

The clearance of population from upland Kildonan and other parts of inland Sutherland in the early nineteenth century, and their relocation on coastal plots, brought many people to parishes such as Latheron (which accounts for the increase in population in the period 1801-1851; Figure 4.2), and to Helmsdale in particular. For James Loch, the principal architect of the policy, Helmsdale was 'the centre of the population, the wealth, and the cultivation of this country' (Sutherland). Loch saw in the decline of Gaelic, the rise in 'moral instruction' and in the general industry of the inhabitants 'a civilising process of cumulative economic improvement'.68 Even there, however, the fishing workforce was not exclusively dependent upon fishing. The Sutherland herring fishing industry, with the exception of Helmsdale, was never as successful as that of Caithness or, from the 1830s, the more specialised fleets of the north-east coastal Lowlands. Caithness fishing differed from the east coast generally in that the population involved, especially in the summer fishing, were crofter-fishermen. Fishing paid the rent but in so doing restricted possibilities of capital accumulation by individuals for the purchase of boats or new equipment. The varying dependency of the north-east fishing population upon the land limited its involvement in the expansion of east coast herring fishing from the 1830s and 1840s. The use by Moray, Shetland, and Banff fishermen of large-scale and expensive equipment, the move to deeper waters, and the extension of curing facilities to virtually every east coast settlement all meant that Caithness, though remaining important as a fishing region, declined in relative significance during the later nineteenth century.

From the 1840s the larger boats of the east coast began to fish northern and western waters. This integration of two regional economies not only symbolised the growing importance of the east coast fishing but brought to the north-west a level of organisation above and beyond the capabilities of the small fisherman-crofter. East coast fishing concerns established curing stations in the Outer Isles and prompted the development of other facilities (Figure 5.3). The involvement of larger, better organised east coast fleets in the north-west had the effect of providing employment for women at the curing and drying of the fish, whilst at the same time over-shadowing the typical small-boat fishing of the area. Numbers employed in curing in places like Stornoway and Castlebay increased greatly in the second half of the nineteenth century but at the height of the fishing in Barra and Lewis in the 1880s, for example, four-fifths of the boats were of east coast origin. Catches provided employment in the west even if the boats were from other parts of Scotland. By 1874 only Wick, Fraserburgh and Peterhead exceeded the herring catch at Stornoway, and at the zenith of the Scottish herring industry in the early 1900s, Stornoway and Castlebay both handled annual catches in excess of 250,000 tons.69 Perhaps more important to the economy of the north-west and to the needs of the crofter particularly was the wage derived from seasonal employment in curing the catches of east coast boats and the financial returns gained by following the herring fleet back to the east for the summer fishing there. This seasonal migration as curers and as extra labour on the boats grew rapidly after the 1850s.

The regional integration of labour and economy sig-nalled by the involvement of east coast boats with north-west fishing did not stimulate local industry or provide an alternative to agriculture in the latter region. Some parishes had a quota of larger boats, but in general the north-west herring fishing was under-capital-ised at a time when surplus capital was being directed to meet rental arrears. And the greater impact of the potato famine and destitution of the later 1840s in that region undermined local initiatives at the moment east coast concerns began to utilise and develop western resources. Even in the prosperous east coast, crofting- fishing communities were affected by the recurrent blights of the mid-nineteenth century. One source noted of Avoch in April 1847, for example, that 'great destitution prevails among the Fishermen's families, in the village - many of whom are known to be on the brink of starvation', and in Latheron parish, things were little better. In Avoch, storms had snapped lines and ruined nets and the population, too poor to afford new nets at 30 shillings each and 'at a great distance from the fishing off the west coast', petitioned the Edinburgh Board for Relief of Destitution for assistance. The Board provided some funds, and in other relief measures of 1849, directed fishermen from Cellardyke in Fife to instruct the natives of Skye and Wester Ross in the techniques of commercial fishing.70 That such instruction should be needed is somehow indicative of the north-west sector as a whole. Line fishing for cod or ling was important to a number of places in the area and for some few, fishing was their means of livelihood. But fishing by line for white fish or net for herring in the north-west sector never provided the majority with the means to quit the land. Small-scale fishing or labour at north-east coast curing stations was certainly a more certain source of income than kelp or textiles during the 1800s, but never led in the north and west Highlands to large-scale commercial fishing by natives or the pursuit of entirely non-agricultural occupations. Capital was largely derived from and circulated by Lowland merchants and entrepreneurs. What expansion of herring fishing did occur in north-western waters in the later 1800s was the result of the commercial penetration of an under-developed local economy by a prosperous regional sector responding to national demand. Caithness, in its language as well as in its organisation of labour around chiefly-fishing and partly-crofting settlements, was not typical of the small-holding Highlands as a whole and did not share to the same degree the problems of adjustment to processes of agricultural transformation. In parts of the south-west Highlands, proximity to the Lowland centres of population meant regular fishing by native boats could provide an adequate income but even there, the move to full specialisation in herring fishing was resisted given the essentially seasonal nature of the industry. Though it provided returns for larger enterprise from the south and east and windfall gains for natives on occasion, the fishing industry in the Highlands as a whole at best offered only temporary prosperity and small-scale supplements to returns from the land.

Lesser industries in the Highlands

Beyond kelp, textiles and fishing, the Highlanders had only a few minor industries and manufactures whose output and employment provided a small income additional to the rewards from agricultural labour. Extractive industries were small scale. Slate quarrying at Easdale and Ballachulish and mining at Strontian provided some alternative to agriculture although the miners at Strontian were nearly all Lowlanders.71 The working of limestone was common to many estates but seldom for commercial ends. Iron-ore furnaces were erected at Invergarry in 1727, at Bonawe in 1753 and Furnace in 1755 by partnerships from the Furness region, and at Glenkinglass and Abernethy in 1727 and 1728 respectively by the York Buildings Company72(Figure 5.3). The association of this limited industrial development with anglicisation and civilisation is clear in the comment of Knox who wrote of Bonawe how 'the verdant fields, and other agreeable consequences on this little spot, plainly indicate the residence of Englishmen'.73 At Brora in Sutherland where coal and salt had been worked since the sixteenth century, development of these mineral resources from 1811 was intended to provide an industrial and manufacturing element to plans for agricultural clearance and the development of fishing on the Sutherland estates. Colliers and other labour were recruited from Lowland Scotland and Wales and by mid-1816 Brora coal was being extracted at the rate of 200 tons per week and used in the local manufacture of bricks and tiles. But by the early 1820s, Brora was suffering from the effects of southern competition and the coal mine closed in 1825.74 Tanning, sack-making, brewing and other manufactures such as nail-making and a rope works in Cromarty were established in parts of the Highlands; shipbuilding was important on a small scale in Easter Ross, and where wood was plentiful.

Woodland covered only about 7 per cent of Highland land area at the time of the Military Survey of 1750 and although commercial woodland management in the Highlands was more common than has been generally supposed, it was never so widespread nor of such a scale during the 1770s and 1800s as to be the basis to industrial production. The more recent interest in large-scale plantations (as opposed to semi-natural woodland or coppice management or the planting of trees for aesthetic and commercial purposes during estate improvement) has seen forestry provide employment in the Highlands, but no such formal attention was given before the twentieth century.75 The deer forests of the nineteenth-century Highlands (Figure 5.3) were areas for stalking and shooting, not timber production. Labour as gillies on estate roads or as guides was important only as a temporary source of wage labour. The tourist 'discovery' of the Highlands was not sufficiently numerous even by the nineteenth century to provide employment; Smout estimates a few thousand or so annual visitors for the 1800s compared with 600,000 visitors in 1965. The Highlands may have been increasingly popular from the later 1700s and in the 1800s especially as the setting for historical association, myth, and as the playground of industrialists, but for the inhabitants, agriculture remained the means for the production and reproduction of Highland life. In only one other industry - distilling - did the Highlands contribute and respond to national commercial expansion. And whisky-making shared with textiles, kelp, and fishing in being an industrial occupation in only certain parts of the Highlands rather than a source of economic advance for the region as a whole.

Distilling in the Highlands expanded from the 1700s because it was an easy means of transforming local grain surpluses into a marketable product.76 Not all distilling was legal. Government legislation of 1786 had attempted to impose a premium of 20 shillings per gallon of still capacity and the result throughout the Highlands was an illicit industry (as there had been before and was afterwards) whose output, labour force, and geographical distribution is difficult to determine. It has been claimed that illicit distilling concentrated particularly in deprived areas bordering regions of grain surplus. This excluded the north and west from large-scale production. Turnock has suggested that the opportunities for people in the eastern Highlands with only small farms and with little capital were great, 'so much so that the industry may be seen as the eastern equivalent to kelping in the west Highlands and Islands'.77 Unlike kelp, however, distilling in the Highlands was hindered 'by generally well-meaning but badly misdirected government interference'.78 The delimitation of a Highland 'zone' in the 1790s (Figure 5.3) separated Scotland into excise regions, but had the effect in the Highlands of further driving the industry underground. Not until legislation of 1823 did many Highland stills and distilleries register as legal. Registered distilleries at the end of the eighteenth century concentrated around Easter Ross (Figure 5.3). By the later nineteenth century, the industry in the Highlands centred around Speyside, Islay and Campbeltown in Kintyre. In this later pattern the industry maintained its traditional dependency upon areas of grain surplus but increasingly located in accordance to matters of water quality and other factors of production influenced by market demand rather than as a response to local economic necessity. Distilling in the later nineteenth and twentieth centuries offered employment and was important for those areas of the Highlands with excess grain, but for much of the eighteenth century and first part of the 1800s, the industry never challenged the primacy of agriculture and was indeed dependent as a part-time industrial pursuit upon agricultural production.

Industriousness and the Failure of Industry

LABOUR MIGRATION AND CULTURAL TRANSFORMATION

The relative failure of schemes for the establishment of commercially-orientated industry in the Highlands should not be taken to mean that the Highlands were at all times and everywhere without an industrial sector and that Highlanders were without the quality of industriousness. The small-scale manufacture of goods, either for subsistence purposes or where markets were available for sale and export to meet the demands of rising money rents, was an established practice and attention to by-employments outside agriculture depended more upon local resources of land use, labour and skill than upon the separation of industry from agriculture. Even the limited making and marketing of goods for sale regularly brought amounts of capital and imported goods into and out of the Highlands. This contact increased from the later 1600s and in the eighteenth and nineteenth centuries took on a particular significance for certain regions where traditionally-held industrial skills had been re-oriented to meet the commercial needs of larger markets. Most such industrial marketing of Highland goods was limited in type and in scale. Neilson's remark below of Morvern in 1755 aptly summarises the regular and commonplace but at the same time only locally-beneficial and small-scale nature of trade and commerce in manufactured products, within the Highland economy and between the Highlands and the rest of Scotland.

> In the spring season there are a number of people with small boats loaded with Beef and mutton in Barrells, Butter, Cheese, Tallow, dry'd fish, Train Oil & that Come from the western Isles bound for Glasgow, who dispose of a good Deal of their Cargo's along this Coast on very reasonable terms. At Glasgow they purchase Broad Cloaths, Linen, wines, Suggars, and such other goods as they have a demand for at home.79

This movement of goods was paralleled by movement of people. In parts of the Highlands, the loosening but not breaking of ties with the land resulting from the commercialisation of agriculture meant many could (or rather had to) pursue by-employments which, with varying success in certain parts of the region, allowed an at least partly-industrial labour force to appear. In this sense, the Highlands reflect to a lesser degree the wider experience of Scotland as a whole in redistributing labour away from agriculture towards either the rurally-located manufacture of textiles or migration to towns. But in the

Industriousness and the Failure of Industry

Highlands where localised industrial development was neither everywhere successful as a means of developing a distinct division of labour (at least between agriculture and industry), nor as a basis to longer-term regional transformation, the creation of surplus labour at times of population growth meant that migration assumed a particular significance and did so variably within different parts of the Highlands. As we have seen, most permanent Highland-Lowland migration in this period was from the south-east 'farming' Highlands with the north-west 'crofting' Highlands not an important source area for permanent out-movement until the later 1800s and then never to the extent of the south and east. But permanent migration by Highlanders to Lowland industry was not directly important in the context of Highland industrial development. Temporary circulation of Highland labour is significant in this context.

Temporary migration was important in several senses: demographically as a factor acting to alter age-specific sex ratios and the seasonality of, and mean age at, marriage; economically, as a means of acquiring cash income and as a vital support to the crofting system of the north and west in particular; and linguistically, in that many returning migrants consciously shifted from Gaelic to English given the relative status of the two languages. Temporary or seasonal migration in context with the processes of material change examined above was thus an important means of cultural transformation.80 In parts of the southern and central Highlands, proximity to the textile industries of Perth and Dundee and the larger concerns in the west central Lowlands influenced permanent population out-movement as from Little Dunkeld, for example, where we are told of population moving 'to Perth and its neighbourhood for employment at the bleachfields and extensive manufactures lately erected there'. And in parts of Easter Ross, the failure of textile schemes there by the 1830s prompted many Highlanders to move to areas of centralised production such as Dundee and Perth.81 Actual decline or relative slump in Highland industry may thus have prompted both permanent and seasonal migration, especially from those areas of the Highlands where textiles were better established. More usual was temporary migration to the Lowlands in consequence of the combined effects of agricultural transformation and the failure of industry in the Highlands to provide employment. The report of 1793 on Kilmartin in Argyll is representative of the types of movement occurring.

Some young men and women, go yearly to serve in

the Low Country, merely in expectation of higher wages, though they generally return within a year or two. A considerable number, particularly of the cottar class, go to the harvest; some as far as the Lothians. Three families, this year, have gone to the cotton work, and some others speak of following them, though it seems to be with reluctance, as they consider the employment to be rather unfavourable to health, having formerly led an active life.82

This labour migration was an important means of language shift. In Kilmore and Kilbride parish, for Lochgoilhead and Kilmorich and South Knapdale, English was being introduced by returning Highlanders in the 1790s; 'The English has of late spread considerably, owing, in a great measure, to young people travelling to the low country, and returning home after they acquired the language' (of South Knapdale in 1797). And even on Barra 'by their frequent excursions to Glasgow, the people have introduced a number of English words'. By the mid-nineteenth century, this process of language change was more widespread than earlier, even in the north and west. In Kilfinichen and Kilvickeon, Kilmartin, Gairloch, Portree, Strath, and Tongue in the 1840s, similar processes of language change resulting from labour migration are recorded; in Gairloch we are told of 'corrupters of both languages, with more pride than good taste, now and then, introduce words of bad English or bad Scotch, which they have learned from the Newhaven or Buckie fishermen, whom they meet with on the coast of Caithness during the fishing season'.83 In the crofting north and west, especially the islands, temporary migration at the east coast fishing or Lowland harvest was a necessary adjunct to the continued existence of the crofting way of life. Such seasonal movement was especially important in the 1800s given the failure of kelp to provide longer-term economic benefit to all classes and the seasonal nature of fishing whose commercial development in the north depended more upon capitalisation by Lowland entrepreneurs than it did upon expansion of smaller indigenous concerns whose labour force had been freed from working smallholdings. It is a curious paradox of the cultural transformation of the Highlands that as industry in the Highlands proved incapable of retaining and utilising the population of the region, many Highlanders were increasingly involved with industry as a result of labour migration to the Lowlands.

CONCLUSION

Explanation of the relative failure of industry in the Highlands lies in understanding the underlying causes of that gap between the ends sought and the means employed in transforming and developing Highland industry, and the ends resulting. Two principal ends-in-view have been identified above: firstly, the directed use (at greater scales and with a different purpose than in traditional subsistence practices) of indigenous skills and products to motivate commercial development within the Highlands to meet national and international as well as local market demand; and secondly, the development of industry as a social quality.

There were several means employed to this combined end. Division of labour was both means and end. Many commentators saw the separation off from agriculture of a body of craftsmen labourers, rurally located in manufacturing 'stations' or gathered together in villages with other more specialised trades, as a necessary basis to the longer-term commercial and industrial development of the region. This division extended also to the processes of production within given manufactures and to the household as the institution of production; in textiles men to weave, women to spin, or in crofting-fishing communities, a distinction between men and women both seasonally and sexually in the time spent and jobs done on the land or at the associated processes of the industry. The creation of a more rigidly-defined occupational structure in the Highlands was intended also as a means of establishing a wage-economy within a region and culture where labour demand for work beyond usual routines was met by customary practices, and where money income was used to pay rents or to buy and sell goods and not commonly for the purchase of regulated labour time with agreed payments. Extending the cash nexus and refining a division of labour depended upon the monetisation and capitalisation of the Highland economy. This involved fixed capital in property (the symbol and means of authority) in the form of fishing and textile settlements and in planned villages. It involved fixed capital also in the technical facilities for production, in the purchase and distribution of standard reels or spinning wheels, for example, or the building of piers, curing sheds, and better boats. It demanded the means of circulating capital or raw material or equipment from one process to another within given Highland industries or throughout the economy generally. In turn, and given the dependence of most Highlanders upon agriculture and the inability of the tenantry to accumulate capital for those

314

reasons discussed above, this necessitated entrepreneurial involvement - by landlords, putting-out merchants and Lowland manufacturers - and direct supervision of these means to extending a spirit of industry by formal institutions.

The ends resulting from the above related means were likewise closely related and varied over different parts of the Highlands, over time, and in their effect upon the classes of Highland society. The build-up of rental arrears meant that capital and the entrepreneurs who controlled its circulation came not from within the region but chiefly from outside it, a process influenced and accelerated by the going of the tacksman, the selling of estates to Lowland graziers, and the failure of landlords to retain and employ a growing population. Those institutions involved in establishing Highland industry - principally the Board of Trustees, the Board of Annexed Estates, the British Linen Company, and the British Fisheries Society - were all well-intentioned towards the Highlands, but failed to provide (perhaps even to understand) the means to longer-term social and economic benefit. Either their period of operation was too short to allow a complete realisation of intended policy (the Board of Annexed Estates), too narrowly conceived to allow wider areas and Highland tenantry to participate more generally (the British Fisheries Society and the Board of Trustees), or the institution was itself under-funded and unable to provide full-time Highland-wide industrial employment at a time of agrarian transformation. In part, these institutions also failed because of the geography of the Highlands - distance from markets and difficulties of transport and communication - and, to an extent perhaps, because of the sometimes expressed reluctance of Highlanders to participate in industrial work.

> If the inhabitants of these countries can procure the bare necessities of life by their labour from the ground they possess their ambition leads them to no further effort, nor do they in general desire to meliorate their condition by any other exertion of industry.84

As justification for a supposed Highland indolence, this observation and the claim by one writer that 'a Highlander never sits at ease at a loom; 'tis like putting a deer in the plough'85 should be dismissed. But there is an element of truth in the opposition of Highlanders to depart from the customary seasonality of labour at industrial by-employments or to alter a recognised division of labour within and between households. Linen spinning as an industrial process was much stimulated in certain parts of the Highlands as a result of the putting-out networks established by agents of the British Linen Company and individual merchants, but in those places and more generally, spinning was never accompanied by a parallel rise in rurally-located Highland weaving by men nor by a comparable expansion in the working of wool. The result was that Highland textiles centred upon particular processes only, provided unequal employment opportunities within the household, and did so only for certain regions in given periods. Fishing was important as a means of earning cash in particular parts of the Highlands, but only for a few settlements in more favoured locations in the south-west Highlands did it provide year-round employment and adequate total income. In fishing, commercialisation of technique, concentration of capital, and entrepreneurial skills all originated beyond the Highlands, albeit that Highland labour was crucial. Other industries never provided more than a local stimulus to commerce and civility. Kelp was a short-lived extractive industry based on seasonal labour and simple processes. It never demanded or determined a division of labour either between processes or within the family, and by its very nature and in the way it was managed, could not separate off an industrial workforce from agricultural labour. In that respect, it symbolises more generally the failure of schemes for industry to stimulate and redirect the inherent industriousness of the Highland population.

In review of the processes of material transformation examined above and in Chapter 4, it is clear that the Highlands shared with other parts of Britain and Europe common experiences of agricultural commercialisation, population increase, the growth of rurally-located manufactures, and so on. At the same time, the culture of the Highlands was being transformed by processes and in circumstances historically and geographically specific to the region. It is clear, too, from the above discussion and the earlier chapters on anglicisation and improvement that material changes were not only at the same moment practically linguistic, intellectual, and ideological - a cultural transformation - but were also effected differently within and across the institutions of Highland society and were, moreover, of varying impact in different parts of the region. To some extent, given the regional scale of analysis, the facts of comparative advantage (within the Highlands and of the Highlands to the rest of Britain and Europe), and the close relationships between agriculture, population and rural industry, the material aspects of Highland transformation reflect some of the hypotheses proposed in the concept of proto-industrialisation. The Highlands was recognised as a distinct region for purposes of material development (as it was for schemes of education and religious instruction); rurally-located industry, especially textiles, developed in association with a predominantly pastoral agriculture; commercially-oriented industry was intended to meet the demands of national and international markets; and, to an extent, towns and planned villages, at least on the southern and eastern borders of the Highlands, provided a locus for marketing and mercantile activity. At more detailed levels of analysis, however, the criteria and hypotheses of the concept of proto-industrialisation do not provide adequate explanation of the transformation of the Highland space economy. In this context, four principal points may be made: the concept minimises the question of scale within the regional level of analysis; in the Highlands proto-industry led not to factory production (though it led Highland labour to factory employment beyond the region), but rather to what one author has called 'repastoralisation'.86 There is no clear evidence to suggest that proto-industrialisation provided the means for early marriage and population growth in the Highlands and there is good reason to believe that continued traditional practices of holding subdivision and occupation, the role of the potato, and the differential ease and degree of out-migration were more significant means of creating a surplus population; and lastly, the concept neglects the place of culture and custom as influencing factors in the course of regional transformation.

Much of the evidence examined has pointed to important geographical differences in scale in the transformation of the Highland way of life. It is interesting to note that each of the three principal manufactures discussed above had particularly local geographies within the region as a whole. As critics of the concept of proto-industrialisation have observed, the question of scale is of paramount importance.87 Not only was the material transformation of the Highlands not unremittingly progressive, its specific historical form and contradictions varied, for example, between the north and west crofting communities and the small holding farmers of the south and east, in which latter area rurally-located manufactures found a more favourable footing. This is the principal geographic division within the Highlands as a whole, but at smaller scales, differences between coastal margins and upland straths in soil type, population pressure, access to market, and returns from industry determined often enduring localisms of landscape and social experience.

The fact that there was commercially-oriented rurally-located manufacturing at all in the Highlands to an extent supports the claims of the proto-industrialisation concept, but as has been detailed above, in none of the three industries was population led from a more complete dependence upon agriculture labour within which industrial production was largely subsistence (Kaufsystem) to a partial dependence upon agriculture with rural industry the mainstay for the production and reproduction of human life (Verlagsystem). In kelping, the accumulation of capital in hands other than the labourers was the result of landlord policy which determined the retention of a labour force only seasonally dependent upon kelp and determined that labour force, after kelp's collapse as a result of comparative scientific advantages, to return to agricultural production - to 'repastoralise' - and to do so without capital and without legal recognition of their customary occupance or duthchas. In fishing, industrial employment continued together with work on the land, the balance varying by place and over time. In textiles, the circulation of capital and of equipment by merchants, often working for formal institutions as well as their own gain, was important particularly in those areas of the Highlands in which towns provided markets. In those two areas, the coming-together of native skill, entrepreneurial talent, markets, capital, perhaps even the finishing processes, was important to the existence of a Highland textile industry looking to supply international markets; it was just that conjunction of elements, of course, that underlay plans to build planned villages and manufacturing stations. In the case of linen textiles in these two areas, the Highlands did have what might perhaps be seen as proto-industrial locales in association with more advanced agricultural practices, but even there, production was only partial and was not sustained by a fundamental shift in the balance between agriculture and industry or by changes in the organisation of family labour sufficient in themselves to allow reliance on manufacturing or the move to centralised production.

There is no clear evidence to suggest that industry in the Highlands freed marriage from the traditional constraints of inheritance and patriarchal control thus providing for earlier marriage and rapid rates of population growth. Kelp allowed population concentration and may have stimulated earlier marriages in the north and west, but population was increasing there as a result of those other forces within the agricultural sector behind the establishment of crofting. Most evidence points to

318

population growth before and together with the rise of kelping. For other industries, particularly textiles, it may even be that the growth of proto-industry in the more commercialised 'farming' Highlands was the cause of population decline since those cleared from the land (in the way Smout has suggested was typical of the nation as a whole), would not all have been employed. Certainly, the connection between this area and levels of out-migration is an established one. Although more research is needed before exact claims may be made, it is possible to suggest in this context that, for the Highlands as a whole, proto-industry absorbed and redirected rather than 'caused' the growth of Highland population.

The concept of proto-industrialisation, in being conceived and commonly understood as a linear and unidirectional means of understanding material relationships between industry and agriculture and different forms of industrial organisation with one another, accords little place to questions of culture and custom. This deficiency has been discussed elsewhere in regard to other regions.88 In the context of the Highlands, it is a serious limitation to explanation. Organisation of the production and reproduction of Highland life was determined not alone by those institutions and processes intent on the region's social and material transformation but by a variety of customs and historical practices intrinsic to the Highland way of life. As has been elsewhere noted, 'A true sense of the place of customary and traditional values and practices as well as alternative types of industrial organisation and production process is lost in the search for impelling dynamics and the key to progress'.89 Explanations that ignore the role of language, religion, the unifying notion of duthchas within the Highland consciousness, for example, and fail to consider how such 'non-economic' variables (within which material practices are embedded) may actually have worked in opposition to the processes of transformation, will remain only partial. It is to such issues of culture and counter-hegemony that the following chapter is addressed.

NOTES

1.   NLS, MS 5319, f.144, George Dempster to the British Fisheries Society, 14 August 1805.

2.   NLS, MS 5201, f.43, William Cross, 'Some Considerations by way of Essay upon the Means of Civilizing the Highlands & Extinguishing Jacobitism in Scotland', 1748.

3.   P. White, <u>Observations on the Present State of the Scotch Fisheries</u> (London, 1791), p.156.

4.   R. Williams, <u>Keywords</u> (London, 1981), pp.165–168; M. Berg, 'Political economy and the principles of manufacture 1700–1800', in M. Berg, P. Hudson, and M. Sonenscher (eds.), <u>Manufacture in Town and Country before the Factory</u> (Cambridge, 1983), pp.33–58; M. Berg, <u>The Age of Manufactures</u> (London, 1985), esp. pp.48–69.

5.   T.C. Smout, 'Where had the Scottish economy got to by the third quarter of the eighteenth century', in I. Hont and M. Ignatieff (eds.), <u>Wealth and Virtue: the Shaping of Political Economy in the Scottish Enlightenment</u> (Cambridge, 1983), pp.70–71.

6.   M. Gray, 'Economic welfare and money income in the Highlands, 1750–1850', <u>Scottish Journal of Political Economy</u>, <u>II</u>, (1955), pp.47–63; <u>idem</u>, <u>The Highland Economy 1750–1850</u> (Edinburgh, 1957); B. Lenman, <u>An Economic History of Modern Scotland, 1660–1976</u> (London, 1977), pp. 89–90; T.C. Smout, 'Scottish landowners and economic growth, 1650–1850', <u>Scottish Journal of Political Economy, XI,</u> (1964), pp.218–234.

7.   E. Richards, <u>A History of the Highland Clearances Volume 2: Emigration, Protest, Reasons</u> (Beckenham, 1985), p.18.

8.   A. Smith, <u>The Wealth of Nations</u> (London, 1977 edn.), pp.135, 204.

9.   Berg, 'Political economy', p.52.

10.   K. Tribe, <u>Land, Labour and Economic Discourse</u> (London, 1978), p.105.

11.   Smith, <u>The Wealth of Nations</u>, pp.362-363.

12. H. Home (Lord Kames), Sketches of the History of Man (Edinburgh, 1807), I, p.97.

13. J. Millar, The Origin of the Distinction of Ranks (London, 1779), p.296.

14. M. McKay (ed.), The Rev. Dr. John Walker's Report on the Hebrides of 1764 and 1771 (Edinburgh, 1980), p.35.

15. G. S. MacKenzie, Letter to the Proprietors of Land in Ross-shire (Edinburgh, 1803), p.17.

16. J. Sinclair, Analysis of the Statistical Account of Scotland (Edinburgh, 1826), pp.180-181.

17. J. Walker, An Economical History of the Hebrides and Highlands of Scotland (Edinburgh, 1808), II, pp.152-153.

18. J. Anderson, Observations on the Means of Exciting a Spirit of National Industry, Chiefly Intended to Promote the Agriculture, Commerce, Manufactures and Fisheries of Scotland (Dublin, 1779), I, p.39.

19. Quoted in A. Chitnis, The Scottish Enlightenment (London, 1976), p.20.

20. NLS, MS 5007, f.26, ff.106-107, f.137, 'Heads of Improvement for the Highlands and Western Islands'.

21. J. Walker, 'An Essay on Kelp', Transactions of the Highland and Agricultural Society of Scotland, I, (1799), pp.1-31; M. Gray, 'The Kelp Industry in the Highlands and Islands', Economic History Review, IV, (1951), pp.197-209; Dr Johnson writes (in 1775) of how kelping was 'lately found' by Highland landlords; Journey to the Western Islands, p.73.

22. Gray, 'The Kelp Industry', p.198 n.4.

23. Ibid., pp.200-201; SRO, GD 46/13/126, State of Lewis kelp 1794-1799.

24. Ibid., pp.202-203; SRO, D 201/5/1228, f.2; CD 201/5/1332, f.7a.

25. SRO, GD 201/5/1228, f.4; Report from the Select Committee appointed to inquire into the condition of the Population of the Highlands and Islands of Scotland, and into the practicability of affording the People relief by

means of Emigration, VI, (1841), Q.795, 2628; J. Macdonald, General View of the Agriculture of the Hebrides (Edinburgh, 1811), pp.117-118.

26. J. Hunter, The Making of the Crofting Community (Edinburgh, 1976), p.31.

27. Macdonald, Agriculture of the Hebrides, pp.119-120.

28. T.C. Smout, Scottish Trade on the Eve of the Union, 1660-1707 (Edinburgh, 1963), pp.232-237; idem, 'Where had the Scottish economy got to by 1776?'.

29. J. Shaw, 'The New Rural Industries: Water Power and Textiles', in M.L. Parry and T.R. Slater (eds.), The Making of the Scottish Countryside (London, 1980), p.312; A. Durie, The Scottish Linen Industry in the Eighteenth Century (Edinburgh, 1979), p.13.

30. Gray, Highland Economy, p.139.

31. L. Leneman, Living in Atholl 1685-1785: a social history of the estates (Edinburgh, 1986), pp.25-31, 205-212.

32. I.R.M. Mowat, Easter Ross 1750-1850: the double frontier (Edinburgh, 1981), pp.53-58.

33. 5 George I, c.20; 12 George I, c.4; 26 George II, c.20; Durie, The Scottish Linen Industry, p.89.

34. Shaw, 'The New Rural Industries', p.301.

35. SRO, NG 1/24/11, f.45, 9 December 1757, Encouragement of Linen Manufacture in the Highlands, 1754-1763; see also NG 1/24/12, Savings on the fund for improvements in the Highlands, 1755-1764.

36. SRO, NG 1/24/14, f.16, 18 November 1757.

37. A. Durie, 'Linen-spinning in the north of Scotland, 1746-1773', Northern Scotland 2(1), (1974-1975), pp.13-36.

38. EUL, La.II. 623, f.17, f.32, Report to the Commissioners for improving fisheries and manufacturers in Scotland on the state of industry and trade in the Highlands and Islands, 1755.

39. SRO, NG 1/1/14, ff.207-208, 30 March 1759.

40. Durie, The Scottish Linen Industry, pp.90-91.

41. Smith, Jacobite Estates, p.117.

42. SRO, E.777/244, p.4.

43. Ibid., pp.13, 29, 36, 43, 49, 56-57.

44. McKay, Walker's Report on the Hebrides, pp.46-47, 103.

45. SRO, E.729/8, p.123.

46. SRO, E.787/24, p.9.

47. Smith, Jacobite Estates, p.132.

48. Ibid., pp.125-126; Archibald Campbell of Knockbuy considered the question of woollen cloths in his 1744 'Epistle about encouraging manufacturing in Argyllshire' - 'I think Argyllshire as fit for carrying on of manufactures of Spinning yarn, making linnine, and course woolan cloaths, as any country in Scotland' - but what little attention was given to textiles focused on linen; SRO, GD 14/17, f.5.

49. SRO, GD 95/1/4, f.57.

50. A. Belches, An Account of the Society in Scotland for Propagating Christian Knowledge, from its commencement in 1709 (Edinburgh, 1774), p.59.

51. Ibid., pp.32, 120, 124, 133, 137, 189; Durie, The Scottish Linen Industry, pp.74, 76-77, 85-86, 89, 155; Shaw, 'The New Rural Industries', p.298.

52. SRO, E.746/94/4; E.746/94/1, f.4, quoted in Smith, Jacobite Estates, p.120.

53. Gray, 'Economic Welfare and Money Income', pp.58-59; N. Murray has noted the persistence of customer weavers in the Highlands, working up the consumer's prepared material to the customer's order, until the early 1830s; The Scottish Hand Loom Weavers 1790-1850: a social history (Edinburgh, 1978), p.13.

54. Durie, The Scottish Linen Industry, p.91.

55. Ibid., p.119.

56. Macdonald, Lewis A History of the Island, pp.100, 102; McKay, Walker's Report on the Hebrides, pp.66, 235; J.R. Coull, 'Fisheries in Scotland in the 16th, 17th and 18th Centuries: the evidence in MacFarlane's Geographical Collections', Scottish Geographical Magazine, 93(1), (1977), pp.5–14.

57. A. Sutherland, A Summer Ramble in the North Highlands (Edinburgh, 1825), p.103.

58. SRO, NG 1/16/1, f.96 An account of the number of Busses employed in the Herring Fishery in Scotland from the commencement of the Parliamentary Bounty in 1756 to 5 January 1777.

59. Mowat, Easter Ross 1750–1850, pp.47–52.

60. J. Dunlop, 'The British Fisheries Society: 1787 questionnaire', Northern Scotland, 2(1), (1974–1975), pp.37–56.

61. In J. Fergusson (ed.), Letters of George Dempster to Sir Adam Fergusson, 1756–1813 (London, 1934), p.138 quoted in Richards, Highland Clearances Volume 1, p.21; Dempster was a sub-director of the British Fisheries Society and a member of the Highland Society of London (Dunlop, ibid., p.42).

62. Quoted in Dunlop, ibid., p.51.

63. SRO, E.729/1, p.12; EUL, La.II.623, f.62.

64. J. Dunlop, The British Fisheries Society 1786–1893 (Edinburgh, 1978),

65. Ibid., p.67.

66. J. R. Coull, 'Fisheries in the North-East of Scotland before 1800', Scottish Studies, 13, (1969), pp.13–24; idem, 'The Scottish Herring Fishery 1800–1914: development and intensification of a pattern of resource use', Scottish Geographical Magazine, 102(1), (1986), pp. 4–17; M. Gray, The Fishing Industries of Scotland 1790–1914: a study in regional adaptation (Aberdeen 1978).

67. Gray, ibid., p.33.

68. Richards, Highland Clearances Volume 2, p.55.

324

69. Coull, 'The Scottish Herring Fishery 1800-1914', pp.14-15; D. Mackinlay, The Isle of Lewis and its Fishermen Crofters (London, 1878), p.xxix.

70. SRO, HD 19/16, 1 April 1847; HD 19/3, 14 April 1847; HD 16/132, ff.1-4 23rd February 1849.

71. A. Cameron, 'A page of the past: the lead mines at Strontian', Transactions of the Gaelic Society of Inverness, XXXVIII, (1937-1941), pp.444-452; A. O'Dell and K. Walton, The Highlands and Islands of Scotland (London, 1962), p.117.

72. S.G.E. Lythe and J. Butt, An Economic History of Scotland 1100-1939 (Glasgow, 1975), p.189; O'Dell and Walton, ibid., p.118.

73. J. Knox, A Tour through the Highlands of Scotland and the Hebride Isles in 1786 (London, 1787), p.18.

74. E. Richards, The Leviathan of Wealth: the Sutherland fortune in the Industrial Revolution (London, 1973), pp.227-228.

75. J. M. Lindsay, 'The commercial use of Highland woodland, 1750-1870: a reconsideration', Scottish Geographical Magazine, 92(1), (1976), pp.30-40; idem, 'The iron industry in the Highlands; charcoal blast furnaces', Scottish Historical Review, LVII, (1977), pp.49-63; idem, 'Forestry and agriculture in the Scottish Highlands, 1700-1850: a problem in estate management', Agricultural History Review, 25, (1977), pp.23-36; idem, 'The Commercial use of Woodland and Coppice Management' in Parry and Slater (eds.), The Making of the Scottish Countryside, pp.271-289; D. Turnock, The Historical Geography of Scotland since 1707 (Cambridge, 1982), pp.246-262.

76. Turnock, Historical Geography of Scotland, pp.97-108; M.S. Moss and J.R. Hume, The Making of Scotch Whisky: A History of the Scotch Whisky Distilling Industry (Edinburgh, 1981); M.C. Storrie 'The Scotch Whisky Industry', Transactions of the Institute of British Geographers, 31, (1962), pp.97-114; Mowat, Easter Ross 1750-1850, pp.58-63.

77. Turnock, op. cit., pp.98, 105.

78. Mowat, Easter Ross 1750-1850, p.60.

79. EUL, La.II. 623, f.14.

80. C.W.J. Withers, 'The Migration of Highland Scots to Urban Lowland Scotland, c, 1750-1891' in R.M. Smith (ed.), Regional Demographic Patterns in the Past (Oxford, forthcoming); T.M. Devine, 'Temporary migration and the Scottish Highlands in the Nineteenth Century', Economic History Review, XXXII(3), (1979), pp.344-359; W. Howatson,'The Scottish Hairst and Seasonal Labour 1600-1870', Scottish Studies, 26, (1982), pp.13-36; H. Jones, 'Evolution of Scottish Migration Patterns: a Social-Relations-of-Production Approach', Scottish Geographical Magazine, 102(3), (1986), pp.151-164.

81. OSA, VI, (1793), p.367; Mowat, Easter Ross 1750-1850, p.57; C.W.J. Withers, Highland Communities in Dundee and Perth 1787-1891 (Dundee, 1986), pp.40-47.

82. OSA, VIII, (1793), p.108.

83. OSA, III, (1792), p.190; XI, (1794), pp.136-137; XIX, (1797), p.325; On Barra, see XIII, (1794), p.341; NSA, 7, (1842-1843), p.307; 7, (1844), p.562; 14, (1841), p.226, p.308; 15,. (1841), p.117; On Gairloch, see 14, (1841), pp.95-96.

84. Quoted in Richards, Highland Clearances Volume 1, p.59.

85. A. Grant, Letters from the Mountains (London, 1807), II, p.103.

86. H. Medick, 'The Proto-Industrial Family Economy: The Structural Function of Household and Family during the Transition from Peasant Society to Industrial Capitalism', Social History, 3, (1976), pp.300-301.

87. D. Coleman, 'Proto-industrialization: a concept too many', Economic History Review, 36, (1983), pp.435-448: R. A. Butlin, 'Early Industrialization in Europe: Concepts and Problems', Geographical Journal, 152(1), (1986), pp.1-8.

88. For a review of those authors who have discussed in details the deficiencies of the proto-industrialisation concept, see Butlin, ibid., passim; on more specifically related criticisms attaching to the utility of the concept in relation to culture and community, see M. Berg, P. Hudson, and M. Sonenscher, 'Manufacture in Town and Country', pp.13-16.

89. Berg, Hudson, and Sonenscher, ibid., p.19.

6

THE GAELIC REACTION TO CULTURAL TRANSFORMATION

> Can you suggest, in general terms, any measure
> which the landlord or other parties could take in
> order to improve your situation? - It is easy to
> answer that. Give us land out of the plenty of
> land that is about for cultivation.1

> If this lawlessness in Lewis be not put down by a
> sufficient force, we shall have, - and deserve to
> have - all the 'unemployed' everywhere demanding
> the redivision of Laws for their support. There
> is no difference between Highlands and Lowlands as
> to the wishes concerned nor as to Doctrines
> preached. That Gaelic speaking men can commit any
> outrage and be sympathised with as heros is really
> too ridiculous.2

To suppose the transformation of the Highland way of life
was without opposition from those whose lives were being
transformed would be to distort seriously the history of
the Highlands. Yet attempts at a more complete understanding of the forms and scale of opposition are hindered both
by the nature of the material available and, to a lesser
degree, by the variety of forms taken in opposition. The
relative paucity of historical documentation from
Highlanders themselves makes it difficult to understand the
cultural productions of the Gaels as opposed to the
cultural productions imposed on them, and, moreover, raises
historiographic issues: 'The scantiness of historical
material from the Highlanders has necessarily reinforced
the idea that their reaction to the clearances was undemon-
strative and unresisting'.3
Gaelic poetry has provided an important body of source
material on protest and is discussed as such below. For
the Highlands, 'the poetic tradition may be unrepresenta-
tive . . . its provenance are usually unclear . . .
survival depended upon the highly selective process of the

oral tradition, and the poetry may well reflect what people wanted to believe about the past, rather than the way the past seemed at the time'. It is in Richards' view 'now possible to connect two sides of the popular response: the poetry of the people and the actual record of physical resistance'.4

Whilst not denying these claims, the question of the Gaelic reaction to cultural transformation is more complex than is implied by the terms 'physical resistance' and 'popular response'. As earlier noted, we may distinguish in theory between three types of opposition to elite cultural hegemony: alternative hegemony, class conscious-ness, and counter-hegemony (see above, pages 29-30). In type, counter-hegemony in the sense of physical resistance took several forms in the Highlands: riotous assembly across whole districts, for example, the deforcement of law officers and tearing-up of orders for eviction, the slaughter of sheep or deer. Instances of opposition were not, however, discrete typological events and may have combined destruction of property and threat to life or other features at one and the same moment. In some cases, the more prolonged and overtly violent instances of physical resistance were met by the renewed assertion of authority in the form of military force, by 'rule' not hegemony. Chronologically, protest was most marked in the late eighteenth century and during the 1800s with some instances in the early decades of the twentieth century. Geographically, most episodes of protest will be shown to have taken place in the northern Highlands, with numerous instances of opposition to enclosure or clearance in Easter Ross and Sutherland in the century from about 1780 and with the food riots of 1847 also concentrating in that region. Rent strikes and the 'land wars' of the 1880s and 1890s were more common in the Outer Isles.

Just as the forms taken in dominant hegemony varied, so physical resistance as counter-hegemony was not the only means of opposition. To an extent, both the retention of Gaelic as the language of spiritual worship and the significance attached to religion in the Highlands may be considered expressions of opposition. It is possible to suggest that both in the retention of Gaelic and, more strongly, in their turning to spiritual comforts at times of material hardship as many did in the nineteenth century, the Highland people were exercising a form of alternative hegemony, albeit that it was largely tacit opposition to externally-derived material change.

Given this suggested variety of reaction to cultural transformation, its chronology and geographical expression, this chapter examines the degree to which it is possible to talk of there being <u>one</u> reaction to cultural transformation. If it is the case that the nature and scale of alternative and oppositional forms 'is itself a matter of constant historical variation in real circumstances', any attempt at understanding the Gaelic reaction to the imposition of a different ideology and a new way of life must consider the extent to which <u>individual</u> incidents of protest shared a root cause or causes, a <u>common</u> ideological and practical justification borne not only out of a mutual understanding by Highlanders of their social relations one to another but also out of a unified and unifying sense of social distinctiveness from other groups in society. Two issues are raised in considering this matter: firstly, the extent to which we may understand the Highland experience by looking only at the Highlands; secondly, the question of the motivating spirit - what from the work of Gramsci, Rude, and others we may term the 'inherent ideology' of a people;5 that regional or class consciousness particular to the Highlands - which informed both individual moments and the general context of protest as it underlay Highland life in general. The Highlands was far from being the only region in Britain or Europe in which tensions between economic imperatives and moral precepts gave rise to social protest by one class or group at the actions and authority of others. Their opposition in riot and poetry is firmly situated within the general history and geography of protest in Britain, events which date in rural Britain from the enclosure riots of the 1540s to the tithe wars and land wars of the 1890s and later and which included land protests, food riots, the destruction of agricultural machinery in the Captain Swing riots, and anti-Poor Law movements; and which in industrial towns and cities, took the form of resistance to erosion of skilled status, or against changes in the technology of production or decline in wages. The work of Tilly and Rude in a European context is of significance here. And as these authors and others have pointed out, the terms used to describe protest - 'food riots', 'mob', 'pressure group' - need to be used in ways that illuminate their local significance without lessening their generally-recognised historical meaning.6

Whilst the Gaelic reaction was part of a wider context of opposition by peasant societies to material transformation, the forms taken in Highland protest were more complex than simply resistance by members of a peasant mode of production to penetration by externally-derived capitalism. In part, the problem is historiographical but two further introductory points may be made. Firstly, 'traditional' Highland society was not homogeneous and without internal conflict or contradiction, either between landlords and tenants or within the tenantry. This has implications for the question of a <u>single</u> Gaelic or Highland ideology or consciousness given the observed separation-out of Highland society into classes during the eighteenth and nineteenth centuries. Secondly, as a result of Highland migration to Lowland cities and in consequence of the expression by Lowland Highlanders and others of political and social class interests that transcended simple questions of regional identity, the Highland reaction to cultural transformation had important non-Highland expressions of Highland issues. The involvement of non-Highland formal institutions and wider interests points to complex issues of class and regional consciousness that are disguised if we consider the ideology and articulations of Highland protest confined only to the Highlands.

The question of Highland identity, a motivating consciousness which informed individual instances and the general context of protest because it operated within and between all layers of Highland society is a difficult one. It has been suggested above that 'The production of ideas, of conceptions, of consciousness, is at first directly interwoven with the material activity and the material intercourse of men, the language of real life', and that the material transformation of societies depends upon the ideas and intellectual force of the ruling classes (see above, pages 26-27). In reacting against material and ideological changes, the Highlanders were asserting claims to what Rude has termed an 'inherent ideology', which should not be considered as 'false consciousness' in the sense of that identity usually imposed upon Highlanders from above and without, but rather as a <u>mentalite</u>, traditionally-recognised ideas and beliefs founded in the established material practices of a given way of life. In addition, there is what Rude has called 'derived ideology', that stock of ideas and beliefs borrowed from others which may, in the context of protest, take the form of structured systems of ideas such as Freedom, the Rights of Man, as they informed reactions against material or political change. Set within the notion of inherent ideology is the peasant's belief in his right to land, the right to buy bread at a 'just' price and the right to invoke traditional 'liberties' if denied. We cannot neglect from our discussion of Highland cultural transformation the notion of <u>mentalite</u>, the <u>sensibilite collective</u> of the common people, albeit that the questions how far did this 'inherent' ideology carry protesters at any given moment and how all-informing was what Thompson has called 'plebian culture' - that 'self-activating culture of the people derived from their own experiences and resources'7 - may be difficult to answer for the Highlands.

The notion of 'legitimation' which has been used to consider the belief by men and women that they were in opposing the claims or actions of authority, 'defending traditional rights or customs; and . . . that they were supported by the wider consensus of the community'8 is of some heuristic value in the Highland context. Three sorts of customs are normally recognised: the general customs of the land which, taken together, form the body of the common law; customs or usages of particular trades; and customs of particular localities which have the force of the law in that locality and which, in replacing the common law in that locality, may even be inconsistent with or in opposition to common law.9 To be valid in law, customs must be reasonable, have been in existence 'time out of mind', have continued without interruption since time immemorial and should refer to some specific locality. Though these distinctions in English law are not strictly comparable with Scottish law or with the sense of rootedness in a place and the belief in traditional rights and practices of occupancy embodied in the term duthchas, it is possible to suggest that the Highlander was seeking through protest to legitimate what were regarded within the locality and the Highland community at large as rightful claims to land and methods of land management, simply because that is what always had been done in those places.

The place of duthchas as a legitimising notion for the use and occupancy of land is thus of some significance. As discussed earlier, the term is rarely defined with precision in tenurial terms but 'The impression given is that whilst it had no force in law, it nevertheless had the force of custom behind it' (and custom here in the sense both of locality and remembered unbroken occupance). As Dodgshon notes, 'Whether this distinction between law and custom could always be drawn is difficult to decide, but either we admit the very real possibility that the Highlander once possessed kin-based hereditary tenures comparable to those disclosed by the Irish and Welsh law codes, of which duthchas may be a hollow survival, or we face the stiffer task of explaining why not'. Behind the implicit connections between duthchas and the related notion of kindly tenure is 'the customary belief that once a family had occupied land for three generations, then the fourth and subsequent generations acquired a secure right to occupancy'.10 In discussing kindly tenure in Lowland Scotland, Sanderson has shown how the term more properly related to why the tenant held land in this way rather than how it was held: 'Kindly tenancy was nothing less than the

claim to customary inheritance, however the tenant held',
It is possible to argue then that what by the sixteenth
century in Lowland Scotland had become 'a firmly established principle of customary landholding, not simply
folk-law but a recognised right which could be renounced,
for which compensation could be asked, and which was upheld
in both local and royal courts', in short 'had become
marketable', had become in the Highlands, in the form of
duthchas, a customary right of and for the holding of land,
legitimated by kinship ties and recognised in the
Highlanders' inherent ideology as a result of remembered
occupance over generations.11 And as customary rights of
inheritance decayed in the Lowlands with the spread of
feuing and the rentier economy, it is possible to claim
that the continued consensus recognition by Highlanders of
the customary notions attaching to the duthchas of a
particular holding further distinguished the area as
'backward' in the eyes of outsiders for whom, as we have
seen, new practices symbolised material progress. To an
extent too, the question of a Highland ideology or
consciousness which centred upon kinship and recognised
rights to land-holding hinges not upon the formal
recognition of duthchas as a real tenurial claim but upon
an ideologically-constituted belief in what the term stood
for as a way of holding and inheriting land. This is not
to say that Highland protest was motivated only by claims
to the past and not by real grievances in their historic
present.   It is to note that important moral and
ideological issues underlie and inform what might otherwise
be treated as a record of physical events.12

Protest in its various forms in the Highlands should be
seen as more than 'popular resistance', and more complex in
its historical expression and cause than the response of
one 'traditional' mode of production in confrontation with
another more 'advanced'.

In examining the question of reaction to cultural
transformation here, an attempt has been made to consider
the principal forms taken - language maintenance and
religious revival, what may be called the 'literary
reaction', and the more evident incidents of physical
resistance to eviction or protest against sheep farms and
deer forests - from the standpoint of Highlanders themselves, their expressed needs, capacities and inherent
ideology.

LANGUAGE, RELIGION, AND GAELIC CULTURAL CONSCIOUSNESS

In giving evidence to the Napier Commission, John Murdoch,

who in several ways was a central figure in campaigns for 'the people's cause' noted that

> The language and lore of the Highlands being treated with despite has tended to crush their self-respect, and repress that self-reliance without which no people can advance. When a man was convinced that his language was a barbarism, his lore as filthy rags, and that the only good thing about him - his land - was, because of his general worthlessness, to go to a man of another race and another tongue, what remained ... that he should fight for?13

Earlier, we discussed the question of Gaelic's status as a symbol of backwardness in the minds of those outsiders engaged in the improvement of the Highlands and noted how the language was replaced by English more quickly and completely as an educational language amongst Highlanders than as the language of religious worship (Chapter 3). This was shown to be principally the result of the relative success of policies of anglicisation though education compared with those acts intended to supply the Highlands with a Gaelic-speaking ministry and thus bring the High-lander to 'civilitie and obedience' and in time to English through the medium of his own language. In part, however, the relative strengths of Gaelic or English in different social domains was the result of Highlanders choosing and adopting English as a school language and seeing in it the means to worldly advance whilst retaining Gaelic as the language of and for God: as the Rev. James Grant of Kilmuir, Skye, noted in evidence to the Napier Commission, 'Highlanders would like their children to be better scholars than themselves, to be able to read the Scripture in Gaelic, but to be also able to speak English and carve their way through the world'. Evidence on differing social domains highlights the difficulty of knowing the extent to which Gaelic was regarded by those who spoke it not merely as the vehicle of expression of the Highland way of life but as the symbol of it, and of knowing, too, to what extent the maintenance of Gaelic by Highlanders in the face of acts of linguistic transformation, and the use of it by non-Highlanders, was a conscious act of opposition.

Language maintenance and Gaelic consciousness

Writing in an issue of The Glasgow Highlander in 1933 one 'disinherited Gael' considered that 'Even in these material-

istic days it is surely worth one's while to learn the
tongue of Ossian and thus imbibe the spirit of which it is
not only the sign and symbol, but the only fitting
vehicle'. Thirty years earlier, Charles Fraser-Mackintosh
had noted that 'There were times when Highlanders used to
be indignant at the abuse and rancour of depreciation of
the Gaelic language; but fortunately we have outlived
these feelings of resentment and indeed such abuse is now
seldom heard'.14 The terms of that abuse and the ideology
which considered the maintenance of Gaelic a barrier to
material advance are exemplified in the below quote from
MacCulloch in 1824. Gaelic it was noted:

> maintains or fosters those ancient habits and
> modes of thinking, which repel what the people
> cannot be taught to consider improvements;
> innovations which they despise, because they
> dislike those by whom they were introduced, or
> which they neglect, because ignorant of their
> value, or, which they abhor because they interfere
> with old habits, or lastly, which they consider
> invarious [sic] of their hereditary or habitual
> rights.

He recognised also the links between the Gaelic language as
intellectual production and the material actions it could
transmit or hinder.

> Opinions are formed in it, and consecrated by it;
> it constitutes, not only the vehicle of ideas, but
> almost the ideas themselves; and it will be in
> vain to attempt to change the current of thought
> and action in the Highlands, while the language is
> allowed to remain.

MacCulloch quoted from Graham's Gartmore Manuscript of 1747
which had likewise argued that Gaelic prevented Highlanders
'from making improvements in the affairs of common like,
and in other knowledge'. Whilst he noted 'This the opinion
of 1747', he argued in conclusion in terms that suggest a
continued hostility toward the language: 'the superiority
in knowledge, art, and industry, in every thing that
constitutes the political strength and value of a population, as well as the happiness and wealth of the constituent individuals, is in favour of those who speak
English'.15
    MacCulloch's is evidence of a certain sort of course,
albeit that it reflects a persistent theme in Highland
transformation, and we should not suppose that that

334

consciousness of what Gaelic represented and the regional identity it embodied would have been the same for Highlanders and non-Highlanders alike. But the fact that some Gaels would have agreed with him, just as there were others like Kirkwood in the later 1690s not of the Highlands prepared to defend Gaelic means the question of language maintenance as opposition is not necessarily a simple one. And the issues are compounded by the fact that in the later eighteenth century especially in context with the 'discovery' of the Highlander as 'antiquarian primitive', some knowledge of Gaelic was considered a necessary cultural attribute within the anglicised upper ranks in society. There are signs of attempts at language maintenance in the 1700s and 1800s, though differences between what some saw as the study and preservation of Gaelic as the dying medium of an archaic society, and active attempts to defend Gaelic as the vehicle and symbol of Highland consciousness need to be borne in mind. The fact, for example, that the Gaelic poet Alexander MacDonald, Alasdair mac Mhaighstir Alasdair, could write in his 1751 Ais-eiridh na Sean-Chanoin Albannaich (Resurrection of the Ancient Scottish Tongue) how Gaelic was 'persecuted and intolerated' (see page 68 above), yet work for the SSPCK and produce a text - A Galick and English Vocabulary (1741) - designed to teach English to Gaelic speakers, further points to the complex combination of opposites underlying the use and retention of Gaelic.

Black has shown how the Highland Society of Scotland, formed in Edinburgh in 1784, had a remit as a sort of 'Gaelic Academy'.16 One of the Society's objects at foundation was to 'pay a proper attention to the preservation of the language, poetry, and music of the Highlands'. This they did through the appointment of a bard, a piper and a so-called 'Professor' of Gaelic, an office discontinued in 1799. The Society gathered together important Gaelic manuscripts and papers, and published a Dictionary and other works. But by 1825 there is evidence of what Black has called 'the Society's deepening distaste for its cultural commitment', and by 1844, the piping competitions, the last vestige of the cultural commitment, had effectively ended. The Society was influential, however, in the founding of the Celtic Chair at Edinburgh University in 1883. Black is correct to see the Highland Society of Scotland as 'a characteristic product of the Enlightenment' and to claim them a significant body without whose work much would have been lost, but it is difficult to see in their 'cultural commitment' the promotion of spoken Gaelic as a means of maintaining a sense of cultural identity in the face of material change.

Whilst some institutions were important in the context
of migrant Highlanders and some others did play a more
formal and direct role in expressing opposition to the
transformation of the Highlands (see below), it is difficult to avoid the conclusion that some Highland institutions derived meaning rather more from the articulation and
transmission of 'false' images of the Highlands - whisky,
tartan, the kilt - than from any involvement with Gaelic
language maintenance as a means of counter-hegemony.
Several individuals, however, put forward claims as to how
Gaelic should be maintained. Turner's 1809 edition of
MacDonald's 1776 poems was produced by an editor 'desirous
to preserve his mother tongue',17 and in a long tract of
1828 entitled <u>The True Method of Preserving the Gaelic
language (or How to Retrieve the Decaying Honour and
Prosperity of the Highlands and Islands of Scotland</u>),
McNish argued for the equal use of Gaelic in all courts and
churches and as a political language. McNish's belief that
'until the Highlander gets this language introduced into
the courts and other places of business, within the Gaelic
districts, it is vain for him to think that he can raise
himself from the situation of a herd'18 was, of course, in
fundamental opposition to the beliefs of those in authority
for whom English, not Gaelic, was the means of social and
cultural advance beyond primitive pastoralism. The work
seems not to have been widely influential and given
prevalent attitudes and the nature of the audience it
sought to motivate, perhaps we should not suppose it should
have been. But in pointing to Gaelic's exclusion from the
courts, the by-then quite common practice of sending
non-Gaelic speaking clergy to Highland parishes and in the
contemporary treatment of Gaelic in education, McNish
identified areas in which Gaelic needed to assert itself.
He recognised, too, that in the matter of language, both
the transformation and the identity of the Highlands was
encapsulated: 'with the language, the glory of our land is
eclipsed'.

Towards the end of the nineteenth century, several
influences came together to support the language: changes
to a small degree in educational policy, the foundation of
the Gaelic Chair at Edinburgh University in 1883, the
establishment of <u>An Comunn Gaidhealach</u> and the Gaelic
Society of Inverness, the work of the Napier Commission,
land law reform movements, and a commitment to political
nationalism which, for some anyway, demanded the use of
Gaelic. This last is perhaps the most surprising since it
involved the acceptance of a common <u>national</u> feeling in
both Highlands and Lowlands, a feeling which cut across
class interests and the established (though not necessarily

correct) images of each other's culture.19   Important in
this context was the involvement with Ireland and Irish
nationalism, as it was to be in matters of land agitation
and land law reform (see below).   John Murdoch was an
important influence in uniting Irish and Highland interests
through his The Highlander.   For Murdoch, the revival of
Gaelic would 'fan the flame of nationality' at least in the
Highlands; 'and who knows how soon it will spread all over
broad Scotland'.20   Hunter has shown how 'Murdoch's
ambition to make the Gaelic Highlands the cradle of a
Scottish national awakening was to be shared by later
nationalists'.   For some of these nationalists, principally
J.S. Blackie and Ruaridh Erskine of Mar, language maintenance and even language revivalism was essential for the
existence of a Gaelic consciousness.   Scotland, not just
the Highlands, had been a Gaelic-speaking nation and should
become one once again.   In Guth na Bliadhna, a journal he
founded in 1912, Erskine of Mar claimed two things were
necessary for Scotland's political salvation: 'the
preservation and propagation of the Gaelic, and the
consolidation of the kingdom under one Celtic aegis "Gun
Chànain, gun Chinneach!"   No Language, No Nation'.21   This
claim mirrors the notion in Gaelic poetic tradition of a
'greater Scotland' once Gaelic but now lost.   In doing so,
the links between language and nationalism may perhaps be
seen as part of the 'inherent ideology' of Highland
consciousness, but in part also, the Gaelic revivalist
movement in the later nineteenth century was more political
than linguistic and derived more from wider interests than
as a means to retain the language only.   More certain
evidence on Gaelic's place as the vehicle for Highland
consciousness comes from examination of the place of
religion in Gaelic society and in the Gaelic literary
response to social change.

Religion in Gaelic society: religious revivals and the Disruption as alternative hegemony, 1740-1843

Put simply, the question of religion in Gaelic society
divides into two issues.   On the one hand are
denominational and institutional matters wherein the
Church, seen by the State as a means of introducing civil
hegemony through godliness, adopted a variety of schemes to
that end in the Highlands, and in which region the conflict
of cultures expressed in and through religion is too often
drawn along rigid sectarian lines.   On the other hand is
the matter of those inherent beliefs, 'ingredients of the
larger complex of Gaelic religious consciousness', which

may more directly have informed people's lives.22 These
issues are distinct but not separate from one another or
from other matters affecting the Highlands. The bond
between Gaelic and religion is today a matter both of
institution and ideology; the fate of the language today
is in several ways, for example, closely bound-up with the
Free Church, at least in the Outer Isles.23 And in the
past, the use of Gaelic religious texts in Highland schools
reinforced the use of Gaelic in a particular social domain
– 'the language of their devotions' – as it also encouraged
the growth of Gaelic literacy. The bond between Gaelic and
religion was evident in several ways: in the fact that as
the language declined, its cessation in church services was
one of the final stages of language retreat; in the
petitioning of Church and presbyterial authorities by
Gaelic speakers, irked at their having non-Gaelic-speaking
ministers resident in Highland charges (see page 139
above); in the importance Highlanders attached to
religious texts, especially to the Gaelic Bible, and in the
expressed worth of those texts in stimulating literacy and
a desire for learning; and not least in the context of
protest and opposition, in the emotional commitment through
Gaelic and God, the feeling of a collective sensibility,
that spiritual worship could bring to a people whose
material and social relationships were being transformed.

Reaction in and through popular religion to the
processes of Highland transformation took two principal
forms in the later eighteenth and nineteenth centuries:
evangelical revivals and the Disruption of the Scottish
Church in 1843. The roots of the first lie in the
1600s.24 But their particular expression as a religious
movement of the common people dates from the late 1700s and
the early 1800s. The 1843 Disruption, when the Scottish
Church was split in two and the Free Church became in the
Highlands the Church of the people, was rooted in wider
debates about patronage and poor law reform in Scotland as
a whole. In the Highlands the Disruption derived
additional momentum from the evangelical revivals and from
the fact that religious sentiment was used to confront
social antagonisms.

Strong evangelical feelings had emerged in parts of the
eastern Highlands in the seventeenth century partly as a
result of the sentiments aroused by the Irish Gaelic Bible
of 1690, but not until the later 1700s were evangelical
revivals important in the Highlands as more generally
internationally.25 Many smaller outbursts of religious
sentiment – in Nigg in 1740, Ardclach in 1776, Kilbrandon
and Kilchattan in 1786, in Breadalbane in 1816, and
throughout the north and west Highlands in the opening

decades of the nineteenth century - were more 'awakenings' than revivals, although these incidents were the foundations to later mass expressions of faith and belief. The Evangelical Revival or Movement of the later 1700s and 1800s was essentially a reaction against the landlords and against the Established clergy: 'it would have been strange if the ordinary tenantry, turning against their landlords, did not also turn against their clergy, who belonged to the same social stratum'.26 In an assessment of the patterns and causes of collective behaviour underlying the Ross-shire revival, Bruce has argued that they were informed by 'an underlying hidden rationality' and were not the result of some sort of pathological reaction born only of anxiety and frustration.27 The rationality of their action against landlords stemmed from opposition to newly-imposed material practices at a time when traditional relationships within Highland society were being undermined and issues of class were outweighing loyalties of rank and kin. The rejection of the Established clergy may be explained in part by the fact that the clergy of the later 1700s and early 1800s were drawn into the middle and upper-middle classes in Highland society (as they had been largely recruited from them) and thus drawn away from the small tenantry who made up the majority of the population and, in part also, because of the general lack of involvement by members of the Established Church during moments of clearance and eviction: 'there can be no doubt that most of the Established clergy gave at least tacit consent to landlords' policies and that their role during the clearances has ever since haunted the reputation of the Church of Scotland in the Highlands'.28 Some ministers did see the clearances as divine retribution for the sins of the Highlander - but we must be careful in making too sweeping a denunciation or arguing only on denominational lines. There were some Established clergy who publicly denounced the clearances and defended the crofting tenantry: Lachlan MacKenzie, minister of Lochbroom from 1782 to 1819, for example, and most notably the brothers Malcolm and Donald MacCallum, the latter of whom was arrested and imprisoned for his activities (see below).

It is true, nevertheless, that in the period in which we have seen the fabric of traditional Highland society greatly weakened, Highland tenantry could not turn to the Established clergy for spiritual guidance or a sense of material security. They turned rather to a popular and fervent evangelism which provided meaning because it was a movement of the people which not only 'helped to create a spirit which was anti-authority in general' and fostered 'the growth of anti-ecclesiastical poetry', but also

underlay that emergence of that own political identity
within the crofting community as a whole.29   Hunter argues
thus:

> On occasion, therefore, the apparent connection
> between religious revivalism and social disloca-
> tion was manifested not only in the fact that
> small tenants . . . were particularly susceptible
> to the new religion, but also in the fact that the
> doctrinal proclamations of the revivals' origina-
> tors and adherents embodied some part of the
> social aspirations just beginning to be formed by
> crofters.

And elsewhere in the same work:

> Evangelicalism and the emergence of the modern
> crofting community are inseparable phenomena if
> only for the reason that it was through the medium
> of a profoundly evangelical faith that crofters
> first developed a forward-looking critique of the
> situation created in the Highlands by the actions
> of the region's landowning and therefore ruling
> class.30

It is true that the Evangelical Movement in the
Highlands was both forward-looking and a critique of
landlord hegemony. The movement was to a degree also
inward-looking, which, because it lacked before 1843 the
social and political institutions through which to channel
class consciousness more directly was, in its first
formation anyway, almost 'a recluse religion' existing only
as an alternative to dominant hegemony. What is interesting in this respect is that several of the people's revival
meetings (as also meetings of the Land League) were held in
sites recognised in Gaelic tradition either as having
associations with the 'fairies', the ancestral dead, or
were at or near other established meeting places.31   This
fact and the fact, too, that revival meetings engendered a
style of congregational psalm-singing which possessed great
elemental and spiritual power for being sung in the
open-air, may suggest that Highlanders saw in revivals a
chance to invest their then present condition with values
derived from established meanings and beliefs. In this
sense, religion acted as an alternative hegemony, function-
ing through maintained beliefs in opposition to the social
changes and attitudes of the time though not until the
later 1800s in open conflict with them.
Prominent in directing revival sentiment were 'the

Men', <u>na daoine</u>, a group of evangelical laymen and men of
the people venerated for their godliness. These figures
exhibited a number of characteristics including a distinct
style of dress; austerity of behaviour; use of mystical
modes of speech and allegorical interpretations of Scripture; and a sense of being members of an intense (and
influential) spiritual brotherhood. In most, it is
possible to note also a continued commitment to criticism,
through popular religion, of the landlord class. Bruce
argues that this 'criticism of the lairds and of the
ministers who supported them' was part of the reason why
the people followed 'the Men'. Other causes are, firstly,
that their more supernaturalist preachings combined more
easily with the beliefs and superstitions of the Highlanders than the Enlightenment-influenced rationalist teachings
of the Established Clergy, and secondly and most importantly, 'the crucial element in the greater plausibility of
"the Men" was their social position'. The fact that they
were <u>of</u> the peasantry is, in this case, at least as significant as the fact that they spoke <u>for</u> the peasantry in
opposition to the landlords; 'these preachers . . .
constituted the first leadership of any sort to emerge from
the crofting population's own ranks'.32 Yet because it was
a leadership that sought to provide an underlying rationality to their Christian concepts by drawing upon notions
inherent to Gaelic culture - second sight and prophecy, for
example - representations of popular religious revivals as
issues of class alone are unsatisfactory.

Nor were 'the Men' the only agents of revival. The
schools of the Gaelic School Society had since 1811 been
engaged in using Gaelic texts to teach Highland children to
read and write in that language, the intention being to
'insure both the extension and use of the English language'. Paradoxically in view of the evidence of the
success of Gaelic schools in furthering English, these
institutions helped strengthen the Highlanders' commitment
to Gaelic as the language of religious expression as they
also provided a means through which Highlanders could turn
in opposition away from the forces of material transformation rather than confront them directly (as they were to do
after 1843 and in the later nineteenth century). In a
number of instances, the establishment of a Gaelic Society
school in a parish was followed by a revival and on several
occasions, the Gaelic school teachers were directly
involved in inciting parishioners to abstain from regular
sabbath attendance. In 1829, the Presbytery of Mull worked
to put an end to the practices of exhortation by two Gaelic
Society school teachers in Ardnamurchan, practices considered 'subversive of all established order and so calculated

to produce the most pernicious consequences'. In Lewis in
the 1830s, John Macleod and Angus MacIver of Bernera were
dismissed from their schools because they had preached to
and catechised the people they also taught, and similar
events characterised parts of Wester Ross in the 1820s.33
    In the Highlands the Disruption of 1843 rested squarely
on these evangelical foundations. The Free Church was
notably anti-landlord in its early years. The principal
issue of difference had been the evangelicals' opposition
to landlords' control of church patronage. Given the
interests and feelings represented by the parties involved,
the Disruption was in the Highlands more a class conflict
than an ecclesiastical dispute.

> The parish church was a common centre where all
> classes met . . . But even religion . . . was
> converted at the Disruption into a new fountain of
> bitterness . . .   There is thus a double point of
> collision between the two ranks - an ecclesiasti-
> cal as well as an agrarian enmity . . .   It is
> consequently almost impossible to find an
> individual in the upper rank who has not a grudge
> against the people, either on the score of their
> Free Churchism, or on the score of their hostility
> to the sheep walk system.34

    The threat to the authority of the landlords - hence
the intensity of proprietorial opposition to the Free
Church - lay in the fact that the Free Church threatened to
end crofters' political isolation. And it did so because
the institutions of the Free Church were rooted in popular
belief and were the heirs to a tradition of religious
dissent: 'the Disruption and the revivals which preceded
it were largely instrumental in welding a disparate
collection of small tenants into a community capable of
acting collectively and possessing a distinctive character
and outlook'.35   As one author has observed:

> the reason why agrarian capitalism did not cause
> disturbances before 1790 in the Highlands clearly
> has a good deal to do with the absence of any
> cultural possibility for the Highlanders to stand
> on their own two feet opposed to the lairds, a
> chance that evangelical Calvinism afforded them
> ultimately.36

Popular religious sentiment as an expression of opposition
to the authority of landlords and Established clergy
derived in part from beliefs inherent to Gaelic culture and

in part also from external issues of social class formation
during periods of material change in which 'formal'
religion could not justify the means taken in that change.
It was a form of opposition underlain by a shared
rationality and principally legitimated by 'the Men' whose
role as leaders through religion of the politically-
emergent crofting population was taken up in the second
half of the nineteenth century by individuals within the
Free Church and the Highland Land League. At the same
time, conscious expressions of Highland identity and
opposition to the processes of transformation and the
claims of authority were to be found in the Gaelic literary
tradition.

GAELIC POETRY AND OPPOSITION TO TRANSFORMATION

A number of authors have discussed the relationship between
Gaelic literature and Highland society and have variously
noted how 'Gaelic literature in every period has grown out
of the life of the common people'.37 Thomson has suggested
that 'Gaelic poetry in the eighteenth century reflects
clearly the changes that had taken place, and were taking
place, in society',38 and others have shown both of the
clearances and the land agitation in the later 1800s how
poetry was part of the popular response to social
change.39 In using literary evidence in this context,
however, several difficulties have to be recognised at the
outset: firstly, given that any literature is part of a
literary tradition as well as a social product, we need to
know something about what we may call the 'representative-
ness' of the source in question. This is particularly true
of the Highlands of which region externally-derived
literary images of romantic glens, rude magnificence,
Ossianic peasants, or 'canny chiels' have too often been
held typical when they are more commonly 'false' images,
barriers to explanation. As one author noted in discussing
'the poetry and prose of the crofter question',

> It is the acknowledged privilege of the Highlands
> and Highlander to be looked at through a veil of
> romance. Poets and novelists from Sir Walter
> Scott to William Black and Professor Blackie have
> encircled them with a halo of idealism that was
> delightfully picturesque so long as it had to be
> viewed only from the picturesque side, but which
> becomes embarrassing in circumstances like the
> present, when the prosaic laws of political
> economy have to be applied.40

Secondly, there is the difficulty of knowing the assumptions to make of evidence which may be an expression rather more of personal commitment than the registered sensibility of a people or an age. The Highlands is only one region among many in which there is literary evidence 'from within' of social change from without. There is a clear tradition of protest poetry and prose going back in Britain to the mid-seventeenth century, even perhaps to More's Utopia of 1516. And in the later eighteenth century and nineteenth century, the poetry of such as Stephen Duck ('the thresher poet'), John Clare, or Oliver Goldsmith may all be used to illuminate change in rural society.41 Whilst these and later sources need to be used in conjunction with other material, there is a need also to consider the historiographical and social context of literary evidence before we may treat it as a source at all or use it uncritically as a 'quarry' for contemporary research, the simple 'reflection' of social change in the past.

In the 150 years after the appearance of the Book of the Dean of Lismore, compiled between 1512 and 1526, four streams of Gaelic poetry have been distinguished: the genuine bardic class; a stream of 'titled amateurs' part bardic in background; a new class of acknowledged poets; and folk-poets proper.42 The first group are represented over this period only by survivors of a bardic class, a decline itself a consequence of a policy of legislative action against the bards begun in 1449; the second group show elements of bardic and popular styles, a transition symptomatic of the going of bardic conventions. The third and fourth streams are of interest here because 'There are hints, throughout the poetry of the 1690s and early 1700s, of change and Anglicisation and the threat to the old order'.43 These hints are more clearly apparent in the eighteenth century if only because the written materials for the study of Gaelic poetry are more available. From this time, Gaelic oral poetry had a double role in Gaelic society; in part as the first phase in written Gaelic vernacular literature, and also as part of a continued oral tradition.44 The fact that Gaelic poetry after 1650 is in one sense more folk-poetry than not does not mean it was homogeneous.

Gaelic poetry and social change in the Highlands, c.1698–1812

Although there are signs in the seventeenth century of comment through poetry on contemporary social change - strictures against the conspicuous consumption of a MacLeod chief in Roderick Morrison's 'Oran do Mhac Leoid Dhun Bheagain' ('Song for MacLeod of Dunvegan'), or on clan politics and the ascendancy of the Campbells in the work of Iain Lom - more certain expressions date from that 'long' eighteenth century between the birth in or about 1698 of Alexander MacDonald, Alasdair Mac Mhaighstir Alasdair, and the death in 1812 of Duncan Ban Macintyre, Donnchadh Bàn.45 The major poets of the period were Alexander MacDonald (c.1698-c.1770), John MacCodrum (c.1693-1779), Duncan Ban Macintyre (1724-c.1812), Rob Donn (c.1715-1778), Dugald Buchanan (1716-1768), William Ross (1762-1791), and later, Ewen Maclachlan (1773-1822).46 Examples of an awareness of social changes in Highland society are to be found in the work of each but are perhaps best seen for our purposes in the poetry of Mac Mhaighstir Alasdair, Mac-Codrum, and Duncan Ban Macintyre.

In his poem 'Ais-eiridh na Sean-Chànoin Albannaich' ('Resurrection of the Old Scottish Tongue') published in the 1751 work of the same title and subtitled 'Moladh an Ughair do'n t-seann Chànoin Ghàidhlig' (The Author's Eulogy for the old Gaelic Language'), it is possible to see in Mac Mhaighstir Alasdair's work a sense of Scottish as well as Gaelic nationalism evident in the historical associations of the language and a recognition of the superiority of the Gaelic language over English (and Latin) for certain purposes. MacDonald emphasises what Thomson has called 'the larger Scottish relevance of the language' and makes still older claims of Gaelic.

> It lived still
> its glory shall not fade
> in spite of guile
> and strangers' bitter hate.
> Scotland spoke it,
> and Lowland carles did too,
> . . . .
>
> Adam spoke it,
> even in Paradise,
> and Eve's Gaelic
> flowed in its lovely wise.47

His son's anthology of 1776 likewise made claim to Gaelic having been 'once the mother tongue of the principal states of Europe'. MacDonald was involved in the 1745 Rising on the Jacobite side - a fact which led to his formal dismissal from the SSPCK - and his 'Oran nam Fineachan Gàidhealach' ('The Song of the Highland Clans') and 'Brosnachadh eile do no Gaidheil' ('Another Incitement for

the Gaels' are exhortations to the need to fight for what
was seen as a just cause, even after 'Culloden's defeat at
the hands of a vile stinking Dutchman'.48

MacCodrum is of interest not because he was in 1763
appointed bard to Sir James MacDonald of Sleat in an
attempt by the landlord to maintain the traditional social
circles of a Highland chief (the last to be so appointed),
but because his work reveals an awareness of national
affairs although he was himself footed firmly in local
issues, a 'village' poet. MacCodrum noted the shift in
loyalty of Highland chiefs who were 'without pity for poor
folk, without kindness to friends; they are of the opinion
that you do not belong to the soil'.49   And in his 'Oran
ar Aghaidh an Eididh Ghallda ('Song Against the Lowland
Garb'), MacCodrum drew attention to the military associations of the kilt - 'Once it was the clothing of the active
heroes' - and to how the proscription of Highland dress was
an injustice to the Gael. Duncan Ban Macintyre was less a
local poet. From 1767 he was a member of Edinburgh's City
Guard, then, like Edinburgh's sedan chairmen, dominated by
Highlanders. Donnchadh Ban's poetry was influenced by that
of Mac Mhaighstir Alasdair and the two are often treated
together although Macintyre fought on the Hanoverian side
at the Battle of Falkirk and politics have little part in
his poetry. In his 'Moladh Beinn Dobhrainn' ('Praise of
Ben Dorain'), however, we find Macintyre making reference
to the way incoming sheep were despoiling the Highlands the
poet knew and loved - he was born in Glen Orchy in Argyllshire, one of the earlier districts to be affected by
commercial sheep grazing and this poem dates to the period
1751 to 1766 - and in his 'Oran nam Balgairean' ('The Song
of the Foxes'), his feelings on the coming of 'the big
sheep' are abundantly clear.

> My blessing be upon the foxes, because that
>   they hunt the sheep -
> The sheep with the brockit faces that have
>   made confusion in all the world,
> Turning our country to desert and putting
>   up the rents of our lands.
> Now is no place left for the farmer - his
>   livelihood is gone;
> Hard necessity drives him to forsake the
>   home of his fathers.
> The townships and the sheilings, where once
>   hospitality dwelt,
> They are now nought but ruins, and there is
>   no cultivation in the fields.50

These examples are among many that illuminate Thomson's claim on Gaelic poetry of the 1700s reflecting social change. Dugald Buchanan's '<u>An Claigeann</u>' ('The Skull') in which several verses are directed at the spread of commercial landlordism and rackrenting lairds, may also be mentioned in this context. In other ways, we hear how Gaelic was sometimes used by the tenantry to deride landlords.51 And as others have shown, there was a continuing tradition in protest songs and poetry in other parts of Scotland, in the balladry of the north-east Lowlands especially, in ways that mirror the evidence for the Highlands in the eighteenth century.52 In discussing political and protest songs in eighteenth-century Scotland, for example, Crawford has noted that many such songs though having spontaneously occurring variations gave expression 'to universal situations and emotions as experienced by the members'.53 In the same way, Gaelic poetry of the eighteenth century had a new vigour in comparison with that of the 1600s; changes affecting Highland rural society are seen to be increasingly part of a common experience.

The poetry of the clearances, c.1790–c.1880

In his discussion of the poetry of the clearances, Maclean has noted several points of interest.54 The first is that much of the Gaelic poetry of the nineteenth century, until the 1880s anyway, is characterised by a nostalgic sentiment and by a 'weakness, thinness and perplexity' which reflected the relative weakness then of any physical resistance to the clearances. Maclean's conclusion on the nostalgic tone of nineteenth-century poetry has found agreement in the work of others. For Thomson, it is the theme of 'homeland'.

> The commonest theme of Gaelic verse in the nineteenth century is that of 'homeland'. This was no doubt to be expected in a period of upheaval and uprooting, much of it of an involuntary nature, whether people were forced to migrate by physical action or by economic circumstances. The homeland is seen primarily in a nostalgic light: a place of youthful associations, family and community warmth, a Paradise lost.55

This sentiment is a reflection in Gaelic poetry of what others have identified in nineteenth-century English poetry and prose as 'a conventional structure of retrospect', a rural rhetoric centred more upon a remembered and often

347

idealised past than upon its actual nature.56 An additional problem in relation to clearance poetry as Maclean notes is the 'absurd tendency to blame the factor more than the landlord', a tendency which operated to undermine any sense of collective resistance.

MacDonell has documented the testimony in poetry of many emigrant Gaels. The extract below from a Skye migrant in his 'Imrich ran Eileineach' ('Emigration of the Islanders') may be held representative in tone and type of much of this evidence.

> A new master has come into the land,
>   a sad woeful matter.
> The people are leaving;
>   their possessions have dwindled.
> They haven't a cow to put to graze.
> Some were put towards rent,
>   others died;
> Rare were those that survived.
> What would it profit me
>   to remain in this land
> Where I can earn nothing by shoemaking.57

Some early clearance poetry did provide expression of popular feeling on traditional rights of occupancy - in Ailean Dall's 'Oran nan Coibarairean Gallda' ('The Song of the Lowland Shepherds'), for example, which is a bitter attack on Lowland shepherds and sheep-farmers and everything they stood for, more pointed but similar in intent and aim to Macintyre's 'Oran nan Balgairean'. For most of the nineteenth century before the 1880s, however, only the poetry of William Livingstone (1808-1870) and John Maclachlan (1804-1874) may be exempted from Maclean's general criticism.

Whilst we may agree with Maclean that 'there is in Clearance poetry a tendency to a vague generalised regret without a definiteness even of indictment', it is less easy to know why this should be so. Several partial answers may be advanced. In part, it was the result of 'a common failure to face the real cause', that is, the shifting loyalty of Highland chiefs and landlords, not the shepherds or factors themselves; in part, too, it may have been because of the scale and intensity of the changes and the evictions and because of the material circumstances of most Highlanders during the 1800s for whom living standards in the previous century may have been remembered as better even when they were not. And in part also, the problem may be historiographical: sandwiched between a vigorous eighteenth-century poetry (and a society still relatively so) and 'the resurgent spirit' of the 1880s (and the political activism of the Gael in that period) comes a period whose poetry and social context can only suffer in comparison. The fact that there is a 'clearance poetry' at all should not be minimised in discussing social and economic change in the early and mid-1800s, but for the reasons advanced above, this poetry was more a passive record of contemporary change than an active element of it. This is less true of poetry of the land agitation.

Poetry of the land agitation, c.1880–c.1892

For Maclean, the resurgence of Gaelic poetry in the 1880s had three main causes: the stirring of a working class Radicalism in the cities; the interest of the Liberal Party in the votes of rural workers they were to enfranchise in 1884; and the example of Ireland. Within this context of broader issues, Meek has distinguished three main types of land agitation poetry: verse composed by the 'village poet'; poetry composed by Gaelic migrants in urban Lowland Scotland for whom Gaelic periodicals and pro-Highlander newspapers were a vital means of publication; and less common than the above, verse 'with a strongly intellectual bias, born of a broad university education, and a study of Gaelic and English literature'.58 The first group were not unaware of general issues: Robertson's song of the Sutherland clearances, for example, written in the 1880s and which includes the lines 'My curse on the big sheep; Where are the children of the kindly folk?; we parted when we were young; Before MacKay's country had become a wilderness', is illustrative of this local reflection upon Highland-wide issues.59 The last two groups, of greater interest, are best represented in the works of two poets; John Smith of Iarsiadar in Lewis, <u>Iain Mac a'Ghobhainn</u>, as the intellectual commentator through poetry on Gaelic land issues in the context of national politics and international issues, and Mary MacPherson, better known as <u>Mairi Mhor nan Oran</u> ('Big Mary of the Songs'), as a city-based land agitation poet. Both Smith and <u>Mairi Mhor</u> and to an extent, too, William Livingstone, were concerned 'with their countrymen's struggle for freedom'. In the work of Smith, Thomson sees 'the most considered and the most damning and scathing indictment of those policies which decimated the Gaelic people'.60

The work of Smith is important because while most land agitation poetry tends to be narrative, his was analytic of the causes of Highland transformation and aware enough to know that Highland changes were part only of wider issues affecting society. In his 'Oran Luchd an Spors' ('Song for Sportsmen'), he considers the policy of turning large parts of the Highlands into sporting estates and deer-forests.

> The noble chieftains who were kind and
> honest have left us;
> imposters have come in their place;
> they have exerted an evil influence on this land.
> The fermenters of barley have come,
> the singed distillers with their tubes,
> who amassed a fortune by plundering drunkards,
> making thousands utterly miserable.
> These are the worthless creatures who have
> taken the place of the others,
> and who rule in the Highlands of Scotland;
> it cannot be that prosperity will be our lot.
>
> Some of them trafficked in opium,
> they gathered a great deal of riches,
> their vice made the Chinamen suffer,
> their people destroyed by the poison;
> men without kindness or mercy,
> who were hard to prick in their conscience;
> in payment for all of their plunder
> they deserved to be stabbed with a whinger.61

Similar ideas inform his 'Spiorad a'Charthannais' ('The Spirit of Kindliness'), written in the wake of the Bernera Riot in 1874 (see below). For Smith, the Bernera Riot was symptomatic of the lack of kindliness shown by men to one another in the Highlands. Whether he understood this to include notions of duthchas or only the sense of kindliness in social relations is difficult to say, but the anti-landlord tone of the poem is clear enough even though it does not include the incitement to violence of his 'Oran Luchd an Spors'.

In that it is part of a larger output of verse from Gaelic emigres, the poetry of Mairi Mhor nan Oran is perhaps more typical of land agitation verse. Her work is said to have contributed to the victory of Land-Law reform candidates in Highland elections in the 1880s. Her 'Brosnachadh nan Gaidheal' ('Incitement of the Gaels') was composed for the 1885 elections and other work praises highly activists in the Land League. Her song 'Eilean a'Cheo' ('The Isle of the Mist') contains an exhortation to the Skye people to stand firm and fight, and her 'A' Choinneamh Chaidreach' ('The Friendly Meeting') argues in part how absentee and indebted landlords were the cause of the Highland land crisis. Other agitation poets make similar points.

> The plough has been placed on the hen-roost,
> and the arable land has been laid waste;
> what our father had on rent has been taken
>   from us;
> and if we got it back again,
> we would not make our complaint against the
>   state
> concerning every danger
> and misjudgement that the landowners have
>   inflicted on the Gaels.62

As Meek makes clear, the view that land was 'the property of the people, and not of any feudal superior' and that this right was beyond dispute yet had been usurped un-naturally by landlords through eviction and deer-forest, lies at the heart of land agitation poetry. Yet land agitation verse is often local and narrative. It offers little by way of analysis of the central issue - land hunger - and leaving aside the work of John Smith of Iarsiadar, 'there is virtually no trace of party consciousness, or of a struggle against a widespread political system'. Perhaps the fact that the verse of this period is only local and narrative with poets seeing agitation in personal terms may explain why it provides a guide to Highlanders' 'emotional reactions' without also providing a means through which generally-recognised sentiments might have been presented in more scathing tones given other events of the time.

SOCIAL PROTEST AND COUNTER-HEGEMONY, c.1780-c.1930

Set within and alongside the expressed opposition in religious revival and protest poetry is the problematical record of physical resistance. It is problematical for reasons of historiography, fact, and interpretation.

In discussing Highland protest, there has been a widely-held and persistent notion that the Highlander was un-resistant to clearance or landlord authority, at least until the Land Wars of the later nineteenth century which are seen as an isolated period in Highland history, triggered by the unique event of the 'Battle of the Braes' in 1882. This historiographical orthodoxy has only recently been overturned. Extending from this persistent interpretation, however, is our second problem; that, paradoxically, much of the evidence on Highland clearances

Is derived from those moments of opposition recorded in legal depositions and by outside observers, a record whose contents belie the interpretation made of them.63 Thirdly, more recent research has shown not only that the beginnings of Highland protest lie in the later eighteenth century if not earlier, but also that resistance to authority took several forms and continued until the first decades of the twentieth century. The problem here is two-fold: firstly to know the extent to which individual episodes of protest in different places at different times shared a common form of expression, and secondly, to know the extent to which they were legitimated by a generally-recognised and understood inherent ideology, a Highland consciousness motivated by consensus claims to the holding and working of land, for example, or in the values of one class over another. A final difficulty in interpretation of the record of physical resistance as counter-hegemony is knowing how far such resistance should be seen as an attempt to counter the advance of new ways and to maintain established beliefs and practices in the face of transformation (as backward-looking, 'residual' elements of oppositional culture), or whether such resistance was intended to argue through force for the incorporation of the demands of Highlanders into dominant social and material relationships as new 'emergent' practices.

The belief that, until the 1880s, Highlanders were passive agents in their own transformation is best expressed in the work of Hanham (1969), although it has earlier roots.64 Hanham's principal conclusions - that by the time of the Sutherland clearances of 1807-1820 'the Highlander had been so far pacified that scarcely a hand was raised against the destruction of much-loved homes'; that 'The Highlanders were notoriously god-fearing and law-abiding, and unwilling to cause trouble'; and that protest began in 1882 - are now no longer tenable. For Hanham, the 'problem' of Highland discontent lay in the origin of the disturbances of 1882, a fact he explained chiefly in terms of outside influences. Given later work on the extent and form of protest, however, some of the central questions of Highland discontent now lie in knowing not why the 1882 Battle of the Braes should have occurred where and when it did, but rather in knowing in what relations this incident stands to other 'Land Wars' of the 1880s and how these wars stand in regard to protest against eviction in the 1780s and 1820s or the food riots of 1847.

The tradition of docility has its origins also in the fact that some nineteenth-century commentators did not know of the extent of formal opposition before the 1880s. Given this, the tenor of much contemporary description is

352

Table 6.1

The characteristics of 'the Highland disturbance' as a four-stage challenge to landlord authority*

Stage	Characteristics
1	Local law officer or landlord agent attempts to serve summons of removal. The first time he is turned away, the second he is subjected to some sort of petty humiliation - his papers burnt, or stripped naked and chased of the land, or cast adrift in an open boat - commonly by the women of the village. [This was usually termed the 'deforcement' of an officer of authority].
2	A posse of constables led by a sheriff and his assistants arrive. Real resistance follows in the form of volleys of sticks and stones from a massed group of the common people, with women invariably in the front line of defence. Sometimes men dressed as women involved. Resistance usually sufficient to push back constables. Common people may have made an appeal to some distant authority; 'the press, local worthies or even the landlord'.
3	Higher legal authorities alerted; Solicitor General, for example, or the Lord Advocate, even the Home Office. Local landowners make repeated claims that disturbances linked with outside agitators and have connections with 'Radicalism'. Talk of radicalism or 'Northern Rebellion' helped persuade authorities of the necessity of military intervention.
4	News of impending intervention usually enough to defuse the resistance; end of resistance often facilitated by mediation of the local minister 'who produced a face-saving formula for the people'.

* From Richards (1973), pp.39-40; idem (1985), pp.333-334.

alarmist and dramatic because the Land Wars and croftor
opposition were considered without precedent. For some,
the crofter of the late nineteenth century was thus alien
to all authority, a view echoing earlier claims to the
inherent lawlessness of the Highlander.

> Could we analyse the soul of a Highland crofter,
> it would disclose a spiritual being quite unique
> in our matter-of-fact civilisation. There would
> be found in it a large percentage of Radicalism to
> start with. . . The poorest and most ignorant serf
> in Connaught is at heart a Tory compared with the
> average crofter. He has his Church to venerate,
> and his priest to obey, even where he has lost all
> respect for civil authority. In a Scotch village,
> and still more in these lonely clachans which defy
> the tempests of the Atlantic, there is no sense
> whatever of obedience to authority as such.65

More recent work has documented the precedents to the
protest of the 1800s. Richards (1973) has argued for the
existence of 'sporadic but repeated eruptions of spontaneous resistance to established authority', within which 'Not
only is there a continuity, but there is also a recurrent
pattern in the record of popular protest'. Given that in
many cases of resistance to landlord policy, 'the common
people seem to have adopted, or conformed to, a recurrent,
almost stylised, mode of action',66 Richards proposed a
composite picture of Highland disturbances (Table 6.1),
although it is likely this model fits best the protest
against clearance. In later work, he identified three
principal sorts of disturbance - induction riots, clearance
riots, and food riots.67

The geography of protest - both in locational terms and
in the way in which topography and communications influenced the form and extent of protest - should not be
neglected. Richards rightly notes:

> Highland disorder was favoured by the fragile
> system existing for the maintenance of civil peace
> in the north. Geographical isolation, the
> awkwardness of the terrain, and the minimal
> establishment of police and militia inevitably
> stretched the capacity of the authorities to
> maintain a sense of security in the region.68

Whilst this helps explain 'the condition of near-hysteria
that often infected law officers and landlord agents during
times of disturbances', it may also be that the facts of

354

geography hindered the development of widespread organised protest beyond the merely local 'sporadic but repeated eruptions'. Richards argues that 'Although the terrain was ostensibly ideal for Hobsbawmian rebels and myths, no outstanding figures emerged'. It may be possible to argue then that although 'ostensibly ideal', Highland geography may have determined the location if not the type of protest - clearance riots only in more fertile areas, for example - and may even have acted against the uniting of shared local events as a unified mass movement of counter-hegemonic opposition given difficulties of communication and organisation. What will be shown below to be the relative lack of combined opposition until the later nineteenth century may owe also to the 'disappearance' of the organisational ranks in Highland society, given the departure of the tacksman and the equivocal position of many clergy.

It is clear from even this brief introduction, however, that the record of Highland protest, though problematic, is neither an unimportant appendix to a more fully understood material and cultural transformation nor itself a uniform response to that transformation. The forms of Highland social protest incorporated local 'apolitical' factors as in later moments they were also politically motivated and part of a wider context of opposition. From the later 1700s, sporadic riots seem to have shared common features and were legitimated by an inherent ideology as they were also motivated by factors and people external to the Highlands. The fact, too, that the response of authority involved on occasion the enforcement of political rule on a variety of scales from armed police to gunboats suggests that questions raised by examination of the record of Highland discontent are central to explanation of the region's transformation.

A tradition of opposition?: resistance, riots, and protest, 1792-1874

The events of 1792 on the Kildermorie estate of Munro of Novar in Alness, Easter Ross, are often regarded as the first collective expression amongst Highlanders of opposition to the new ways of farming and the authority of landlords. In brief, the events of 1792 are these. The people of the area resisted the entry of sheep owned by incoming Lochaber shepherds, a resistant itself stemming from their re-location on poorer-quality land, with their black cattle, in 1791. Their intention was to round-up all the sheep and drive them out of the northern Highlands. With this intention clear from the outset and given the that that messages which sent to adjacent parishes to co-ordinate resistance, the reaction of local landlords was total panic. The authorities responded by mobilising three companies of the Black Watch. After a brief confrontation at Boath, eight ringleaders were apprehended. They were later released.69

The events of 1791-1792 made a permanent impression on Highland consciousness; 1792 is remembered as Bliadhna Nan Caorach, 'The Year of the Sheep'. The resistance was grounded in opposition to material change and to an extent provided inspiration for defiance in future years. It was organised as a local matter but with the intention of widening its effects – messages were sent through churches and public houses in Easter Ross, the Black Isle and parts of Sutherland 'calling the people to meet on a certain day for collecting the Whole Sheep and driving them off the Country'.70 It was concluded by the threat of military force and the arrest of local leaders, having exposed the inadequacy of local authority and drawn the matter to public attention.

Strictly speaking, the events of 1792 embraced three separate episodes: the establishment of a sheep farm by 'south-country' shepherds (in this case the Camerons from Lochaber); the seizure of stray cattle by the Camerons who simultaneously restricted access to traditionally-recognised hill grazing; and the release of their cattle by the tenantry and the plan to evict the sheep. Taken together, the protests of 1792 were 'the product of a direct clash between traditional practices of black cattle rearing and the new sheep farms, rather than the eviction of all the tenantry' although the threat of eviction was contained within the continued advance of sheep farming.71 The 1792 'insurrection' thus highlights some of the difficulties involved in assessing the evidence for the existence of a 'tradition' of Highland protest; protest against changes in agriculture may not have taken the same form as resistance to eviction or food riots; what were often only local matters were often interpreted by landlords to be the reflection on a small scale of general 'radicalism' or a 'Highland Rebellion', and there remains the danger of seeing single incidents as somehow typical when they may not have been.

The ability to answer the question as to when exactly Highland resistance to cultural transformation began is limited by the surviving source material. Moreover, records of physical resistance in various forms should not neglect the more passive resistance of Highlanders to social change. Given this, the search for an absolute beginning to formalised opposition is a fruitless one.

Cregeen has noted, for example, 'a legacy of mistrust and hostility' amongst the tenantry involved in the improvements of the 1730s in Tiree and Morvern, a sentiment of passive resistance which proved 'an almost insurmountable obstacle to the Argylls'.72 Elsewhere we find opposition in the 1720s to the placement of non-Gaelic-speaking clergy in Highland charges, a pattern mirroring the induction riots which Richards sees originating in 1777. For the 1740s, we are told of an incident in Durness in which an SSPCK schoolmaster and catechist and his wife were physically harassed by parishioners and their supply of peat for fuel continually wetted because his Gaelic was too poor to benefit the population. We do not know how many similar incidents went unrecorded. Smith has recorded protest on the Annexed Estates in 1764, and Logue has outlined an incident in 1782 when a Lowland sheep-farmer was fired at and assaulted by natives of Letterfinlay in Lochaber after having inspected the suitability of nearby lands for a sheep farm,73 and we have already discussed the slaughter of sheep on the estates of Ross of Balnagown in 1782. This latter incident of 1782 paralleled directly the above events of a decade later in Kildermorie and Strathrusdale in attempting to restrict the advance of sheep farming and return the land to its former use as grazing for the cattle of evicted tenants. Elsewhere and at other times, Highlanders rebelled against military service - the Black Watch mutinied in 1743, the Seaforth Highlanders and 76th Highlanders in 1778, the Gordon and Grant fencibles in 1794 - and opposition to recruitment and the Scottish Militia Act was common in parts of the Highlands in the later 1790s.74

If we include recorded opposition to ministers in the early eighteenth century, recruitment protests, and those more widely-recognised instances of protest bracketed by the induction riots of 1777 in Clyne and the Bernera Riot of 1874, we may identify fifty-eight incidents of opposition and protest in the period 1704 to 1874 (Table 6.2); incidents falling into seven categories rather than the three proposed by Richards (1973) (Table 6.1). Their geographical distribution may be seen from Figure 6.1. This schema should be seen only as a guide. In some cases, the act of opposition involved both the illicit slaughter of the landlord's sheep and protest against clearance, or a written petition against induction to the presbyterial authorities with no further action being taken; in others, riot against the induction of an unsuitable minister, or over the continued exporting of meal at times of shortage in the Highlands. It is likely other incidents remain unrecorded, of course, and the difficulty in enumerating

Figure 6.1 The location of protest and disturbance in the Highlands, 1777–1929. Inset A shows the location of incidents in the 'Land Wars'

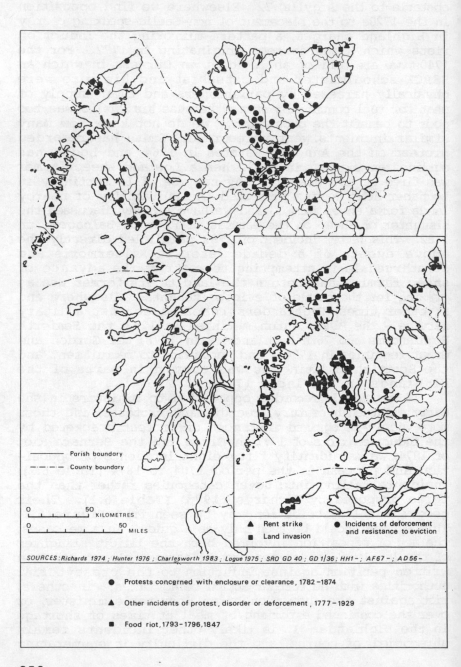

Parish boundary

County boundary

0   50
|—|—|—|—|—| KILOMETRES
0   50
|—|—|—|—|—| MILES

A

▲ Rent strike   ● Incidents of deforcement
■ Land invasion   and resistance to eviction

SOURCES: *Richards 1974; Hunter 1976; Charlesworth 1983; Logue 1975; SRO GD 40; GD 1/36; HH1-; AF67-; AD56-*

● Protests concerned with enclosure or clearance, 1782–1874

▲ Other incidents of protest, disorder or deforcement, 1777–1929

■ Food riot, 1793–1796, 1847

358

Table 6.2

Locations and types of Highland protest, 1704-1874*

Location and year	Type of protest	Officers deforced	Stoning	Police or troops called	Women prominent	Prisoners taken
Inverness 1703-1704	WPI					
Argyll 1708-1717	WPI					
Weem 1711	WPI					
Little Dunkeld 1723	WPI					
Port of Menteith 1725	WPI					
Tiree and Morvern 1739	RPO					
Durness 1740	I(+)				✓	
Glenmuick Tullich and Glengairn 1758	WPI					
Clyne 1777	I		✓		✓	✓
Lochaber 1782**	C		✓		✓	
Ross-shire 1782**	SS				✓	
Easter Ross 1792	C		✓	✓	✓	
Inverness 1793-1796	FR					
Dingwall 1796	FR					
Lewis 1793	OR					
Weem 1797	OR					
Creich ~811	I		✓	✓	✓	
Clyne 1812	C					

(Continued overleaf.)

Table 6.2 (Continued)

Location and Year	Type of protest	Officers deforced	Stoning	Police or troops called	Women prominent	Prisoners taken
Kildonan 1813	SS/C(1)	✓	✓	✓		
Assynt 1813	I	✓		✓		✓
Sutherland and Caithness 1815–1819	SS(2)					
Culrain 1820–1821(++)	C	✓	✓	✓	✓	✓
Gruids 1820–1821**	C	✓	✓	✓	✓	✓
Achness 1820–1821	C	✓	✓	✓	✓	
Unapool 1820	C	✓			✓	✓
Croy 1823	I				✓	
Kinlochbervie 1834	I	✓				
Dunbeath 1835	C(3)				✓	
Harris 1839	C	✓	✓		✓	
Durness 1840–1841(++)	C	✓	✓	✓	✓	
Culrain 1840	C	✓	✓	✓	✓	
Lochsheil 1842	C		✓		✓	
Logie and Resolis 1843	I	✓		✓	✓	
Glencalvie 1842–1845	C					✓
Ballindalloch 1843	C	✓		✓		✓
Avoch 1847	FR	✓		✓		
Balintraid 1847	FR	✓		✓		

Table 6.2 (Continued)

Location and Year	Type of protest	Officers deforced	Stoning	Police or troops called	Women prominent	Prisoners taken
Beauly 1847	FR			✓		✓
Castletown 1847	FR			✓		✓
Evanton 1847	FR			✓		
Invergordon 1847	FR			✓		
Rosemarkie 1847	FR			✓		
Thurso 1847	FR			✓		✓
Wick 1847	FR					✓
Sollas 1849	C	✓	✓	✓	✓	
Strathconan 1850	C	✓	✓	✓		
Strathaird 1851	C					
Elphin 1851	C					
Knockan 1851	C					
Coigach 1852–1853	C	✓	✓	✓	✓	✓
Strathcarron 1853	C	✓	✓	✓	✓	✓
Knoydart 1853	C					✓
Ullapool 1853	C				✓	✓
Greenyards 1854	SS/C(4)	✓	✓	✓		✓
Boreraig and Suisnish 1853–1854	C					
Dervaig 1857	C					
Treshnish 1857	C					
Bernera 1874	C					

(Continued overleaf.)

Table 6.2 (Continued)

* The form and the principal characteristics of the table of protests is based on Richards (1974), p.96; additional entries are based on sources documented in this text.

C = Protest against clearance and eviction
FR = Food riots, meal riots
I = Induction riot
OR = Opposition to recruitment
RPO= Recorded passive opposition
SS = Slaughter of sheep
WPI= Written protest against induction

(1) This also involved threatening letters.

(2) A total of 4834 sheep are recorded to have been 'lost' as a result of tenant hostility; J. Macdonald, 'On the agriculture of the County of Sutherland', Trans. Royal Highland and Agric. Soc. of Scotland, XII (1880), p.64.

(3) This also involved arson against peat stacks and threatening letters.

(4) Forty of the landlord's cattle destroyed here; SRO, AD56/309/3, 3.

** Firearms used
(+) Protest against catechist/schoolmaster
(++) Minister involved

'passive opposition' amongst tenantry is that a collective sensibility of discontent over changes in pasture rights or other estate improvements may have existed for some time before that sentiment of hostility (noted in the poetry, for example), took the physical forms represented in Table 6.2.

Richards has considered that three incidents - the events of 1792 ('a climacteric moment in the transformation of the Highlands'), the campaign against Patrick Sellar in 1813-1816, and the Culrain riots of 1820-1821, should be regarded as 'episodes of unusually ambitious resistance, marked by sustained and co-ordinated pressure' which together posed 'a generalised threat to the progress of the clearances'.75 Attention is given here to particular events only to highlight certain elements within the recurrent pattern. Three 'episodes' are discussed here; the Kildonan riots of 1813 as an illustration of opposition to clearance, the protests against clearance on the Coigach estates in 1853 as an example of successful though limited resistance, and the 1874 Bernera Riot because it demonstrates the changing nature of protest by the later 1800s. Of perhaps greater importance is the geography of the disturbances, the forms taken in protest, and the ideological claims motivating the acts themselves.

Like the insurrection of 1792, the Kildonan protests of 1813 were based on opposition to the expansion of commercial sheep-farming and the take-up by sheep of traditional grazing grounds. Additionally, the Kildonan protests were against the forced removal of tenants from the Strathnaver district to new lotted lands on the coast. Clearances began in 1806 and 1897 in an atmosphere of resentment and lack of co-operation from tenantry. From 1809 the improvement of the estates was under the direction of two Morayshire agriculturalists, William Young and Patrick Sellar. Resentment at removal flared into open conflict against authority in 1812. In December 1812 the strath of Kildonan was divided into three sheep farms, the tenantry having been given notice to quit eight months earlier. From January 1813, popular feeling was directed at the shepherds - 'those English Devils' as one tenant called them - and threats of violence (unrealised) were made against them as they were driven off the land. A petition was delivered to the Sheriff Substitute from 'the tenants of Kildonan' in which the tenants denied they were motivated by radical political views. Of greater importance is their claim to the land used as hill grazings.

> And therefore we expected that Mr. Young would
> give us the first offer of our present possessions

> or provide us such Larachew [from the Gaelic
> larach, situation in the sense of a holding] that
> we may have some Hill Grass as the Highlanders
> mostly depends on the Hill Grass.

The tenants also argued that they were permitted the
working of these lands because many had sons serving in the
army. What more generally alarmed the authorities,
however, was the reported widening of disturbances by the
involvement of tenants from other districts and the fact
that the protest, in aiming 'to drive the Sheeps out of the
country', threatened the whole basis to economic improvement in Sutherland and the northern Highlands. After
sheriff-officers had been deforced in February 1813,
Cranstoun the Sheriff-Depute of Sutherland arranged for
troops to be despatched from Fort George. The impending
arrival of this force ended resistance in March 1813.76
The Kildonan 'Rebellion' illustrates many of the
'classic' features of protest against clearance in the
nineteenth-century Highlands. The authorities were alarmed
both by the spirit of opposition and by its organisation.
Economic improvement demanded a willing tenantry. Young
wrote in February 1813 how 'such a set of savages is not to
be found in the wilds of America . . . if Lord and Lady
Stafford do not put it in my power to quell this banditti
we may bid adieu to all improvement'. Important, too, was
the widespread publicity of the event even although the
protest itself was a failure. But the issues had been
brought to public attention. Most crucial was the repeated
claim to the land itself and to established ways of land
use. Patrick Sellar noted how the Kildonan rioters argued
'they were entitled to keep possession of their Grounds and
would allow no shepherd to come to the country'. Selkirk
argued that Kildonan people possessed 'so much of the old
Highland Spirit as to think the land their own'.

> According to the ideas handed down to them from
> their ancestors, and long prevalent among high and
> low throughout the Highlands, they were only
> defending their rights and resisting a ruinous,
> unjust and tyranical encroachment on their
> property.77

In this we have perhaps the crux of the problem: protest
was the result of irreconcilable ideological differences
between the moral economy of a tenantry for whom land was
inalienably theirs through occupation (though with no
legality to their claim) and the political economy of the
improving classes for whom legal right of removal, hindered

364

by opposition and deforcement, was carried out by force tempered by public opinion. The fact that dissent was directed at the shepherds and farmers not at the landlords (a point made of clearance poetry above) may hint also at a residual deference amongst Highlanders for whom landlords were perceived (wrongly) as providing patriarchal leadership.

This pattern of resistance and the characteristics of protest against clearance as a four-stage model (Table 6.1) was repeated throughout the Highlands in the nineteenth century. In some protest there was more widespread violence as at Culrain in 1820-1821 where women were bayoneted and at Greenyards in 1854 where contemporary commentators recorded 'the slaughter' as police baton-charged the crowd seriously injuring several women. In most cases, the attempted restriction upon the actions of authority failed although each event increasingly drew the depressed position of the tenantry to the attention of wider audiences. But in Coigach in 1852 and 1853, however, resistance was more successful.

On the less remunerative and over-crowded lands of the north-west, the problem lay in the twin matters of land hunger and low rentals. Clearance of part of Coigach estate began in 1852 with the removal of eighty tenants and the agreed relinquishing of hill grazings. The intention was to clear the 'surplus' tenants and improve the standard of agriculture. It was not successful. Sheriff-officers were deforced in serving the writs. There was further and greater resistance in 1853. The factor, Andrew Scott, considered that 'the people in that district have lost all respect for Constituted Authority'. What is true, however, of the Coigach case is that local authority was unable to enforce the law; 'We have not a local police force of sufficient strength to protect the officers in the service of the summonses [wrote the Sheriff-Substitute to Loch] and I doubt, from all that I have seen and heard, whether a reinforcement from Glasgow even will be able to do so'.78 At the same time, public opinion was mounting. Coigach figured in newspapers such as the North British Daily Mail, the Northern Ensign, and the Scotsman. Works such as Donald Ross's Real Scottish Grievances did much to raise public consciousness of the issues (Figure 6.2). It was the fact of greater public sensitivity to Highland issues that stayed the landlord's hand at Coigach; that and because the tenants were 'unduly obstinate' and the estates too distant for the forces of authority to have effective control. Nevertheless, the Coigach tenants did win. At a time of increased public interest and political involvement in Highland matters, the affair may justifiably be seen as

Figure 6.2   The iconography of eviction: eviction of tenantry from Ross's Real Scottish Grievances (Glasgow, 1854) (Reproduced with the permission of the Mitchell Library)

a prelude to the Land Wars of the 1880s. Closer in time and form to these events was the Bernera Riot of 1874.

This event centred upon a dispute about the appropriation by Donald Munro, factor to Matheson (proprietor of Lewis), of grazing land belonging to Bernera islanders. The principal grievance of Lewis crofters was the small size of their holdings; holdings which had to be continuously cropped owing to the number of people dependent upon them whilst adjacent farms used once cultivated areas for pasture only. Disputes over boundary dykes and straying stock were common. Traditional pasture lands on the Lewis mainland had been removed in 1850 and in 1872 further grazing lands were appropriated and restrictions laid down on the use of the remaining areas. In 1874 all grazings remaining on Lewis were removed; the tenants refused to co-operate, and Munro began proceedings to remove them completely from Bernera. The sheriff-officer serving the summons was deforced and after one of the ringleaders was arrested, a crowd marched to Stornoway to confront Matheson who, sympathising with them, took no action. Munro had taken all his actions without the authority of his employer. He lost his post. The riot was seen at the time as a breakthrough for the rights of the common people, and has been more recently considered as 'a first victory for the Island crofters against officialdom'.79 It was a victory because of that increased consciousness amongst crofters of their own political strength, because of their belief in the traditional claim to land and in part also because the issues of land reform and rural social protest were far more politicised as public issues by the 1870s than during the sporadic episodes of the 1780s and 1820s.

Within this changing context of opposition, several points merit examination in reviewing the evidence for a tradition of protest in the century from 1792. Leaving aside the Land Wars, the geography of disturbance reveals a marked concentration in the eastern districts of Ross and Cromarty and Sutherland (Figure 6.1). Most of the protests against clearance of tenantry or the enclosure of hill grazings for sheep were located in the fertile straths seen by Lowland shepherds and Highland landlords as the best areas for the new commercial pastoralism. Elsewhere in the Highlands, incidents of disorder show no such relative clustering leaving aside the food riots of 1793–1796 and 1847 in which the challenge to authority was over setting 'the right price' to food and involved most commonly staying the transport of grainstuffs from ports and markets at times of shortage. Resistance to clearance, and, in the case of the riots on the Sutherland estates, to schemes for improvement involving new divisions of labour may, in part, have derived emphasis from support between the different communities involved, especially in parts of Easter Ross and east Sutherland where communication was easier.

Such mutual understanding of each other's position in opposing material changes was apparent in 1792 for several places in Easter Ross. Recognition of the context of resistance may have been wider still: the protestors in Culrain in eastern Ross and Cromarty pledged assistance in 1820 to the people of Unapool over thirty miles distant in west Sutherland 'if they had the spirit to resist'. Geographical proximity may thus not always have been important in stimulating that 'folk memory' surrounding and motivating the events. In the initial attempt to serve eviction notices at Greenyards in 1854, the sheriff-officers were deforced and carried to the Braes of Dounie, the site of the Culrain riots of 1820. It is possible that the relatively minor geographical constraints imposed by the topography and settlement pattern of the north-eastern Highlands allowed for the greater organisation of opposition amongst the peasantry in those regions. In the north and west, concerted action was more difficult to orchestrate until dispersion into coastal locations and crofting townships in the later 1800s allowed for the easier exchange of knowledge on incidents of protest and, later, a more coherent general reaction.

Highland social protest was to a large degree women's protest. In twenty-five incidents of opposition to clearance from Lochaber in 1782 to Greenyards in 1854, women played a prominent role in sixteen of them (Table 6.2). The involvement of women in the front line of opposition seemed to result from belief (quickly shown to be false) that they would be immune from attack. In the Ross-shire disturbances of 1853 and 1854 Mackenzie, the Sheriff of the county, considered that the chief cause of disorder was the women who were not only responsible for organising opposition but also for the commonplace acts of humiliation when the sheriff-officer was stripped naked and his summons papers burnt.80 Quite why Highland women should have acted as they did in opposition is uncertain. Their reaction was consistent with the role of women in other periods of pre-industrial protest, a reaction stemming perhaps from the central place of women in the management of the peasant domestic economy. One author has suggested that the role of women in Highland protest was an expression of much older beliefs concerning the matriarchal basis to Celtic society.81 Most historians agree that ministers played a minor role in the context of physical resistance. With few exceptions who may have sanctioned the clearances or, like Donald MacCallum who supported the tenantry, the clergy commonly, to quote Richards, 'cast their influence against the spontaneous resistance of the people'. This fact may explain why popular evangelicism took such a firm hold in the Highlands before 1843. By the later nineteenth century, those ministers who both expressly opposed the clearances and sanctioned the resistance to them had a greater degree of popular political support for their opposition, through the Free Church, a sympathetic public, and in the politics of land reform.

In review, Richards argues that the record and pattern of popular Highland resistance before 1882 performed three important tasks, albeit that such resistance he elsewhere noted was inchoate, dispersed, sporadic, spontaneous, and never a continuous threat to the landlords: 'it attracted public attention which eventually had a cumulative effect; it checked the full exercise of landlord power; and it sabotaged plans of economic reconstruction'.82 Given these effects, the various forms taken in protest, and the fact, too, that public opinion and other matters contextual to the actual incidents were of increasing significance during the 1800s, the question of a motivating or legitimating ideology informing these individual acts as part of a tradition of resistance is more complex than at first appears. Smout has advanced the idea of 'the Highland ideology' in which 'the crofter put home before wealth, the possession of land before the dubious opportunity to gain enrichment by a better income as an industrial worker, or even as a landholder overseas'.83 In contrast, Richards has claimed that there was 'a fundamental lack of a rallying ideology for the common Highlanders' or, at least, that opposition was 'reactionary' and 'backward-looking' in seeking only to protect established ways.

> The people believed that they had traditional
> tribal rights to their land and that the landlords
> were usurping those rights, and acting against
> real justice. This basic assumption was not given
> effective political expression until the 1870s.
> So far as one can tell, much of the thinking in
> the Highlands was essentially backward-looking.
> There was much discussion of lost rights - but
> little radical thought was devoted to any consider-
> ation of the future of the Highland society and
> economy - or even to any notion of an alternative
> to landlordism.84

Highland protest in the century from 1780 may be better explained by reference to the notions of 'inherent' and 'derived' ideology. Central to the inherent ideology of

369

Highlanders was the expressed belief in their customary occupation of land. And it is a notion that persists throughout the century as before and after. It appears as a claim in most of the incidents of resistance to clearance. It was a customary belief of particular localities and one recognised across the Highlands. The belief finds its expression in clearance poetry, in the notion of duthchas, and in incidents of protest and resistance from 1882 onwards. 'Land' was the predominant issue, expressed variously as traditional grazing rights, a remembered occupance, and even as something to be reclaimed through 'land raids' (see below). The key difficulty lay, however, in the fact that this inherent belief was without foundation in law as a recognised custom or in security of tenure. The constituent ties of the clan system through which land was distributed offered little support as material and social changes replaced a moral economy with issues of political economy, land 'values', and class consciousness. To a degree, Highland protest was 'backward-looking', a residual element of a new social formation, if by backward we mean that such opposition was rooted in claims to traditional rights that practitioners of any new method of landholding would have found archaic and outmoded. But in the context of the historic present, expressed beliefs in rights of occupation of land (though not its ownership) should also be seen as 'forward-looking' in the sense that Highlanders claimed such rights in order to maintain a continued presence, to be allowed to hold and work land in the future as they had done in the past. At the same time, Highland protest was increasingly legitimated by events and attitudes contextual both to the region proper and to the actual incidents themselves. In part this was evident only 'in formation' in the form of religious revivalism but by the 1840s and 1850s, counter-hegemony was motivated by a class consciousness stemming from material change, was evident within the crofter community particularly, and apparent in the direct action of the common people against authority in the form of food riots. In combination with this political consciousness from within, the principal derived influence upon the context of Highland protest by the second half of the nineteenth century was public opinion and political pressure from without. Some episodes of protest were also motivated by the ruin of arable crops on restricted holdings. And it is arguable that the relative economic prosperity of the 1860s and 1870s may have weakened the spirit of resistance. But what is undeniable is that with greater awareness and political action from without and an increased class consciousness from within, the context of

social protest had changed by the nineteenth century. This
is not to suggest that the form of protest or the legitimating beliefs behind opposition changed. Because land and
land rights remained the principal issue, we may talk of
Highland protest as a single tradition of opposition
informed by an inherent ideology, punctuated by moments of
violent resistance and more and more influenced by the
later 1800s by outside events and wider questions of
politics and class.

> Thus, whereas in 1850 the popular cry was,
> essentially, that the landlords should be stopped
> in their work of eviction, by 1880 the initiative
> had changed hands. Thenceforward the crofters
> took the battle to the landlords.85

The Highland Land Wars and the wider context of protest, 1882–c.1930

The Highland 'Land Wars' that began in Skye in 1882 and
continued until the 1940s (if by then only intermittently)
may be divided for convenience into three periods: an
initial phase from 1882 to 1886, a period punctuated by the
work of the Napier Commission in 1883–1884 but throughout
characterised by rent strikes and claims to traditional
grazing rights; a second period from 1886 to about 1896 in
which reaction to the Napier Commission and the 1886
Crofters' Act and continued landlessness was evident in
land 'raids' and in increased military intervention; and a
more protracted phase from 1897 which followed the establishment of the Congested Districts Board.86 Land raids
continued as late as 1948 but protest over the appropriation of ancestral lands and their use by landlords as sheep
farms or deer forests was particularly apparent in the
period 1882 to c.1930. A number of factors highlight this
period and the land wars as crucial. Firstly, protest
shifted in its geography away from the farming regions of
eastern Ross and Cromarty and Sutherland towards the
crofting north and west, to Lewis and Skye especially
(Figure 6.1). Secondly, the forms of protest changed from
resistance to eviction towards more direct action against
the landlords, chiefly the occupation of hitherto appropriated land, and refusal to pay rent. Thirdly, this period
was marked by greater military involvement than earlier
protest as well as by continued legislation on the 'land
problem'. Most important was the wider context in which
this later protest took place. This context was the result
of several factors in combination; the influence of Irish

land agitation and political issues, issues that allowed the emergent class consciousness of the crofting population to find expression in institutions of counter-hegemony such as the Highland Land Law Reform Association (HLLRA) and in 'Crofters' Party' members of parliament; and the involvement and role of Highland newspapers and Gaelic and Highland societies in directing and reflecting public opinion and questions of class consciousness.

The events of the 1880s and later took place within a depressed agricultural economy, in the Highlands as throughout Britain.87 The 1860s and 1870s had witnessed an upturn in the economy of the crofting regions, although it was a prosperity relative to more usual hardship and one resting on uncertain foundations. These foundations were shaken by a bad harvest in the Highlands in 1881; by poor rewards from the east coast herring fishing and storms in the western Highlands which severely damaged native boats and limited returns from local fishing; and, given potato crop failure, by a rapid rise in grain prices. None of these factors was alone sufficient to motivate opposition, but as background they cannot be neglected. In some respects, they directly influenced the form of protest. Poor harvests and low prices for limited stock, for example, highlighted only too well the restricted holdings of crofters in contrast to the larger extents of sheep farm and deer forest. And given the necessity for temporary employment outwith the crofting regions, seasonal migration of labour influenced the times of the year in which confrontation occurred.

The 'Land Wars' are generally recognised to have begun in the Braes district of Skye in 1882. But earlier events - the Bernera Riot, the Leckmelm evictions of 1879 in Lochbroom where tenants were forced to become employees in a remodelled estate economy or be evicted, and the refusal in 1880-1881 of the crofters of Valtos and Elishader townships on the Kilmuir estates in Skye to pay rent given continued rack-renting of their holdings - illustrate that spirit and continuity of discontent underlying the later 1800s before the incidents of 1882. And the passing of the Irish Land Act in 1881 which had conceded several of the demands of the Irish Land League - principally security of tenure and fair rents - was important in further raising the consciousness of Highlanders on matters of agitation and opposition to the authority of landlords. The principal events making up the land wars have been outlined in Table 6.3. It is likely this table under-represents the actual incidents of protest and it is unlikely, too, that all events will ever be fully documented. Several of the entries include periods of protest marked by a continued

Table 6.3

The principal events of the Highland land wars, c.1882–c.1930*

Location and year	Basis to protest	Form taken in protest
Valtos, Skye 1880–1881	Rack-renting	Rent strikes
Braes, Skye 1881–1884(+)	'Grazing rights' (1)	Petition; rent strikes;'confrontation' (2)
Glendale, Skye 1882–1884(+)	Grazing rights; 'tenurial restrictions' (3)	Petition; rent strikes; confrontation
Rogart 1882(+)	Eviction	Confrontation
Lochcarron 1882(+)	Eviction	Confrontation
Strome Ferry 1883		Sabattarian Riot

[Autumn–Winter 1883: Establishment of the Highland Land Law Reform Association]

Barra 1883	Tenurial restrictions	'Land seizure' (4)
Tiree 1883–1884	Grazing rights	Rent strikes
South Uist 1884(+)	Grazing rights	Land seizure; rent strikes
North Uist 1884	Grazing rights	Petition
Melbost, Lewis 1884(+)	Grazing rights	Land seizure – 'harassment' (5)

[September 1884: HLLRA's manifesto outlined in 'The Dingwall Programme']
[1884: Napier Commission publishes its Report]

Lewis 1884–1885	Grazing rights	Harassment; rent strikes
Skye 1884–1886(+)	Grazing rights	Land seizure; rent strikes

[September 1884: Police in Skye armed]

(Continued overleaf.)

Table 6.3 (Continued)

[November 1884: Marines in Skye under Sheriff Ivory]

Fort William 1885(+)	Eviction	Confrontation
Ardnamurchan 1885	Grazing rights	Harassment; rent strikes

[1886: Crofters Act; Crofters Commission; 4 Crofter MPs elected to Westminster]

Kintail 1886	'Land shortage'(6)	Land seizure
South Uist 1886	Tenurial rights	Land seizure
Benbecula 1886	Land shortage	Land seizure
Tiree 1886–1887(+)	Land shortage	Land seizure
Skye 1886(+)	Land shortage	Land seizure; rent strikes

[October 1886: Sheriff Ivory's Skye expedition]

Park, Lewis 1886–1887(+)	Land shortage	Land seizure; 'attack on stock'(7)
Borve, Lewis 1887(+)	Land shortage	Land seizure
Aignish, Lewis 1887–1888(+)	Land shortage	Land seizure; petition; attack on stock; confrontation
Lewis 1887–1888(+)	Land shortage	'Dyke-breaking'(8)
Clachmore, Sutherland 1887	Land shortage; grazing rights	Land seizure; dyke-breaking
Saddell and Skipness 1888	Eviction	Confrontation
Clyth 1888–1889	Land shortage	Land seizure

[Withdrawal of troops from Lewis]

Table 6.3 (Continued)

Ullapool 1889	Land shortage	Land seizure
Glendale, Skye 1888–1889(+)	Land shortage	Land seizure
Berneray 1890, 1892(+)	Land shortage	Land seizure
Park, Lewis 1891–1892(+)	Land shortage	Land seizure
Lynedale, Skye 1892(+)	Land shortage	Land seizure
Kilmuir, Skye 1893	Land shortage	Land seizure
Plockton 1893		Sabattarian riot
Lewis 1895	Land shortage	Land seizure; dyke-breaking
North Uist 1895–1896(+)	Eviction	Confrontation

[1897: Congested Districts Board established]

Embo 1898	Eviction	Confrontation
Lewis, Harris, Skye, North Uist, South Uist	Land shortage	Land seizure; dyke-breaking
Tiree 1899–1929(+)		

[1911: Small Landowners (Scotland) Act;
Crofters Commission and Congested Districts Board abolished;
Board of Agriculture for Scotland established]
[1919: Land Settlement (Scotland) Act]

Knoydart 1948	Land shortage	Land seizure

(Continued overleaf.)

Table 6.3 (Continued)

* Based on incidents recorded by Hunter (1976), pp.131–206 and events documented in the following MSS: SRO; AF 67; GD 1/36; GD 40; HH 1/–; AD 56/5.

(+) Incidents in which deforcement took place and police and/or troops called for.

(1) By this is meant that protest was based on claims to traditionally-recognised grazing grounds that had been appropriated, usually for sheep, at some earlier date.

(2) A catch-all term to denote physical violence resulting from the meeting of a mob of peasants with a law officer, land agent, or factor.

(3) Protest made against clauses in lease which, for example, restricted the areas from which seaweed or peat could be obtained, forbade the keeping of dogs, or limited the amounts of land to be ploughed.

(4) The illegal occupation of land, usually the landlords' but occasionally non-cooperative tenants'.

(5) This varied from blocking the roads with boulders, or threatening letters, to the burning of hay ricks or buildings, usually directed against the landlords but occasionally against tenants who did not join the Land League.

(6) An expressed feeling that the individual's holdings were too limited and that crofters' arable land in general was inadequate in extent.

(7) Slaughter of livestock (see Table 6.1); usually in the land wars, the killing of deer (as at Park in 1887), but also involving the killing or maiming of the landlords' sheep or horses.

(8) The over-turning of turf or stone dykes and the tearing-up of wire fences.

refusal to pay rent, the constantly-recurring destruction of boundaries or encroachment on to landlords' property. In many of these incidents, law-officers were also deforced or the forces of authority - civil or military or both - were employed at the outset. But throughout the period, land, as appropriated rights, or as something to be occupied given restricted holdings or as waste to be ploughed up, remained the central issue.

In the case of the Braes incidents in 1882, the land at issue was an extent of grazing in Ben Lee which, since the early 1800s, had been beyond the officially-recognised boundaries of the three townships at its foot. To the people of these townships, however, Ben Lee was an integral part of their holdings and always had been. Refused a plea to have these lands returned when the lease came up for renewal in 1881, the response of the tenants was refusal to pay rent. Given the earlier Valtos rent strike, this was not a novel means of opposition. But what characterised the Braes affair as critically important was the refusal to pay rent not to force a rent reduction (as at Valtos), but to force through political and economic action the return of appropriated land to which crofters felt they had a moral claim. And equally important, as Hunter notes 'by recognising that a rent strike could be used not merely to enforce a rent reduction but to coerce a proprietor into giving more land to small tenants, the Braes crofters had adapted the principal weapon of the Irish Land League to Highland circumstances'. The Braes events unfolded along the lines of incidents before and since (Table 6.1). Eviction notices were given. Deforcement of the serving officers took place. Following deforcement, the Sheriff of Inverness-shire, William Ivory, requested and got Glasgow policemen to assist in the execution of the law, local police being too few. On 19th April 1882, after arresting the ringleaders of the rent strike, the contingent of police was stoned and several tenants severely injured in the series of running charges and skirmishes known now as the 'Battle of the Braes'.88 At the same time, other parts of Skye were expressing discontent at the authority of the landlords. At Glendale in north-west Skye, protest was against tenurial restriction - the fact that tenants still had exacting labour dues, for example - as well as over claims to 'hill land which was taken from us'. A rent strike began in March 1882. The situation was aggravated by the handing-over of a farm in Waterstein to the estate factor, Donald MacDonald, at a time when the crofting tenantry had petitioned for its return. The action of the tenants was to drive their stock on to the disputed grazings. Threats were made against MacDonald that his stock would be driven over cliffs into the sea. What also characterised the Glendale protests was concerted action by tenants to ensure a united front. The below notice was put up at Skinidin, one of the townships of Glendale, in March 1882: 'Any of the Tenants of Skineden [sic] who will pay Rent, not only his house and property but his life will be taken away or any one backsliding'.89 Similar notices and threats against those tenants who did pay rent or refuse to join the HLLRA were made on numerous occasions. At Glendale and in other places – North Uist in 1884 and Kilmuir in 1885, for example – actions were taken against fellow tenants (burning hay ricks, property damaged, stock mutilated), though no instance of assassination is known. But the fact that such action took place within the tenantry (and that there were many in positions of authority who sympathised with the crofters) illustrates the danger of caricaturing the land wars as the reaction of a 'backward-looking' tenantry uniformly opposed to the actions of authority per se, landlord or sheriff-officer, without recognising the issues of class and political representation and even of opposition 'from within' that informed and limited consensus claims to land. By the summer and autumn of 1882, Skye was beyond the control of civil authority. Law officers in Portree hoped that discontent would be defused by the departure of the men to the herring fishing although as one reported, the involvement of Highlanders with Irish fishing was a cause for concern given fears over Irish agitators: 'I am confident that all is quiet till winter when the men will return from the Irish fishings – what will be done then I consider depends on the state of Ireland'. But that summer there was 'a thrift of fish'; fewer men departed than usual. Extra police were recruited by November 1882. Joshua Maclennan, procurator fiscal in Portree considered that unless unrest in Skye was firmly dealt with 'the present state of things [in Glendale] is likely to spread not only over the whole of Skye but also over the whole Outer Hebrides from Lewis to Barra and also over the whole West Coast of Scotland'.90 There is evidence that tenants in any one township or island watched developments elsewhere. Archibald Chisholm, procurator fiscal in Lochmaddy North Uist wrote thus to Sheriff Ivory: 'The people of the district are not excited over their agitation about land, they are watching the course of events in Skye, and I believe the show of force made there will keep [them] in awe'.91 Events proved Maclennan correct.

Protest was both geographically widespread and well organised. The Glendale tenantry were armed with scythes lashed to poles, had sentries posted on hill tops ('each sentry has got a horn to give notice to the other tenants if any one is seen coming'), were 'united as one man' and were prepared to meet force with force: 'it was the avowed intention of the people to meet any force being sent to the district to serve writs with determined opposition'.92 In part, the tensions of 1883 were ameliorated by the arrest in February without violent confrontation of several wanted crofters in Glendale, but in being imprisoned as were their fellows at Braes and released to widespread public acclaim, crofters' leaders became 'martyrs' to the popular cause. More important in 1883 was the establishment of the Highland Land Law Reform Association, and of the royal commission of inquiry into 'the condition of the Crofters and Cottars in the Highlands and Islands of Scotland' under the chairmanship of Lord Napier. The first was important because it institutionalised the existing political lobby in support of crofters and gave to the crofters' movement a political and organisational structure – 'attributes which were to enable it to transcend the limitations initially imposed on it by geographical circumstances'.93 The second was important because the possibility of legislative action on the question of land grievances stilled the violence. But as this proved false illusion, the authority and actions of the HLLRA increased as did the scale and extent of unrest.

What was distinctive about the protest that immediately followed the Napier Commission was not only its widespread nature (Table 6.3) but also the use of terror tactics by crofters. To meet this, the authorities took two steps: the first, in September 1884, was to arm the Skye police; the second involved for the first time the large-scale use of troops as a means of asserting the law. The Skye military expedition of 1884-1885 was the first such force in the Highlands since the Jacobite Rebellion. It comprised a troopship, H.M.S. Assistance, and the gunboats Forester and Banterer, with 350 marines and 100 bluejackets, and the steamer Lochiel carrying Ivory and his party. Overall, however, the expedition was a failure; troops were not allowed to perform duties normally executed by the civil authorities, although they did assist in restoring order in the serving of individual eviction notices.94

Throughout 1884 and 1885 unrest continued, rent strikes being the most widespread form of opposition. What lent the events of protest and atmosphere of opposition additional strength was the election in 1885 of four Crofters' Party MPs to Westminister. By 1885, parliamentary authority was ready to consider the Highland land problem and to propose, in the 1886 Crofters' Act and

the establishment of the Crofters' Commission, a legislative reform which affected all those holdings consisting
of arable land held with rights of common pasture where
tenants paid, annually, money rents of less than £30.

The Crofters' Act was a success in that it guaranteed
security of tenure and gave crofters the right to claim
compensation for any improvements made on the holdings. In
two respects, however, it was a failure: it made almost no
provision for making more land available and, in so doing,
automatically excluded cottars from consideration. The
result was renewed protest chiefly by cottars in the form
of land raids. One such event in 1886 led to the deforcement of forty police officers on Tiree in July and the
arrest, after 250 marines had assisted police, of eight
crofters. Their imprisonment raised a storm of protest and
petitions from Highland and Radical societies in the
Lowlands. The fact that a military force of such size
should be used points to a renewed vigour on the part of
authority to quell disturbance, but it is clear also that
marines were seen as something of a last resort and were
used because the forces of civil authority were inadequate
in number and too widely distributed to be useful when
whole districts and islands were in a state of unrest.95
Military action was, however, a commonplace in 1886 and
1887. Sheriff Ivory led a second Skye expedition in 1886.
The below resolution of the Glendale crofters of May 1886
summarises many of the claims made by tenantry. In the
eyes of Alexander MacDonald, the principal factor on the
island, it represented 'a state of utter anarchy and
lawlessness unparalleled for centuries'.

> The Crofters of Glendale are resolved to go in a
> body to the Parish of Bracadale and reinstate the
> descendants of the evicted in the Arable land
> which will be allotted amongst them: that we are
> firm in this resolve and will not withdraw from
> our purpose until turned back by a stronger force
> than ourselves.96

Numerous arrests were made in Skye in 1886, including that
of the Rev. Donald MacCallum who was arrested on a charge
of 'unlawful agitation' and 'inciting class hatred'. By
the winter of 1886-1887, the combined action of the
military and the police had quelled open resistance in Skye
if not stemmed the recurring clandestine destruction of
dykes and fences.

In Lewis, however, where crofts were smaller and
temporary employment more important to the local economy,
the relative failure of the herring fishing in the years

380

prior to 1887 had placed the native population in a state of destitution. The failure of the fishing 'has caused, for two successive seasons, the return penniless from the East Coast of hundreds - nay thousands - of able-bodied men whose position but a few years ago was one of affluence'.97 The consequence was renewed agitation over land, evident in land raids or action against occupying stock. At Park in south-east Lewis in 1887, 700 men, principally cottars, drove deer out of the Park deer forest and killed at least 100 of them, perhaps 300. In the eyes of Sheriff Fraser of Stornoway, the flouting of estate authority, the scale of the action and the use of arms demanded swift response, preferably by military force. For Fraser this display of force was doubly necessary to deter further protest amongst the tenantry of Clashmore in Assynt, Sutherland, then 'in a state of great unrest'. Eighty men of the Royal Scots came from Stornoway to the Park area and H.M.S. <u>Jackal</u> and H.M.S. <u>Seahorse</u> brought parties of marines. H.M.S. <u>Ajax</u>, with 400 marines, was disabled en route from Greenock and never arrived. The leaders were arrested but found 'not guilty of mobbing and rioting' and were released. The Rev. Donald MacCallum celebrated the Park deer raid in his poem '<u>Ruaig an Fheidh</u>' in which he wrote 'We are no plunderers, as is stated in lies; we are brave people being ruined by want'.98

The claim that crofters and cottars 'had come to retake the homes of their ancestors' was made again and again in land raids of the later 1880s and 1890s. Barra crofters were resolved in 1888 to ignore civil authority 'until every inch of land available for cultivation is occupied by tenants', and unless their grievances were swiftly met, 'they will be forced to apply their ploughing implements to the land lying waste - for which they are willing to pay a reasonable rent'.99 Events at Aignish in Lewis in 1888 illustrate these claims although the scale of protest is not typical. Aignish sheep farm was claimed by the tenants of nearby townships 'to provide holdings for the starving landless cottars and their families in the district, whose ancestors had it under cultivation'.100 The planned appropriation of the farm by 1000 tenants was met by police, Royal Scots and marines, and after the Sheriff of Stornoway had read the Riot Act in Gaelic and in English the opposing parties met in bloody confrontation (Figure 6.3). The Aignish riot was the last of the land riots to take place on such a scale, although land raids, dyke breaking, and rent strikes continued in the 1890s and into the 1900s wherever the crofting population saw the retention as sheep farms of lands 'formerly tilled by their ancestors for centuries'. What characterised these later

Figure 6.3 The iconography of confrontation: the Sheriff of Stornoway reading the Riot Act at Aignish Farm
(Reproduced with the permission of the Illustrated London News Picture Library; from ILN, 21 January 1888)

events of protest, however, was the recognition by authority of the need for legislation on the land problem.101
This was slow in coming hence the continued protest but it
did come. The Congested Districts Board, founded in 1897,
was the first step. This Board allowed some assistance for
local industry in the north and west but was handicapped in
the longer term by financial restrictions. The 1911 Small
Landholders (Scotland) Act which abolished the Crofters'
Commission and the Congested Districts Board and set up a
Board of Agriculture for Scotland initially promised the
redistribution of crofting and farm lands, in the Hebrides
especially, but was likewise under-funded and depended to
too great a degree on the co-operation of those very
landlords whose lands would be re-organised. For this
reason the 1911 Act failed. Many of the land raids after
the 1914-1918 war drew additional strength from a feeling
that fighting for one's own land was more just than
fighting for one's country: 'We fought for this land in
France [declared one land raider in Lewis in 1919] and
we're prepared to die for it in Lewis'. The 1919 Land
Settlement (Scotland) Act extended the powers of the Board
of Agriculture and gradually, during the 1920s, land
settlement schemes eased over-crowding and allowed the
expansion of crofter holdings as sheep farms and deer
forests were broken up. By 1930 land raids were largely
unknown.

To a greater degree than the preceding century,
Highland protest in the period 1882 to c.1930 was influenced in its expression and extent by the geography and
economy of the area in which it took place. Seizure of
those lands and grazing grounds appropriated at some
earlier date to make way for sheep farm or deer forest was
a relatively easy matter in comparison with halting their
initial lay-out. The necessity for temporary employment
outwith the crofting region at times limited protest,
seasonally and in terms of men involved - women and boys
more than once deforced law officers when the men were at
the fishing. And the returns from fishing or other
temporary employment over good or bad seasons acted to
weaken or strengthen agitation. Principally, however, the
facts of geography and economy presented difficulties to
the civil authorities. On a local scale, dykes and fences
were easy to remove by concerted action at night but law
officers could not be spared to oversee their reconstruction and maintenance or to guard landlords' stock. More
generally, gunboats and military force had to be employed
because of the difficulties of travel and communication, a
fact recognised by those in authority throughout the
period. In places, the presence of troops only aggravated

383

the protest - as Tyvory wrote to Lord Lothian in 1895: 'The real administrative difficulty lies in determining in which cases the presence of police is likely to suggest and foster resistance, and in which it is more likely to repress or overawe it'.102 But the fact that troops were used in such numbers points, in the closing decades of the nineteenth century especially, to the renewal of authority by 'rule' rather more than by coercive means.

In most respects, the crofters' wars were little different from events in that tradition of earlier protest examined above. Above all, the inherent ideology on the question of land as ancestral claim and present 'right' was unchanging. This widespread ideological commitment was without foundation in law, but as motivating belief for the land raids (as for earlier opposition to eviction), claims to traditionally-recognised lands and to customary practices of management provided the principal legitimation for protest in the 1800s as much as they had in the 1780s. This belief is exemplified in the below words by the Rev. Donald MacCallum:

> There are two kinds of laws. The laws which are
> the moral law, and laws of expediency - the land
> law. The moral law was never made, it is. The
> land law was made to suit circumstances. When the
> circumstances change so must the law. They are
> made for man, not man for them. The land for the
> people is the principle.103

Given that Highlanders' inherent ideology was consistently felt (if at times differently expressed), the reason why the protest of the later nineteenth century was more successful in achieving legislative recognition lies in factors exogenous to the Highlands.

The politics of Highland land reform focus in part upon the connection with Ireland's land agitation. To many in authority during the protest of the 1880s, Irish agitation was the cause of Highland disturbance.

> Ireland was certainly the origin of the Skye
> agitation. The return of the fishermen from
> Kinsale immediately preceded the first note of
> discontent in the Braes, near Portree; an Irish
> emissary, Mr. McHugh, followed, and his presence
> was succeeded by the lawless outbreak in
> Glendale; publications of socialistic tendency
> were, and still are, widely circulated among the
> population through agencies in London and other
> large towns, some of which bear to have been

printed in Dublin; cartoons, showing mitred
ecclesiastics crushing a snake marked "Landlordism", were distributed; and, finally, local
agents were employed, and liberally paid from some
source which does not appear.104

The principal link between Irish agitation and Highland
land issues was John Murdoch who not only saw in the Irish
and Highland land question the foundation to a political
(and cultural) nationalism, but who also, with John Stuart
Blackie, helped shape the increasing public sympathy on
Highland affairs into institutional form. Murdoch's
objective was to encourage crofters to overthrow 'the
vicious land system' and to ensure that Gaelic societies in
the urban Lowlands and farther afield involved themselves
in the struggle.105 To this end Murdoch helped found in
1878 the Federation of Celtic Societies which brought
together a number of such bodies in Scotland and
elsewhere. Although the Federation was itself of little
consequence as a means of political reform, it provided as
did Murdoch's The Highlander a basis to the later actions
of the HLLRA.

The HLLRA, the principal institution working on behalf
of crofters, followed the example of the Irish Land League
in working for fair rents, durability of tenure, and
compensation for improvements. From August 1883, branches
were established throughout the Highlands (the HLLRA was
initially based in London). These local associations may
be seen as a means of counter-hegemony in the context of
Highland protest; as the editor of the Oban Times, Duncan
Cameron, noted in September 1883, 'The opposing force is
thoroughly and efficiently organised and it is only by
thorough and efficient counter-organisation that it can be
successfully coped with'.106 The first branch was established in Glendale, Skye, on 5 December 1883. By June 1884
the HLLRA had a membership of about 5000. Their expressed
intent was 'to effect by unity of purpose and action such
changes in the land laws as will promote the welfare of the
people' and their 'Dingwall Programme' of September 1884
outlined radical proposals to redistribute land in favour
of crofters. What gave the HLLRA greater power was the
enfranchisement of crofters under the Third Reform Bill
and, in 1885, four 'Crofters' Party' MPs – D.H. MacFarlane
(Argyll); Charles Fraser-MacKintosh (Inverness-shire);
Roderick MacDonald (Ross-shire); and Gavin Clark (Caithness) – were returned to a parliament by then devoting more
time to Highland affairs than any of its predecessors since
the 1740s. In 1886 the HLLRA was re-named the Highland
Land League. Internal dissensions split the group,

however, during the later 1880s. By 1895, the Highland Land League had ceased to exist (although a new Highland Land League was established in 1909, which, after it became the Scots National League in 1921, was one of the founding organisations of the Scottish National Party). Over the period 1883 to 1895, however, the Highland Land League was a vital means of articulating the sentiment of crofters within wider political circles. It was successful because it forced the Highland question 'to the forefront of British politics'. It did so by providing an institutional basis for notions of ancestral lands and land hunger, and by allowing questions of class and expressions of class consciousness on Highland issues (from within and without the region) to be realised politically: to become 'emergent' features of a new social formation rather than remain alternative oppositional forms expressed in a poetry of dissent, in apolitical riotous assembly, or through popular religion. The Highland Land League did not ignore these other notions however: many of their meetings, for example, were held on the sites of earlier revivals; the HLLRA had the widespread support of the Free Church in the Highland elections of 1890; and many agitators sought justification in the scriptures for their expressed claims to land.107

The HLLRA was also successful because it could draw upon a strong vein of support for Highland affairs from within society generally. Partly, this was the result of the 'discovery' of the Highlands by royalty and tourists, itself evident in the sentimentalisation in art and literature particularly during the 1880s of Highlanders as loyal and worthy peasants, and the treatment of Highland scenery as playground rather than moral landscape. Chiefly, however, it was the result of newspapers and journals which drew the events of the land wars to public notice and the work of Gaelic societies in the Lowlands in agitating for land reform.

There were a number of Gaelic periodicals published, chiefly in the Lowlands, from the early 1800s, many of which in the later nineteenth century carried information on events of protest.108 Many of these were short-lived however. Most important in providing radical support through the press was John Murdoch's The Highlander which ran from 1873 to 1881. The Highlander carried articles in Gaelic, was openly outspoken in support of Highland land reform and worked to foster, even to re-awaken, a collective sensibility in the Gaelic mind between tir is teanga, land and language.109 It provided an outlet for men such as J.S. Blackie to acquire funds for the Celtic Chair at Edinburgh University and publish articles on a range of subjects to do with the Highlands. Other newspapers and journals provided news on Highland affairs - The Oban Times, The Celtic Magazine (1875-1888), The Highland Echo (1877-1878), The Highland Monthly, (1889-1893), for example.

Rather more important in stimulating the public conscience about Highland matters - destitution in the 1840s, protest in the 1880s - were national papers such as The Scotsman or the more radical Glasgow-based North British Daily Mail. Hanham has argued that 'it was not until the foundation of The Highlander in 1873 and the development of Radical policy by the Oban Times under Duncan Cameron that there was a recognised medium for the expression of Highland discontent' - a view which later research has substantiated although the place of agitation poetry as a form of journalism should not be minimised. But in arguing thus and in noting 'Whether these papers had a large following in the Highlands may be doubted',110 Hanham neglects the by then vital fact that it was not so much in the Highlands that these and other newspapers had their effect as in the urban Lowlands where they could draw upon and reflect the support of Gaelic societies, migrant Highlanders, and the shared interests of particular class groups.

In the context of social protest against landlessness or, earlier, over clearance for sheep, Gaelic and Highland migrant communities not only provided a source of opposition through clearance and land agitation poetry, but also and more importantly provided financial and political assistance for the crofters' movement. In an address to Perth Gaelic Society in 1880, J.S. Blackie argued that Gaelic societies had 'a distinct and well-marked sphere of action . . . to do something towards the preservation and maintenance of a race of genuine Highlanders in the Highlands'. He argued that all such societies should follow a consistent programme of action: to compile 'an annotated Book of the Clearances'; to have as their aims the radical reform of the land laws - 'to secure for the tenants a free basis of operations, to secure for the Highlands a resident middle-class'; 'Gaelic Societies must take particular note of the accession to the depopulating forces by the artificial extension of deer forests'; to work for improved methods of husbandry; encourage schools to study Gaelic; establish funds to enable Gaelic students to study at Edinburgh University; and appoint collectors of Gaelic material in areas of Gaelic recession.111 Charles Fraser-Mackintosh similarly argued that 'Every Gaelic-speaking Highlander should belong to a Highland Association in his neighbourhood', to form such associations if none existed and 'to federate and affiliate themselves with more important Societies in the great centres of population'.

Several points may be made in this context. As has been elsewhere noted, there were many different sorts of Gaelic and Highland societies. Some had a defined 'cultural commitment' in the way Black has identified for the Highland Society of Scotland; others, however, were the reflection in kilt and ceremony of that combination of opposites that characterised the later nineteenth-century Highlands; J.F. Campbell considered the Highland Society of London in 1871, for example, 'not the genuine article but Londoners making believe to be Highlanders', and there were many others of like nature. Others, such as the Glasgow Highland Society and the Gaelic chapels in the Lowland cities, provided an important source of support for urban Gaels but were less commonly involved in political agitation. Several Highland institutions were so involved however; particularly prominent was the Gaelic Society of Inverness founded in 1871, the Edinburgh Sutherland Association and, in Glasgow, the Argyllshire Society (1851), the Islay Association, the Sutherland Association (1860), the Skye Association (1865), the Tiree Association (1870), the Lewis Association (1876), the Mull and Iona Association, the Ross-shire Association, the Lochaber Society, the Appin Society, the Coll Society, and the Ardnamurchan, Morvern and Sunart Association.112 Many Highlanders shared common membership of a number of these institutions engaged in land reform issues and the links were, at times, wider still; Charles Cameron the Glasgow Liberal MP who was president of the Federation of Celtic Societies was also the owner of the pro-Highlander The North British Daily Mail.113 These Scottish Highland societies also had their counterparts overseas. A number of Highland institutions in the New World, as also individuals, voiced their dissent at the actions of landlords. In India in 1822, for example, 'The Expatriated Highlanders of Sutherland' raised funds for victims of the Sutherland clearances and groups in the United States, Canada, and Australia did likewise.114 This expression of concern on eviction, landlessness, and protest should be seen as the representation in particular form of that wider sentiment of interest in Highland affairs that has underlain the region's material and social transformation. We have seen this to be evident in those people of non-Highland background (in addition to emigre Gaels) whose moral commitment to the education and improvement of the Highlander was apparent in their subscriptions to the SSPCK or Gaelic Schools Society. It is evident in the lists of subscriptions for the relief of Highland destitution at the time of the famine; not just, as one might expect, from Gaelic chapels and urban Highlanders but from congregations, institutions, and individuals from all classes throughout Britain and overseas.115 It has been apparent, of course, in the ideological claims and realised actions of these persons engaged, at any moment, in the transformation of the Highlands. In the context of protest and opposition to that transformation in the nineteenth century, it is evident in petitions from migrant Highlanders, who although they were not _in_ the region were _of_ it and who, it may be argued, would have understood more completely the inherent ideological claims to land and language. Articulation of counter-hegemony was evident, too, in the widespread involvement of radical political associations - in Scotland, Ireland and North America - who, at a time of increased class consciousness and political activism, saw in the Highland land wars and in that tradition of protest in which the antagonism between crofter and landlord was set, the reflection of wider class conflicts in society.

CONCLUSION

This chapter has suggested that the cultural transformation of Highland Scotland was in various ways opposed by persons outside the region as well as by Highlanders themselves. It has suggested, too, that the forms taken in opposition were composed of 'inherent' notions of shared beliefs and consensus claims to land and of 'derived' notions of class and class consciousness. The central legitimating ideology or principal underlying and motivating Highland social protest has been the expressed collective belief in the inalienability of land; not in the sense of its formal appropriation through law as property or as a materially measurable commodity, but in the sense of land as _their_ land, an inherited occupance, a physical setting with which Highlanders were indissolubly tied through continuity of social and material practices. Albeit that it was a belief without legal validity, it persisted throughout the period under review here and found recognition in various ways: in the concept of _duthchas_, in the claim to 'ancestral' arable holdings which had been expropriated at some earlier time and laid out in new ways or in the form of 'rights' to traditionally-recognised grazing grounds; and in poetry it was more usually viewed in retrospect as 'homeland' or contrasted with the then contemporary lack of 'kindliness'.
   Whilst it can be argued that Highland social protest

389

has been a continuous tradition of opposition, the geography of counter-hegemony in the sense of physical resistance to the appropriation of land as enclosed arable, sheep farm, or, later in the nineteenth century, deer forest, has varied. In the century from 1782, protest was concentrated particularly in the more fertile areas of the north-east Highlands. There, a largely subsistence mixed farming economy whose limited commercial output (chiefly in grain) was directed to and through nearby market towns was replaced by a form of agriculture whose markets lay further to the south and whose managers were likewise 'south-country' men. This replacement not only demanded the take-up by sheep of traditional hill grazings but also the re-apportionment of tenants' arable land either as sub-divided holdings to accommodate a growing population or, more usually, its conversion to pasture as the tenants were moved to coastal holdings or migrated. In either case, customary rights and practices were extinguished. Protest in that region and in other areas at the same period where sheep farming was the principal change affecting Highland agriculture thus centred, simultaneously, upon opposition to the advance of sheep farming as a given 'new' form of land use, to the eviction that that advance demanded, to the Lowland graziers and shepherds who were its principal agents, and to the new and enforced division of labour that it entailed.

By the later nineteenth century, however, protest was concentrated in the north and west, in the crofting Highlands. In that region, especially in the Outer Isles, protest was directed not so much at the _advance_ of sheep farming or at the _processes_ of establishment of sheep farming or deer forests, as at their later _results_ in terms of the overall _pattern_ of landholding and the individual restricted size of crofters' holdings. Pressure upon these holdings had been accentuated in earlier decades, it should be remembered, by the relative rates of population growth and permanent migration in the north and west compared with the farming Highlands, by the policy of landlords with kelp-producing estates to retain labour, and by the relative failure of schemes for industry and a new division of labour. Protest in the north and west in the 1880s and later was more forceful than at earlier periods and in other places and took the form of 'raids' to reclaim ancestral grazings and holdings and to put under the plough areas of waste or the pasture grounds and deer forests of landlords.

The relative success of later protest was the result of several factors in combination: the geography and economy of the area which had determined since the early 1800s a

390

resident crofting population in the north and west in contrast to the south and east where population was more regularly 'drawn off' ; the result of the class consciousness of crofters themselves, particularly in the second half of the nineteenth century; and, both as result of and influence upon this emergent class consciousness from within, a 'derived' identity from without given public opinion, parliamentary legislation on the land question and the involvement of non-Highland groups and individuals. These reasons may also suggest (if only by their absence) why the articulated protest of the 1780s and first decades of the nineteenth century was not as successful as later protest. Only by the later nineteenth century was there an identifiable class consciousness amongst crofters - the crofting community was largely in the process of formation before then. The alternative hegemony represented by religious revival, 'the Men', and by a poetry of opposition did not itself provide political motivation for, or a leadership of, protest. And what we have discussed here as 'derived' influences - parliamentary legislation, sympathetic public opinion, and an articulated regional and class consciousness drawn both from migrant Highlanders and others of similar social class - were not as important in the context of eighteenth-century protest. The parliamentary influences of landlords and the landed interest was much stronger then. And concerned as it was at that time more with questions of Ossianic authenticity and the ideologically unchallengeable 'improvement' of the Highlands through education and industry, public opinion had not yet been drawn in support towards the Highland tenantry in the way it was by the later 1800s.

NOTES

1.   Napier Commission Report (1884), XXXII, pp.4-5.

2.   SRO, GD 40 16/35, ff.24-24v, Duke of Argyll to Lord Lothian, 11 January 1888 re Highland disturbances.

3.   Richards, Highland Clearances Volume 2, p.389.

4.   Richards, Highland Clearances Volume 2, p.293.

5.   G. Rude, Ideology and Popular Protest (London, 1980); G. Lichtheim, The Concept of Ideology and Other Essays (New York, 1967).

6.   For works on this general context of protest, see for example A. Charlesworth, Social Protest in a Rural Society: the spatial diffusion of the Captain Swing disturbances of 1830-1831 (HGRG Research Series, Publication 1, 1979); idem, (ed.), An Atlas of Rural Protest in Britain 1548-1900 (London, 1983); idem, 'Labour protest 1780-1850' in J. Langton and R.J. Morris (eds.), Atlas of Industrialising Britain 1780-1914 (London, 1979); J. Dunbabin, Rural Discontent in Nineteenth-Century Britain (London,1974). J. Stevenson and P. Quinault (eds.), Popular Protest and Public Order (London, 1974); C. Tilly, 'Collective Violence in European Perspective' in H.D. Graham and T.R. Gurr (eds.), Violence in America: Historical and Comparative Perspectives (New York, 1969); idem, 'The Pre-Industrial Crowd' in G. Rude, Paris and London in the Eighteenth Century (London, 1970); E.P. Thompson, 'Eighteenth-Century English Society: Class Struggle without Class?', Social History, III (1978), pp.137-165; idem, 'The Moral Economy of the English Crowd in the Eighteenth Century', Past and Present, 50 (1971), pp.76-136; G. Wootton, Pressure Groups in Britain 1720-1970 (London, 1975); G. Rude, The Crowd in History (New York, 1964).

7.   E.P. Thompson, 'Patrician Society, Plebian Culture', Journal of Social History, VII (1974), pp.382-405.

8.   Thompson, 'Moral Economy of the English Crowd', p.78.

9.   J.W. Wellwood, 'Custom and Usage' in Halsbury's Laws of England (London, 1975), Volume 12. On the application of custom to locality and as the basis to law in a given locality see, for example, C. Fisher, Custom, Work and Market Capitalism: the Forest of Dean Colliers 1788-1888

(London, 1981).

10. Dodgshon, <u>Land and Society . . .</u>, pp.110, 115.

11. M. Sanderson, <u>Scottish Rural Society in the 16th Century</u> (Edinburgh, 1982), pp.60-61. This notion of remembrance is most clearly expressed in terms of family ties and kin links. Cregeen has argued persuasively that 'most Highlanders are genealogists by nature': E.R. Cregeen, 'Oral Sources for the Social History of the Scottish Highlands and Islands', <u>Oral History, 2</u> (1974), p.25.

12. A point made by most of those authors referred to above (nn. 7 and 8), but specifically in the Scottish context, see T.C. Smout, 'An Ideological Struggle: the Highland Clearances', <u>Scottish International 5(2)</u> (1972), pp.13-16; E. Cowan (ed.), <u>The People's Past</u> (Edinburgh, 1980); more generally on this point see the introductory comments in C. Ginzburg, <u>The Cheese and the Worms</u> (London, 1980); and N. Daniel, <u>The Cultural Barrier</u> (Edinburgh, 1975).

13. J. Hunter, <u>For the People's Cause: from the writings of John Murdoch</u> (London, 1986); <u>Napier Commission Report</u> (1884), XXXVI, Q.44463.

14. ('A Disinherited Gael') 'The Cultural Value of Gaelic', <u>The Glasgow Highlander, 1(3)</u> (1933), 7 October; C. Fraser-MacKintosh, 'Gaelic at the Close of the 19th century. What of the next?', <u>The Celtic Monthly, IX(4)</u> (1901), p.74.

15. J. MacCulloch, <u>The Highlands and Western Isles of Scotland</u> (London, 1824), IV, pp.187-189 (pp.184-227 is a section on 'The Gaelic Language'). For a detailed critique of MacCulloch's opinionated claims, see J. Browne, <u>A Critical Examination of Dr. MacCulloch's Work on the Highlands and Western Isles of Scotland</u> (Edinburgh, 1825).

16. R. Black, 'The Gaelic Academy: the cultural commitment of the Highland Society of Scotland', <u>Scottish Gaelic Studies, XIV(II)</u> (1986), pp.1-38.

17. <u>Comh-Chruinneachadh Orain Ghaidhealach le Roanull MacDhomnuill Ann an Eilein Eigg (Ath-Leasaichte le Paruig Tuairner)</u> (Glasgow, 1809).

18. N. McNish, <u>The True Method of Preserving the Gaelic</u>

Language (Glasgow, 1928), p.11.

19. R. Mitchison, 'Nineteenth Century Scottish Nationalism: the Cultural Background', in R. Mitchison (ed.), The Roots of Nationalism: Studies in Northern Europe (Edinburgh, 1980), pp.131-142.

20. The Highlander, 13 April 1878; quoted in J. Hunter, 'The Gaelic Connection: the Highlands, Ireland and Nationalism, 1873-1922', Scottish Historical Review, LIV(2) (1975), pp.178-204 (quote on p.184).

21. Hunter, 'The Gaelic Connection', pp.185, 193

22. J. MacInnes, 'Religion in Gaelic Society', Transactions of the Gaelic Society of Inverness, LII (1980-1982), pp.222-242.

23. D.S. Thomson, 'Gaelic Scotland', in D.S. Glen (ed.), Whither Scotland (London, 1971), pp.136-137.

24. J. MacInnes, The Evangelical Movement in the Highlands of Scotland (Aberdeen, 1951); Withers, Gaelic in Scotland, pp.145-147.

25. On this point, see S. O'Brien, 'A Transatlantic Community of Saints: the Great Awakening and the First Evangelical Network, 1735-1755', American Historical Review, 91(4) (1986), pp.811-832.

26. MacInnes, 'Religion in Gaelic Society', p.235.

27. S. Bruce, 'Social Change and Collective Behaviour: the revival in eighteenth-century Ross-shire', British Journal of Sociology, XXIV(4) (1983), pp.554-572.

28. J. Hunter, 'The Emergence of the Crofting Community: the Religious Contribution 1798-1843', Scottish Studies, 18 (1974), p.99.

29. MacInnes, p.239. On this spirit of evangelism, see A. Auld, Ministers and Men of the Far North (Wick, 1868); D. Sage, Memorabilia Domestica (Edinburgh, 1889); A. MacGillivray, Sketches of Religion and Revivals of Religion in the North Highlands during the last century (Inverness, 1859).

30. Hunter, 'The Emergence of the Crofting Community', pp.101, 112.

31. MacInnes, 'Religion in Gaelic Society', p.241

32. Bruce, 'Social Change and Collective Behaviour', pp.564-567; Hunter, 'The Emergence of the Crofting Community', p.105.

33. SRO, CH2/273/3, 23 April 1829; D. Macdonald, Lewis: a History of the Island (Edinburgh, 1978), p.151.

34. R. Somers, Letters from the Highlands (London, 1848), p.66.

35. Hunter, 'The Emergence of the Crofting Community', p.112.

36. T.C. Smout in reviewing A. Charlesworth (ed.),An Atlas of Rural Protest in Scottish Historical Review, LXIII(2) (1984), p.19.

37. T.M. Murchison, 'Highland Life as reflected in Gaelic Literature', Transactions of the Gaelic Society of Inverness, XXXVII (1938), p.221.

38. D.S. Thomson, An Introduction to Gaelic Poetry (London, 1977), p.156.

39. S. Maclean, 'The Poetry of the Clearances', Transactions of the Gaelic Society of Inverness, XXXVIII (1938-1941), pp.293-324; D. Meek, 'Gaelic Poets of the Land Agitation', Transactions of the Gaelic Society Inverness, XLIX (1977), pp.309-376; see also the much less valuable A.J. MacAskill, 'Life in the Highlands in the 17th and 18th Centuries: as seen through the Eyes of the Poets of that Period', Transactions of the Gaelic Society of Inverness, XLI (1951-1952), pp.157-177; M. Maclean, The Literature of the Celts (London, 1926); idem, The Literature of the Highlands (London, 1926).

40. M. Chapman, The Gaelic Vision in Scottish Culture (London, 1978); C.W.J. Withers, 'The Image of the Land: Scotland's Geography through her Languages and Literature', Scottish Geographical Magazine, 100(3) (1984), pp.37-53; the quotation is from W.R. Lawson, 'The Poetry and Prose of the Crofter Question', National Review, 4 (1884-1885), pp.593-594.

41 R. Williams, The Country and the City (London, 1975); J. Turner, The Politics of Landscape: Rural Scenery and Society in English Poetry 1630-1660 (Oxford, 1979).

42. D.S. Thomson, 'Scottish Gaelic Folk-Poetry ante 1650', Scottish Gaelic Studies, VIII (2) (1958), pp.1-17.

43. Thomson, Introduction to Gaelic Poetry, p.146; idem, 'Gaelic Writers in Lowland Scotland', Scottish Literary Journal, 4(1) (1977), pp.36-46.

44. J. MacInnes, 'The Oral Tradition in Scottish Gaelic Poetry', Scottish Studies, XII (1968), pp.29-43.

45. D. Stevenson, Alasdair MacColla and the Highland Problem in the 17th Century (Edinburgh, 1980), p.191; Thomson, Introduction to Gaelic Poetry, pp.118-127. The date of 1698 for Mac Mhaighstir Alasdair's birth is taken from Black, Mac Mhaighstir Alasdair, p.5.

46. Thomson, Introduction to Gaelic Poetry, pp.156-217; Chapman, The Gaelic Vision . . ., p.53.

47. Thomson, ibid, p.159; Black, Mac Mhaighstir Alasdair, p.26; A. and A. MacDonald (eds.), The Poems of Alexander MacDonald (Inverness, 1924), p.4.

48. Although, as Black had pointed out, MacDonald had left their employ in 1744; see also J.L. Campbell (ed.), Highland Songs of the Forty-Five (Edinburgh, 1984), pp.35, 141.

49. Thomson, Introduction to Gaelic Poetry, p.191; W. Matheson, The Songs of John MacCodrum (Edinburgh, 1938), pp.200-201.

50. Quoted in Richards, Highland Clearances Volume 2, p.285. 'Brockit' here means 'having a white stripe down its face' or 'having black and white stripes or spots'.

51. L. MacBean, Buchanan: the Sacred Bard of the Scottish Highlands (London, 1920), p.114; C. Fraser-Macintosh, Antiquarian Notes: a series of papers regarding families and places in the Highlands (Inverness, 1865), pp.60-61.

52. On this point, see H. Henderson, 'The Ballad, the Folk and the Oral Tradition', in Cowan, The People's Past, pp.69-107; D. Buchan, The Ballad and the Folk (London, 1972); G. Ross Roy, 'The Jacobite Literature of the 18th Century, Scotia, 1(1) (1977), pp.42-55; W. Donaldson, 'Bonny Highland Laddie: the Making of a Myth', Scottish Literary Journal, 3(2) (1976), pp.30-50.

53. T. Crawford, 'Political and Protest Songs in Eigh-teenth Century Scotland' (Part I), Scottish Studies, 14(1) (1970), pp.1-34; (Part II) in 14(2) (1970), pp.105-132.

54. S. Maclean, 'The Poetry of the Clearances', Transac-tions of the Gaelic Society of Inverness, XXXVIII (1938-1941), pp.293-324.

55. Thomson, Introduction to Gaelic Poetry, p.223.

56. Williams, The Country and the City, p.91; M.J. Weiner, English Culture and the Decline of the Industrial Spirit 1850-1980 (Cambridge, 1982), pp.3-10, 46-50.

57. M. MacDonell, The Emigrant Experience: Songs of Highland Emigrants in North America (Toronto, 1982); 'Imrich nan Eileineach' by Calum Ban MacMhannain (1758-1829) in MacDonell, ibid, pp.108-109; quotation from lines 49-60.

58. Meek, 'Gaelic Poets of the Land Agitation', p.311.

59. J. MacInnes, 'A Gaelic Song of the Sutherland Clearanc-es', Scottish Studies, VIII (1964), pp.104-106.

60. Thomson, Introduction to Gaelic Poetry, p.239.

61. Meek, ibid, p.343; Thomson, Introduction to Gaelic Poetry, p.240. A 'whinger' is a short stabbing sword.

62. Meek, ibid, pp.322; 352-3.

63. Richards, Highland Clearances Volume 2, p.293.

64. H.J. Hanham, 'The problem of Highland Discontent 1880-1885', Transactions of the Royal Historical Society, 19 (1969), pp.21-65. On earlier expressions of passivity, see J.P. Day, Public Administration in the Highlands and Islands of Scotland (London, 1918); and the excellent review offered in E. Richards, 'How Tame were the Highland-ers during the Clearances?', Scottish Studies, 17 (1973), pp.35-50; see also the earlier works by J.G. Kellas, 'The Crofters' War', History Today, XII (1962), pp.281-288; D.H. Crowley, 'The "Crofters' Party" 1885-1892', History Today, XXXV (1956), pp.110-126.

65. Lawson, 'The Poetry and Prose of the Crofter Ques-tion', p.595.

66. Richards, 'How Tame were the Highlanders during the Clearances?', p.36.

67. E. Richards, 'Patterns of Highland Discontent 1790–1860', in J. Stevenson and R. Quinault (eds.), Popular Protest and Public Order, pp.75–114; idem, 'Agrarian Change, Modernisation and the Clearances' in D. Omand (ed.), The Ross and Cromarty Book (Golspie, 1984), pp.159–183; E. Richards, 'The Last Scottish Food Riots', Past and Present, Supplement 6 (1982); idem, 'Food Riots in 1847' in Charlesworth (ed.), Atlas of Rural Protest, pp.108–111.

68. Richards, Highland Clearances Volume 2, pp.301–302.

69. Richards, Highland Clearances Volume 1, pp.249–283; idem (1974), pp.78–79; idem (1984), pp.170–172; K. Logue, Popular Disturbances in Scotland 1780–1815 (Edinburgh, 1979), pp.56–64.

70. Quoted in Logue, ibid, p.60.

71. Richards, op.cit. (1983), p.51.

72. E.R. Cregeen, 'The House of Argyll and the Highlands' in I.M. Lewis (ed.), History and Social Anthropology (London, 1968), pp.154–157

73. SRO, CH/2/78, f.194; Smith, Jacobite Estates, p.11; Logue, Popular Disturbances, pp.55–56.

74. K. Logue, 'Eighteenth-Century Popular Protest: Aspects of the People's Past', in Cowan (ed.), The People's Past, pp.108–130. On the mutiny of the Highland regiments, see also J. Prebble, Mutiny: Highland Regiments in Revolt 1743–1804 (London, 1975).

75. Richards, Highland Clearances Volume 2, p.301. The phrase 'a climacteric moment . . .' is taken from Richards, Highland Clearances Volume 1, p.252.

76. SRO, AD14/13/9; E. Richards, The Leviathan of Wealth (London, 1973), pp.179–183, 213–216, 251–252.

77 Quoted in ibid, pp.179, 181.

78. E. Richards, 'Problems on the Cromartie Estate 1851–1853', Scottish Historical Review, 52 (1973), p.160.

79. D.S. Thomson, Companion to Gaelic Scotland (Oxford, 1983), p.23; D. Macdonald, Lewis: a History of the Island (Edinburgh, 1978), p.172.

80. SRO, AD56/309/3, 3(ii), letter from R. Taylor, Sheriff-Substitute, Tain, to Lord Advocate, 12 April 1854.

81. O. Hufton, 'Women in Revolution 1789-1796', Past and Present, 83 (1971); H. Henderson, 'The Women of the Glen: some thoughts on Highland History' in R. O'Driscoll (ed.), The Celtic Consciousness (Dublin, 1982), pp.255-264.

82. Richards, Highland Clearances Volume 2, pp.335, 345.

83. Smout, 'An Ideological Struggle: the Highland Clearances', p.14.

84. Richards, 'How Tame were the Highlanders during the Clearances?', pp.41-42.

85. Richards, Highland Clearances Volume 1, p.473.

86. The history and development of the Highland Land Wars has been documented in detail by J. Hunter in his The Making of the Crofting Community (Edinburgh, 1976), pp.131-206. I am grateful to Dr. Hunter for his permission to draw from this material.

87. Hunter, ibid, pp.131-132; T.W. Fletcher, 'The Great Depression in English Agriculture 1873-1896', Economic Historical Review, XIII (1961), pp.417-432; P.J. Perry, 'Where was the Great Agricultural Depression?', Agricultural History Review, 20(1) (1977), pp.30-45; I.M.M. MacPhail, 'Prelude to the Crofter' War 1870-1880', Transactions of the Gaelic Society of Inverness, XLIX (1977), pp.159-188.

88. SRO, GD1/36/Box 1. The report by Alexander Gow of the Dundee Advertiser, an eye-witness to the 'Battle', appears in full in Hanham, 'The Problem of Highland Discontent', pp.24-30.

89. SRO, GD1/36/1, 20 March 1882.

90. SRO, GD1/36/1, 21 May 1882; GD1/36/1/12, f.25.

91. SRO, GD1/36/1/18, f.62, 21 November 1884.

92. SRO, GD1/36/2/1, f.1, 17 January 1883.

93. Hunter, The Making of the Crofting Community, p.145.

94. I.M.M. MacPhail, 'The Skye Military Expedition of 1884-1885', Transactions of the Gaelic Society of Inverness, XLVIII (1972-1974), pp.62-94.

95. SRO, GD40/16/4, 26 July 1886.

96. SRO, GD1/36/1/9/10, 12 May 1886.

97. SRO, AF67/402, p.7, Report to Her Majesty's Secretary of State for Scotland on the Condition of the Cottar Population of the Lews.

98. SRO, AF 67/35, 23 November 1887; Macdonald, Lewis: A History of the Island, p.174; MacCallum quoted in M.Maclean and C. Carrell, As an Fhearann: from the land – (Stornoway, 1986), p.31.

99. SRO, AF67/35, 23 January 1888.

100. Quoted in Hunter, The Making of the Crofting Community, pp.174, 177.

101. On disturbances and protest in the 1900s, see Hunter, ibid, pp.184-206; SRO, AF67/36-66 (Crofting disturbances in Lewis, Sutherland and Skye 1887-1926); AF67/95-159 (Crofting disturbances in Lewis 1888-1923); AF67/160-161 (Crofting disturbances in Caithness 1888, 1919-1920); AF67/162-168 (Crofting disturbances in Skye 1901-1919); AF67/324-335 (Land seizures in Lewis 1919-1921); AF67/367-369 (Land agitation in Skye 1910).

102. SRO, AF67/117, 7 December 1895.

103. Quoted in Lawson, 'The Poetry and Prose of the Crofter Question'. p.596.

104. SRO, GD40/16/32, f.3, M. McNeill, 'Confidential Report to the Secretary of State for Scotland on the Condition of the Western Highlands and Islands', October 1886.

105. Hunter, The Making of the Crofting Community, p.129; idem, 'The politics of highland land reform 1873-1895', Scottish Historical Review, LIII (1974), pp.45-68.

106. Hunter, 'The politics of highland land reform', p.51.

107. Hunter, 'The politics of highland land reform', p.567; <u>idem</u>, 'The Emergence of the Crofting Community', pp.108-109.

108. M. Maclean, <u>The Literature of the Celts</u> (London, 1926), p.345; D.J. Macleod, 'Gaelic Prose', <u>Transactions of the Gaelic Society of Inverness, XLIX</u> (1974-1976), pp.198-230.

109. Hunter, <u>For the People's Cause</u>, p.29.

110. Richards, <u>Highland Clearances Volume 1</u>, pp.472-505; Hanham, 'The Problem of Highland Discontent', p.51.

111. J.S. Blackie, <u>Gaelic Societies, Highland Depopulation and Land Law Reform</u> (Edinburgh, 1880), pp.15-17; <u>idem</u>, <u>The Scottish Highlanders and the Land Laws</u> (London, 1885).

112. MacPhail, 'Prelude to the Crofters' War', pp.169-170; 'Directory of Highland and Celtic Societies', <u>The Celtic Magazine, (IV)</u> (1879), pp.35-38; Hanham, 'The Problem of Highland Discontent', p.38 has a list of the constituent founding bodies of the 1878 Federation of Celtic Societies.

113. J.G. Kellas, 'Highland migration to Glasgow and the Origin of the Scottish Labour Movement', <u>Bulletin, Society for the Study of Labour History, 12</u> (1966), pp.9-12.

114. Richards, 'How Tame were the Highlanders during the Clearances?', p.46.

115. SRO, HD16/70 (List of Subscriptions for the Relief of Highland Destitution); GD1/36/13 (List of Subscribers to the Destitute Highlanders, 1847).

7

CONCLUSION: THE TRANSFORMATION OF A CULTURE REGION

> The schemes that have been suggested for the
> improvement of the Highlands are numerous and
> discordant, as might be expected. Theories are
> pleasing in perspective, and, apparently, easy of
> execution; but the history of all attempts to
> effect a total and instantaneous revolution in
> Highland sentiment and manners, demonstrates the
> fallacious nature of the views entertained. The
> Highlanders, like all other people, are to be
> operated upon by gradual means. Convince them of
> the superiority of your mode of thinking and
> acting; but do not attempt force.1

Anderson's observation above, made in his 1831 Essay,
aptly summarises several of the points made at greater
length here on the transformation of the Scottish Highlands: how, for example, there was often a gap between the
intended changes in 'sentiment and manners' and the actual
results in practice; how transformation of the Highland way
of life involved, simultaneously, changes in the mode of
thinking and acting, in intellectual production as well as
in material practice; and how changes were not instantly
successful but were more often realised 'by gradual means'
- through the hegemonic assertion of dominant values rather
than by force or 'rule'.
Whilst the transformation of the Highlands as a culture
region has been then, in great part, the story of attempts
by outside authority 'to convince them' [Highlanders] 'of
the superiority' of a different intellectual and material
mode of production, the above chapters have suggested also
that the processes of cultural transformation have varied
over time and space in their effect and that they have been
continually modified and recreated 'from within' the
structures of external authority as they have at times been
directly opposed by Highlanders themselves. In addition,
what is meant here by transformation has involved questions

402

of consciousness; differences in regional consciousness between what may be understood as 'the outsiders image' of the Highlands and the Highland, or perhaps more properly Highlanders', regional consciousness. And other issues – of class and class formation, of differences in 'traditional' social structure and in the productive capacity of certain parts of the Highlands – have been shown to underlie and inform these questions of intellectual and material change.

This book has tried to show how the transformation of the Highlands may be considered a cultural phenomenon and that cultural change be seen as a more complex and contradictory dialectic than is usually implied by those interpretations of the historic Highlands which see change in the region as the result either of political, linguistic or other 'superstructural' factors or the inevitable consequence of 'uneven' (hence regional) development of the economic 'base' to Scottish and Highland life. Several issues have been considered particularly important: the question of the dominant ideology and the relationship between the expressed need for transformation and the principal effecting institutions involved; the complex nature of the material changes in the Highland way of life; and the differences in image held of the Highlands.

THE IDEOLOGY AND INSTITUTIONS OF CULTURAL TRANSFORMATION

The acculturation of the Highlands has been pursued in various ways within an ideology of 'improvement' which has seen 'culture' or 'civility' as an achieved (and achievable) social state.

The ideology of 'improvement'

The ideology of 'improvement' is particularly associated with eighteenth-century beliefs on material progress which, expressed in terms of stages of economic development and in relation to a predominant notion of culture as a process of individual and societal advance, contrasted 'savage' or 'primitive' Highland society with the civilised values of urban Lowland Scotland.

Although it took historically specific forms in the 1700s, the ideology of improvement was not the product of the eighteenth century. It has earlier origins in 'the move toward one Commonwealth' in the 1600s involving as it did then questions of civility, obedience (to the Crown and central authority), religious unification, and attempts to

Conclusion

make Highlanders 'speak and write the English tongue'.
Further, the ideology of improvement (which at any moment
in the Highlands embraced agricultural and industrial
advance, the division of labour, issues of literature,
private property, social propriety, and education as it was
also expressed and represented in the use of a 'correct'
English as the symbol and means of authority), has not been
particular to that region. Lowland Scotland in the past
was subject to processes of anglicisation in schools and to
what Young considered 'the aping of English language and
manners by the Scottish ruling classes' in addition to
changes in the material basis to life. In this sense, the
ideology of improvement and cultural 'enlightenment' may be
seen as class-related rather than only regionally particular.

But from the later 1600s, in the context of a region
which had long been considered 'uncultivated', with a
different language and social system and socially and
geographically distant from all notions of civility and
culture, the ideology of improvement has had particular
significance. In the context of Highland culture, this
ideological and intellectual production had two principal
functions: of, firstly, identifying the region and its
people as inferior, an 'inferiority' which demanded
amelioration by 'superiors'; and secondly, of legitimating
and rationalising those processes of change directed by
superiors at cultural forms in which rested, to the outside
('superior') eye, the region's material and intellectual
backwardness. It may be suggested then that the actual
transformation of the Highlands as a culture region rested
not alone in all-impelling forces of economic and capitalistic integration (as many have supposed), but in addition
involved as a motivational force the creation of a specific
intellectual image of the Highlands which provided ideological justification for the actions taken and policies
pursued by the institutions and agents of authority. The
Highland region and more crucially, Highlanders themselves,
were 'made' as an intellectual production as they were at
the same time made and re-made materially.

Anglicisation, educational institutions and cultural-hegemony

The principal formal institutions involved in the cultural
transformation of the Highlands were those concerned with
anglicisation and religious unification. In the 1600s, the
relations between Church and State were close and the
planting of schools, parish churches and Gaelic-speaking

404

Conclusion

clergy and probationers was part of a unified move toward 'civilitie and obedience'. In the eighteenth and nineteenth centuries, formal institutions for religious supervision and educational provision were largely separate organisations working to the same end. The SSPCK was the single most important institution of anglicisation in the 1700s and continually modified its operating policies to achieve the desired end of 'rooting out their Irish language'. While it is the case, however, that anglicisation was simultaneously an economic and a cultural activity (and for the SSPCK and Gaelic Schools we have seen how these organisations drew financial and moral support for their Highland schools and educational policies from particular social ranks and institutions elsewhere in Scotland), the hegemonic assertion of a 'correct' spoken English as expressing and representing authority should not be considered the simple and direct result of formal institutions alone.

The spread of English was the result of seasonal labour migration, and the in-movement of non-Gaelic speakers in addition to anti-Gaelic educational policies. The family or household as an 'institution' also had an important role in language shift. There is evidence not only of different use of Gaelic or English by generation within the family but also of differences in the use of one language or another for given social purposes: English for schooling, commerce, as a symbol of culture and individual social progress; Gaelic for religious worship, the heart and the hearth but with no contemporary 'value' attached to it by outsiders (and some Gaels) as a language of social advancement.

The assertion of anglicisation as the expression of the dominating interests of one class over another was common throughout eighteenth and nineteenth-century Scotland not just in the Highlands, and was evident in the status attached to speech styles and dialects elsewhere in Britain. But the fact that by the second decade of the nineteenth century the scholars of several Gaelic schools in the Highlands were paying to retain their school-master and have English lessons means also we should be cautious in seeing the assertion of a particular use of language as the only correct one as the straightforward consequence of class consciousness and material relationships. There were Highlanders who welcomed the expansion of anti-Gaelic educational policies; ministers who spoke against the language as a school medium for example, parents who saw no 'reward' in its use, school inspectors who as late as the 1890s spoke out against its employment as a school language (as they did also against Scots). At the same time, there were individuals from within the structures of authority prepared to oppose educational policies antithetical to Gaelic. And from the later nineteenth century, in institutions like the Gaelic Society of Inverness, in Gaelic's place in schools (albeit minor until 1918), and in the establishment of the Celtic Chair at Edinburgh University, there was a belated shift away from centuries of anti-Gaelic sentiment.

Institutions of industry and industriousness

Those several formal bodies and societies established to stimulate 'a spirit of industry' in the Highlands had variable effect regionally and chronologically and were restricted both by 'internal' matters - poor administration and under-funding - and by difficulties imposed by communication in the Highlands and relative distance from principal markets. In a few places - in several Highland towns and villages where population numbers and commercial expansion allowed occupational specialisation, in the more prosperous fishing settlements, or in parts of Highland Perthshire and Easter Ross where textile manufacturing was successfully linked to larger external markets - the effect of institutional activity and the development of planned 'industrial' settlements did lead to a more clearly-defined division of labour. Most usually, however, the development by direct institutional initiative of a division of labour between and within given tasks and occupations was not successful at the regional level. The intended separation-off of a rurally-located but increasingly (if not wholly) industrially-dependent market-oriented section of the population from the bulk of the peasantry was only successful in parts of the southern and eastern Highlands in regard to textiles and in parts of the south-west Highlands later in the nineteenth century in relation to fishing. Particular locales there did specialise in one occupation or another - partly in consequence of proximity to Lowland markets and the capital, materials, and entrepreneurial skills of putting-out merchants and clothiers or larger fishermen, and partly because of related changes in the patterns of land-holding. Even in these areas, however, the impact upon the household as the unit or institution of production is still not fully understood. In the textile areas, traditionally-seasonal rhythms of spinning by women were not everywhere and all times accompanied by a parallel expansion in weaving by men. In the north and in the north-east fishing villages, most households centred around a part-agricultural and

406

Conclusion

part-fishing occupational pluralism. And in the north and west and island parishes especially, this occupational pluralism was crucial to the origin and continuance of crofting. But for most Highland households throughout the period under review, the means to continued existence lay in agriculture and in coping or not with the changes in the constituent relationships and agreed customs of Highland rural society.

PROCESSES AND PATTERNS OF MATERIAL TRANSFORMATION

Leaving aside local differences in outlook, in the balance between arable or pastoral farming, and in the relationships of given parts of the region with outside markets, Highland rural society was based upon recognised principles of land management and customs of occupance which were simultaneously demographic, economic, and moral. As suggested above, however, it was not a society without internal tensions - between clans, between landlord and tenant, and within the tenantry - and for this reason, we should not suppose the observed changes in the Highland economy to have been alone the result of outside influences. But from the end of the seventeenth century, the inherent tensions within what Gray has termed the 'constant conflict between the demands of productive efficiency and the old obligations of class to class' were replaced. They were replaced at first gradually and in the south-west Highlands and then more rapidly throughout the region by new contradictions and social antagonisms. The origins of these tensions lay in the externally-derived commercial penetration of the Highlands. The principal results were firstly, and in general terms, the separation of Highland social structure into two classes and secondly, the eventual creation of a sense of their identity - a class consciousness - from within the Highland peasantry itself.

Demographic factors

Although not all is known of the rate and causes of change in Highland demographic structures, enough is known of the principal elements to state three things in conclusion: firstly, population increase was more marked and longer maintained in the north and west Highlands than in the south and east. This fact is not in itself significant but is so in relation to the extent to which the potato was adopted as the main staple of the Highland diet and given the policy of landlords in the north and west in retaining

Conclusion

population. Secondly, population increase in the north and west demanded the re-organisation of runrig at a time when the population was largely employed in kelping. The result was the continued sub-division of holdings on land that was being neglected by tenants whilst becoming more and more on land that was being neglected by tenants whilst becoming more and more 'marginal', both to the expanding sheep farms and deer forests and to the demands of efficient production. These facts underlay the emergence of the crofter and the cottar as particular forms of tenant in the outer islands. Thirdly, population pressure was relieved by emigration and clearance and for the crofting parishes especially, by seasonal migration to the Lowlands. This migration - permanent and temporary - led to imbalances in the sex and age ratio of the Highland population. Delay in marriage and decline in age-specific marital fertility were additional principal causes of decline in the region from the mid-nineteenth century.

Capitalisation and the Highland economy

From the second half of the seventeenth century, increased importance was attached in the Highlands to the money portion of the principal rent. Although in parts of the Highlands by the later 1700s (and until the 1820s), this cash portion derived from labour on the kelp or the part-time manufacture of textiles, it chiefly derived for most tenantry from the sale of black cattle. At a time of rise in rent and change in established practices, however, opportunities for most tenants to improve their holdings or to save capital were limited. More usual was the build-up of rental arrears. This indebtedness which was apparent even at times of prosperity had two effects in the later 1700s and early 1800s. Firstly, it restricted development by tenants of their holdings. Secondly, it had the effect of leaving landlords either with financial overheads that seriously undermined any longer-term policies of well-intentioned estate rationalisation or it disposed landlords towards the wholesale clearance of the tenantry and the bringing-in of sheep in place of people - the replacement of moral relationships by what to landlords anyway were seen as economic imperatives. Continued rental arrears in the nineteenth century - often at least as large as the total rental (Table 4.5) - meant depleted levels of fixed and circulating capital in the Highlands. And what capital was concentrated was often held by Lowland incomers - south-country shepherds and graziers, Perthshire putting-out merchants, English-born landlords and sportsmen

- whose concern was not the maintenance of established practices and recognised customary rights but rather (and only) the level of financial return.

Economic change and class formation

Highland society operated within and through a graduated structure of recognised ranks with the three principal divisions of chief, tacksman, and tenant being underlain by generally-recognised rights to land as also by subtle internal contradictions of status (even of caste). By the second half of the eighteenth century, this social system, admittedly typified here, was changing rapidly. It was changing for several reasons: the increased involvement of Highland landlords with commercial rather than social values; because of the emphasis placed upon money rents; and by virtue of the departure of the tacksman as the principal mediating layer. Although it is not strictly historiographically correct to talk of 'classes' by the late 1700s, it is possible to note by this period the division of Highland society into two 'layers', landlords and a stratified peasantry. And from the 1800s it is suggested, it is possible to talk not only of social classes in an 'absolute' occupational sense, but also (and increasingly more important during the course of the nineteenth century), to consider class in terms of 'relative' identity - class <u>consciousness</u> - as the majority of Highlanders became aware of their own interests as they also became aware of the largely oppositional and dominant claims of landlords. It has been suggested here - as it was commonly noted by commentators in the nineteenth century - that the Highlands were without a middle class. A commercial middle layer was almost non-existent outside of the towns. And where such a middle class did exist it was often made up of estate factors and land agents whose position as the officer of landlord authority in running estates was often complemented by their role as local justices of the peace, sheriff's officers, overseers of poor law administration or health board inspectors.

It is possible to suggest, as has Hunter, that these processes of class formation were delayed in their actual expression by what we might understand as some sort of collective psychological trauma within the Highland peasantry. This trauma was occasioned more perhaps by residual deference to kin loyalties (particularly in relation to the reverence attached to a chief) than it was the simple result of 'the shock of the new' in terms of the imposition of 'modern' agricultural methods. For most

409

Conclusion

Highlanders, it was the fact that it was often unjust, in their new role as <u>commercial</u> landlords, that made the changes in material circumstance so hard to come to terms with and questions of loyalty and agreed behavioural patterns so difficult to depart from. Thus, argues Hunter, 'the weight of traditional loyalty to the chief rendered more difficult the appreciation of the social and economic transformation than would have been the case if the landlord had been expropriated and swept into oblivion as happened in Ireland'. And as he further observes, 'The undermining of the belief that "if our landlord knew our circumstances well he would give us justice" was an immensely slow process which had its origins in the eighteenth century and is by no means complete even today'.2 The above chapters have pointed to several ways in which this idea may be expanded upon.

The fact of this persistent residual deference and of attachment to established ways within the Highland peasantry at a time when that peasantry was itself coming into existence as a class may suggest also that while the notion of class is sufficient in relational terms to describe the positions of landlord and tenant in the social and material relations of production in the Highlands, the notion of class consciousness to describe the simple recognition of other class groups or even a sense of opposition to the interests of other classes may not be sufficient to allow for those issues of loyalty, custom, and inherent ideology that we have seen to be set within and between classes. It is possible to suggest, too, that the rearticulation of these traditional behavioural relationships along class lines had a geographical expression. In the north and west, where the crofting community was 'made' as a particular social class as a result of the retention of population and continued subdivision of holdings, ideas of loyalty and custom may have been more strongly and longer held than in parts of the south and east Highlands. There the processes of material change and class formation had been earlier and less abrupt and established beliefs may have been subsumed within the practices and claims of a tenant class whose relative levels of mobility and employment outside agriculture may in any case have acted against the maintenance of agreed rights and customs. The relative geography of protest from within the Highland peasantry is important in this context. Opposition to enclosure and Lowland factors and graziers centred before 1860 in the more fertile districts of Easter Ross and east Sutherland. Later protest at the extinction of customary rights and the appropriation of land was more common in the north and west and islands where ideas of custom and loyalty perhaps

Conclusion

persisted longer where the claims to these traditional rights as legitimation for opposition was the result both of this persistence and the delayed but more abrupt nature of material change in those parts.

In addition, this book has tried to show how the processes of class formation in the Highlands stemmed not just from the clash within the region of 'inherent' ways and beliefs with 'imposed' forms of capitalism, but drew also from 'derived' notions of class identity and political power from outside the Highlands. This was the result of the involvement of Highlanders and urban Highland institutions in wider issues of land reform and national politics from the mid-nineteenth century and the involvement of persons, not of Highland birth but of the same class interests, in Highland affairs.

The geography of transformation

It is evident from the above explorations that local geographical differences in society and economy, in the rate and scale of change, in the balance between arable and pastoral, and even in matters of loyalty underlie what has been discussed here as regional transformation. It is possible that recognition of internal differences in culture occurred as early as the 1590s when James VI contrasted mainland Highlanders 'that are barbarous for the most parte, and yet mixed with some shewe of civilitie'. This perceived distinction finds common expression in the eighteenth century (as we might expect it should at that time). The perception and recognition by outsiders of differences within the Highlands is more usually confined, however, to issues of towns as isolated commercial points, to questions of soil type and other topographic distinctions, and from that to matters of agricultural productivity, and to the generally south-to-north adoption of 'improved' ways. Thus, for Anderson in referring to the question of attachment to traditional social relations at a time of economic change:

> The pressure of high rents has already done away, in a great measure, the hereditary notions of obedience and devotedness to the chief, on the part of the dependent, in Argyllshire; but in the secluded parts of the counties of Ross and Inverness, we may yet see the interesting spectacle of a people preserving the habits of former times, and affected by the relations of feudal and patriarchal attachment.3

Conclusion

Several points may be made in conclusion on this issue. Firstly, whilst the processes of cultural transformation did in fact have a varying geography over time within the Highlands as a whole, many contemporary commentators treat as fact what were often only perceived differences in economy or in rate of adoption of new practices. Secondly, the question of scale is important. Argyll, the central Perthshire Highlands, Easter Ross, and the more fertile parishes around Inverness were 'leading' areas. Relatively, the north and west lagged behind. But differences in soil type and in productivity and not least in the commercial attitudes of the landlords and tenantry occurred on often very small scales. The representation of change as always Highland-wide and as the gradual encroachment by 'waves' of outside influences should perhaps be replaced by understanding the geography of transformation as the appearance of 'islands' - of outside capital (in the form of sheep farms, deer forests, or manufacturing stations), or of authority and English-speaking (in the form of churches and schools) - within a shrinking Highland 'sea'.

THE HIGHLANDS IDENTIFIED

Given these variations in ideology, geography, and economy, and the fact that processes of cultural transformation and class formation in the region were the result neither of economic factors alone nor of things that happened only in the Highlands, it is possible to suggest that that persistent historiographical tradition which has represented change in the Highland way of life as the result of impersonal economic forces and of a conflict between Highlands 'versus' Lowlands ought now to be abandoned. This exploration has tried to suggest, for example, how issues of class affecting the Highlands have transcended the region itself, how anglicisation was not particular to that region, and has sought to explain why these processes took the particular cultural form they did in the Highlands. It is also true, however, that our understanding of Highland cultural transformation has been critically influenced by adherence more to the outsiders' image of the region than by recognition of the fact of Highland regional consciousness.

The outsiders' image of the Highlands

The outsiders' image of the Highlands has been founded both

412

on perceived notions of separateness and cultural 'inferior-ity' and on persistent claims to a lack of culture in relation to given 'real' levels of economic and social development. It was this sense of separateness that motivated the ideology of improvement (see above). But this ideology and the outsiders' image of the region have both reflected and directed wider intellectual 'forma-tions'. The outsiders' image has also been lent a particu-lar (and self-serving) emphasis from the later 1600s by things particularly Highland, by the imagined 'wildness' of the Highland clans especially. The <u>idea</u> of wildness was reinforced by the <u>fact</u> of the Jacobite risings. In Highland society, a chief's personal status was largely synonymous with military prowess, not only with individual skill and daring in battle, but also with the number of loyal kin a chief could call upon at time of war. From the mid-eighteenth century, this military function was no longer possible. But from 1745, the real martial qualities of the Highlander were incorporated as part of the ideologi-cal creation and re-creation of the Highlands in the minds of outsiders. The processes of incorporation as a given image took two forms: firstly, the evident 'wildness' of rebellion was further reason to improve 'the barbarian' Highlander; secondly, certain cultural traits of the region were absorbed as Highland 'tradition' into the dominant culture of the higher ranks and classes of Scottish and British society. Aspects of Highland culture became 'residual' in the sense identified above of values or expressions 'which cannot be expressed in terms of the dominant culture yet remain lived and practised as part of the residue of some previous social formation' (Chapter 1 page 30). Indeed, in some ways, the incorporation as tradition of these 'residual' elements - the kilt, bagpipe music, Highland regiments, 'Ossianic' glens (cf. Figure 2.1) - has been so persistent and unchallenged as an image since the later 1700s that things Highland and the region itself have come somehow to symbolise Scotland as a nation.4 This ideological incorporation (as 'false consciousness') of aspects of Highland culture was influ-enced, too, by literary interpretations of the Highlands as romantic wilderness and as a result of the investiture in and through a certain type of literature of all Highlanders (but especially the peasantry) with qualities of virtue and noble humility.5

Highland regional consciousness

The notion of the inalienability of land has been crucial

Conclusion

to the Highlander. Land was seen as their land, not just in the sense of the physical basis on which agriculture was practised, but also and more importantly, as the basis to the maintenance of established social systems, given patterns of inheritance and land management, and to the continued occupancy of a people possessed of a given way of life. This is not to argue, however, that the attachment of Highlanders to their land and, therefore, their preparedness to oppose the cultural transformation of given habits of mind and material practices was rooted in an ideal past without internal contradiction although as several authors have shown, the pastoral myth of the clan as a system of equality and the Highlands before 1745 as a land of milk and honey has been apparent in Highland historiography.6 It is to note that the Highland consciousness or _mentalité_ rested upon consensual recognition of ideas and material practices that were at basis different from (though not _necessarily_ in opposition to) the ideas and productive forces of that society and mode of production with whom the Highland people were increasingly in contact from the later 1600s.

Of particular importance is the notion of _duthchas_. This concept or agreed belief provided legitimation in the minds of Highlanders for their claim to land as ancient possessions, and motivation for their reclaiming of those lands appropriated by the assertion of capital over custom. The slow adoption of leases, for example, largely stemmed from the belief that to accept a written lease was to surrender this recognised right. And the notions of _duthchas_ and customary rights appear in various oppositional forms in the course of Highland transformation: as part of what some have seen to be a backward-looking tradition of poetry and protest before about 1870; in the poetry of the land agitation as 'lack of kindliness'; in emigration verse on the 'home-land'; and most forcefully in the counter-hegemony of the land wars and protests of the later nineteenth century in which 'the land of our forefathers' was re-occupied, and reinstated as the foundation to Highland culture. These forms of opposition were themselves rooted in the fact that what was for the Highland peasant traditional custom and inherent ideology was for the improving landlord an outmoded sentiment without foundation in law whose survival only further identified the Highlander as backward, without culture. At a time when emphasis in society was increasingly on the demands of capital, ownership of property, and the authority of one rank or class over another, it was this ideological clash of custom-as-culture with other, dominant, intellectual and material productions

414

Conclusion

that framed the transformation of the region.

Given the above points on class formation and on other differences within the Highlands, it is possible to suggest in conclusion then that what has been considered as a <u>single</u> Highland regional consciousness be replaced by the idea of regional <u>class</u> consciousness. The expression of oppositional hegemony and inviolable rights to land, for example, was much more the tenants' claim than the landlords who were either neglecting their moral relationships to clan and land in favour of economic ties or were themselves replaced by outsiders for whom notions of <u>duthchas</u>, loyalty, and ancient possessions counted for nothing. Whilst he lost his land, the tenant kept his beliefs, in part as alternative hegemony unrealised in physical form before the later eighteenth century. By the later 1800s, these ideas and the sense of their own identity that they represented for the tenantry, were successful as counter-hegemony and were so in part because of issues of public opinion, class formation and change in political sympathy outside the region proper. And the fact that crofters were in the same period acting to ensure unity of opposition from within their own class by taking action against the property and stock of fellow crofters points to complex processes of hegemony as 'a lived experience' underlying what has been understood here as the cultural transformation of the Highlands.

NOTES

1.   J. Anderson, 'Essay on the present state of the Highlands and Islands of Scotland', Transactions of the Highlands and Agricultural Society of Scotland, NS, II, (1831), pp.58-59.

2.   J. Hunter, The Making of the Crofting Community, (Edinburgh, 1976), p.91.

3.   Anderson, 'Essay on the Present State of the Highlands...', p.22.

4.   M. Chapman, The Gaelic Vision in Scottish Culture (London, 1978), p.9; As An Fhearann (from the land): A century of images of the Scottish Highlands (Stornoway, 1986); It is evident in film too - in films like Local Hero.

5.   I. Carter, 'The changing image of the Scottish peasantry, 1745-1890', in R. Samuel (ed.), People's History and Socialist Theory (London, 1981), pp. 9-14; C. W. J. Withers, 'The Image of the Land: Scotland's geography through her languages and literature', Scottish Geographical Magazine, 100(3), (1984), pp.37-53.

6.   Hunter, Making of the Crofting Community, pp.92-93 has a good discussion of this point; see also D. Stewart, Sketches of the Character, Manners and Present State of the Highlanders of Scotland (Edinburgh, 1825); Argyll, Scotland as It Was and Is (Edinburgh, 1887).

BIBLIOGRAPHY

MANUSCRIPT SOURCES

Scottish Record Office

Account of losses sustained by robberies of the Highlanders	GD 52.76
Breadalbane Muniments	GD 112
Campbell of Balliveolan Papers	GD 13
Campbell of Barcaldine Papers	GD 170
Campbell of Duntroon Papers	GD 116
Campbell of Stonefield Papers	GD 14
Clanranald Papers	GD 201
Crofters Commission MSS	AF 67
Forfeited Estates Papers	E.701
	E.727
	E.728
	E.729
	E.730
	E.741
	E.746
	E.777
	E.787
	E.783
	E.788
Highland Destitution Papers	HD 1, _et seq._
Home Office Papers (Highland disturbances)	HH 1/-
Home Office Papers	RH 2/4
Lord Advocate's Papers	AD 56
Lord MacDonald MSS	GD 221
MacDonald of Sanda Muniments	GD 92
MacKay of Reay Papers	GD 84
Maclaine of Lochbuie Papers	GD 174
Marquess of Lothian Muniments	GD 40
Memorial anent the true state of the Highlands of Scotland before the '45	RH 2/5

Bibliography

Scottish Record Office (Continued)

Reay Papers	GD 84
Records of the General Assembly of the Church of Scotland	CH 1/1 and CH 1/2
Records of the Royal Commission on the Highlands and Islands, 1883	AF 50
Register Minutes of the Assembly of the Free Church of Scotland	CH 3/665
Register Minutes of the Committee Meetings of the Society in Scotland for Propagating Christian Knowledge, 1709–1878	GD 95/2
Register Minutes of the Free Church of Argyll	CH 3/26
Register Minutes of the General Meetings of the Society in Scotland for Propagating Christian Knowledge, 1709–1878	GD 95/1
Register Minutes of the Presbytery of Chanonry	CH 2/66
Register Minutes of the Presbytery of Dunkeld	CH 2/106
Register Minutes of the Presbytery of Lewis	CH 2/473
Register Minutes of the Presbytery of Lochcarron	CH 2/567
Register Minutes of the Presbytery of Tain	CH 2/348
Register Minutes of the Presbytery of Uist	CH 2/361
Register Minutes of the Royal Bounty Committee (Scroll minutes, correspondence)	CH 1/5
Register Minutes of the Synod of Argyll	CH 2/557
Register Minutes of the Synod of Caithness and Sutherland	CH 2/345
Register Minutes of the Synod of Glenelg	CH 2/568
Register Minutes of the Synod of Moray	CH 2/271
Register Minutes of the Synod of Ross	CH 2/312
Register of a visit to the SSPCK schools by P.Butter	GD 95 9/3
Register of SSPCK schools, 1701–1761	GD 95/9
Report by Messrs. Hyndman and Dick appointed by the General Assembly to visit the Highlands and Islands	CH 8/212/1 CH 8/212/2 CH 1/5/79
Seaforth Muniments	GD 46
Sheriff Ivory Papers	GD 1/36
Some considerations to induce the people of South Brittain to Contribute to the Designe of Propagating Christian Knowledge to the Highlands and Isles of North Britain	

418

Bibliography

Scottish Record Office (Continued)

and of Civilizing the Barbarous Inhabitants of these parts of the Kingdom, 1708	GD 95/10/57
SSPCK Papers (other than Committee and General Meeting Minutes)	GD 95/10
	GD 95/11
	GD 95/13

National Library of Scotland

Contract of James VI and I regarding the suppression of lawlessness in the Highlands, 1612	MS Ch 798
Correspondence on schools, etc. in Highlands, 1728-1736	MS 3431
Delvine Papers	MS 1034
Disposition of Troops in the Highlands, 1749	MS 5129
Highland and Land Law Reform Association	MS 2636
	MS 2644
Improvements for the Highlands, 1812	MS 5007
'Informations' regarding the Highlands, c.1750	MS 98
Letters concerning the Highlands, 1805, 1809	MS 5319
Letters on distress in Highlands, 1837	MS 1054
Letters re distress of 1846-7	MS 9702
	MS 9713
Letters regarding commission for settlement of Highlands, 1678-1679	MS 975
Memorial on law against Highland dress, c.1748	MS 5127
Memorial on the State of the Highlands	Adv.MS 81.1.5
Observations on the improvements of Highland Estates in the North west Coast of Scotland	Adv.MS 20.5.5
Observations on the North of Scotland, 1796	MS 1034
Order for disarming of Highlands, 1725	MS Ch.2594
Papers concerning the disorders in the Highlands, c.1635	MS 1915
Papers on the State of the Highlands in the 1750s	MS 2200
Proposal for encouragement of sailors to settle in Highlands	MS 5006
Proposals concerning Highlands, 1748	MS 5201
Recruiting in the Highlands, 1791	MS 1048
Report &c relating to the Highlands, 1724	MS 7118

Bibliography

National Library of Scotland (Continued)

Rental of Kintyre, 1678	MS 3367
Society for the Reformation of Manners	MS 1954
Some Remarks on the Highland Clans and Methods Proposed for Civilising them	Adv.MS 16.1.14 Adv.MS 32.4.6
Statistics on Relief given to poor in 1842	MS 15047
The Highland Man's Observation on the Alteration of the Times	MS 301
The King's Answer on the Highlands 1667	MS 7033

Edinburgh University Library

Essay by Sir Aeneas Macpherson on the establishment of inland villages in the Highlands of Scotland	La.II.412
Letters of Dempster, George, on the state of the northern parts of Scotland and the means pursued for their improvement	La.III.379
Minutes of a Committee of the General Assembly for Administering Funds for Gaelic-speaking students, 1763-1787	La.III.341
Miscellaneous papers of the SSPCK	La.II.482
Miscellaneous papers of the SSPCK and the Royal Bounty Committee	La.II.484
Report to the commissioners for improving fisheries and manufactures in Scotland on the state of industry and trade in the Highlands and Islands, 1755	La.II.623
Some hints to HRH the Duke of Cumberland concerning the Highlands of Scotland	Dc.6.70/2
Tribuum gemitus, or the Highland clanns sad & just complaint, 1698	La.III.319

New College Library

Highland Library Material	L.5.1.6.1., 5-12
Letters regarding the Gaelic Bible	L.5.1.6.1., 1-4
Kirkwood MSS	
Kirkwood MSS (articles of amendment to printed versions of 1697 pamphlet)	Box 2 21(36)

Bibliography

British Museum

Walker's Report on the Hebrides, 1764   King's MS 105

Bibliography

PRINTED PRIMARY SOURCES

Parliamentary Papers

Highland Churches ... the present State of the New Churches and Manses in the Highlands and Islands of Scotland, P.P., 1831-1832, XXX

Report from the Select Committee on the State of Education in Scotland, P.P., 1837-1838, VII

First Report from the Select Committee on Emigration, P.P., 1841, VI

Report of the Agent General for Emigration on the Applicability of Emigration to relieve Distress in the Highlands (1837) P.P., 1841, XXVII

Report from the Select Committee appointed to inquire into the condition of the Population of the Highlands and Islands of Scotland, and into the practicability of affording the People relief by means of Emigration, P.P., 1841, VI

Committee of Council on Education's Correspondence with the Education Committee of the General Assembly of the Church of Scotland, P.P., 1843, XL

Report on the Poor Laws, Scotland, P.P., 1844, XXVII-XXXVI

Documents relative to the Distress and Famine in Scotland in the Year 1783, in consequence of the late Harvest and Loss of the Potato Crop, P.P., 1846, XXXVII

First Annual Report of the Board of Supervision for the Relief of the Poor in Scotland, P.P., 1847, XXXVIII

Report of the Central Board for the Relief of Destitution in the Highlands and Islands of Scotland (1847), P.P., LIII

Report to the Board of Supervision, by Sir John McNeill, G.C.B. on the Western Highlands and Islands, P.P., 1851, XXVI

Report on the State of Education in the Hebrides by Alexander Nicolson, P.P., 1867, XXV

Gaelic Census (Scotland), P.P., 1882, L

Bibliography

Parliamentary Papers (Continued)

Commission of Inquiry into the Condition of Crofters and
Cottars in the Highlands and Islands of Scotland, P.P.,
1884-1885, XXXII-XXXVI

Reports of Societies and Institutions

Address from the Presbytery of Paisley to Friends Interest-
ed in the Moral, and Spiritual Welfare of the Highlanders,
Residing out of Paisley, and within the Bounds of the
Presbytery, Paisley, N.d.

Annual Reports of the British and Foreign Bible Society
(London, 1805-1871)

Annual Reports of the Dundee Auxiliary Gaelic School
Society (Dundee, 1820, 1823-1825)

Annual Reports of the Highland Missionary Society (Edinburgh, 1821, 1822, 1826, 1829-1836)

Educational Statistics of the Highlands and Islands of
Scotland, 1833 (Edinburgh, 1834)

First Report of the Ladies Association in Support of Gaelic
Schools in Connection with the Church of Scotland (Edinburgh, 1847)

First Report of the Society in Paisley and its Vicinity for
Gaelic Missions to the Highlands and Islands of Scotland
(Paisley, 1818)

Gaelic Schools Society, Annual Reports (Edinburgh Society
for the support of Gaelic Schools) (Edinburgh, 1811-1861,
1871, 1875)

Moral Statistics of the Highlands and Islands of Scotland,
compiled from returns received by the Inverness Society for
the Education of the Poor in the Highlands (Inverness,
1826)

Regulations of the Highlands Missionary Society, for
Promoting Religious Instruction in the Highlands and
Islands of Scotland (Edinburgh, 1819)

Reports of the Committee of the General Assembly for
Increasing the Education and Religious Instruction in

<u>Scotland, particularly</u> in the <u>Highlands and Islands</u>
(Edinburgh, 1827-1833)

<u>Newspapers consulted</u>

<u>An Gaidheal</u> (1871-1966)

<u>An Teachdaire Gaelach</u> (1829-1831)

<u>Celtic Magazine</u> (1875-1888)

<u>The Celtic Monthly</u> (1893-1917)

<u>The Edinburgh Review</u> (1802-1889)

<u>Guth na Bliadhna</u> (1904-1925)

<u>The Highland Monthly</u> (1889-1893)

<u>The Highlander</u> (1873-1881)

<u>The Oban Times</u> (1880-1980)

<u>Scots Magazine</u> (1739-1817)

SECONDARY SOURCES

Adam, M.I. 'The Highland Emigration of 1770', <u>Scottish
Historical Review</u>, XVI, 1919

Adam, M.I. 'The Causes of the Highland Emigration of
1783-1803', <u>Scottish Historical Review</u>, XVII, 1920

Adam, R.J. (ed.), <u>John Home's Survey of Assynt</u> (Edinburgh,
1960)

Adam Smith, J. 'Some Eighteenth-Century Ideas of Scotland',
in N.T. Phillipson and R. Mitchison (eds.), <u>Scotland in the
Age of Improvement</u> (Edinburgh, 1970)

Adamson, W.I. <u>Hegemony and Revolution</u> (Berkeley, 1980)

Agnew, J.A. and Duncan, J.S. 'The transfer of ideas into
Anglo-American human geography', <u>Progress in Human Geography</u>, 5(1) 1981

Agnew, J., Mercer, J. and Sopher, D. (eds.), <u>The City in</u>

Cultural Context (Boston, 1984)

Allardyce, J. (ed.), Historical Papers Relating to the Jacobite Period 1699-1750 (Aberdeen, 1899)

An Comunn Gaidhealach The Teaching of Gaelic in Highland Schools (London, 1970)

An Comunn Gaidhealach Report of the Special Commission on the Teaching of Gaelic in Schools and Colleges (Glasgow, 1936)

Anderson, G. and P. Guide to the Highlands and Islands of Scotland (London, 1834)

Anderson, J. Observations on the Means of Exciting a Spirit of National Industry, Chiefly Intended to Promote the Agriculture, Commerce, Manufactures and Fisheries of Scotland (Dublin, 1779)

Anderson, J. An Account of the present state of the Hebrides and Western Coasts of Scotland (Edinburgh, 1785)

Anderson, J. Prize Essay on the State of Society and Knowledge in the Highlands of Scotland; particularly in the Northern Counties in 1745 (Edinburgh, 1827)

Anderson, J. 'Essay on the Present State of the Highlands and Islands of Scotland', Transactions, Highland and Agricultural Society of Scotland, II, 1831

Anderson, P. 'The antimonies of Antonio Gramsci' New Left Review, 100, 1977

Anon. The Highland Complaint (London, 1737)

Anon. The Highlander Delineated (London, 1745)

Apter, D.E. (ed.), Ideology and Discontent (New York, 1964)

Ash, M. The Strange Death of Scottish History (Edinburgh, 1980)

Auld, A. Ministers and Men of the Far North (Wick, 1868)

Baker, A.R.H. and Billinge, M.D. (eds.), Period and Place: research methods in historical geography (Cambridge, 1982)

Baker, A.R.H. and Gregory, D. (eds.), Explorations in

Bibliography

<u>Historical Geography</u> (Cambridge, 1984)

Barrell, J. <u>English Literature in History 1730-1780: an equal wide survey</u> (London, 1983)

Barron, J. <u>The Northern Highlands in the Nineteenth Century</u> (Inverness, 1903-1913)

Barrow, G.W.S. <u>The Kingdom of the Scots</u> (London, 1973)

Bates, T.R. 'Gramsci and the theory of hegemony', <u>Journal of the History of Ideas</u>, 36, 1975.

Beaton, A.J. <u>The Social and Economic Condition of the Highlands since 1800</u> (Stirling, 1906)

Beaton, D. <u>Bibliography of Gaelic Books, pamphlets and magazine articles for the counties of Caithness and Sutherland</u> (Wick, 1923)

Beattie, J. <u>Scoticisms, arranged in alphabetical order, designed to correct improprieties of speech and writing</u> (Edinburgh, 1791)

Belches, A. <u>An Account of the Society in Scotland for Propagating Christian Knowledge from its Commencement in 1709</u> (Edinburgh, 1774)

Berg, M. <u>The Age of Manufactures</u> (London, 1985)

Berg, M., Hudson, P., and Sonenscher, M. <u>Manufacture in Town and Country before the Factory</u> (Cambridge, 1983)

Billinge, M.D. 'Hegemony, Class and Power in late Georgian and early Victorian England: towards a cultural geography', in A.R.H. Baker and D. Gregory (eds.), <u>Explorations in Historical Geography</u> (Cambridge, 1984)

Black, G.F. <u>MacPherson's Ossian and the Ossianic Controversy: a contribution towards a Bibliography</u> (New York, 1926)

Black, R.I. 'The Gaelic Academy: the cultural commitment of the Highland Society of Scotland', <u>Scottish Gaelic Studies</u>, XIV(II), 1986

Black, R. <u>Mac Mhaighstir Alasdair: The Ardnamurchan Years</u> (Inverness, 1986)

Blackie, J.S. <u>The Gaelic Language: its Classical Affini-</u>

ties and Distinctive Character (Edinburgh, 1864)

Blackie, J.S. Ought Gaelic to be taught in Highland Schools (Edinburgh, 1877)

Blackie, J.S. Gaelic Societies, Highland Depopulation and Land Law Reform (Edinburgh, 1880)

Blackie, J.S. The Language and Literature of the Scottish Highlands (London, 1881)

Blackie, J.S. Altavona, Fact and Fiction from my life in the Highlands (London, 1883)

Blackie, J.S. The Scottish Highlanders and the Land Laws (London, 1885)

Blaut, J.M. 'A radical critique of cultural geography', Antipode, 12(2), 1980

Boud, R.S. 'Scottish agricultural improvement societies 1723-1835', Review of Scottish Culture, 1,1984

Bowen, E.G. 'Les Pays de Galles', Trans.Inst.Brit.Geogrs., 26, 1959

Briggs, A. and Saville, J. (eds), Essays in Labour History (London, 1957)

Brown, T. Annals of the Disruption (Edinburgh, 1890)

Browne, D. History of the Highlands and of the Highland Clans (Glasgow, 1838)

Bruce, S. 'Social change and collective behaviour: the revival in eighteenth-century Ross-shire', British Journal of Sociology, XXIV(4), 1983

Bryson, G. Man and Society: the Scottish Enquiry of the Eighteenth Century (Princeton, 1945)

Buchanan, D. Laoidhe Spioradail le Dughall Bochannan (Duinedin, 1767)

Buchanan, J.G. Travels in the Western Hebrides (London, 1793)

Bumsted, J. The People's Clearance 1770-1815 (Edinburgh, 1982)

427

Burt, E. Letters from a Gentleman in the North of Scotland to his friend in London (London, 1754)

Butlin, R.A. 'Early industrialization in Europe: concepts and problems', Geographical Journal, 152(1), 1986

By a Highlander The Present Conduct of the Chieftains and Proprietors of Lands in the Highlands of Scotland (London, 1773)

Caird, J.B. 'Land use in the Uists since 1800', Proceedings of the Royal Society of Edinburgh, 77(B), 1979

Cameron, A.C. Go Listen to the Crofters (Stornoway, 1986)

Cameron, G. A History and Description of the Town of Inverness (Edinburgh, 1847)

Cameron, J. Celtic Law (London, 1937)

Campbell, D. The Language, Poetry and Music of the Highland Clans (Edinburgh, 1862)

Campbell, J. A Full and Particular Description of the Highlands of Scotland (London, 1752)

Campbell, J.L. Gaelic in Scottish Education and Life (Edinburgh, 1950)

Campbell, J.L. Highland Songs of the Forty-Five (Edinburgh, 1984 edn.)

Campbell, M. Argyll: the Enduring Heartland (Edinburgh, 1977)

Campbell, R.H. Scotland Since 1707: the Rise of an Industrial Society (Oxford, 1965)

Campbell, R.H. and Skinner, A. (eds.), The Origins and Nature of the Scottish Enlightenment (Edinburgh, 1982)

Carmichael, A. Carmina Gadelica (Edinburgh, 1900-1971)

Carter, I. 'Economic Models and Recent History of the Highlands', Scottish Studies, 15, 1971

Carter, I. 'Marriage patterns and social sectors in Scotland before the eighteenth century', Scottish Studies, 17(1), 1973

Bibliography

Carter, I. 'The changing image of the Scottish peasantry 1745-1890', in R. Samuel (ed.), People's History and Socialist Theory (London, 1981)

Chapman, M The Nature of Scottish Gaelic Folk Culture, Unpublished B.Litt., University of Oxford, 1977

Chapman, M. The Gaelic Vision in Scottish Culture (London, 1978)

Charlesworth, A. Social Protest in a Rural Society: the spatial diffusion of the Captain Swing disturbances of 1830-1831 (HGRG Publication 1, Norwich, 1979)

Charlesworth, A. (ed.), An Atlas of Rural Protest in Britain 1548-1900 (London, 1983)

Charlton, D.G. New Images of the Natural in France (Cambridge, 1984)

Cheal, D. 'Hegemony, ideology and contradictory consciousness', Sociological Quarterly, 20, 1979

Chitnis, A. The Scottish Enlightenment (London, 1976)

Coleman, D. 'Protoindustrialization: a concept too many', Economic History Review, 36, 1983

Condry, E. The Scottish Highland Problem: Some Anthropological Aspects, Unpublished B.Litt., University of Oxford, 1977

Cooper, D. Road to the Isles: travellers in the Hebrides 1770-1914 (London, 1979)

Cosgrove, D. 'Towards a radical cultural geography', Antipode, 15(1), 1983

Cosgrove, D.E. 'Prospect, perspective, and the evolution of the landscape idea', Transactions, Institute of British Geographers, 10(1), 1985

Coull, J.R. 'Fisheries in the North-East of Scotland before 1800', Scottish Studies, 13, 1969

Coull, J.R. 'Fisheries in Scotland in the 16th, 17th and 18th centuries: the evidence in MacFarlane's Geographical Collections', Scottish Geographical Magazine, 93(1), 1977

Bibliography

Coull, J.R. 'The Scottish Herring Fishery 1800-1914:
development and intensification of a pattern of resource
use', Scottish Geographical Magazine, 102(1), 1986

Cowan, E.J. (ed.), The Historical Highlands: a Guide to
Reading (Edinburgh, 1977)

Cowan, E. (ed.), The People's Past (Edinburgh, 1980)

Craig, D.M., Scottish Literature and the Scottish People
(London, 1961)

Craven, J.B. (ed.), Records of the Diocese of Argyll and
the Isles 1560-1860 (Kirkwall, 1907)

Cregeen, E.R. (ed.), Argyll Estate Instructions 1771-1805
(Edinburgh, 1964)

Cregeen, E.R. 'The Changing Role of the House of Argyll in
the Scottish Highlands', in I. Lewis (ed.), History and
Social Anthropology (London, 1968)

Cregeen, E.R. 'The Tacksmen and their Successors: a Study
of Tenurial Reorganisation in Mull, Morvern and Tiree in
the Early Eighteenth Century', Scottish Studies, 13(2),
1969

Cregeen, E.R. 'Oral Sources for the social history of the
Scottish Highlands and Islands', Oral History, 2, 1974

Crowley, D.H. 'The "Crofters' Party" 1885-1892', History
Today, XXXV, 1956

Daiches, D. The Paradox of Scottish Culture: the
Eighteenth-Century Experience (Oxford, 1964)

Day, J.P. Public Administration in the Highlands and
Islands of Scotland (London, 1918)

Defoe, D. A Tour through the Whole Island of Great Britain,
Divided into Circuits or Journeys (London, 1742)

Devine, T. (ed.), Lairds and Improvement in the Scotland of
the Enlightenment (Strathclyde, 1978)

Devine, T. 'Temporary Migration and the Scottish Highlands
in the Nineteenth Century', Economic History Review,
XXXII(3), 1979

Bibliography

Devine, T. 'The Highland Clearances', ReFRESH, 4, 1987

Dickinson, H.T. Liberty and Property: Political Ideology in Eighteenth Century Britain (London, 1977)

Dickinson, W.C. Scotland from the Earliest Times to 1603 (Edinburgh, 1961)

Dickson, T. (ed.), Scottish Capitalism: class, state and nation from before the Union to the Present (London, 1980)

Dodgshon, R.A. Land and Society in Early Scotland (Oxford, 1981)

Donajgrodski, A.P. Social Control in Nineteenth-Century Britain (London, 1977)

Donaldson, W. '"Bonny Highland Laddie": the Making of a Myth', Scottish Literary Journal, 3(2), 1976

Douglas, T. [Earl of Selkirk] Observations on the Present State of the Highlands of Scotland with a view of the Causes and Probable Consequences of Emigration (Edinburgh, 1806)

Dunbabin, J. Rural Discontent in Nineteenth-Century Britain (London, 1974)

Duncan, J.S. 'The superorganic in American cultural geography', Annals, Association of American Geographers, 70(2), 1980

Dunlop, J. The British Fisheries Society 1786-1893 (Edinburgh, 1978)

Dunsford, M. and Perrons, D. The Arena of Capital (London, 1983)

Dupré, L. Marx's Social Critique of Culture (Yale, 1983)

Durkacz, V. 'The source of the language problem in Scottish education 1688-1709', Scottish Historical Review, LVII, 1978

Durkacz, V.E. 'The Church of Scotland's eighteenth-century attitudes to Gaelic preaching', Scottish Gaelic Studies, XIII(II), 1981

Durkacz, V.E. The Decline of the Celtic Languages (Edinburgh, 1983)

Bibliography

Durie, A. 'Linen-spinning in the north of Scotland 1746-1773', Northern Scotland, 2(1), 1975

Durie, A. The Scottish Linen Industry in the Eighteenth Century (Edinburgh, 1979)

Ennew, J. The Western Isles Today (Cambridge, 1980)

Fairhurst, H. 'The evolution of Highland rural settlement with particular reference to Argyllshire', Scottish Studies, 6, 1962

Fairhurst, H. 'Agrarian improvement and the development of enclosure in the south-west Highlands of Scotland', Scottish Historical Review, 42, 1963

Fairhurst, H. 'The surveys for the Sutherland clearances 1813-1820', Scottish Studies, 8, 1964

Farquharson, A. An address to Highlanders respecting their Native Gaelic showing its and the Broad Scotch's superiority over the Artificial English (Edinburgh, 1868)

Femia, J. 'Hegemony and consciousness in the thought of Antonio Gramsci', Political Studies, 23, 1975

Femia, J. Gramsci's Political Thought (Oxford, 1981)

Ferguson, W. 'The Problems of the Established Church in the West Highlands and Islands in the Eighteenth Century', Records, Scottish Church History Society, XVII(I), 1972

Ferguson, W. Scotland 1689 to the Present (Edinburgh, 1978)

Fergusson, A. Essay on the History of Civil Society (Edinburgh, 1767)

Fleischer, H. Marxism and History (London, 1973)

Flinn, M.W. (ed.), Scottish Population History (Cambridge, 1977)

Flinn, M. 'Malthus, emigration and potatoes in the Scottish north-west, 1770-1870', in L.M. Cullen and T.C. Smout (eds.), Comparative Aspects of Scottish and Irish Economic and Social History 1600-1900 (Edinburgh, 1977)

Forgacs, D. and Nowell-Smith, G. Antonio Gramsci - Selections from Cultural Writings (London, 1983)

Bibliography

Fraser Darling, F. West Highland Survey (Oxford, 1955)

Fraser-Mackintosh, C. Antiquarian Notes (Inverness, 1865)

Fraser-Mackintosh, C. 'Present Claims on Gaelic-speaking Highlanders', Celtic Magazine, III, 1878

Fullarton, A. and Baird, C.R. Remarks on the Evils at Present Affecting the Highlands and Islands of Scotland, with some suggestions as to their Remedies (Glasgow, 1838)

Gailey, R.A. 'Settlement and population in Kintyre 1750-1890', Scottish Geographical Magazine, 76, 1960

Gailey, R.A. 'Mobility of Tenants on a Highland Estate in the Early Nineteenth Century', Scottish Historical Review, 77, 1961

Gaskell, P. Morvern Transformed (Edinburgh, 1968)

Gaskill, H. '"Ossian" Macpherson: towards a rehabilitation', Comparative Criticism, 8, 1986

Geddes, A. The Isle of Lewis and Harris (Edinburgh, 1955)

Geertz, C. The Interpretation of Culture (New York, 1973)

Giddens, A. The Class Structure of the Advanced Societies (London, 1973)

Gilpin, W. Observations on the Highlands of Scotland (London, 1789)

Glen, D. (ed.), Whither Scotland? (London, 1971)

Goodenough, W.H. Culture, Language and Society (Massachusetts, 1971)

Graham, H.G. The Social Life of Scotland in the Eighteenth Century (London, 1906)

Gramsci, A. Prison Notebooks (London, 1970)

Grant, A. Letters from the Mountains (London, 1807)

Grant, I.F. The Economic History of Scotland (London, 1934)

Grant, I. Highland Folk Ways (London, 1967)

Bibliography

Gray, M. 'The Kelp Industry in the Highlands and Islands', Economic History Review, IV, 1951

Gray, M. 'Settlement in the Highlands, 1750-1950: the documentary and written record', Scottish Studies, 6, 1952

Gray, M. 'The Abolition of Run-rig in the Highlands of Scotland', Economic History Review, IV(2), 1952

Gray, M. 'Economic welfare and money income in the Highlands, 1750-1850', Scottish Journal of Political Economy, II, 1955

Gray, M. 'The Highland Potato Famine of the 1840s', Economic History Review, VII, 1955

Gray, M. The Highland Economy 1750-1850 (Edinburgh, 1957)

Gray, M. 'The Consolidation of the Crofting System', Agricultural History Review, V, 1957

Gray, M. 'Crofting and Fishing in the North West Highlands 1890-1914', Northern Scotland, 1, 1972

Gregory, D. The History of the Western Highlands and Isles of Scotland (Edinburgh, 1881)

Grey, R. 'Bourgeois hegemony in Victorian Britain', in The Communist University of London (ed.), Class, Hegemony and Party (London, 1977)

Grimble, I. The Trial of Patrick Sellar (London, 1962)

Grimble, I. The Survival of a Celtic Society in the Mackay Country formerly called Strathnaver in Northern Scotland, from the Sixteenth Century, Unpublished Ph.D., University of Aberdeen. 1963

Grimble, I. The World of Rob Donn (Edinburgh, 1979)

Haldane, A.R.B. The Drove Roads of Scotland (Edinburgh, 1952)

Haldane, A.R.B. New Ways Through the Glens (Edinburgh, 1962)

Hamilton, H. Industrial Revolution in Scotland (London, 1966)

434

Bibliography

Hanham, H.J. 'The Problem of Highland Discontent 1880-1885', Transactions, Royal Historical Society, XIX, 1969

Harding, A.W. Sgoilean Chriosd: a study of the Edinburgh Society for the Support of Gaelic Schools, Unpublished M.Litt., University of Glasgow, 1979

Harris, M. Cultural Materialism (New York, 1979)

Hechter, M. Internal Colonialism: the Celtic Fringe in British National Development 1536-1966 (London, 1975)

Henderson, H. 'The Women of the Glen: some thoughts on Highland History', in R. O'Driscoll (ed.), The Celtic Consciousness (Dublin, 1982)

Henderson, J. General View of the Agriculture of Sutherland (London, 1812)

Heron, R. General View of the Natural Circumstances of those Isles, adjacent to the North-West coast of Scotland (Edinburgh, 1794)

Heron, R. Scotland Delineated (Edinburgh, 1797)

Heron, R. Scotland Described: or A Topographical Description of all the Counties of Scotland (Edinburgh, 1797)

Hildebrandt, R.N. Migration and Economic Change in the Northern Highlands During the Nineteenth Century, with Particular Reference to the Period 1851-1891, Unpublished Ph.D., University of Glasgow, 1980

Hoare, Q. and Nowell-Smith, G. (eds.), Selections from the Prison Notebooks of Antonio Gramsci (London, 1971)

Holmes, D.T. Literary Tours in the Highlands and Islands of Scotland (Paisley, 1909)

Home, H. [Lord Kames] The Gentleman Farmer (Edinburgh, 1776)

Home, H. [Lord Kames] Sketches of the History of Man (Edinburgh, 1807)

Home , J. The History of the Rebellion in the Year 1745 (London, 1802)

Bibliography

Hont, T. and Ignatieff, M. (eds.), Wealth and Virtue: the shaping of political economy in the Scottish Enlightenment (Cambridge, 1982)

Howatson, W. 'The Scottish Hairst and Seasonal Labour 1600–1870', Scottish Studies, 26, 1982

Hunter, J. Diocese and Presbytery of Dunkeld (London, 1918)

Hunter, J. 'Sheep and deer: Highland sheep farming, 1850–1900', Northern Scotland, 1(2), 1973

Hunter, J. 'The emergence of the crofting community: the religious contribution 1798–1843', Scottish Studies, 18, 1974

Hunter, J. 'The politics of Highland land reform, 1873–1895', Scottish Historical Review, LIII, 1974

Hunter, J. 'The Gaelic Connection: the Highlands, Ireland and nationalism, 1873–1922', Scottish Historical Review, LIV(2), 1975

Hunter, J. The Making of the Crofting Community (Edinburgh, 1976)

Hunter, J. For the People's Cause: from the writings of John Murdoch (London, 1986)

Innes, C. Origines Parochiales Scotiae (Edinburgh, 1851–1855)

Innes, J.L. 'Landuse changes in the Scottish Highlands during the 19th century: the role of pasture degeneration', Scottish Geographical Magazine, 99(3), 1983

Innes, T. A Critical Essay on the Ancient Inhabitants of the Northern Parts of Britain or Scotland (London, 1729)

Irvine, A. An Inquiry into the Causes and Effects of Emigration from the Highlands and Islands of Scotland (Edinburgh, 1804)

Jackson, K.H. Language and History in Early Britain (Edinburgh, 1953)

Johnson, S. A Journey to the Western Isles of Scotland (London, 1775)

Bibliography

Jones, H. 'Evolution of Scottish Migration Patterns: a social-relations-of-production approach', Scottish Geographical Magazine, 102(3), 1986

Keesing, F.M. Cultural Anthropology (New York, 1959)

Keesing, F.M. 'Theories of culture', Annual Review of Anthropology, 3, 1974

Kellas, J.G. 'Highland Migration to Glasgow and the Origin of the Scottish Labour Movement', Bulletin, Society for the Study of Labour History, 12, 1966

Kellas, J.G. 'The Crofters' War', History Today, XII, 1962

Keltie, J.S. A History of the Scottish Highlands, Highland Clans and Highland Regiments (Edinburgh, 1875)

Kirkwood, J. An Answer to the Objection against Printing the Bible in Irish, as being prejudicial to the Design of Extirpating the Irish Language out the Highlands of Scotland (Edinburgh, 1687)

Knox, J. A View of the British Empire more especially Scotland with some proposals for the Improvement of that country (London, 1784)

Knox, J. Observations on the Northern Fisheries (London, 1786)

Knox, J. A Discourse on the Expediency of Establishing Fishing Stations (London, 1786)

Knox, J. A Tour through the Highlands of Scotland and the Hebride Isles in 1786 (London, 1787)

Kolakowski, L. Main Currents of Marxism (Oxford, 1978)

Kyd, J.G. (ed.), Scottish Population Statistics (Edinburgh, 1952)

Lang, A. (ed.), The Highlands of Scotland in 1750 (Edinburgh, 1898)

Langton, J. and Morris, R.J. (eds.), Atlas of Industrializing Britain 1780-1914 (London, 1986)

Lawson, W.R. 'The poetry and prose of the crofter question', National Review, 4, 1885

Bibliography

Lehmann, W.C. Henry Home, Lord Kames, and the Scottish Enlightenment (The Hague, 1971)

Leneman, L. Living in Atholl: a social history of the estates 1685-1785 (Edinburgh, 1986)

Lenman, B.P. Integration, Enlightenment and Industrialization (London, 1981)

Lettice, J. Letters on a Tour through Various Parts of Scotland in 1792 (London, 1794)

Levitt, I. and Smout, T.C. The State of the Scottish Working Class in 1843 (Edinburgh, 1979)

Lichtheim, G. The Concept of Ideology and Other Essays (New York, 1967)

Lindsay, J.M. 'The commercial use of Highland woodland, 1750-1870: a reconsideration', Scottish Geographical Magazine, 92(1), 1976

Lindsay, J.M. 'Forestry and agriculture in the Scottish Highlands, 1700-1850', Agricultural History Review, 25, 1977

Lindsay, J.M. 'The iron industry in the Highlands: charcoal blast furnaces', Scottish Historical Review, LVII, 1977

Lobban, R.D. The Migration of Highlanders into Lowland Scotland c.1750-1890, with particular reference to Greenock, Unpublished Ph.D., University of Edinburgh, 1969

Loch, J. An Account of the Improvements on the Estates of the Marquess of Stafford in the Counties of Stafford and Salop, and on the Estate of Sutherland (London, 1820)

Logan, J. The Scottish Gael; or Celtic Manners as preserved among the Highlanders (London, 1831)

Logan, J. Sketch of the Origins and Progress of Scottish Societies in London and Elsewhere (London, 1840)

Logue, K. Popular Disturbances in Scotland 1780-1815 (Edinburgh, 1979)

Lythe, S.G.E. and Butt, J. An Economic History of Scotland 1100-1939 (Glasgow, 1975)

438

Bibliography

MacAskill, A.J. 'Life in the Highlands in the 18th and 19th Centuries: As seen through the eyes of the poets of the period', Transactions, Gaelic Society of Inverness, XXXXI, 1952

MacBean, L. Buchanan: the Sacred Bard of the Scottish Highlands (London, 1920)

MacCulloch, J. The Highlands and Western Isles of Scotland (London, 1824)

MacDhomnuill, R. Comh-Chruinneach Orainnaigh Gaidhealach Ann' N Eilean Eigg (Dun-Eideinn, 1776)

MacDonald, A. Leabhar a Theasgarc Ainminnin (Dun-Eideinn, 1741)

MacDonald, A. Ais-Eiridh na Sean-Chanoin Albannaich (Dun-Eideinn, 1751)

MacDonald, A. and MacDonald, A. The Poems of Alexander MacDonald (Inverness, 1924)

MacDonald, C.M. History of Argyll (Glasgow, 1950)

MacDonald, D. Lewis: a History of the Island (Edinburgh, 1978)

MacDonald, D.F. Scotland's Shifting Population (Glasgow, 1937)

MacDonald, J. General View of the Agriculture of the Hebrides (Edinburgh, 1811)

MacDonald, J. 'On the agriculture of the county of Sutherland', Transactions, Highland and Agricultural Society of Scotland, XII, 1880

Macdonald, W. 'On the agriculture of Inverness-shire', Transactions, Highland and Agricultural Society of Scotland, IV, 1872

MacDonell, M. The Emigrant Experience: Songs of Highland Emigrants in North America (Toronto, 1982)

McElroy, D. Scotland's Age of Improvement: a survey of eighteenth-century literary clubs and societies (Washington, 1969)

439

Bibliography

MacGill, W. Old Ross-shire and Scotland as seen in the Tain and Balnagown Documents (Inverness, 1909)

MacGillivray, A. Sketches of Religion and Revivals of Religion in the North Highlands during the last century (Edinburgh, 1859)

Macinnes, A.I. 'Scottish Gaeldom 1638-1651: the vernacular response to the Covenanting dynamic', in J. Dwyer, R.A. Mason and A. Murdoch (eds.), New Perspectives on the Politics and Culture of Early Modern Scotland (Edinburgh, 1984)

MacInnes, J. The Evangelical Movement in the Highlands of Scotland (Aberdeen, 1951)

MacInnes, J. 'A Gaelic song of the Sutherland Clearances', Scottish Studies, VIII, 1964

MacInnes, J. 'The Oral Tradition in Gaelic Poetry', Scottish Studies, 12, 1968

MacInnes, J. 'Gaelic poetry and historical tradition', in L. Maclean (ed.), The Middle Ages in the Highlands (Inverness, 1981)

MacInnes, J. 'Religion in Gaelic society', Transactions, Gaelic Society of Inverness, LII, 1982

Mackay, M. (ed.), The Rev. Dr. John Walker's Report on the Hebrides (Edinburgh, 1980)

Mackenzie, A. The History of the Highland Clearances (Glasgow, 1946)

Mackenzie, G. A General Survey of the Counties of Ross and Cromarty (London, 1810)

MacKenzie, G.S. Letter to the Proprietors of Land in Ross-shire (Edinburgh, 1803)

Mackenzie, W.C. The Western Isles: their history, traditions and place-names (Paisley, 1932)

McKerral, A. 'The Tacksman and his holding in the S.W. Highlands', Scottish Historical Review, 26, 1947

McKerral, A. Kintyre in the Seventeenth Century (Edinburgh, 1948)

440

Bibliography

MacKinlay, D. The Isle of Lewis and its Fishermen Crofters (London, 1878)

MacKinnon, D. 'Education in Argyll and the Isles 1638-1709', Records, Scottish Church History Society, 6, 1938

MacKinnon, K.M. The Lion's Tongue (Inverness, 1974)

MacKinnon, K.M. Language, Education and Social Processes in a Gaelic Community (London, 1977)

MacLaren, A.A. (ed.), Social Class in Scotland: Past and Present (Edinburgh, 1978)

Maclean, D. Typographia Scoto-Gadelica (Edinburgh, 1915)

Maclean, D. 'Highland Libraries in the Eighteenth Century', Records, Glasgow Bibliographical Society, VIII, 1923

Maclean, D. 'Highland Libraries in the Eighteenth Century', Transactions, Gaelic Society of Inverness, XXXI, 1923

Maclean, L. The History of the Celtic Language (London, 1840)

Maclean, M. The Literature of the Celts (Glasgow, 1926)

Maclean, M. The Literature of the Highlands (Glasgow, 1926)

Maclean, M. and Carrell, C. As An Fhearann: from the land (Stornoway, 1986)

Maclean, S. 'The Poetry of the Clearances', Transactions, Gaelic Society of Inverness, XXXVIII, 1939-1941

McLellan, D. Marx: the first 100 years (London, 1982)

Macleod, D.J. 'Gaelic Prose', Transactions, Gaelic Society of Inverness, XLIX, 1974-1976

MacNaughton, P. Lecture on the Importance of the Gaelic Language to Highlanders (Perth, 1885)

McNish, N. The True Method of Preserving the Gaelic Language (Edinburgh, 1828)

MacPhail, I.M.M. 'The Skye Military Expedition of 1884-1885', Transactions, Gaelic Society of Inverness,

Bibliography

XLVIII, 1974

MacPhail, I.M.M. 'Prelude to the Crofters' War, 1870-1880', Transactions, Gaelic Society of Inverness, XLIX, 1974-1976

MacPherson, A.G. 'An old Highland parish register' (Part I), Scottish Studies, 11, 1967

MacPherson, A.G. 'An old Highland parish register' (Part II), Scottish Studies, 12, 1968

MacPherson, A.G. 'Migration fields in a traditional Highland community, 1350-1850', Journal of Historical Geography, 10(1), 1984

MacRae, A. Revivals in the Highlands and Islands in the Nineteenth Century (London, 1905)

MacTavish, D.C. (ed.), Minutes of the Synod of Argyll (Edinburgh, 1943-1944)

Markus, T.R. (ed.), Order in Space and Society: architectural form and its context in the Scottish Enlightenment (Edinburgh, 1982)

Martin, A. Kintyre: the hidden past (Edinburgh, 1984)

Marshall, W. General View of the Agriculture of the Central Highlands of Scotland (London, 1794)

Martin, M. A Description of the Western Isles of Scotland (London, 1703)

Mason, J. 'Scottish Charity Schools of the Eighteenth Century', Scottish Historical Review, XXXIII, 1954

Matheson, W. (ed.), The Songs of John MacCodrum (Edinburgh, 1938)

Medick, H. 'The proto-industrial family economy: the structural function of household and family during the transition from peasant society to industrial capitalism', Social History, 3, 1976

Meek, D. 'Gaelic Poets of the Land Agitation', Transactions, Gaelic Society of Inverness, XLIX, 1977

Mewett, P. 'Occupational Pluralism in Crofting: the Influence of Non-Croft Work on the Patterns of Crofting

Bibliography

Agriculture in the Isle of Lewis since about 1859', The Scottish Journal of Sociology, 2(1), 1977

Mikesell, M.W. 'Tradition and Innovation in Cultural Geography', Annals, Association of American Geographers, 68(1), 1978

Millar, A. (ed.), A Selection of Scottish Forfeited Estates (Edinburgh, 1909)

Millar, J. The Origin of the Distinction of Ranks (London, 1779)

Millar, J.H. A Literary History of Scotland (London, 1903)

Mitchell, A. (ed.), Inverness Kirk - Session Records (Inverness, 1902)

Mitchell, A. (ed.), Alexander Macfarlane's Geographical Collections Relating to Scotland (Edinburgh, 1906)

Mitchell, D. History of the Highlands and Gaelic Scotland (Paisley, 1900)

Mitchell, R.D. 'Economic Development and Cultural Change: a Highland Review', Historical Geography Newsletter, 5(1), 1975

Mitchison, R. Agricultural Sir John: the Life of Sir John Sinclair of Ulbster 1754-1835 (London, 1962)

Mitchison, R. 'The Government and the Highlands 1707-1745', in Phillipson, N.T. and Mitchison, R. (eds.), Scotland in the Age of Improvement (Edinburgh, 1970)

Mitchison, R. (ed.), The Roots of Nationalism: studies in Northern Europe (Edinburgh, 1980)

Morren, N. Annals of the General Assembly of the Church of Scotland (Edinburgh, 1838)

Morris, R.J. Class and Class Consciousness in the Industrial Revolution 1780-1850 (London, 1979)

Moss, M.S. and Hume, J.R. The Making of Scotch Whisky: a History of the Scotch Whisky Distilling Industry (Edinburgh, 1981)

Mowat, I.R.M. Easter Ross 1750-1850 (Edinburgh, 1981)

Bibliography

Munro, R.W. Taming the Rough Bounds: Knoydart 1745-1784 (Coll, 1984)

Murchison, T.M. 'Highland Life as reflected in Gaelic Literature', Transactions, Gaelic Society of Inverness, XXXVIII, 1937-1941

Murchison, T.M. 'The Presbytery of Gairloch 1724-1750', Transactions, Gaelic Society of Inverness, XLIV, 1964-1966

Murdoch, A. The People Above: politics and administration in mid-eighteenth century Scotland (Edinburgh, 1980)

Murison, D. 'Linguistic Relationships in Mediaeval Scotland', in Barrow, G.W.S. (ed.), The Scottish Tradition: Essays in Honour of R.G. Cant (Edinburgh, 1974)

Murray, J.A.H. The Dialect of the Southern Counties of Scotland (London, 1873)

Neale, R.S. Class in English History 1680-1850 (Oxford, 1981)

Neale, R.S. 'Cultural materialism', Social History, 9(2), 1984

Nicholson, R. Scotland in the Later Middle Ages (Edinburgh, 1974)

Norton, W. 'The meaning of culture in cultural geography: an appraisal', Journal of Geography, 83(4), 1984

O'Dell, A. and Walton, K. The Highlands and Islands of Scotland (London, 1962)

Ommer, R.E. 'Primitive accumulation and the Scottish clann in the Old World and the New', Journal of Historical Geography, 12(2), 1986

Orr, W. Deer Forests, Landlords and Crofters (Edinburgh, 1982)

Osborne, R. 'The movements of people in Scotland 1851-1951', Scottish Studies, 2, 1958

Parkin, F. Class Inequality and Political Order (London, 1971)

Parry, M.L. and Slater, T.R. (eds.), The Making of the

Bibliography

Scottish Countryside (London, 1980)

Pennant, T. A Tour in Scotland (London, 1769)

Pennant, T. A Tour in Scotland and Voyage to the Hebrides in 1772 (London, 1774)

Peterkin, A. Records of the Kirk of Scotland containing the Acts and Proceedings of the General Assemblies from the Year 1638 Downwards (Edinburgh, 1838)

Phillips, K.C. Language and Class in Victorian England (Oxford, 1984)

Phillipson, N.T. and Mitchison, R. (eds.), Scotland in the Age of Improvement (Edinburgh, 1970)

Piggott, S. Ruins in a Landscape (Edinburgh, 1976)

Playfair, J. A Description of Scotland, Geographical and Statistical (Edinburgh, 1819)

Price, G. 'Gaelic in Scotland at the End of the Eighteenth Century (Part I)', Bulletin, Board of Celtic Studies, 27, 1978

Price, G. 'Gaelic in Scotland at the End of the Eighteenth Century (Part II)', Bulletin, Board of Celtic Studies, 28, 1979

Pryde, G.S. A New History of Scotland (Edinburgh, 1962)

Ramsay, A. History of the Highland and Agricultural Society of Scotland (Edinburgh, 1879)

Ramsay, J. A Letter to the Right Honourable the Lord Advocate of Scotland on the State of Education in the Outer Hebrides in 1862 (Glasgow, 1863)

Ravenstein, E.G. 'On the Celtic Languages in the British Isles: a Statistical Survey', Journal of the Royal Statistical Society, 1879

Rees Pryce, W. 'The idea of culture in human geography', in Grant, E. and Newby, P. (eds.), Landscape and Industry: essays in memory of Geoffrey Gullett (London, 1982)

Reid, J. Bibliotheca Scoto-Celtica (Glasgow, 1832)

445

Bibliography

Reid, W. and Hume, J. Edinburgh Gaelic Chapel (Edinburgh, 1969)

Rendall, J. The Origins of the Scottish Enlightenment (Edinburgh, 1978)

Richards, E. 'The Prospect of Economic Growth in Sutherland at the time of the clearances, 1809-1813', Scottish Historical Review, XLIX, 1970

Richards, E. 'How Tame were the Highlanders during the Clearances?', Scottish Studies, 17(1), 1973

Richards, E. 'Problems on the Cromartie Estate, 1851-3', Scottish Historical Review, 52, 1973

Richards, E. The Leviathan of Wealth (London, 1973)

Richards, E. 'Patterns of Highland Discontent, 1790-1860', in Stevenson, J. and Quinault, R. (eds.), Popular Protest and Public Order 1780-1820 (London, 1974)

Richards, E. 'The Last Scottish Food Riots', Past and Present, Supplement 6, 1982

Richards, E. A History of the Highland Clearances Volume 1: Agrarian transformation and the evictions (London, 1982)

Richards, E. 'Agrarian change, Modernisation and the Clearances', in D. Omand (ed.), The Ross and Cromarty Book (Golspie, 1984)

Richards, E. A History of the Highland Clearances Volume 2: Emigration, protest, reasons (London, 1985)

Richards, E., Hunter, J. and Sutherland, S. 'The Sutherland Clearances', Northern Scotland, 2(1), 1975

Robertson, I.M.L. 'The head-dyke: a fundamental line in Scottish geography', Scottish Geographical Magazine, 65, 1949

Robertson, J. General View of the Agriculture in the County of Inverness (London, 1808)

Robson, J. General View of the Agriculture in the County of Argyll, and western parts of Inverness-shire (London, 1794)

Ross, I.S. Lord Kames and the Scotland of his day (Oxford,

Bibliography

1972)

Rossi, I. (ed.), <u>The Logic of Culture</u> (London, 1982)

Ross Roy, G. 'The Jacobite Literature of the 18th Century', <u>Scotia</u>, I(1), 1977

Rude, G. <u>The Crowd in History</u> (New York, 1964)

Rude, G. <u>Ideology and Popular Protest</u> (London, 1980)

Sage, D. <u>Memorabilia Domestica</u> (Edinburgh, 1889)

Sahlins, M. <u>Culture and Practical Reason</u> (London, 1976)

Sanderson, M.H.B. <u>Scottish Rural Society in the 16th Century</u> (Edinburgh, 1982)

Schneider, L, and Bonjean, C.M. (eds.), <u>The Idea of Culture in the Social Sciences</u> (Cambridge, 1973)

Shaw, F. <u>The Northern and Western Islands of Scotland: their economy and society in the seventeenth century</u> (Edinburgh, 1980)

Shaw, J. <u>Water Power in Scotland, 1550-1870</u> (Edinburgh, 1985)

Shaw, W. <u>An Analysis of the Gaelic Language</u> (London, 1778)

Shaw, W. <u>An Enquiry into the Authenticity of the Poems Ascribed to Ossian</u> (London, 1782)

Sider, G. 'The ties that bind: culture and agriculture, property and propriety in the Newfoundland village fishery', <u>Social History</u>, 5(1) 1980

Sims-Williams, P. 'The Visionary Celt: the construction of an ethnic pre-conception', <u>Cambridge Medieval Celtic Studies</u>, 11, 1986

Sinclair, J. <u>Observations on the Scotch Dialect</u> (Edinburgh, 1782)

Sinclair, J. <u>General View of the Agriculture of the Northern Counties and Islands of Scotland</u> (London, 1795)

Sinclair, J. <u>Observations on the Propriety of Preserving the Dress, the Language, the Poetry, the Music, and the</u>

Bibliography

Customs of the Ancient Inhabitants of Scotland (London, 1804)

Sinclair, J. An Account of the Highland Society in London (London, 1813)

Sinclair, J. Analysis of the Statistical Account of Scotland (London, 1826)

Skene, W.F. Celtic Scotland (Edinburgh, 1876-1883)

Smith, A. The Wealth of Nations (London, 1776)

Smith, A. 'Annexed Estates in the Eighteenth-Century Highlands', Northern Scotland, 3(1), 1978

Smith, A. Jacobite Estate of the Forty-Five (Edinburgh, 1982)

Smith, J. General View of the Agriculture of the County of Argyle (London, 1805)

Smout, T.C. 'Scottish landowners and economic growth 1650-1850', Scottish Journal of Political Economy, XI, 1964

Smout, T.C. A History of the Scottish People 1560-1830 (Glasgow, 1969)

Smout, T.C. 'An Ideological Struggle: the Highland Clearances', Scottish International, 5(2), 1972

Smout, T.C. 'Tours in the Scottish Highlands from the eighteenth to the twentieth centuries', Northern Scotland, 5(2), 1983

Somers, R. Letters from the Highlands (London, 1848)

Stedman Jones, G. Languages of Class (Cambridge, 1983)

Stevenson, D. Alasdair MacColla and the Highland Problem in the Seventeenth Century (Edinburgh, 1980)

Stevenson, J. Popular Disturbances in England 1700-1870 (London, 1979)

Stevenson, J. and Quinault, R. (eds.), Popular Protest and Public Order 1780-1820 (London, 1974)

Stewart, D. Sketches of the Character, Institutions and

Bibliography

Customs of the Highlanders of Scotland (Edinburgh, 1822)

Stewart, W.G. Lectures on the Mountains, or the Highlands and Highlanders as they were and as they are (London, 1860)

Storrie, M.C. 'Landholdings and settlement evolution in West Highland Scotland', Geografiska Annaler, 47, 1965

Sutherland, A. A Summer Ramble in the North Highlands (Edinburgh, 1825)

Telfer-Dunbar, J. History of Highland Dress (London, 1962)

Thomas, K. Man and the Natural World: changing attitudes in England 1500-1800 (London, 1983)

Thomas, D.S. The Gaelic Sources of MacPherson's Ossian (Edinburgh, 1951)

Thomson, D.S. 'Scottish Gaelic Folk Poetry Ante 1650', Scottish Gaelic Studies, VIII(1), 1955

Thomson, D.S. 'Bogus Gaelic Literature c.1750-c.1820', Transactions, Gaelic Society of Glasgow, V, 1958

Thomson, D.S. '"Ossian" MacPherson and the Gaelic World of the Eighteenth Century', Aberdeen University Review, XL, 1963

Thomson, D.S. 'Gaelic Learned Orders and Literati in Medieval Scotland', Scottish Studies, 12, 1968

Thomson, D.S. An Introduction to Gaelic Poetry (London, 1974)

Thomson, D.S. and Grimble, I. (eds.), The Future of the Highlands (London, 1968)

Thomson, D.S. (ed.), Companion to Gaelic Scotland (Oxford, 1983)

Thompson, E.P. 'The moral economy of the English crowd in the eighteenth century', Past and Present, 50, 1971

Thompson, E.P. 'Patrician Society - Plebian Culture', Journal of Social History, 2, 1974

Thompson, E.P. The Poverty of Theory (London, 1974)

Bibliography

Thompson, E.P. 'Eighteenth-century English society: class struggle without class?', Social History, 3, 1978

Thompson, E.P. The Making of the English Working Class (Harmondsworth, 1980)

Trevor-Roper, H. 'The invention of tradition: the Highland tradition of Scotland', in E. Hobsbawm and T. Ranger (eds.), The Invention of Tradition (Cambridge, 1984)

Tribe, K. Land, Labour and Economic Discourse (London, 1978)

Turnair, P. Comh-Chruinneadhadh Orain Ghaidhealach le Raonull MacDhomnuill Ann an Eilein Eigg (Glasgow, 1809)

Turner, J. The politics of landscape: rural scenery and society in English poetry 1630-1660 (Oxford, 1979)

Turnock, D. Patterns of Highland Development (London, 1970)

Turnock, D. 'The retreat of settlement in the Grampian uplands', Northern Scotland, 4(1-2), 1981

Turnock, D. The Historical Geography of Scotland since 1707 (Cambridge, 1982)

Wagner, P.L. and Mikesell, M.W. (eds.), Readings in Cultural Geography (Chicago, 1962)

Wagner, P.L. 'The themes of cultural geography rethought', Yearbook, Association of Pacific Coast Geographers, 37, 1978

Walker, R. A Short Account of the Rise, Progress, and Present State of the Society in Scotland for Propagating Christian Knowledge (Edinburgh, 1748)

Walker, J. 'An Essay on Kelp', Transactions of the Highland and Agricultural Society of Scotland, I, 1799

Walker, J. An Economical History of the Hebrides and Highlands of Scotland (Edinburgh, 1808)

Wallerstein, I. The Politics of the World Economy (Cambridge, 1984)

Walton, K. 'Population changes in north-east Scotland, 1696-1951', Scottish Studies, 5, 1961

Bibliography

Watson, W.J. 'The Position of Gaelic in Scotland', <u>Celtic Review</u>, X, 1916

Weiner, M. <u>English Culture and the Decline of the Industrial Spirit 1850-1980</u> (Cambridge, 1982)

White, L.A. <u>The Science of Culture</u> (New York, 1949)

White, L.A. 'The concept of culture', <u>American Anthropologist</u>, 61, 1959

White, P. <u>Observations on the Present State of the Scotch Fisheries</u> (London, 1791)

Whittington, G. and Whyte, I. (eds.), <u>An Historical Geography of Scotland</u> (London, 1983)

Whyte, I.D. <u>Agriculture and Society in Seventeenth-Century Scotland</u> (Edinburgh, 1980)

Williams, G.A. 'The concept of egemonia in the thought of A. Gramsci', <u>Journal of the History of Ideas</u>, 21, 1960

Williams, R. <u>Culture and Society 1780-1950</u> (London, 1963)

Williams, R. 'Base and superstructure in Marxist cultural theory', <u>New Left Review</u>, 82, 1973

Williams, R. <u>Marxism and Literature</u> (Oxford, 1977)

Williams, R. <u>The Country and the City</u> (London, 1975)

Williams, R. <u>Keywords</u> (London, 1981)

Williams, S. <u>The Concept of Culture and Human Geography: a review and reassessment</u> (Keele, 1983)

Williamson, K. 'Lowland Scots in Education: an historical survey' (Part I), <u>Scottish Language</u>, 1, 1983; (Part II), 2,1983

Wills, V. (ed.), <u>Reports on the Annexed Estates, 1755-1769</u> (London, 1973)

Wills, V. (ed.), <u>Statistics of the Annexed Estates, 1755-1756</u> (London, 1973)

Withers, C.W.J. 'The Highland parishes in 1698: an examination of sources for the definition of the Gaidhealtachd',

Bibliography

Scottish Studies 24, 1980

Withers, C.W.J. 'The geographical extent of Gaelic in Scotland, 1698-1806', Scottish Geographical Magazine, 97(3), 1981

Withers, C.W.J. 'The Image of the Land: Scotland's geography through her languages and literature', Scottish Geographical Magazine, 100(3), 1984

Withers, C.W.J. Gaelic in Scotland 1698-1981: the geographical history of a language (Edinburgh, 1984)

Withers, C.W.J. 'Highland migration to Dundee, Perth and Stirling, c.1753-1891', Journal of Historical Geography, 11(4), 1985

Withers, C.W.J. Highland Communities in Dundee and Perth 1787-1891 (Dundee, 1986)

Withrington, D.J. 'The SSPCK and Highland Schools in the Mid-Eighteenth Century', Scottish Historical Review, XLI, 1962

Withrington, D. 'Education in the 17th century Highlands', in L. Maclean (ed.), The Seventeenth Century in the Highlands (Inverness, 1986)

Wittig, K. The Scottish Tradition in Literature (Edinburgh, 1958)

Wootton, G. Pressure groups in Britain 1720-1970 (London, 1975)

Young, J.D. The Rousing of the Scottish Working Class (London, 1979)

Youngson, A.J. 'Alexander Webster and his "Account of the Number of People in Scotland in the Year 1755"', Population Studies, 15, 1961

Youngson, A.J. After the Forty-Five (Edinburgh, 1973)

Youngson, A.J. Beyond the Highland Line (London, 1974)

Zaring, J. 'The romantic face of Wales', Annals, Association of American Geographers, 67(3), 1977

454

Fairs 90
False consciousness 25,
330, 413
Famine 179, 182, 203, 215,
236-45, 248, 258, 275,
307, 389
Farr 161, 184, 231
Federation of Celtic
Societies 385, 388
Ferguson, Adam 62, 67
Feudalism 3, 4, 59, 76, 78,
80, 96
Fife 89, 308
Fishing 9, 57, 59, 78, 87,
91, 92, 94, 189, 222, 227,
241, 243,252, 276, 281,
299-308, 313, 316, 372,
380-1
Fishing Act (1808) 304
Flax 94, 220, 290, 291-9
Flinn, Michael 178, 236,
245
Food riots 30, 243, 328,
329, 352, 367
Forbes, Duncan 81
Forbes, John 94
Forestry 1, 9, 210, 227,
309-10
Forfeited Annexed Estates
7, 10, 12, 61, 82-3, 84-6,
87, 92, 121, 140, 181,
197, 199-200, 209, 220,
224, 291, 293, 294, 295-7,
300, 315, 357
Fort Augustus 87, 90, 279
Fort George 87, 90, 364
Fort George Agricultural
Society 62
Fort William 87, 90, 141,
279, 374
Forth, Firth of 3, 82
Fortrose 296
Fraserburgh 307
Fraser Darling, Frank 227-8
Fraser-Macintosh, Charles
253, 334, 385, 387-8
Free Church of Scotland
154, 155, 338, 342-3, 369,
386

Furnace 281, 309

Gaelic Bible 120, 123, 154,
338
Gaelic Society of Inverness
163, 336, 388, 406
Gailhealtachd 3, 4, 5, 17,
33, 161
Gairloch 184, 208, 313
Galltachd 4
Game Act (1831) 247
General Assembly Committee
for the Highland Libraries
136-7
General Assembly of the
Church of Scotland 15,
111, 115, 117, 120-1, 131,
134, 136-7, 138, 139-40,
144, 154, 155-64
Gentleman Adventurers 89
Gigha and Cara 280
Glasgow 91, 155, 209, 243,
311, 313, 365, 377
Glasgow Auxiliary Bible
Society 154, 155
Glasgow Highlander 233
Glasgow Highland Society
155, 388
Glencalvie 248, 360
Glendale 373, 375, 377-9,
380, 384
Glendaruel 209
Glenelg 241, 291
Glenfinnan 82
Glengarry 82
Glenkinglass 309
Glenmoriston 82, 291
Glenmuick Tullich and
Glengairn 139, 359
Glenorchy 189, 207, 228,
346
Glensheil 184
Graham, Nicol, of Gartmore
15, 81, 211
Grain 5, 90, 201, 203, 205,
209, 220, 229, 235, 242,
257-8, 273-4, 310, 367
Gramsci, Antonio 27, 28,
31, 329

Montrose, Duke of 74, 118
Morar 242
Moray 3, 91, 115, 135,
 221, 306
Morrison, Roderick 345
Mortality crises 179, 197,
 203, 236, 245
Mortlach 161
Morvern 8, 9, 82, 209, 213,
 220, 293, 311, 357, 359
Moulin 290, 293
Muck 142
Mull 8, 81, 149, 182, 208,
 209, 213, 224, 225, 227,
 231, 241, 285, 300, 302,
 341
Murdoch, John 332-3, 337,
 385, 386

Nairn 3, 82, 88, 154
Napier and Ettrick, Lord
 253, 379
Napier Commission 163, 253,
 254-5, 257, 332, 333, 336,
 371, 379
Nasmyth, Alexander 70
Netherlorn 209, 219
New Zealand 246
Nicolson, Alexander 253
Nigg 338
North British Daily Mail
 365, 387, 388
North Carolina 189
Northern Ensign 365

Oban 279
Oban Times 385, 387
Oral tradition 344-5
Orkney 241, 243, 283
Oronsay 225
Ossian 67-70, 334, 391
Overtures for teaching the
 Societies Schollars to
 understand and Speak the
 English Language 124

Paisley 191
Paisley and East Renfrew
 Bible Society 154

Paisley Society for Gaelic
 Missions 154
Park Raid 374, 375, 381-2
Passenger Act (1803) 221
Pastoralism 42, 72, 175,
 219, 222-9, 367
Pennant, Thomas 194
Perth 82, 94, 185, 312
Perth Gaelic Society 387
Perthshire 1, 85, 90, 115,
 126, 140, 190, 203, 208,
 224, 231, 239, 258, 281,
 290, 295, 296, 298, 412
Peterhead 307
Picturesque, ideas on 66-7,
 343
Pine Coffin, Sir Edward 242
Plague 197
Planned villages 91-5,
 108n, 209, 222, 278-9,
 302, 314
Plockton 375
Police 359-61, 365, 373,
 379, 384
Political policies towards
 the Highlands 5, 6, 7-8,
 14, 57, 72-86, 87-8, 95-6
Poor Law 244, 248, 329,
 338, 409
Population 1, 6, 9, 91, 92,
 178-204, 218, 226, 255-6,
 273, 284, 287, 304-5, 316,
 317, 407-8
Portree 90, 184, 233, 235,
 240, 242, 243, 251, 313,
 378
Potato 9, 178, 182, 192,
 198, 201-4, 217, 220, 229,
 239-45, 249, 317, 372
Presbyterianism 8, 137
Prices 229-36, 242, 246,
 248, 283, 288, 292
Private property,
 civilising influence of
 62, 63, 277, 314, 404
Privy Council 59, 73, 76,
 112, 113, 114
Probationers 115-17, 118,
 119, 137, 138, 140, 153

461

464